Instructional Strategies
for Teaching
the Gifted

JEANETTE PLAUCHÉ PARKER

University of
Southwestern Louisiana

ALLYN AND BACON, INC.
Boston   London   Sydney   Toronto

Library of Congress Cataloging-in-Publication Data

Parker, Jeanette Plauché.
    Instructional strategies for teaching the gifted / Jeanette
Plauché Parker.
        p.   cm.
    Bibliography: p.
    Includes index.
    ISBN 0-205-11676-0
    1. Gifted children--Education--United States--Curricula.
2. Teachers of gifted children--Training of--United States.
I. Title.
LC3993.9.P37 1989
371.95'3--dc19   88-14436
                                                                            CIP

Printed in the United States of America
10 9 8 7 6 5 4 3 2 1   92 91 90 89 88

L9417545.
22.20

LEAA

To my mentors, family, and friends
who made it all possible

Contents

Foreword

Some truly profound changes have been taking place in education. Many educators are unaware that these changes have occurred. Not every teacher training program, school system, and textbook has changed. But enough changes have taken place to make a big difference in how and what children are learning and in how they use what they have learned. As early as 1975, John Flanagan reported that tenth graders in a national sample (PROJECT TALENT) scored higher than their counterparts of 1960 on tests of creativity and abstract thinking. In a more recent examination of a large sample of students, Tammy Safter and I found that students at all grade levels are more adept in using creative thinking skills than their counterparts of a few years ago.

In a Space Age conference in 1960, I made the following prediction regarding educational change:

> One of the most revolutionary changes I foresee is a revision of the objectives of education. Today we proclaim that our schools exist for learning. We say that we must get tougher and make pupils learn more. Schools of the future will be designed not only for *learning* but for *thinking*. More and more insistently, today's schools and colleges are being asked to produce men and women who can think, who can make new scientific discoveries, who can find more adequate solutions to impelling world problems. . . . This is the creative challenge (*Education and the Creative Potential*, 1963, p. 4).

In the 1980s, we have seen the gradual appearance of textbooks and teacher training courses emphasizing thinking skills, productive thinking, creative thinking, problem solving, creative problem solving, and the like. Before the 1980s, textbooks and courses like these were extremely rare. The last two years have seen the greatest surge in books and courses on thinking, problem solving, and creativity.

Dr. Jeanette Parker's text is one such example. She has described how the psychology of learning and the process of learning can be fused or integrated and applied to objectives in all of the traditional disciplines. The history of education has shown us that no educational idea, theory, or innovation has much of a chance to survive unless someone "spells it out" in the form of textbooks, evaluation tools, teaching materials—today we would say "technology." Much technology has been developed in this field, and one of the greatest strengths of this text is that the author introduces you to much of this technology.

Another outstanding characteristic of this book is that Dr. Parker has shown how technology in the areas of creative process, creative thinking and problem solving, productive thinking, decision making, critical thinking, and the like can be used in any subject matter. She gives examples subject by subject.

From ancient beginnings to the present time, educational theorists and practitioners have differed on whether processes such as creative thinking should be taught through the regular curriculum or whether they must be taught as separate disciplines. I first became aware of this controversy when R. E. Myers and I began to market *Can You Imagine?* and other creative thinking programs of this sort. Our sales were fairly good, but they were not good enough for the publisher. Efforts to sell them to school administrators met with "We like them, but they are not language arts; they are not social studies; they are not science. We buy by subject matter."

Edward de Bono, one of the most honored scholars in this field, has taken the position that thinking skills must be taught outside of the curriculum—otherwise they will give way to the curriculum and be neglected. When I went to Japan in 1978, the first question I was asked by education professors was: "Which side are you on? Should creativity be taught separately or should it be taught through all of the curriculum?" My reply was the latter. Dr. Parker has shown how it can be done. Her applications are almost "generic"—that is, some of the applications mentioned for science could be used in language arts, many of those suggested for mathematics would be useful in social studies, and the like. Teachers therefore should consider all of the strategies presented in the text in the light of the various disciplines, expanding on the author's suggestion to develop new applications in their own fields.

E. Paul Torrance
Athens, Georgia

Preface

In his 1971 report to the U.S. Congress, Commissioner of Education Sidney P. Marland, Jr., defined gifted and talented students as those who "require differentiated educational programs and services beyond those normally provided by the regular school program in order to realize their contribution to self and society."[1] A landmark in the history of gifted child education, the Marland report shocked the nation into realizing how little was being done for our future leaders. Since the publication of this study, much progress has been made in the training of this important segment of America's school population. Similar strides have been made in the area of professional education for teachers of the gifted. In 1980, the National Association for Gifted Children sponsored the First Annual Institute for Professional Training in Gifted Education. During its five years of work, participants in the Professional Training Institutes developed guidelines that have been widely used by institutions developing teacher training programs in gifted education.

In spite of the progress that has been made over the last ten to fifteen years in improving the quality of services available for our gifted and talented children and youth and the programs that train their teachers, much work is still needed. In order to prepare our teachers adequately for serving the needs of the gifted and talented, our training programs must have a healthy balance of the two major elements of education: the theoretical and the pragmatic. In the area of theory, numerous volumes have provided background material to aid teachers in the development of curriculum—books presenting a variety of paradigms ranging from Renzulli's *Enrichment Triad Model* (1977),[2] designed as a basis for gifted education programs, to Guilford's complex

---

[1] S. Marland, Jr. (1972). *Education of the gifted and talented.* Report to the Congress of the United States by the U.S. Commissioner of Education. Washington, D.C.: U.S. Government Printing Office.

[2] J. S. Renzulli (1977). *The Enrichment Triad Model: A guide for developing defensible programs for the gifted and talented.* Mansfield Center, CT: Creative Learning Press.

cube (1967),[3] representing the structure of the human intellect. Other texts (e.g., Clark, 1983; Davis and Rimm, 1985; Gallagher, 1985)[4,5,6] have presented a broad overview of the field of gifted education, emphasized the nature and needs of gifted children and youth, and/or suggested programmatic and curricular provisions for meeting the diverse needs of these students. Still others have presented individual strategies such as thinking skills, values clarification, simulation, and creative problem solving, for use by teachers at all levels of education. Although the purposes espoused by the authors of such works have been well served, professionals in the field have continued to need one important resource—a single volume presenting a model for curriculum development along with detailed strategies for accomplishing its goals. *Instructional Strategies for Teaching the Gifted* is designed to serve this need.

This book was written for four specific audiences:

- University professors teaching strategies (or "methods and materials") courses in gifted education
- Supervisors and consultants conducting staff development and inservice training workshops
- Teachers employed to provide special services to gifted students through accelerated core curriculum or enrichment programs
- Teachers desiring to differentiate the educational experiences offered to the gifted students in their regular education classes

Acknowledging that no single work can serve all of the needs of any segment of the gifted education spectrum, this book makes the following assumptions:

1. Knowledge of the characteristics and problems of gifted students and a variety of theoretical models on which differentiated curriculum may appropriately be built should be prerequisite for any university course or inservice training workshop in which this book is used as a text.

2. The practitioner using this book as a reference should first become familiar with the nature and needs of gifted students and the theoretical foundations on which differentiated curriculum may be appropriately based.

---

[3] J. P. Guilford (1967). *The nature of human intelligence.* New York: McGraw-Hill.
[4] B. Clark (1983). *Growing up gifted* (2nd ed.). Columbus, OH: Merrill.
[5] G. A. Davis & S. B. Rimm (1985). *Education of the gifted and talented.* Englewood Cliffs, NJ: Prentice-Hall.
[6] J. J. Gallagher (1985). *Teaching the gifted child* (3rd ed.). Boston: Allyn and Bacon.

Instructional Strategies for Teaching the Gifted is built around the philosophy that leadership training should be the primary goal of special programs for gifted students. For this reason my Leadership Training Model is referenced frequently throughout the text. It is acknowledged, however, that there are many effective gifted programs that do not espouse the leadership perspective in their goals. Thus, it should be emphasized that the strategies presented herein are applicable in all gifted program prototypes. It should also be noted that many of the strategies discussed in this book are appropriate for use in the regular education program. Indeed, it is my philosophy that many of the experiences that are typically reserved for the gifted resource room should be made available to all students. If we can succeed in incorporating thinking skills, democratic values, problem solving, and related skills and concepts in our curricula for all students, regardless of their educational levels, then the products of our schools will improve greatly, and gifted program teachers will be able to concentrate on meeting those unique needs of gifted students that cannot be adequately met within heterogeneously grouped classes.

ORGANIZATION OF THE TEXT

In keeping with my belief that programs for the gifted should be based on a leadership training perspective, Section I of this text presents the Leadership Training Model—a comprehensive model on which gifted programs may be based. Following the initial overview of the model, the strategies recommended for leadership training are presented with a research rationale, instructions for their use, and examples of activities that may be used to teach them. Sections II, III, and IV are organized as follows:

Cognitive Strategies (thinking skills, research, and futuristics)

Affective Strategies (interpersonal communication, role playing, and decision making)

Creative Strategies (creativity theory, creative problem solving, and strategies for fostering creativity in the gifted)

The final section, A Strategies Approach to Content Area Teaching, presents methods of incorporating the foregoing strategies into the core curriculum—whether in an accelerated program for gifted students or in a regular classroom including gifted students. To facilitate the teacher's use of this section, it is organized according to the major content areas of the regular curriculum: language arts, mathematics, science and social studies, and art; also included are chapters on the use of media in gifted education and the use of instructional units for organizing the presented strategies into curriculum for the gifted.

I would like to make one final comment with regard to the form of writing used in this book. In the last several years writers have made special efforts to use nonsexist language in their work. Although these efforts are admirable, they often result in the use of cumbersome verbiage that interrupts the reader's continuity of thought. In order to enhance the readability of the book while adhering to currently preferred trends, I have chosen to alternate by chapter the use of masculine and feminine pronouns and their adjectival forms when the gender is either unknown or irrelevant.

Jeanette Plauché Parker

Acknowledgments

As with any work of value, this project depended on the assistance of numerous friends, authors, readers, and publishers. Although it is not possible to name all who influenced the development of this book over the years, I would like to acknowledge certain individuals who contributed directly to the production of the final manuscript. Probably the most influential was my husband, George Parker, whose encouragement and patient understanding allowed me to complete my terminal degree and embark on the "mid-life career change" which permitted this book to become a reality. Next I must mention my mentors—notably Paul Torrance, my major professor at the University of Georgia from whom I learned what creativity was all about. Also important were those who led, taught, or otherwise influenced me in the early days of my gifted education career—Merritt Beadle, my former principal; Dorothy Sisk and Linda Addison; and my fellow doctoral students and friends Jack Mirabile and Gail Lewis Robinson. Gail also served as my most "avid critic" (if such is not a paradox) and personal editor.

Others who contributed their thoughts and feedback on various sections included many of the Lafayette Parish (Louisiana) Gifted Program faculty, especially Program Coordinator Jan Morris and teachers Jean Caruthers, Annette Chapman, Nancy Ehret, Madelyn Maragos, Brenda Reamer, and Cynthia Vige, as well as Dr. Jane Ellen Carstens, Dr. Billy Duncan, and other colleagues at the University at which I am employed. Other friends who read selected chapters and contributed their expertise include Donna Mirabile and Jeanne Daigle King. I wish also to give credit to my University's Administration, who have encouraged my research and all of the good things that we have done in gifted education; without their support, this project would not have been possible.

I also gratefully acknowledge the invaluable assistance of my office staff at the USL Center for Gifted Education: my wonderful secretary, Barbara Doucet; my graduate assistants, Suzanne Dupre, Darby Fontenot, Ellen Hargrave, and Therese Puyau; and my student aides, Marsha Milburn and Laura Trahan. And Paul Solaqua, former editor at

Allyn and Bacon, who advised, cajoled, and encouraged me almost to the end before leaving for other endeavors, must certainly receive a piece of the credit.

I am indebted to those authors and publishers who granted me permission to use their materials: my sometimes co-author, Dr. Jeannie Kreamer; Dr. Marvin Gold, publisher-editor of *The Gifted Child Today;* the wonderful, talented Dr. Mary Hunter Wolfe; Don Thornton; film animation experts Chris Nelson (Coordinator of Gifted Programs for the State of Georgia) and Jim Rogers (teacher in the Lafayette Parish Gifted Program); Dr. Jim Flaitz (our resident statistics professor who assisted greatly in the writing of my statistical research section); Michelle Zeitlin, a talented young actress whose high school freelancing provided me with a fine example of simulation, and Priscilla Hansen of the *Los Angeles Times* who helped me locate Michelle; and Suzanne Bourgeois, who shared the secrets of her beautiful talent for teaching children to write poetry. Finally, I wish to thank the World Future Society; the National Council for the Social Studies; Teleometrics, Inc; Pyramid Film & Video; and ETC. Publishers for their kind permission to use numerous passages from their outstanding publications and films.

It is to all of these wonderful people, without whose help this book would not have been published, that my first volume is dedicated.

Instructional Strategies
for Teaching
the Gifted

Section I

EDUCATING THE GIFTED FOR LEADERSHIP

Leaders are the custodians of a nation's ideals, of the beliefs it cherishes, of its permanent hopes, of the faith that makes a nation out of a mere aggregation of individuals.

Walter Lippman

Gifted education is progressing rapidly. A 1979 survey conducted by the Office of Civil Rights revealed that direct services were being offered to approximately 35 percent of the gifted students in the nation (Lyon, 1980). A more recent update reported that all but six states had allocated funds for gifted education, with annual allotments as high as $16 million. Thirty-nine states have developed guidelines for the identification of students for gifted programs, and fourteen currently require special certification for teachers of the gifted (Mitchell, 1986). All but one state and the District of Columbia have assigned coordinators or consultants to the area of gifted education, with at least half of these persons assigned full-time to this position. And teacher training programs are on the increase, having grown from 39 degree programs registered with the United States Office for Gifted and Talented in 1979 to 134 such programs, reported by Parker and Karnes in 1987.

Without question, our schools are currently serving a larger segment of our gifted population than at any other time in history. But what can we say about the quality of these services?

Note: The material in Section I is largely excerpted from a previously published article and is reproduced herein with the permission of The *Gifted Child Today* (formerly *G/C/T*), P.O. Box 6448, Mobile, AL 36660.

THE GOALS OF GIFTED EDUCATION

The last fifteen years have witnessed hundreds of articles and presentations advocating differentiated educational programming for the gifted. Although Public Law 94-142 did not identify the gifted as an exceptionality in need of special education, it did lay the groundwork for the development of individualized educational programs for gifted students. The landmark Marland (1972) report had previously examined this issue thoroughly, pointing out that, if democratic education implied "appropriate educational opportunities to benefit" (p. 25), then the offering of differentiated educational provisions was imperative. Marland further pointed out, however, that special programming for the gifted was needed for the benefit and survival of democracy itself. His contention mirrored Torrance's earlier observation that the survival of our civilization depended on the creative imagination of future generations. As Torrance reminded us, "Democracies collapse only when they fail to use intelligent, imaginative methods for solving their problems. Greece failed to heed such a warning by Socrates and gradually collapsed" (1962, p. 6).

The necessity for differentiated programming needs no new advocates. We must, however, examine the reasons why gifted education is essential for the survival of our democratic society. If the gifted students in today's schools are to become tomorrow's leaders, we must make leadership training a major goal of programs for the gifted. In formulating philosophy and goals for gifted programs, program developers must consider the development of integrated leaders from our gifted population to be the overall major goal of such programs. In keeping with this philosophy, Section I of this book presents the Leadership Training Model, a comprehensive model for gifted programs whose major goal is leadership development among the gifted.

REFERENCES

Lyon, H. C. (1980). The federal perspective on gifted & talented. *Journal for the Education of the Gifted, IV,* 3–7.

Marland, S., Jr. (1972). *Education of the gifted and talented. Report to the Congress of the United States by the U.S. Commissioner of Education.* Washington, D.C.: U.S. Government Printing Office.

Mitchell, B. (1986). Current state efforts in gifted/talented education in the United States. *Roeper Review, 8,* 272–273.

Parker, J. P., & Karnes, F. A. (1987). Graduate degree programs in education of the gifted: Contents and services offered. *Roeper Review, 9,* 172–176.

Torrance, E. P. (1962). *Guiding creative talent.* Englewood Cliffs, NJ: Prentice-Hall.

1

Leadership Training for the Gifted

Leaders have a significant role in creating the
state of mind that is society.
                                    John Gardner

Essentially there are two principal schools of thought on leadership. The trait theory suggests that leaders are born and not made (i.e., effective leadership qualities are innate and cannot be developed). Modern theorists do not agree, however. If their contentions are correct, we must provide leadership training for our gifted students. Differentiated programming for the gifted can no longer be justified exclusively on the basis of one's legal right to an appropriate education. Whereas this right is indisputable, it must be complemented with a second point: society cannot nor will not survive without intelligent, imaginative leadership. Leadership training is therefore mandatory for those members of our population who have the intellectual and creative potential to lead.

If the development of future leadership is to become a major goal in programs for the gifted, we must structure these programs around a leadership perspective. Current literature suggests that four skill areas are involved in the development of effective leadership: Cognition, Problem Solving, Interpersonal Communication, and Decision Making. Cognition and Problem Solving are left-brain functions; Interpersonal Communication and Decision Making are based in the right brain. Gifted programs must be designed to produce integrated leaders—individuals who can make the fullest possible use of both hemispheres of the brain.

Built upon the philosophy that leadership training should be the major goal of programs for the gifted, the Leadership Training Model (LTM) provides a core around which gifted programs and their curricula can be structured. This chapter presents an overview of the model's four components and the stages for developing the skills that make up leadership. The remainder of this book will present specific strategies designed to strengthen these skills and thus to build integrated leadership among the gifted.

RELEVANCE OF LTM TO CURRENT NEED

Leadership has been defined as "ability that facilitates the handling and the representing of people as well as the initiating of events and situations on their behalf" (Khatena, 1982, p. 55). If this is truly what leadership is all about, then our only chance for survival as a society is to develop gifted citizenship with the intellect and the imagination to lead. The Leadership Training Model offers a framework within which such leaders can be developed.

Gleaned from research on the abilities, characteristics, and styles of leaders whose successes are written in history, the components of the LTM provide a combination of abilities that any philosophy of gifted education can readily espouse. The intertwining of academic exercise (cognition and problem solving) with the affective components that are all too often relegated to the enrichment resource room (practice in interpersonal communication and decision-making skills) lends a balance that integrated curriculum demands. If we accept the findings of recent research on the necessity to utilize both hemispheres of the brain, then we must similarly accept the essential nature of balance in the curriculum. It is toward this end that the LTM is offered as a comprehensive, integrated approach to programming for the gifted. (See Figure 1–1.)

Cognition

Cognition implies factual knowledge. A steadily increasing number of educators are accentuating the need for advanced cognitive preparation in gifted education. Gifted students do not need more rote learning, nor more emphasis on the lower levels of Bloom's Taxonomy. What is needed is a swing toward training in cognitive process and greater emphasis on the higher levels of thinking. Also essential is the freedom to use one's own most efficient learning style. With these goals in mind, the Cognition component of LTM comprises four stages: Exploration, Specialization, Investigative Skill Training, and Research.

Exploration is the first step in the drive for cognitive strength. Essential for the development of a strong content base, the exploration of a wide variety of cognitive areas can be accomplished through such strategies as the use of community resources (field studies, guest speakers, mentors), classroom learning centers, and effective use of

Figure 1–1.   The Leadership Training Model

<u>Cognition</u>

Exploration
Specialization
Investigative Skill Training
Research

<u>Interpersonal Communication</u>

Self-Realization
Empathy
Cooperation
Conflict Resolution

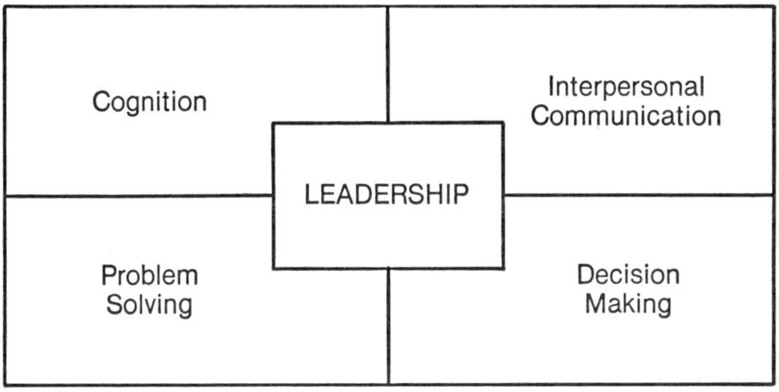

Cognition		Interpersonal Communication
	LEADERSHIP	
Problem Solving		Decision Making

<u>Problem Solving</u>

Problem Perception and Definition
Incubation
Creative Thinking
Analysis
Evaluation
Implementation

<u>Decision Making</u>

Independence
Self-Confidence
Responsibility
Task Commitment
Moral Strength

media. Equally important is the acknowledgment of, and programming for, the differing learning styles of leadership trainees.

Specialization involves the narrowing process that results from exposure to a broad conceptual base. In this stage of the Cognition component, the student is encouraged to focus on a particular topic or problem for in-depth investigation. The skill of problem definition, an extremely relevant and important stage of the creative problem-solving process, must be taught as a cognitive skill as well.

Investigative Skill Training provides the skills necessary for and appropriate to a topic or problem that the student wishes to investigate in depth. Of particular importance in this stage is the development of efficient research skills. A sequential plan for training gifted students in research is presented in Chapter 3.

Research, or the application of the skills acquired in the previous stage, culminates the training process and prepares the student experientially for innovative and cognition-based leadership. The Type Three product of Renzulli's (1977) *Enrichment Triad Model* is an excellent example of this type of application. With its completion, the final product of reality-based investigation and research culminates the Cognition component of the Leadership Training Model, preparing the student for the lifelong continuous acquisition of new skills and information.

Activities for Developing Cognition.   In addition to the four steps of the LTM Cognition component, several strategies are appropriate for developing the cognitive abilities of gifted students. These include the use of community resources (field study excursions, resource speakers, and mentorships or internships) and audiovisual media. Teachers are cautioned against adopting the "field trip curriculum" that has become so popular in gifted programs; to be meaningful, relevant, and valuable, field study excursions must be more than simply visits to the local factory, planetarium, or state capitol. Essential to the use of this strategy are extensive advance preparation and follow-up. (It should be noted further that, in view of the expense, time, and risks involved in taking classes away from school, field study should be used only when an equally valuable experience cannot be gained within the classroom.) Similar criteria should be used in selecting resource speakers; it is also essential to consider the speaker's expertise in the area, and her ability to present effectively to (and respond appropriately to questions from) gifted students. Speakers should be prepared by the teacher with information on the age/grade levels of the students, the backgrounds they will have had prior to the visit, information and methods the teacher would like to have covered, and the like. With proper preparation, these types of experiences can be invaluable in building cognitive skills and informational backgrounds in the gifted.

Problem Solving

If we believe that investigative research must involve the inquiry method, then the acquisition of problem-solving skills must be an integral part of the leadership training process. The Leadership Training Model proposes a six-step approach to creative problem solving: Problem Perception and Definition, Incubation, Creative Thinking, Analysis, Evaluation, and Implementation. This process is discussed in Chapter 9.

Activities for Teaching Problem Solving.   The process for teaching problem solving to gifted students is discussed in detail in Chapter 9 of this text. Essential to the effective use of this process within a leadership perspective is the skill of brainstorming (with careful attention to the rules discussed in the problem-solving chapter). Also necessary is practice in futuristic problem solving (a future-oriented adaptation of the creative problem-solving process) and in the scientific method of problem solving (or inquiry). At the secondary level, students should be introduced to conflict resolution techniques, which may be found in a wide variety of materials on leadership in management.

Interpersonal Communication

One of the primary characteristics of an effective leader is the ability to work with other people. The development of interpersonal communication skills is an essential part of leadership training. The LTM proposes the following continuum: Self-Realization, Empathy, Cooperation, and Conflict Resolution. These stages in the development of interpersonal communication skills are presented in detail in Chapter 5 of this text.

Activities for Developing Interpersonal Communication Skills. A major responsibility of the effective gifted-program teacher in any type of program is the extensive use of group interaction activities. Ideally, the teacher of the gifted should have training and experience in group counseling; this technique can be used to great advantage with gifted students in an isolated setting. Although counseling techniques are not included in this text, other strategies for developing interpersonal communication skills are discussed in some detail in Chapter 5. With young children, instruction in etiquette and other social skills is important. In the higher elementary grades, the popular Trust Walk, Broken Squares, and activities designed to help students recognize the value of all contributions will help them to develop group dynamics skills. When students reach the secondary level, more advanced communication skills such as Parliamentary Procedure, argumentation and debate, conflict resolution, and public speaking of all types should be taught. Interpersonal communication skills are possibly the most essential abilities for gifted leaders to possess. Through a well-planned program of group interaction activities from the earliest to the most advanced years of school, this goal of leadership training can become a reality.

Decision Making

The ability to make intelligent, rational, and responsible decisions is also an essential quality for effective leadership. Effective decision making requires independence of thought and action, self-confidence, acceptance of responsibility, task commitment, and moral strength. The Leadership Training Model proposes a series of planned experiences designed to develop these aspects of decision making. This component of LTM includes the development of realistic goals, ability to organize and implement plans for meeting these goals, and both formative and summative evaluation. Strategies that lend themselves well to the development of decision-making skills include values education, role playing, and counseling. Activities for developing these skills are presented in Chapters 6 and 7 of this text.

Values Education.   One important prerequisite of decision-making ability is moral development, particularly the development of a clear values system to guide one's decisions. Curriculum developers should carefully select values-oriented activities that will enable gifted program facilitators to clarify and strengthen the democratic values brought to the class situation by the individual student and to influence those students whose values do not agree with the concept of democracy (honesty, justice, respect for others, etc.). It is important that the facilitator's personal values *not* be forced upon the students, as a dogmatic attitude may prove counterproductive in the development of independent decision-making skills.

Role Playing.   One of the most effective strategies for building group process skills is the use of role-playing activities, particularly simulation and sociodrama. Role playing enables the actor to learn by experience, within a physically and psychologically safe environment. It encourages both creative and critical thinking, builds interpersonal communication skills, and strengthens the decision-making skills of the participants.

Counseling.   For many years it has been recognized that the common characteristics of the gifted carry with them a set of recognizable but solvable problems. The acknowledgment of these problems as common among their peers helps gifted students to reach the first step in problem resolution. Piaget believed that social interaction would help children to outgrow their early egocentricity. Group interaction with intellectual peers in the gifted classroom must be an integral part of any differentiated program for gifted students. Group counseling techniques used effectively by a trained teacher will go a long way toward guiding the potential leader to the development of a healthy self-concept, the first prerequisite for interpersonal communication.

Activities for Developing Decision-Making Abilities.   At all levels of education, careful attention should be paid to the development of democratic values in all students. Values education is therefore discussed in some detail in the affective section of this book. Chapter 6 further presents strategies such as simulation and sociodrama, which offer many alternatives for the development of decision-making abilities in the gifted. Social action projects can be encouraged in students of all ages—cleanup of the school grounds for the younger students, community service projects for the secondary levels. Intercultural simulations are useful for helping students to work more effectively with others in their community, and practice in argumentation and debating skills—taught in conjunction with a sound values education—will develop leaders with the courage of their convictions.

REFERENCES

Bellows, R. (1959). *Creative leadership.* Englewood Cliffs, NJ: Prentice-Hall.

Hyman, R. T. (1974). *Ways of teaching* (2nd ed.). Philadelphia: J. B. Lippincott.

Khatena, J. (1982). *Educational psychology of the gifted.* New York: Wiley.

Maslow, A. H. (1959). Creativity in self-actualizing people. In H. Anderson (Ed.), *Creativity and its cultivation.* New York: Harper and Row.

Osborn, A. F. (1963). *Applied imagination.* New York: Charles Scribner's Sons.

Parker, J. P. (1983, September/October). The *Leadership Training Model:* Integrated curriculum for the gifted. *G/C/T*, pp. 8–13.

Renzulli, J. S. (1977). *The Enrichment Triad Model: A guide for developing defensible programs for the gifted and talented.* Wethersfield, CN: Creative Learning Press.

Rogers, C. (1969). *Freedom to learn.* Columbus, Ohio: Merrill.

Simon, S. B.; Howe, L. W.; & Kirschenbaum, H. (1972). *Values clarification: A handbook of practical strategies for teachers and students.* New York: Hart.

Toffler, A. (1972, January 17). Alvin Toffler: Study the future. *Junior Scholastic*, Teacher's Edition, 3–4.

Torrance, E. P. (1964). Creativity and the teacher. In Gowan, J. C., & Demos, G. D. (Eds.), *The education and guidance of the ablest.* Springfield, IL: Charles C. Thomas.

Torrance, E. P. (1974). *Norms-technical manual for Torrance Tests of Creative Thinking.* Lexington, MA: Ginn & Co.

Wallas, G. (1926). *The art of thought.* New York: Harcourt, Brace & Co.

Section II

COGNITIVE STRATEGIES

The brighter you are, the more you have to learn.

Don Herold

Some years ago, a major study was undertaken at Harvard University to determine what the major goals of higher education should be. It was the intent of the Harvard committee to develop a general statement setting forth those elements that would be needed to fulfill the requirements of an educated person toward the end of the twentieth century. According to their report, an educated American should:

1. think and write clearly and effectively;
2. have a critical appreciation of the ways in which we gain and apply knowledge and understanding of the universe, of society, and of ourselves—specifically, knowledge of aesthetics, literature, and the arts; of history as a way of understanding the processes and problems of mankind; of modern social science concepts and techniques; of philosophical analysis; and of the mathematical and experimental methods of the natural sciences;
3. think globally in terms of other cultures and other times;
4. have some understanding of, and experience in thinking about, moral and ethical problems; and
5. possess in-depth knowledge in some field of human endeavor.

On the basis of these premises, Harvard developed a core curriculum that set a precedent for others, acknowledging that our educational institutions were responsible for developing educated persons for this century and the next. To summarize the Harvard report, the educated person must be able to think and write clearly, must have critical appreciation of the arts and the natural and social sciences, and must have in-depth knowledge in some cognitive area.

John Dewey observed that "we can have facts without thinking, but we cannot have thinking without facts" (1933). If we wish to develop effective leaders for the future, we must facilitate the cognitive growth of our gifted students. It is this philosophy on which the first component of the Leadership Training Model is based. Section II of this text will explore three aspects of Cognition—thinking skills, research, and the study of the future—all crucial parts of the future leader's potential.

REFERENCE

Dewey, J. (1933). *How we think: A restatement of the relation of reflective thinking to the educative process.* Boston: D. C. Heath.

2

Teaching Gifted Students to Think

*Thinking is the hardest work there is, which
is the probable reason why so few engage
in it.*
                              Henry Ford

One of the most identifiable characteristics that distinguishes gifted persons from their less capable peers is their intellectual thinking ability. Unfortunately, all too often thinking skills remain undeveloped, and the productive application of this innate potential fails to materialize. As Henry Ford so aptly phrased it, thinking (especially productive thinking) is hard work.

Recent research has produced a wide variety of publications in the area of cognitive psychology. Since cognitive processing does not occur apart from thinking, much attention has also been devoted to the development of thinking skills. Many forms of thinking have been explored in the literature: critical, creative, and productive thinking; scientific and reflective thinking; convergent and divergent thinking; metaphorical, analogical, and logical thinking; and so on. Each has its appropriate uses, and each must be mastered if it is to contribute to the balanced development of the individual's cognitive functioning.

Exactly what *is* thinking? What kinds of thinking should we teach in our schools? How can we develop effective thinkers among our students, particularly those gifted students who will be the leaders of the future? Although some writers consider critical thinking to be in conflict with creative thinking, many others speak of thinking in problem-solving terms.

Burton, Kimball, and Wing (1960) claimed that thinking occurs when a problem is acknowledged and a serious effort toward solution is undertaken. And Torrance (1974) defined creativity as "a process of becoming sensitive to problems, deficiencies, gaps in knowledge, missing elements, disharmonies, and so on; identifying the difficulty; searching for solutions, making guesses, or formulating hypotheses about the deficiencies; testing and retesting these hypotheses and possibly modifying and retesting them; and finally communicating the results" (p. 8).

There are literally hundreds of companies that publish materials for teaching thinking skills in the elementary and secondary schools. Thinking skills programs such as those produced by Midwest Publications are widely used in special programs for the gifted. Many writers have promoted the use of Bloom's taxonomy to assure an emphasis on the "higher levels of thinking," and the Guilfordian operations (especially convergent and divergent production and evaluation) are frequently used to assure the same balance in gifted education.

Thinking skills constitute the foundation of all of the so-called "basics" of school. In the development of his unique paradigm, Guilford (1967) theorized that each of the various components of intellect controlled one or more human intellectual functions. Presenting educational applications of Guilford's model, Meeker (1969) contended that strengthening the components of intellect in which an individual lacked competence would in turn strengthen his ability to function effectively in the corresponding academic skills on which school learning is based. Similarly it may be assumed that the development of efficient thinking skills will enable any individual to perform more effectively in the academic subject matter of which each of these skills forms a foundation. Some of these relationships include:

- Analogy as a basis for mathematical preparation (e.g., the study of ratio and proportion or other bases to help students understand their own decimal system) or creative problem solving (particularly synectics)
- Comparison and contrast as a tool for building language facility (synonyms and antonyms, simile and metaphor) and classification skills (essential to scientific problem solving)
- Critical thinking as a building block for logical reasoning and problem solving, as well as for the development of inferential comprehension skills
- Metaphor as a method of enhancing creative writing and the understanding of literature
- Analysis of cause and effect as a basis for inquiry

In turn, the resulting skills are essential to effective leadership. The development of the basic thinking skills, then, might be seen as the cognitive backbone of a leadership training program for the gifted.

Prior to the twentieth century, it was commonly believed that thinking could take place only through the medium of logic. Even in modern times the art and science of logical thinking have been confined largely to university courses in philosophy. Only recently, with the introduction of thinking skills curricula such as *Philosophy for Children* and materials developed by Black and Black, Epley, Harnadek, and others, has attention been given to the urgency of training young people in this important area.

John Dewey once commented that "learning is learning to think," and the Harvard report emphasized that an educated person must be able to think and write clearly. If these claims are accurate (and if Einstein was not mistaken in his claim that "imagination is more important than knowledge"), our modern educational systems have been sadly remiss in the discharge of their duties. Even today, many "Back-to-Basics" advocates consider the inclusion of thinking skill instruction and practice to be a frill rather than a necessity.

Research has confirmed the importance of including thinking skills instruction in the curriculum. Some findings that document this need are:

1. National educational assessments and standardized test scores have shown that the thinking, reasoning, and problem-solving abilities of today's students are rapidly declining.
2. Instruction in thinking skills helps to improve writing skills, as composition is simply the written expression of thought.
3. Visual and auditory discrimination, practiced in thinking skill instruction, are essential for the development of reading ability, and critical thinking is a necessary part of reading (particularly inferential) comprehension.
4. Understanding science and social science concepts—particularly the use of the inquiry approach, the interpretation of history, and the recognition of trends—requires an efficient command of thinking skills (e.g., patterns and relationships, inference, observation and other science processes, and inductive and deductive reasoning).
5. Efficient test taking requires efficient thinking.
6. Problem finding has been recognized by many writers as the most essential—and yet the most difficult—step of the problem-solving process. Critical thinking is essential to an effective command of problem-finding skills.
7. Analytical thinking is necessary for the identification of appropriate problem-solving techniques in mathematics, science, and other areas of the curriculum.
8. Understanding social science concepts—particularly the interpretation of history and the recognition of trends—requires an effi-

cient command of patterns and relationships. Effective thinking skill instruction includes practice in these skills.

9. Visual and auditory discrimination, practiced in thinking skill instruction, are essential for the development of reading ability.

On the basis of the documented need for including thinking in the curriculum, one of the most commonly avowed goals of education today is to teach students to think for themselves. Torrance (1962) stressed civilization's need for thinkers and problem solvers when he pointed out that, "democracies collapse only when they fail to find intelligent, imaginative methods for solving their problems. Greece failed to heed such a warning by Socrates and gradually collapsed" (p. 6). Recognizing this urgent need, what specific skills should we be teaching in our schools, and particularly with our gifted children and youth? This chapter addresses the thinking skills that appear to be basic to those cognitive strategies commonly required in school and in life; for organizational purposes, these skills are herein classified as critical thinking, relational thinking, and productive thinking. Also included is a brief section on memory training, as the gifted student who is weak in memory will surely become an underachiever.

CRITICAL THINKING

Critical thinking has been defined as "principled thinking" (Siegel, 1980, p. 8), that is, goal-directed thinking that uses logical reasoning and objective criteria as foundations for evaluation and decision making. In order to develop our future leaders into critical thinkers, we must teach them to develop logical, objective criteria and to use these criteria in the evaluation of ideas and solutions for real-life problems. We must also teach the principles and methods of creative thinking, since creative and critical thinking complement rather than conflict with each other.

A wide variety of approaches to teaching critical thinking can be found in the literature. Primarily, critical thinking involves two major components: analysis and logic.

Analysis

In his Taxonomy of Educational Objectives, Bloom (1956) listed analysis as one of the higher levels of thinking. He defined analysis as "the breakdown of the material into its constituent parts and detection of the relationships of the parts and of the way they are organized" (p. 144). Commenting further that analysis is requisite for evaluation, Bloom made it clear that analytical ability is an important component of critical thinking. As with any other skill, the most effective method of acquiring analytical skills is through practice. Analysis is used in many forms in both school and life. When students read a passage and attempt to interpret the author's meaning, they are conducting an analysis of the material read. When engineers consider a mathematical problem, they must use analytical thinking to determine the methods that must be used to solve the problem. In making comparisons of any kind, the thinker must first analyze to determine the attributes or functions of the first component before he can compare it to the second. For example, in completing a client's tax return, an accountant must analyze expenditures to determine which are legal deductions. How can analytical skills be taught? A few suggestions for classroom instruction in analysis are offered below:

———

1. Teach students to distinguish between relevant and irrelevant facts. Newspaper articles and advertisements offer many good examples of this contrast.

2. Help students to discern the difference between fact and opinion. Use newspaper editorials, television commentaries such as "Sixty Minutes," and other types of nonfiction reporting to provide practice.

3. Use examples from the Communist newspaper *Pravda* to demonstrate the political use of propaganda. Help students to derive principles from these examples. Look for other examples of propaganda based on similar principles (e.g., advertising, political campaign speeches). Have students develop imaginative new products or run for imaginary (or school) offices, including the writing of promotions that use propaganda. Ask them to analyze newspapers and magazines for other examples of this technique.

4. Acquire a copy of *How to Lie with Statistics* (Huff, 1954). Show students how statistics are often used out of context to support a writer's position on an issue. Use this lesson to teach methods of determining whether or not a set of statistical data is relevant and properly used.

5. Teach notetaking and outlining procedures. Demonstrate how these forms of organization fit into the pattern of analysis. (See Chapter 3 for further information on notetaking and outlining.)

———

Logic

Logic may be defined as a method for evaluating and structuring arguments on the basis of inference. Essentially there are two types of logic: induction and deduction. *Induction* (or inductive reasoning) may be defined as inference that starts with specific information and leads to generalization. *Deduction* (or deductive reasoning), on the other hand, is inference that begins with a general statement and proceeds to the specific. Reasoning inductively from her observation that all gifted students she had taught had been high achievers, a teacher drew the assumption that all gifted students perform well academically. Naturally those who have taught gifted students will immediately recognize the fallacy of this statement. In some cases the inductive method of reasoning can lead to probability; however, it does not lead to certainty. Deductive reasoning, on the other hand, permits a greater degree of certainty. Consider, for example, the following deductive reasoning pattern:

> All certified teachers have college degrees.
> Jan is a certified teacher.
> Therefore Jan has a college degree.

The contrast between the two modes of reasoning is obvious.

John Stuart Mill was quoted by Dewey as saying that the drawing of inferences is "the great business of life" (1933, p. 21). Dewey believed that critical thinking and other thought processes not only are essential for academic success but (even more significant) could be transferred from an academic context to real life. Logic, frequently reserved for philosophy courses at the postsecondary level, is a method of drawing inferences; logic is commonly thought to be deductive. An example of a simple logic problem might be:*

> Marlene is taller than Jessica, who is taller than Tania. Richard, who likes only girls who are shorter than he is, measures 5'5" in height. If Jessica is also 5'5" tall, which of the three girls is Richard apt to like best?

The *New London Problem*, a more intricate example involving the use of logical (deductive) reasoning, is presented in Appendix A.

RELATIONAL THINKING

Much of the thinking that takes place in the human mind involves one type of relationship or another. When we compare or contrast two or more items or concepts, we are thinking in terms of relationships. Relational thinking comprises two specific areas: simple comparison and contrast, and the more complex techniques of analogy.

---

*The solutions to this and other problems in this text may be found in Appendix B at the back of the book.

Comparison and Contrast

When we consider the relationship between two concepts in order to determine whether they are similar or different, we are making one or more comparisons. Comparison and contrast are involved in simile and metaphor, in attribute listing, in the use of synonyms and antonyms, in classification, and in recognizing and following patterns or sequences.

Similes and metaphors are figures of speech used to compare two items or concepts that are normally considered to be different. In the case of a simile, the word *like* or *as* is used in the comparison (as in the old song, "A Pretty Girl Is *Like* a Melody"). A metaphor makes a similar comparison, but without *like* or *as* (as in "Jezebel was a ball of fire"). Similes and metaphors are employed widely in literature, as their use helps writers to describe characters, places, and other aspects of their writing more vividly. The use of metaphor is also useful in developing creative thinking.

An important strategy included by Frank Williams in his popular "Model for Implementing Cognitive-Affective Behaviors in the Classroom" (1970) was *attribute listing*. Based on Crawford's earlier concept, the recognition of attributes is an essential step in making comparisons. Attribute listing has also come to be acknowledged as an excellent method for developing ideational fluency and, hence, creativity. Simply defined, attributes are characteristics or properties that make persons, animals, objects, or concepts unique. Attributes may be colors, sizes, textures, shapes, or even characteristics that are neither visible nor tangible (e.g., curiosity, sensitivity, bitterness). Attribute listing may be used to develop ideational fluency (thus enhancing creative production), or it may be employed in the context of a subject area to help students internalize a concept. To use attribute listing to build creative fluency, instruct students to brainstorm the attributes of hobbits, green beans, fire, July 4, the Mona Lisa, a public park, or any other imaginative person, animal, place, object, or concept (see Chapter 10 for information on brainstorming). To build this strategy into a content area, have students list traits of effective leaders (social studies), characteristics of insects (science) or tesselations (mathematics), or attributes of Impressionistic paintings or Baroque music (arts).

Synonyms are words with similar (if not identical) meanings, and *antonyms* are words with opposite meanings. The teaching of synonyms and antonyms is essential to vocabulary development and to the building of relational thinking. Their use is discussed further under the section on analogical thinking and in the vocabulary-building section of Chapter 11.

Classification is widely recognized as an important scientific process. If for no other reason than its contribution to science, classification should be taught throughout the school years; however, there are many other uses for this essential skill. In the more advanced levels of relational thinking, classification skills are important to the recognition of relationships between items or concepts. In teaching classification, teachers should provide practice in grouping together items that have common characteristics (or attributes). Classification can be a useful tool in problem solving, as demonstrated in "The Newlyweds," found in Appendix A.

Patterns may be defined as arrangements of figures or words, created by combining two or more attributes into some type of relationship. Patterns may be figural, such as a pattern for building a piece of furniture, or verbal, as in poetic form (e.g., Haiku, which requires a specific number of syllables for each line). They may be geometric, as in tesselations (see Chapter 12), or numeric (e.g., a numerical sequence such as 5, 10, 15, 20). In order to recognize, analyze, and reproduce a pattern, it is necessary first to identify its attributes. A *sequence*, such as the numerical sequence mentioned above, is simply a specific type of pattern. The ability to sequence is important in reading comprehension, in understanding history, in setting and applying priorities, and in working all types of problems. A few activities that may be used in training students in the use of pattern and sequence, an important part of relational thinking, are included here.

Fill in the blank with the missing element of the sequence:

1. Numerical Sequences:
   48, 35, 24, _____, 8, 3
   (The correct answer is 15; each multiplicand is reduced by one for the next product: 48 is 8 × 6; 35 is 7 × 5; 24 is 6 × 4; 15 is 5 × 3; etc.)
2. Letter Sequences:
   ABACADAABBAACCA _____
   (The correct answer is ADD, completing the second part of the sequence, AADDAACCAADD.)
3. Mixed Sequences:
   X6XX5XXX4XXX _____ XX2XXXXXX1
   (In this pattern, the numerals decrease by one, while the number of letters increases between the numbers. Therefore, the correct answer is X3XXX.)

Analogical Thinking

The final type of relational thinking is analogy (or analogical thinking). An analogy is simply a relationship between two concepts. When the President compares today's astronauts to the explorers of earlier times, or when a mathematician uses ratio and proportion, each is using analogy to express relationships. Of all the thinking skills that we need to develop in our gifted students, analogy is one of the most important. Why does analogy play such a significant role in thinking skills instruction?

First, persons who reason analogically have corresponding high levels of mental ability. In his widely used *Structure of Intellect* model, Guilford (1967) identified *Relations* as one of the major products of human intelligence. Analogies involve both cognition and convergent production of Guilford's Figural, Semantic, and Symbolic Relations, suggesting that the ability to think analogically comprises a major segment of intelligence. Sternberg (1977) supported Guilford's theory that analogical reasoning ability is a component of intelligence. On the basis of his research, Sternberg concluded that intellectual skills (such as analogical thinking) could be improved, strengthening the case for the teaching of skills which correlate with intelligence.

Second, research has documented that persons who are adept at solving analogy problems tend to perform well academically, especially in the area of vocabulary. Sternberg (1985) cited studies that produced high correlations between scores on the *Miller Analogies Test* and the vocabulary subtest of the major intelligence measures, as well as others which demonstrated that students who follow deliberate processes for solving analogies will achieve more efficiently in school than those who simply use free-association techniques for this type of problem solving.

Third, analogy problems are included in many of the standardized tests that our brighter students will encounter throughout their academic careers. Parker and Karnes (1987), for example, reported that forty-seven institutions of higher education required the *Graduate Record Examination* (GRE), and others required the *Miller Analogies Test* (MAT), for admission to graduate degree programs in education of the gifted. Both of these instruments include significant numbers of analogy problems.

Finally, analogical thinking presents the teacher with a strategy for helping students to internalize new concepts by comparing them to concepts with which they are already familiar. For example, the Civil Rights movement can be more clearly understood when compared to the causes espoused in the American Revolution; computer learning can be explained as "artificial intelligence"; and so on.

In teaching students to develop analogical reasoning skills, several factors should be considered, particularly the various forms and types of analogy, and strategies for solving analogy items.

Forms of Analogy.   Analogies encountered in testing are frequently defined as "relationships between relationships." Usually these items take the form of A:B::C:D, which should be read as "A is to B as C is to D." In testing, one or more of the four elements of the analogy are omitted, and several options are provided from which the student selects the correct response. Sternberg (1981, 1982) points out that such items may take any one of the following forms:

A:B::C:(____)	Example:	white:black::up:(down,high, back,top)
A:B::(____):D	Example:	top:bottom::(top,high,up,off):down
A:(____)::C:D	Example:	iris:(cornea,eye,retina,toe): :finger:hand
(____):B::C:D	Example:	(ocean,road,river,bay):sea: :village:city
A:B::(C:D)	Example:	white:black::(up:down; jump:off; low:up)
A:(B::C):D	Example:	meat:(eat::milk; milk::soda):drink
(A:B)::C:D	Example:	(poverty:wealth; yesterday:today)::poor:rich
A:(B::C:D)	Example:	sock:(toes::glove:fingers; foot::mitten:hand)
(A:B::C):D	Example:	(mansion:room::skyscraper; skyscraper:mansion::room):office

Types of Analogy.   Gordon (1961) presented three types of analogy that can be used in synectics, a problem-solving method that he developed. These three types—direct, personal, and symbolic analogy—are discussed in Chapter 10 as a method of creative problem solving.

A different view of the types of analogy—specifically, those which appear as items on standardized tests—will be presented here as approaches to specific thinking skill instruction. These types of analogy, which are discussed below, may express any of the following relationships:

1. Semantic relationships
2. Symbolic relationsips
3. Phonetic relationships
4. Class relationships
5. Functional relationships

6. Quantitative relationships

7. Pattern relationships

Semantic Relationships: Semantic relationships are those that involve similarities or differences in meaning. Examples of analogies with semantic relationships might include:

large:big::elderly:old (synonyms)

beginning:end::first:last (antonyms)

8:92::−6:−19 (positive or negative numbers)

good:bad::always:never (positive or negative concepts)

6:8::9:11 (even or odd)

collapse:owe::argue:occur (all same part of speech)

implicit:massive::oblivion:security (both members of each pair are the same part of speech)

Symbolic Relationships: Symbolic relationships are those that are comparable purely in terms of the symbols (e.g., letters or numbers) that make up their components, with no respect to their meanings. Some examples of symbolic analogies are:

foe:coelocanth::conceit:height (same internal letter patterns)

ten:ago::amaze:blind (same number of letters)

egomaniac:hypochondriac::computer:magazine (same number of syllables)

mom:dad::see:tot (same word configuration or shape)

Phonetic Relationships: Two pairs of words may be said to have phonetic relationships if they sound alike in some way. Phonetic analogies might involve the use of homonyms, rhymes, or similar internal sounds. Examples are:

sew:so::two:too (homonyms)

fool:suit::tough:rug (same medial vowel sound)

squeeze:peel::receive:conceit (same vowel blend sound)

grieve:peeve::crime:rhyme (rhyme)

Class Relationships: In class relationships, both members of each pair (and sometimes both members of both pairs) belong to the same classification; one is an attribute, a division or branch, a class, a component, or a kind of the other. For example:

hair:mammal::feather:bird (one is an attribute of the other)

poodle:pug::Holstein:jersey (both members of each pair belong to the same classification, although the classification is not the same for both pairs) cockatoo:parrot::lovebird:budgerigar (all are the same classification)

micropaleontology:geology::topology:mathematics (one is a branch of the other)

novel:book::painting:picture (one is a type of the other)

snake:reptile::crawfish:arthropod (one is a class of the other)

page:book::hydrogen:water (one is a component of the other)

Functional Relationships: If one item changes into the other, acts or performs on the other, or is used for the other, the two items have a functional relationship. Examples of functional analogies are:

foot:football::hand:volleyball (one acts on the other)

screw:screwdriver::nail:hammer (one performs on the other)

rain:sleet::vapor:snow (one changes into the other)

egg:larva::baby:child (one develops or changes into the other)

cane:support::washcloth:wash (one is used for the other)

Quantitative Relationships: Relationships that are expressed as similarities or differences as to quantity, degree, or number, may be said to be quantitative in nature. Some quantitative analogies are:

full:empty::wide:narrow (degree)

meter:yard::liter:quart (length or quantity)

4:16::8:64 (square roots and squares)

group:person::gaggle:goose (number)

phenomena:data::moose:geese (all plural)

Pattern Relationships: Pattern relationships are those that possess similar figural attributes (size, shape, pattern, color). Some examples of pattern relationships are:

$$\square : \diamondsuit :: \triangledown : \triangleright$$

$$\bigcirc : \square :: \otimes : \boxtimes$$

$$\circ : \bigcirc :: \scriptsize\square : \square$$

$$\oslash : \diagbox :: \bigcirc : \square$$

Developing Analogical Reasoning Skills.   Having previously established the existence of some degree of hierarchy among the various levels of what is herein called "relational thinking," we must assume that the understanding of attributes and patterns, simile and metaphor, synonyms and antonyms, and the other lower level relationships must be developed before addressing the higher levels of analogical reasoning. It is essential, then, that the teacher provide simple practice in the recognition and application of all kinds of relationships before proceeding to analogical thinking.

After developing a sound concept of basic relational thinking among the students, the teacher is ready to begin the teaching of analogy. These steps might be followed:

1. Relate analogy to simile and metaphor—all address similarities among otherwise dissimilar concepts. For example, consider the familiar expression, "I am up to my elbows in alligators." It is obvious that no true-to-life alligators are present, but the concept is clear: the speaker is overwhelmed with work. The statement is a metaphor; the work is analogously compared to alligators because both are so difficult to conquer.

2. Instruct students to identify other analogous relationships, showing how dissimilar concepts can be perceived as similar. Extend these analogies to concepts in the subject area (e.g., apartheid as slavery, communism as an infectious disease, the computer as an artificial brain).

3. Present the formats of analogy problems, the different types of relationships that analogy problems can have, and strategies for solving them.

Strategies for Solving Analogy Problems.   When attempting to solve analogy problems, it is essential to adhere to a specific, deliberate set of steps. The following sequence, based on Sternberg's (1981) model, is suggested:

1. Read the entire analogy item.

2. Make note of the parts of speech used (not all words must be the same part of speech, but no more than two different parts of speech may be used for a parallel analogy—except in the case of items that examine the elements of a relationship without reference to meaning, as in phonetic or symbolic analogies).

3. Examine the primary relationship first (i.e., determine the way in which the first two words are related to each other, then apply that relationship to the second pair). If the primary relationship is not immediately obvious, consider the various types of analogies that

can be used, and try to narrow to no more than two or three possibilities.

4. If no relationship can be determined with respect to the primary pair of elements, then (and only then) consider the secondary relationship (i.e., the relationship of the first element to the third and the second to the fourth). Sternberg cautions against examining incorrect relationships; he especially warns against reversing the order of the analogy. For example, in the analogy *calico:cat:: (vertebrate,class,woman,species):human*, one might be tempted to select vertebrate, since a human being is one kind of vertebrate. This procedure, however, constitutes a reversal. In the first pair, calico is a kind of cat; in the second, the first response must name a type of human (as opposed to the other way around). The correct choice is woman, as a woman is a type of human. To say that one type of vertebrate is a human is to reverse the order of the initial relationship and therefore is erroneous.

It should be noted that, although analogies must follow the types of relationships described above, they are commonly presented in educational materials as verbal analogies (relationships between words), figural analogies (relationships among pictures), or numerical analogies (relationships among numbers). In an effort to simplify the presentation of analogy examples in the classroom, a teacher should provide examples of these categories for practice.

PRODUCTIVE THINKING

In his model of the human intellect, Guilford (1967) included two operations that may be grouped under the heading of productive thinking: convergent production and divergent production. *Convergent production* is the type of thinking that is most commonly called for in the traditional school classroom; contrary to popular misconception, it is not the simple regurgitation of facts presented and memorized. Like divergent production, this skill requires the production of new information from given information. In convergent production, however, the emphasis is on the production of expected responses. *Divergent production*, on the other hand, stresses the variety and quality of the response (Meeker, 1969). The primary difference, as demonstrated in the terms themselves, is between focusing (or converging) and branching out (or diverging). Convergent production is required in mathematical problem solving; it is also called upon in the following test items:

1. Using an Insect Classification Key, classify each of the following insects into the class to which it belongs: moth, fly, cricket, grasshopper.

2. List five synonyms for the word *important*.

3. Rearrange the following events in their correct sequence: discovery of America, First World War, invention of cotton gin, Industrial Revolution.

4. List attributes of an effective leader.

Divergent production is commonly associated with creativity; however, the two concepts are not identical. It is important to recognize, for example, that the fluent production of a variety of thoughts does not necessarily constitute divergent production, as divergent production requires the generation of divergent but relevant and useful information. Divergent production is particularly important in gifted education because its open-ended nature encourages students to approach their potential more effectively than does convergent production. Examples of items that require divergent production might include:

1. In what other ways might this character be portrayed?

2. Arrange these blocks in as many different patterns as possible.

3. What paths might you follow to go from point A to point B?

4. How many smaller words can you make from the word *transfiguration*?

5. Brainstorm as many uses as you can think of for a paper clip.

6. Complete an unfinished story.

Synthesis, often considered the opposite of analysis, is the "putting together of elements and parts so as to form a whole" (Bloom, 1956, p. 162). Originally placed by Bloom among the higher levels of thinking, true synthesis requires that the elements be combined in a new way. When a scientist uses the findings of others as background information and then builds on these findings, adding personal interpretations to produce new information, he is forming a synthesis. Students can be taught to synthesize, even in the early grades, through activities that cause them to draw conclusions from a collection of facts. Essay questions ask a student to synthesize, as do research assignments. Like divergent production, synthesis requires creativity and encourages independent thinking. Practice in synthesizing helps to develop the skills involved in extemporaneous speaking, drawing conclusions, and decision making—all important strengths for effective leadership.

MEMORY TRAINING

Meeker (1969) defines memory as the "retention or storage, with some degree of availability, of information in the same form it was committed to storage and in response to the same cues in connection with which it was learned" (p. 16). Of all the operations of Guilford's model, memory is probably the one that is strongest among the gifted. As Meeker has pointed out, the gifted student who is lacking in memory strength will become an underachiever. It is unfortunate that educators do not place more emphasis on creative memory-building techniques (as opposed to rote memorization and recitation). There are a number of modern strategies that can and should be used to develop the memory skills that are so essential to our gifted youth today. Memorizing facts for use in testing and problem solving, dramatic roles for play production, music for programs and recitals, and speeches and literary passages for public performance will strengthen memory skills. Two other techniques, the use of imagery and mnemonics, will be presented here.

Imagery has been cited by many authors as an excellent tool for memory enhancement. One method of using imagery for memory building is to allow the senses to "image" an event, a set of objects, or a sequence of topics in a presentation. For example, to recall a series of historical events, the learner might be asked to make creative associations with each event (e.g., the smell of tea brewing to mark the Boston Tea Party, the feeling of being outdoors during an ice storm to recall Arctic explorations, a memory of canoeing down a peaceful river to designate the voyages of a famour explorer, or the beauty of the earth from outer space to remember the Apollo missions).

Another technique, used informally for many years by people of all ages, is the use of *mnemonic* devices. The familiar trick of tying a string around one's finger is a type of mnemonic—a strategy intended to help a person remember something that might otherwise be forgotten. A mnemonic is used when a person makes a sentence or other grouping of words using the first letter of each item in a list. For example, to remember the order of the colors in the visible light spectrum, students could memorize the fictitious name *Roy G Biv*, the letters of which are the first letters of red, orange, yellow, green, blue, indigo, and violet. In another mnemonic, one might learn a song, sung to the tune of *Swanee River*, which helps in recalling the order of the planets in their distance from the sun: "My very educated mother just served us nine pizza pies" (representing the nine planets, Mercury, Venus, Earth, Mars, Jupiter, Saturn, Uranus, Neptune, Pluto). A speaker attempting to memorize a planned presentation might make a list of the concepts to be covered, and select a key word to represent each concept. To memorize the list of key words, the speaker might develop a mnemonic similar to those above, using either a statement (the first letter of which signals the first letter of the corresponding key word) or a name (each letter of which is the first letter of the corresponding key word). Another system, which dates back to the classical ages, uses visual images to represent items to be memorized in sequence. For example, a speaker might force an association between each new topic (or key word) in her presentation and a piece of furniture in her living room. Once the selected associations are committed to memory, the speaker simply recalls them in the order of their corresponding objects' location.

Research has confirmed that the development of one's own mnemonic devices (as opposed to using mnemonics developed by others) results in more efficient and longer retention of information. Thus, the devices mentioned above should be used only as examples to help students originate their own systems for remembering that which is important to them.

REFERENCES

Alexander, P. A. (1984). Training analogical reasoning skills in the gifted. *Roeper Review*, 6, 191–193.

Black, H., & Black, S. (1984). *Building thinking skills*. Pacific Grove, CA: Midwest Publications.

Bloom, B. S. (Ed.) (1956). *Taxonomy of educational objectives: The classification of educational goals. Handbook I: Cognitive domain*. New York: David McKay.

Bruner, J. S.; Goodnow, J. J.; & Austin, G. A. (1956). *A study of thinking*. New York: John Wiley & Sons.

Burton, W. H.; Kimball, R. B.; & Wing, R. L. (1960). *Education for effective thinking*. New York: Appleton-Century Crofts.

Costa, A. L. (1984). Thinking: How do we know students are getting better at it? *Roeper Review*, 6, 197–199.

Covina, W. A.; Zandy, B. V.; & Kay, D. A. (1982). *Cliffs Graduate Record Examination Aptitude Test preparation guide*. Lincoln, NE: Cliff Notes.

Crawford, R. P. (1937). *Think for yourself*. New York: Whittlesey House (McGraw-Hill).

Crocetti, G. (1985). *Graduate Record Examination General (Aptitude) Test: Complete preparation for the NEW test*. New York: Arco Publishing.

Detterman, D. K., & Sternberg, R. J. (1982). *How and how much can intelligence be increased?* Norwood, NJ: ABLEX Publishing.

Dewey, J. (1933). *How we think: A restatement of the relation of reflective thinking to the educative process*. Boston: D. C. Heath.

Drake, J. A. (1976). *Teaching critical thinking: Analyzing, learning, and teaching critical thinking skills*. Ithaca, NY: Ithaca College Department of Education.

Epley, T. M. (1982). *Models for thinking: Activities to enhance modes of thought*. Ventura, CA: Ventura County Supt. of Schools Office.

Gallagher, J. J. (1985). *Teaching the gifted child*. (3rd Ed.). Boston: Allyn and Bacon.

Gordon, W. J. (1961). *Synectics: The development of creative capacity*. New York: Harper & Brothers.

Guilford, J. A. (1967). *The nature of human intelligence*. New York: McGraw-Hill.

Huff, D. (1954). *How to lie with statistics*. New York: W. W. Norton.

Hurley, P. J. (1985). *A concise introduction to logic*. (2nd Ed.). Belmont, CA: Wadsworth.

Karnes, F. A., & Collins, E. C. (1984). *Handbook of instructional resources and references for teaching the gifted*. Boston: Allyn and Bacon.

Kitano, M. K., & Kirby, D. F. (1986). *Gifted education: A comprehensive view*. Boston: Little, Brown, & Company.

Meeker, M. (1969). *The Structure of Intellect: Its interpretation and uses*. Columbus, OH: Charles E. Merrill.

Parker, J. P., & Karnes, F. A. (1987). Graduate degree programs in education of the gifted: Program contents and services offered. *Roeper Review, 9,* 172–176.

Siegel, H. (1980). Critical thinking as an educational idea. *The Educational Forum, 45,* 7–23.

Sternberg, R. J. (1977). *Intelligence, information processing, and analogical reasoning: The componential analysis of human abilities*. Hillsdale, NJ: Lawrence Erlbaum Associates.

Sternberg, R. J. (1981). *Barron's How to prepare for the MAT: Miller Analogies Test*. (3rd Ed.). Woodbury, NY: Barron's Educational Series.

Sternberg, R. J. (Ed.) (1982). *Advances in the psychology of human intelligence, Volume I*. Hillsdale, NJ: Lawrence Erlbaum Associates.

Sternberg, R. J. (1985). Teaching critical thinking, Part I: Are we making critical mistakes? *Phi Delta Kappan, 67,* 194–198.

Torrance, E. P. (1962). *Guiding creative talent*. Englewood Cliffs, NJ: Prentice-Hall.

Torrance, E. P. (1974). Ways gifted children can study the future. *Gifted Child Quarterly, 18,* 65–71.

Wagner, P. A., and Penner, J. (1982). Games, logic, and giftedness. *Roeper Review, 4,* 14–15.

Wagner, P. A., & Penner, J. (1984). A new approach to teaching forms of reasoning to the gifted. *Roeper Review, 6,* 188–191.

Walsh, D., & Paul, R. W. (no date). *The goal of critical thinking: From educational ideal to educational reality*. American Federation of Teachers Educational Issues Department.

Weinstein, J., & Laufman, L. (1980). Teaching logical reasoning to gifted students. *Gifted Child Quarterly, 24,* 186–190.

Wenger, W. (1980). *Solving unsolvable world problems*. Gaithersburg, MD: Psychegenics Press.

Williams, F. E. (1970). *Classroom ideas for encouraging thinking and feeling*. Buffalo: D.O.K.

3

Research: The Art of Investigation

Research is formalized curiosity: It is poking
and prying with a purpose. It is a seeking that
he who wishes may know the cosmic secrets
*of the world and they that dwell therein.**
                              Zora Neale Hurston

It is the initial thesis of this book that the primary goal of gifted education should be leadership training. And it is a major thesis of the Leadership Training Model that the identification and solution of real-life problems should be the ultimate cognitive goal of any leadership training program. Primary and requisite to the solving of real-life problems is the ability to conduct realistic investigations. Skills of search are therefore an essential segment of the road that leads to leadership success.

All too often, particularly in the elementary school, the writing of reports—most commonly based on (if not copied from) the classroom encyclopedia—is equated by teachers with research. By the time gifted students reach the secondary level, they should have acquired—developmentally, systematically, and at their individual pace—a rather effective command of basic research techniques that can be transferred easily to more advanced levels, carried into the later years of education, and applied to real-life adult problems.

It is the purpose of this chapter to present a system for teaching research skills in gifted education.

---

*Zora Neale Hurston (1942). *Dust tracks on a road* (2nd ed.). Chicago: University of Illinois Press.

TRAINING GIFTED RESEARCHERS

As with most skills, the training of researchers is developmental. Before one can apply the methodologies used by professionals, a firm base of knowledge must first be established. At this stage students should be introduced to the primary types of research, along with their purposes and their uses, exposed to a wide variety of advanced resources from which to gather data for conducting original research, and taught the methodologies for using those resources.

Teachers should not be skeptical of the research abilities of young gifted students. Ideally, in order to avoid the repetition each year of training in encyclopedia usage (often the elementary student's idea of the only way to "do research"), a developmental scope and sequence should be established, with diagnostic testing used at each grade level to enable the students to progress along a defined continuum at their own pace. With this end in mind, a sequence for such a program is suggested in Table 3–1.

It should be understood that the suggested sequence is intended only as a guide to the presentation of the concepts listed herein, and that each concept or process mentioned at the lower levels should be systematically incorporated at increasingly more complex levels of difficulty throughout the grades. Thus the skill of conducting simple experiments in the primary grades would be expanded into more complex experiences as students become capable of handling them in their progression through the school years.

With these ideas in mind, the following organizational plan in presented in this chapter:

Types of Research

The Scientific Method of Problem Solving

Gathering and Processing Data

Statistical Analysis

Preparing the Research Report

Although gifted students have the ability to learn independently, the teacher's role in helping them to acquire research skills is crucial. It is suggested that the following sections be used as a manual for teaching the necessary skills; with this goal in mind, an attempt has been made to cite examples through which students can become more familiar with the various steps discussed herein. The teacher is encouraged to extrapolate from these examples, developing other applications in accordance with individual student interests wherever possible. When students have become thoroughly familiar with the various skills presented, they can make their own applications as needed to develop real-life investigations in their areas of special interest.

Table 3-1. Research Skills for the Gifted: Suggested Scope and Sequence

	Lower Elementary Grades	Middle Grades	Junior/Senior High School
Library Resources	Card Catalog Dictionary Encyclopedia Simple biographies and other elementary nonfiction books	Popular magazines and newspapers *Reader's Guide to Periodical Literature* Specialized reference books Documents and pamphlets Microforms of intermediate resources	Professional magazines and journals Indexes to professional literature Microform indexes
Nonlibrary Resources	Simple experiments Simple weather instruments Simple interviews (friends, parents, teachers)	Surveys Human resources Questionnaires Public records Rating scales Inventories Checklists More complex weather instruments	More advanced mechanical devices (dynamometer, etc.)
Statistical Design and Analysis		Random sampling techniques Frequency distribution Measures of central tendency	Test instruments Historical research Stratified samples Planning simple statistical designs Measures of variability Tests of significance
Processing Skills	Sentence and paragraph construction Reading and summarizing/paraphrasing brief, simple passages	Scientific method of problem solving Note taking Crediting sources Outlining Classroom newspapers Paraphrasing and summarizing Simple review of literature Practice in identifying and stating problems Editing (proofreading, using thesaurus)	Using proofreaders' marks Editing work of others

33

TYPES OF RESEARCH

Descriptive Research

Descriptive research is designed to contribute new knowledge or new understandings of existing knowledge in a particular area. When a researcher gathers information on a topic from a variety of sources, organizes or synthesizes it in an original way, and draws conclusions that were not previously reached by earlier researchers, she is conducting descriptive research. There are several types of studies that may be classed in this category.

Surveys. Surveying is one of the most popular methods of conducting research. Surveys are used by business and industry, by politicians, and by educational researchers. They may be used to forecast the results of elections, to determine improvements needed in a product, or to evaluate the degree to which goals have been met. The data collected may report the opinions of others or provide factual information. Surveys may be conducted in written format (e.g., questionnaires, rating scales, checklists) or verbally (public opinion polls). A well-constructed survey can provide a wealth of information that can be analyzed and reported with relative ease. Frequently, however, survey questions are too open-ended, resulting in vague responses and making objective analyses of the data difficult if not impossible. The following guidelines are suggested for the development of an effective questionnaire:

1. Construct questions to elicit specific rather than general responses. Multiple-choice formats, Likert scales, and checklists lend themselves to objectivity and specificity and thus are easy to analyze.
2. If any term used in a questionnaire is open to interpretation, clearly define the context in which it is to be read. If different respondents read different meanings into a question, their responses will be difficult to standardize.
3. If using a multiple-choice format, provide either an "other" option, permitting respondents to write in their own thoughts, or a "none of the above" option, which simply allows the freedom not to agree with any of the provided choices.
4. Be concise, asking only questions that are directly relevant to and significant in determining a solution to the research questions under investigation. In our survey-ridden society, lengthy questionnaires that require extensive time on the part of the respondent often are discarded.

5. Accompany the survey with a letter that (a) explains the purpose of the research, (b) emphasizes the importance of the study, (c) diplomatically solicits and thanks respondents for their cooperation, (d) specifies the date by which return is requested, and (e) offers to provide respondents with an analysis of the data and the conclusions reached.

6. Enclose a self-addressed, stamped envelope with the survey for return of the completed form.

   Examples of the survey methods mentioned include:

- The Multiple-Choice Questionnaire:

  _____ 5. Which of the following issues do you consider to be MOST crucial for this session of the legislature? (Select only ONE.)

     A. Balanced budget
     B. Funding for education
     C. Repeal of blue laws
     D. New legislation for fighting crime
     E. Other

- The Likert Scale:
  Please rate each of the following issues as to their importance for this session of the legislature, by circling:

  5 (extremely important)
  4 (moderately important)
  3 (neither crucial nor insignificant)
  2 (of little importance)
  1 (should not be considered)

1. Balanced budget	5	4	3	2	1
2. Highway construction	5	4	3	2	1
3. Educational funding	5	4	3	2	1

- The Checklist:
  Please check all of the items below that you feel should be considered in this session of the legislature:

  _____ Balanced budget
  _____ Educational funding
  _____ New legislation for fighting crime

- The Priority Rating Scale:
  Please rank all of the following items in order of their importance for this session of the legislature:

(1=most important, 2=second in importance, etc.)

_____ Balanced budget

_____ Educational funding

_____ New legislation for fighting crime

The analysis of survey data may be made by considering their frequency or their relationships (discussed later in this chapter).

Relational Studies.   Many studies conducted by scientists, social scientists, and educational researchers are designed to determine the relationship(s) between or among any of a wide variety of factors, conditions, or phenomena. Studies that might be enhanced through the use of this method ask questions such as (1) What is the relationship between creativity and professional success? or (2) Which factors in the home environment contribute to juvenile delinquency? To determine the answers to these questions, correlational analyses or tests of significance may be used (discussed later in this chapter).

Developmental Studies.   Developmental studies are designed to determine what changes occur over a specified period of time. Here we will consider two types of developmental research: longitudinal studies and trend analyses.

   Longitudinal (long-term) studies are used primarily to examine the changes in growth that occur in living things (plants, animals, humans) over a period of time—for example, a study designed to determine the effects of certain types of light on plants. Another type of study of interest to a gifted adolescent might examine the relationship between scores on creativity tests administered in a primary gifted program and similar tests administered in high school. Such a study might be intended to determine whether creativity training in the elementary school helps students become creative producers as adults.

   Trend analyses consider current trends for the purpose of forecasting future events or conditions. Trend extrapolation, the extension of current trends into the future, is discussed in Chapter 3 as a strategy for futuristic studies. Essentially, this type of research examines issues such as (1) If the population continues to grow at this rate, what will be its effect on the housing/food supply in the year 2200? or (2) If sales continue to decrease at the current rate, how many years can we expect to derive a profit without developing new products?

Historical Research

The historical researcher utilizes relics (items of historical significance such as tombstones, excavated pottery, items of clothing, fossils) or documents (printed or written materials such as family Bibles, birth or death records, newspaper accounts of battles) to put together a comprehensive picture of a period of history, a geographical area, a cultural pattern, a scientific process, or some other type of historically significant synthesis. In gathering data, the historical researcher must assess carefully the authenticity and accuracy of each relic, document, or other source or type of information collected before utilizing it as a part of the completed puzzle. Students conducting historical research might investigate questions such as (1) What factors caused the population of our city to increase rapidly in the second half of this century? or (2) Do all Louisiana citizens with the family name of Plauché have a common ancestor?

Experimental Research

Experimental research differs from descriptive and historical research in that it utilizes comparable groups of subjects (humans, animals, plants, etc.) and controls, modifies, or manipulates isolated variables to determine the effects of these variables. For example, a student might (1) compare the academic achievement patterns of students exposed to gifted resource rooms with those in accelerated curriculum programs, or (2) examine the effects of different colors on student achievement.

THE SCIENTIFIC METHOD OF
PROBLEM SOLVING

Whichever type of problem a researcher is investigating, the scientific method of problem solving, often called the inquiry method, is generally considered the most valid procedure to follow. This section discusses the five steps of the scientific method and is followed by examples of student projects that utilize this procedure.

Steps of the Scientific Method

State the Problem.   Having determined a general topic area in which to conduct research, the investigator must narrow the search to a specific problem or question to be investigated. The problem may be phrased as a question (Which factors in the classroom environment are most conducive to creative production?) or as a relationship to be studied (The Effects of the Classroom Environment on Creative Production).

Formulate Hypotheses. The second step in the scientific method is the formulation of one or more hypotheses. Essentially a hypothesis is simply an educated guess which the researcher attempts to test through her investigation. Ordinarily a hypothesis is stated in what is known as "null" (or negative) format; for example, "There is no statistically significant relationship between creativity and intelligence." The accuracy of this statement is then tested, and the hypothesis is accepted or rejected on the basis of statistical analysis.

*Collect the Data.** The data collection process involves reading and studying the findings of others that might be relevant to or have an influence on the conditions the researcher wishes to examine. Additionally, there is a need to gather raw data (pieces of information such as test scores, survey responses, or numbers of events observed, as opposed to prior analyses of these data). Two factors are essential to the data collection process: (1) the researcher must be able to synthesize a complete picture from the data gathered, and (2) the data must be organized in a manner that allows their orderly use.

Analyze the Data. Having gathered a representative collection of raw data—pieces of information that have an impact on the total story under investigation—the researcher is ready to analyze the data in the search for a solution or an answer to the question being investigated. There are many ways in which data can be organized and analyzed, and an infinite number of solutions that can be reached. Since most classroom teachers do not have a background in statistics, and most gifted program students have not completed sufficient mathematical training to be able to work with complex statistical procedures, this chapter presents a limited number of elementary analytical techniques, carefully selected to provide a variety of possibilities for research in the elementary or secondary school.

Act on the Hypotheses and Draw Conclusions. Once the data have been analyzed, the researcher reconsiders and acts on (i.e., accepts or rejects) the research hypotheses and extrapolates her findings to the target population. These conclusions or generalizations, then, form a possible answer or solution to the problem initially identified for investigation.

---

*The teacher should explain to the students that the word *data* is the plural form of the word *datum*, a Latin word meaning fact.

Application of the Scientific Method:
Two Illustrations*

Pierre: Development of an Automated Assembly Cell.   Pierre, a thirteen-year-old student in eighth grade, had for several years been fascinated by robotics. The previous year he had built a robotic arm for his Science Fair project; this year, however, he wanted to go a step farther—to invent a robotic system that could actually be used to produce something. The result, a highly creative product, earned him an award at the regional fair, giving him the opportunity to compete at the state level.

The purpose of Pierre's project was to build an automated assembly cell. After gathering information on assembly cells from trade magazines and design engineers, he began to draw rough sketches of items that his cell might be used to assemble. Since he also had an interest in automobiles, he worked in this area and finally decided on a wooden ambulance for the final assembly product.

Although Pierre did not formally record a hypothesis, he experimented with several materials and designs for his cell and its product, including the control system and its timing mechanism. Through the process of elimination (actually an informal method of hypothesis testing), he isolated the most effective materials and design for developing his final product.

After cutting out the pieces for his vehicle, Pierre began drawing the assembly system. For the assembly cell he used clear plastic, to allow easy viewing, and a pneumatic system for control. As he worked to synchronize the meeting of the parts of his ambulance, Pierre found that timing, a crucial factor in the assembly process, was difficult to adjust. After extensive experimentation, however, he succeeded in developing a successful product—a working automated assembly cell.

Jennifer: The Effects of Rooting Media.   Jennifer, another thirteen-year-old eighth grader, had for some time taken a continuing interest in her father's garden, developing a keen interest in plant propagation and growth. Under the guidance of her science teacher, Jennifer expanded her outside interest into a winning Science Fair project, qualifying her to compete in the state fair. Entitled "The Effects of Different Rooting Media on *Tradescantia Albiflora* and *Begonia Semperflorens* Root Initia-

---

*Jennifer Speyrer and Pierre Lanusse are students at Opelousas (Louisiana) Catholic High School. The author is indebted to Jennifer, Pierre, and their parents for their permission to cite their projects; to Captain Richard Meaux, principal of the school, for his assistance; and to Mrs. Wanda Dupuis, the science teacher who provided much help and guidance to the students in the development of their projects.

tion and Formation," Jennifer's project followed more formally the scientific method of problem solving. Her steps, as outlined in her project report, were as follows:

Problem Statement:
The purpose of this project was to determine

1. which rooting media produced the best results under a given set of environmental conditions,
2. which concentration of Butyric Acid produced the most rapid growth of roots in a given period of time,
3. which rooting medium worked best, and
4. which cultivar produced the greatest amount of root growth in all of the experiments combined.

Hypotheses:
1. *Tradescantia Albiflora* and *Begonia Semperflorens* will root in all five rooting media.
2. Vermiculite, perlite, and sand will produce stronger and healthier roots.
3. Different concentrations of Butyric Acid will stimulate root initiation and formation, with the 0.8% solution producing the best results.

Procedures:
After reviewing ten sources of information on plant propagation and related topics, Jennifer prepared 120 soft-wood cuttings, 60 of each of the two types of plant material. Three groups of 30 cuttings each (three of each type of plant material in each of five rooting media) were treated with varied concentrations of Butyric Acid (0.8%, 0.3%, and 0.1%, respectively), and a fourth group of 30 cuttings was left untreated as a control.

Trays containing the planted cuttings were kept in a Quonset greenhouse constructed of double-layer six mil polyethylene plastic with forced air blown between the two layers, allowing direct light through. Pans containing the trays of plants were placed on an electric rooting pad at a bottom heat of 80°F. Leaves were misted daily, and cuttings were watered with 150 ml of water per pan every other day for three weeks. Root initiation, average root length, and average number of roots were checked and recorded every Saturday. At the end of three weeks, all cuttings were checked, and observations were made to determine which rooting medium and which concentration of Butyric Acid gave the best results.

Results:
1. Cuttings planted in vermiculite showed the greatest root initiation and development. Jennifer attributed these results to:
   a. retention of optimum moisture
   b. aeration of rooting media
   c. provision of proper support
   d. nutrient content of the medium.
2. In the cuttings planted in sand, Miracle Mulch, and perlite, root initiation was slow and sparse.
3. Treatment with 0.1%, 0.3%, and 0.8% concentrations of Butyric Acid produced good results.

Conclusions:
1. Sand, perlite, Miracle Mulch, and milled sphagnum should not be used as rooting media for *Tradescantia Albiflora* and *Begonia Semperflorens*.
2. Cultivars treated with 0.1%, 0.3%, and 0.8% concentrations of Butyric Acid will produce healthier and stronger roots with larger numbers of root hairs.

Recommendations for Future Research:
Further experimentation should be conducted to determine

1. which combination of rooting media and Butyric Acid would produce the best results and
2. whether or not one combination would give satisfactory results for all types of plant material.

GATHERING AND PROCESSING DATA

Sampling Techniques

As we have seen in the previous discussions, it is often necessary for a researcher to use a carefully selected sample of the population being investigated because the general population is too large to use directly. For example, consider a study whose purpose is to determine whether sixth-grade boys perform better in mathematics than girls of the same age group. Since it obviously is not possible to examine the grades and achievement test scores of all sixth-grade boys and girls in the nation, the student might select a sample of this group from her state or local district. Since the validity of the findings will be largely dependent on the similarity of the sample to the general population, it is essential that great care be taken in selecting the subjects from whom the data will be gathered. For purposes of training gifted students in elementary research tactics, this chapter will cover the two sampling techniques that are generally considered the most likely to allow selection of a group that reasonably represents the general population: random sampling and stratified sampling.

Random Samples.   We all are familiar with the "drawing from a hat" technique of selecting a random volunteer. Statistically, however, this is not the best method of obtaining a random sample—one that gives every member of a group an equal chance of being selected. There are two primary methods of selecting random samples. The first, using a table of random numbers, is feasible only when such a table is available. Perhaps more practical for the classroom is the systematically drawn random sample. Theoretically the first digit should be drawn from a table of random numbers. A more accessible system, however, would be to have a disinterested party select a number with which to begin. For example, if we wanted to select a random sample of 100 out of a district population of 500 eighth-grade girls, we would ask for a number between 1 and 5 (since we need 100/500, or 1/5 of the total). Out of the alphabetized list of eighth-grade girls in the district, we would then begin with the selected number and record every fifth name thereafter. At the end of the process, we would have our random sample of 1/5 of the names, or 100 subjects.

Stratified Samples.   A second method of sampling, which when properly employed offers the advantage of a more systematically representative group from which to gather data, is the stratified sampling technique. In this method, a characteristic or set of characteristics typical of the general population to be sampled is used as a criterion for subject selection. This method produces a still greater representation if the sample is drawn from the characteristic strata in the same proportion as is found in the general population under investigation. For example, if students are being polled to determine their parents' preferences for a coming election, the sample should contain proportionately the same racial mixture, socioeconomic status, professional/occupational distribution, religious preferences, ages, and so on, as the general population of the district. Having divided the potential sample into these units, the researcher then selects randomly from each group the sample to be used for investigation.

Instruments for Use in Research

Interviews.   Even the youngest gifted child in the primary grades is capable of conducting a simple interview with parents, teachers, or friends. In preparing for such an assignment, the teacher should (1) help students identify the purpose of the interview, (2) guide them in formulating a brief list of questions relevant to their purposes, and (3) provide time in class for the students to practice by interviewing each other, supervising closely to assure that proper techniques are used. As students progress through the grades, more complex interview questions can be utilized, and community professionals can be interviewed to add credibility to the projects.

Written Instruments. Older students (beginning in the middle grades) can be taught to construct a variety of written instruments that can provide much valuable information. Some of these include surveys and rating scales (discussed earlier in this chapter), inventories, checklists, and a variety of tests.

Mechanical Devices. Beginning in the earliest years of school, students can be taught to use and interpret data from simple mechanical devices. Because the study of weather is popular among young children, simple weather instruments such as the thermometer are ideal for teaching primary students to use mechanical devices for gathering data. In the middle grades, the more complex instruments (barometer or hygrometer) can be used, followed by more sophisticated devices of other types (e.g., the dynamometer) in the junior and senior high school years.

Library Resources

Probably the most essential research skill for the gifted student is the use of the library. Without an efficient understanding of what this vast resource offers and the ways of making the most of its wealth, the researcher at any level will miss much of the information that is available at her command. Concepts that should be taught to students from the early years include the use of the card catalog, periodical publications, reference materials of various types, microforms, indexes, and a variety of other resources that can provide the necessary background for any research undertaking to be a success.

Card Catalog. The primary teacher should spend one or more periods per week in the library, instructing students on methods of locating information. After students have been instructed regarding appropriate library behavior and the general types of material that are found in a library, the first resource that should be presented is the card catalog. Even young gifted students, once they have mastered the basics of searching through alphabetized material, can learn to locate books by subject, author, or title. When this skill has been thoroughly assimilated, the students will have virtually unlimited access to the greatest majority of resources the school library has to offer.

Nonfiction Books.   Having mastered the use of the card catalog, the student is ready to search for and use a variety of nonfiction books as references. Biographies and a number of books on a wide variety of topics are available at all levels and can provide students of all ages with much material from which to select.

Journals, Newspapers, and Other Periodicals.   As students progress through the grades, they become familiar with periodicals as sources of information. Through magazines such as the *National Geographic Explorer, Ranger Rick,* and other primary level publications, even the youngest children can begin to learn the rudiments of periodical research; at the upper levels, a more sophisticated level of reading can begin, ultimately resulting in the use of the professional journals.

The use of the newspaper is an essential skill that can be taught on a modified scale beginning with the primary classroom news weekly. Around the middle grades, students should be given intensive instruction in the reading and use of adult newspapers, including the makeup of the newspaper, types of information found, and the like. (Local newspapers often provide filmstrips and other instructional materials for schools free of charge, especially in connection with National Newspaper Week.) A popular activity for helping students learn about the use of the newspaper is the writing of a class paper, either about class or school activities or in connection with a unit of study. For example, sixth-grade social studies classes may enjoy developing a newspaper that might have appeared in ancient times. The teacher should help students to identify sections of the newspaper and the content to be contained in each (e.g., students who are sports-minded might write on the chariot races; those who are fashion-conscious could research the costumes of the times).

Dictionaries and Encyclopedias.   Probably the first reference books that students learn to use in the primary grades are the dictionary and the encyclopedia. Technically, although this concept may contradict what students have been taught since their early years, the encyclopedia is *not* a research tool. Certainly it is a resource that we must all learn to use, as the encyclopedia is helpful for gaining an overview of a general area and narrowing it to a particular topic for further study or for locating a concise answer to a specific question about a given topic. Similarly, the dictionary, a reference tool that is used by many on a regular basis, is necessary for students to master but is really not a research tool in itself. Field Enterprises, the publisher of *World Book Encyclopedia,* provides at nominal cost several levels of instructional materials (teachers' guides and student workbooks) for use in teaching dictionary and encyclopedia skills in the elementary school.

Documents and Pamphlets.   Two other valuable sources of information are government documents and pamphlets published by professional societies and other agencies. Although these materials may require a reasonable level of sophistication for efficient use, they often provide data not available from other sources.

Indexes, Abstracts, and Retrieval Systems.   One of the most important criteria in the selection of research sources is the recency of the information. Since school library collections are often outdated, the conscientious junior investigator must search elsewhere to assure that information is current. For this reason, the regular use of periodical literature is essential. Just as the index to a book helps the reader locate information quickly without the necessity of searching laboriously through the pages, periodical indexes are invaluable in the researcher's quest for articles that provide needed information. Along with the periodical literature, then, the student must begin at an early stage to use the periodical indexes. The *Readers' Guide to Periodical Literature*, probably the simplest such index, can provide access to a great amount of current information, and its use can serve as practice for the later use of professional indexes in the upper grades. Since the *Readers' Guide* is available in most school libraries and includes most periodicals that students are likely to utilize in the early years of research, it is an essential tool for the gifted student to master. (Note: The *Abridged Readers' Guide* is the edition most often available in middle, junior high, and small senior high school libraries, with the complete *Readers' Guide* usually found in the larger high school collections.) In later years, students may be introduced to indexes that provide access to professional journals of the fields in which they are interested in acquiring current, in-depth knowledge.

In addition to the periodical index, which references a great many magazines, newspapers, journals, and other literature of this sort, more useful resources are now available to assist the researcher in the narrowing of references relevant to the topic of study. Unlike early writers who had a relatively small number of resources on which to base their background searches, today's researchers are faced with a wide variety of sources that must be evaluated with respect to their relevance to the investigation. In recent years publishers have developed abstract volumes, reference books in index form which include not only the information needed to locate the referenced articles but also brief abstracts (or synopses) of the articles, with listings of the key terms and concepts about which they are written. Through the use of these abstract indexes, a brief glance at title and description can often tell the researcher whether or not an article will be useful for the project. Perhaps the most commonly used abstracts among educational researchers are the two volumes published by ERIC (the Educational

Resources Information Center): RIE (*Resources in Education*) and CIJE (*Current Index to Journals in Education*), and the similar *Psychological Abstracts* (PA), which indexes and abstracts articles dealing with the behavioral sciences. Like the indexes, abstract volumes are available in most professional fields, providing the researcher with an invaluable resource that saves many hours of searching.

Along with the indexes and abstracts that are now available for help in locating references, modern technology has provided researchers with a relatively new tool—the computerized information retrieval system. Through the use of data bases such as ERIC and PA these systems allow the researcher to input into the computer certain types of information regarding the study (key words or topics, data bases to be used, recency criteria, and the like), and give back lists of references (with abstracts, if desired) for the reader's consideration. What a saving of time these new systems afford for the busy researcher who in past years spent countless hours in the quest for material to support her research!

Specialized Reference Books.   In addition to the preceding materials, there are many reference books that serve specific purposes and that should not be overlooked as valuable sources of information. Among these are guides designed to assist researchers in locating the types of materials they need. One excellent example of this type of reference is Eugene P. Sheehy's *Guide to Reference Books*, 9th edition, and supplements (Chicago: American Library Association, 1976).

Also to be considered are specialized encyclopedias (e.g., *Encyclopedia of Education*) and dictionaries (e.g., *Dictionary of Contemporary Quotations*). Other types of reference books include statistical references (almanacs, statistical abstracts, the popular *Guinness Book of World Records*), directories, and others.

Microforms.   With the flood of periodical literature that has resulted from the knowledge explosion and from the countless professional societies, each with its own journals and other publications, libraries have begun to face an inevitable problem—a lack of space for storing all of the materials needed for the sophisticated researcher. Again, thanks to modern technology, we now have a variety of microforms (microfilm and microfiche) available, enabling the researcher to examine firsthand a wide variety of materials that otherwise would have been inaccessible: rare and out-of-print books and manuscripts; old, foreign, or specialized newspapers; doctoral dissertations; unpublished documents; and many other types of reference material. Microforms have become the storage medium of the future; in combination with the information retrieval systems that index them, they provide an incomparable source of data for the researcher who has limited time.

Nonlibrary Sources

Human Resources. Not to be overlooked are those resources that cannot be indexed yet often provide information that printed material may never contain—human beings. In the early grades, children should be encouraged to talk with their parents, teachers, and friends, asking questions structured to provide information of interest to them. As students approach the later school years, interviews can grow into more sophisticated searches in which human resources provide historical data, often taped for safekeeping, that cannot be duplicated in any other way. Resource persons might include senior citizens, individuals who have hobbies or special interests or talents in students' own areas of interest, public officials, museum curators, university faculty members, or community professionals in areas that the students are studying.

Other Resources. When beginning a teaching segment on research skills, the teacher of the gifted should first determine the level of sophistication of each student with regard to research. An early technique that is most effective at the beginning of such a study is to have the class brainstorm possible sources of information. In addition to the resources named above, gifted students pressed for creative production will eventually come up with ideas such as the use of public records (real estate sales, birth and death records, law enforcement and court statistics, census records), church records (birth, marriage, and death records dating from years prior to the keeping of public records), family Bibles, genealogies, tombstones, and a treasury of other sources that should be considered when searching for information. At this point the teacher should encourage creative thinking and provide access to as many different forms and sources of data as the students are able to handle. The variety is limitless, and the teacher of the gifted must model flexibility if her students are to become researchers in the truest sense of the word.

Processing Information

When teaching the process of data gathering, it is crucial that students be given simultaneously the skills for processing the information they find. This section will comment briefly on several skills that are essential to the organizational process and that should be mastered before the data-gathering process begins: notetaking, outlining, paraphrasing, summarizing, crediting sources, and editing.

Notetaking. When a researcher begins to gather information, whether from printed sources, human sources, or experimental observation, she must first decide on a system for taking and organizing notes. Contrary to the belief held by many teachers, the ability to take efficient notes is *not* an inborn skill—it must be taught! When teaching students to take notes, the following guidelines should be followed:

1. Before beginning to make notes from a given source, enter at the top of the page or card a complete bibliographic reference for the source, including those pieces of information that will be used in footnotes or reference lists, as well as any additional information that might be needed in later stages of the research. Examples of such notations are shown here.

    For a book:
    Leonard, George B. *Education and Ecstasy.* New York: Dell
    Publishing Co., 1968.
    or
    Leonard G. B. (1968). *Education and ecstasy.* New York: Dell
    Publishing Co.

    For an article:
    Lyon, Harold C., Jr. "Humanistic Education for Lifelong
    Learning," *International Review of Education,* Vol. 20, No.
    4 (1974), pp. 502–505.
    or
    Lyon, H. C., Jr. (1974). Humanistic education for lifelong
    learning. *International Review of Education, 20,* 502–505.

2. Early in the process of teaching research skills, familiarize the students with the word *plagiarism,* its meaning and its implications. Help them understand that any use of someone else's writing without proper credit is contrary to law. Model your own belief of the importance of this concept by citing credits on every handout you give to your students that is not your own original work! Provide the format you wish the students to use, and insist that they follow this format precisely. Stress that direct quotations should be used only when the exact wording used by an author is significant, and that ideas not quoted directly should be paraphrased and credited. (In taking notes, the researcher should paraphrase the ideas that are important and place quotation marks around any material that is to be quoted exactly, except in the case of very long quotations, which are indented in block form). Page numbers should be recorded when taking notes on any material, although they are included in the final writing only for direct quotations.

3. Provide practice in taking informal notes, indenting slightly to indicate subtopics. Practice can be provided for the entire class through the use of brief written passages or verbally presented material.

4. Also worthy of consideration is what might be called "right brain notetaking"—the recording of information by creative, visual methods. Such methods might include photocopying key passages or pages and underscoring or highlighting with color coding or numerical indications in the margins of sections to which selected sections pertain, organization by webbing (a manner similar to the future wheel concept), and the like.

Outlining.   After all notes have been taken from the selected materials, a topic outline should be developed, reflecting all of the types of information contained in the notes. When teaching outlining skills, it is important to caution against the following pitfalls that frequently appear in outlines developed by inexperienced writers:

1. Dividing a single topic (using an A without a B). Elementary students commonly make this mistake, as do college students who have not been taught the proper method of outlining. Consider the following outline on creativity:

I. The creative process
    A. Blocks to the creative process
        1. Lack of time
        2. Lack of knowledge
        3. Inability to withhold judgment
II. The creative person

Note that under the topic The Creative Process only one subtopic is included. Why, then, is the subtopic Blocks to the Creative Process not included as a part of the main topic? The principle demonstrated here is simple: If there are not at least two subtopics, there is no reason to divide or break down to a lower level. In other words, never use an A without a B or a 1 without a 2.

2. Failure to indent when indicating subtopics. Again note the above example. Although the division of topics is incorrect, the indentation format is used correctly. All first-level topics (designated by Roman numerals) are lined up vertically, all second-level topics (designated by upper-case letters) are lined up vertically, and so on. Note also that after the second level the subtopics are indicated by Arabic numerals. If additional levels are warranted, they should be indicated by lower-case letters, followed by Arabic numbers in parentheses, and finally by lower-case letters in parentheses. It is unlikely that further analysis is needed, as most details can fit into one of the five specified levels. Remember also that each indented piece of information should pertain directly to the topic that is above and to the left of it.

After the topic/subtopic outline has been developed, representing the organizational plan from which the report will be written, each piece of information recorded in the notetaking process should be classified and grouped according to classification. Once this process has been completed, the ordered notes can be used for writing.

Paraphrasing and Summarizing. During the notetaking process, notes that are not to be quoted directly should be recorded in paraphrased form. Like the other skills mentioned here, paraphrasing is a skill that must be taught. In the primary years, young children can be taught to paraphrase and summarize by asking them to "tell me this story in your own words." Older students can be given textbook passages to rephrase; then, when notetaking practice is begun, they will be ready for and adept at paraphrasing.

Crediting Sources. Teachers can never stress too strongly the importance of giving credit in the text of the report to each source from which information is obtained. There are numerous forms that are approved by professional societies, journals, and publishers for this purpose; the teacher may wish to consider the following simple formats:

> Jensen (1973) pointed out that students were not permitted to communicate with each other in the classroom.

or

> Leonard (15) visualizes humanistic education as a philosophy which will "return man to himself."

Editing. Once the rough draft of a report has been completed, the work is ready to be edited. Since the first draft is written primarily with the aim of organizing ideas on paper, several tasks must be accomplished in the editing process:

1. Read the paper straight through for content. Does the report get across to the reader a clear picture of what you want to say?
2. Reread the paper one paragraph at a time. Check carefully for good sentence and paragraph structure. Does each paragraph treat a single topic, clearly signalled by a well-constructed topic sentence? Is the wording concise and to the point, lacking redundancy? Are grammar and spelling correct? (Check the dictionary for words about which you are uncertain as to spelling and/or usage.) If words are repeated, overly simplified, or uninteresting, use a thesaurus to improve your expression.
3. Put the edited paper aside at least overnight. Pick it up again later and reread it without stopping (marking in the margin any section to which you wish to return). Go back and make any corrections or

revisions you wish to make. Are you satisfied with the quality of your work? Have you covered your topic well? If so, your task is complete.

STATISTICAL ANALYSIS

Essentially the term *statistics* refers to the mathematically based science of analyzing numerical data for the purpose of drawing conclusions about a given group that is the target of study. Researchers and teachers who teach statistical procedures to students must keep firmly in mind that statistics is simply a research tool and not an end in itself. Teaching statistics totally out of context, without relevant examples of its use is, as Renzulli (1977) says with regard to the isolated use of "Type II Enrichment" activities, like a basketball team practicing but never playing a game. Nonetheless, if gifted students are to become investigators of real-life problems, they must have a command of at least an elementary level of statistical procedures.

This section will treat those areas of statistics that can be used with limited samples of data from which generalizations, assumed to be true of the general population, can be drawn and which gifted students can appropriately use with a limited amount of training. These procedures include both descriptive statistics (frequency distributions, measures of central tendency, measures of variability, and simple correlation) and inferential statistics (sampling procedures and tests of significance).

Frequency Distributions

When an investigator has gathered all the data that apply to the stated research question, the data must be organized in a fashion that makes analysis relatively simple to accomplish. The frequency distribution is a popular organizational tool because it is simple to understand, use, and interpret in drawing conclusions from data. In using frequency distributions, three steps must be followed:

1. Determine the range (subtract the smallest value from the largest value and add one).
2. Select an interval for grouping values on the frequency distribution table (divide the range first by 10 and then by 20; select an odd number between the two—preferably a multiple of 5 for ease of manipulation).
3. Prepare a table showing the number of values, called the *frequency (f)* falling into each class or group of scores.

Consider the following example in applying these steps.

Jacob, a highly gifted student in Marvin Taylor's fifth-grade class, had for some time been concerned about his small school district's need for a gifted program. Although Mr. Taylor was an exceptional teacher and provided many opportunities for Jacob to work at his own pace on advanced projects of interest to him, he realized that Jacob's needs could not be totally met in any traditional classroom setting. In social studies, the class had recently heard a law enforcement office talk about the high incidence of school dropouts among juvenile delinquents. Noting Jacob's interest in the speaker's topic, Mr. Taylor encouraged him to pursue the subject further. Having recognized from reading class that Jacob's research skills were advanced for his age and grade level, Mr. Taylor gave him some personalized instruction in basic statistical procedures and guided him in the development of a study that combined his new interest with their perceived need for a gifted program.

When Jacob was ready, his mother took him to the city police station, where a cooperative officer carefully screened out the names of the violators and provided Jacob with a valuable set of numerical data with which to work—test scores on high school dropouts who had been arrested for area crimes within the past five years. Examining this information closely, Jacob was amazed to find the following IQ scores:

120, 112, 133, 135, 104, 140, 106, 145, 124, 100, 110, 90, 130, 146, 110, 122, 132, 119, 139, 150

Following the guidelines provided by Mr. Taylor, Jacob first determined the range of scores (150 − 90 + 1 = 61). Dividing the range by 10 (6.1) and then by 20 (3.05), he selected an interval of 5 (and odd number between 3.05 and 6.1 that was a multiple of 5). Thus each class would have a spread of 5. In order to avoid overlapping of the scores on his table, Jacob began with 89.5 (just below the lowest score) and ended with 154.5 (just above the highest score). Now Jacob prepared a frequency distribution table, showing the number of cases in each class (Table 3–2).

Recognizing that a simple chart was not dramatic enough to demonstrate to a public body the significant of his findings, Jacob prepared a frequency histogram, graphically illustrating the nature of the problem. The graph, which he drew on a large poster in preparation for the next School Board meeting, is show in Figure 3–1. (Note that the numbers of the horizontal axis represent the highest value in each class of the table, the numbers on the vertical axis represent the frequency, and the scores are plotted between these numbers.) Now Jacob was ready to learn about other methods of using statistics to prove a point.

Table 3–2. Frequency Distribution Table

Class	Tally	Frequency
149.5–154.5	I	1
144.5–149.5	I	1
139.5–144.5	II	2
134.5–139.5	II	2
129.5–134.5	III	3
124.5–129.5		0
119.5–124.5	III	3
114.5–119.5		0
109.5–114.5	IIII	4
104.5–109.5	I	1
99.5–104.5	II	2
84.5– 99.5		0
89.5– 94.5	I	1

Figure 3–1. Frequency Histogram

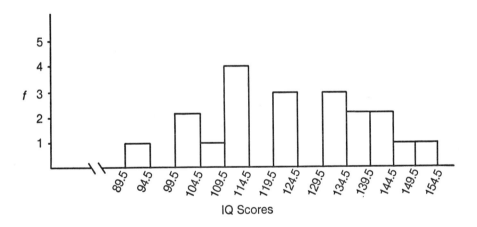

Measures of Central Tendency

Measures of central tendency are measurement concepts that assist the researcher in locating and describing the "center" of a distribution of scores. For example, if a teacher wished to judge the academic achievement of a group of students, she might to do so by determining how each score on a given achievement test varied from a measure of central tendency. These measures, then, are simply reference points with which a comparison may be made. There are three measures of central tendency: the mean, the median, and the mode.

The Mean.   The mean, usually designated symbolically as $\bar{X}$, is simply the arithmetic average of a group of values. The mean is calculated by adding the numbers in a group and dividing the total by the number of values included. For example, if five students made scores of 92, 68, 89, 75, and 96 on a certain test, the mean score of the group would be:

$$\frac{92 + 68 + 89 + 75 + 96}{5} = 84.$$

The mean is probably the most commonly used measure of central tendency because the value of each score enters into its calculation. Thus, descriptions of variability are most often described in terms of an individual's deviation from (distance above or below) the mean.

The Median.   The median is the midpoint of an ordered group of scores. In the above example, the median would be 89, because there are exactly two scores greater than and two scores less than 89. (If there were an even number of scores, the median would be found by calculating the average of the two middle scores.) The median is employed primarily to give a general idea of an individual's standing in comparison to a group. Its use has one primary advantage: If there are extremely high or extremely low values in a group, the mean will be skewed, or influenced, in their direction. For example, the mean of a group of scores including 60, 95, 83, 91, 94, 43, 91, 82, and 36 would be 76, whereas the median of this group would be 84. Since the median is not influenced by the magnitudes of the individual scores in the group, it is often thought to present a more realistic picture of a group that contains extreme values. If no extremes are present, the mean and median may be very close in value, if not identical. Finally, the median should be used in situations in which the scores represent ranks (such as percentiles); in such circumstances, the mean is not an appropriate measure.

The Mode.   The mode of a group of numbers is simply the value that appears most frequently. For example, in a group of test scores including 78, 80, 82, 90, 75, 80, 67, 95, 80, and 78, the mode would be 80, because there are three occurrences of this score. Although the mode is the easiest central measure to determine (since it can be seen visually without the necessity of calculation), it is also the least reliable value to use in a comparative judgment. In groups considered on the basis of numerical data in which either mean or median is available, the mode is usually used as only one facet of a general description of the group. However, the mode is quite useful in cases that do not involve numerical values (e.g., considering the number of males versus the number of females, the number of Democrats versus the number of Republicans, etc.).

———————

Jacob's Work Continues

By now Jacob's work had begun to draw the interest of the community. The word was spreading that a gifted fifth grader had uncovered an above average level of intelligence among juvenile delinquents in the area. As the date of the next School Board meeting approached, Jacob began to refine his analysis. Remembering what Mr. Taylor had taught him about measures of central tendency, Jacob examined his scores more closely. To his delight, he found that the median (middle I.Q. score of his group was 118, the mode (most common score) was also 118, and the mean (or average) score was 119.85! Since Jacob's state endorsed the *Revolving Door Identification Model* (Renzulii, Reis, and Smith, 1981) for identification and placement of gifted students in special programs, students with I.Q. scores of 120 and above would qualify for placement in talent pools, to revolve into gifted programs as their needs demanded. Jacob and Mr. Taylor grew more excited as their "day in court" approached. Still, Jacob felt that he should explore every possible avenue for convincing the Board that gifted programs were needed in his school district. Mr. Taylor then taught Jacob one more area of statistics: measures of variability.

———————

Measures of Variability

Although measures of central tendency are important for describing a group as a whole, or for comparing groups to each other on the basis of their overall characteristics, these measures are not sufficient for comparing individuals to members of other groups or to others within their own groups. Furthermore, two sets of scores can have identical central tendencies but different distribution patterns. In such cases, measures of variability (also called measures of variation, scatter, dispersion, or deviation) must be used. The following concepts are essential to the understanding of variability: range, quartile, percentile, stanine, standard deviation, and the normal curve.

Range. Range, the simplest measure of variability of determine, is simply the difference between the highest and lowest values of a group. Suppose a teacher gave her students a pretest to determine their current level of knowledge on a given topic. She could then use the range of pretest scores in deciding where to begin and how to proceed with instruction. If the range were small (4–5 points), she would know that most students possessed roughly the same degree of preparation on the topic. A wider range (20–30 points), on the other hand, would indicate that the students' background in this area differed substantially and that some individual instruction might be needed for the lower-scoring students.

Quartiles, Percentiles, and Stanines.   In educational circles, the term *percentile* is commonly used. Simply stated, a percentile (as distinguished from a percent or percentage) is a measure that describes an individual in terms of the number (percent) of scores below her score. If, out of 100 students, Marsha makes the tenth highest score, with 90 scores below hers, she can be said to have scored at the 90th percentile (or within the top 10 percent). Statistically speaking, the 50th percentile is considered "average," that is, it can be assumed that half of the general population would score above and half below that score. It should be noted that it is not possible to score at the 100th percentile on a test that has been standardized on a large population, as a score of 100 percent correct by even one person during the standardization process would eliminate the possibility of any future testing yielding a score above it.

Another measure that is similar to the percentile is the quartile. Whereas the percentile refers to the percent of scores falling below a given score, the quartile refers to quarters (or 25 percent increments) of a group. Out of a group of 100 scores, then, the 25th score would be at the top quartile or the 75th percentile. (In other words, 75—or 75 percent—of the scores would fall below it.) The second quartile (Q_2), or the middle score, is therefore equal to the 50th percentile (P_{50}), or the median. (Recalling that the median defines the middle score—the score that has an equal number of scores above and below it—the reader will recognize that Q_2 and P_{50} are also ways of classifying the median score.)

A third measure commonly used in comparing test scores is the stanine. Whereas the quartile system divides all scores in a group into four intervals, the stanine system divides such scores into nine. Thus, a score in the fifth, or middle, stanine (comparable to the 50th percentile, the second quartile, or the median) may be said to be "average" for the particular test. Actually, because few scores are exactly at "average," and since the possibility of measurement error is great, the stanine system (which describes ranges rather than specific scores) provides a safer basis for interpretation than the percentile or the quartile. In practice, any score that falls in stanine 4, 5, or 6 (or the middle one-third of the scores) is considered to be in the average range, making scores at stanines 7–9 above average and those in stanines 1–3 below average. Because of their clarity and the ease of understanding the concepts that they represent, stanines are often used in place of percentiles and quartiles for interpreting scores on standardized tests of mental ability or academic achievement to others.

Jacob Completes His Project

Now Jacob acquired a table of national norms on the intelligence test that had been administered to the dropout delinquents in his study and compared their scores to these norms. Knowing that the School Board traditionally examined test data on the basis of comparisons with national samples, Jacob found the percentiles and stanines corresponding to the scores of his subjects. He had data to prove that nine (or 45 percent) of the delinquents had scored in the top (or ninth) stanine, and eleven (or 55 percent) had scored within the top 10 percent nationally! In the belief that Jacob's findings would persuade the School Board to authorize a new gifted program, his teacher acquired IQ test scores on all students in the district, and Jacob found that 10 percent of these students would qualify for such a program under state guidelines.

When the evening of the Board meeting arrived, Jacob confidently went forward and presented the results of his study. At the end of his impressive presentation, the Board voted unanimously to begin a program for the gifted students in his district. His study of statistics had proved a valuable point!

Standard Deviation.   The most statistically exact (and consequently the most frequently used) method of indicating score variability is the standard deviation. Conceptually, the standard deviation can be defined as the average amount by which the scores in a group, taken collectively, deviate from their mean. Thus, the standard deviation will be large for score groups that vary greatly among themselves, whereas those score groups whose values are relatively similar will have small standard deviations. Consider this example.

Mrs. Johnson's eighth-grade class earned the following scores on their latest science test: 59, 62, 70, 77, 52, 58, 64, 55, 47, and 56. Joseph, usually an "A" student, was disappointed because his grade was only 77, normally a "C." How might he more realistically compare his score with those of his classmates?

Procedure:

1. Calculate the mean score (the sum of the scores divided by the number of scores): 760/10 = 76.
2. Calculate the standard deviation (see calculations below):
   a. Determine each score's deviation (distance above or below the mean [x]).
   b. Square each deviation.

Score (X)	x	x^2
59	− 1	1
62	+ 2	4
70	+10	100
77	+17	289
52	− 8	64
58	− 2	4
64	+ 4	16
55	− 5	25
47	−13	169
56	− 4	16
		688

   c. Sum the squared deviations   (688).
   d. Calculate the average x^2 (688/10=68.8).
   e. The square root of the average x^2 is the standard deviation ($\sqrt{68.8}$ = 8.29).

———

In the above example, the total squared deviations (688) would be divided by the number of scores (10), producing an average deviation of 201.4. The square root of the average deviation, 8.29, is the standard deviation for this group of scores.

An alternate method of calculating the standard deviation is described below:

1. Square each of the scores.
2. Total the column of scores (ΣX. In the above example, this total would be 60.
3. Total the column of squared scores (ΣX^2). In the above example, the total of squared scores would be 36,688.
4. Using s to represent the standard deviation, and n to represent the number of scores (in this case, 10), insert the above figures into the

following formula and solve the equation; the result will be the standard deviation.

$$s = \sqrt{\dfrac{\Sigma X^2 - \dfrac{(\Sigma X)^2}{n}}{n}}$$

The experience gained by statisticians using the standard deviation has resulted in the establishment of certain useful information. For example, most score distributions extend only three to four standard deviations above or below their respective means. From this knowledge we could conclude that a test score as many as two standard deviations above the class mean would represent a quite respectable test performance. Of even greater utility is the observation that when distributions of scores are mound-shaped (that is, when most scores of a group fall in the middle of a histogram on which they have been plotted, causing a bulge in the middle), approximately 2/3 (68 percent) of all scores will be within one standard deviation of the mean (± 1 s.d.). Approximately 95 percent of all scores will fall within two standard deviations of the mean (± 2 s.d.), and approximately 99 percent of all scores will be within three standard deviations of the mean (± 3 s.d.). This knowledge helps us pinpoint more precisely and more meaningfully the relationship between a known score and the average score. When the standard deviation is combined with the normal curve (discussion follows), the researcher can achieve even greater precision in describing scores and consequently can begin to compare scores from different distributions.

Normal Curve.   During the late nineteenth and early twentieth centuries, scientists discovered that the distribution characteristics of many physical phenomena could be described with a normal curve. For example, if we measured and plotted the heights of fourteen-year-old males, we would find that most were near the average height, whereas increasingly fewer were taller or shorter than the average. Equally useful was the discovery of several important mathematical and statistical properties of the normal (or bell) curve. One such mathematical property is the equality and identical location of the mean, median, and mode for any normal distribution. (Since the curve of a normal distribution is perfectly symmetrical, the mean, median, and mode of such a distribution always fall exactly in the center of the curve.) A second important feature of the normal curve is that there is an exact relationship between standard deviations and percentages of area under the normal curve. We must keep in mind that for a given distribution each standard deviation is the same size. However. the area of the curve associated with each standard deviation varies in a predictable fashion as a function of the rise and fall of the curve. Thus, the area between the mean and one standard deviation above the mean is 34.13 percent of the total area of the curve. (Note: Since the area of the normal curve represents the total number of scores in the distribution, it is also true that 34.13 percent of all scores will be found in the interval from the mean to one standard deviation above the mean.) A third important feature of the normal curve is its symmetry. Consequently, 34.13 percent of all scores will also be found in the interval from one standard deviation below the mean to the mean. Other corresponding areas are shown in Figure 3–2.

Using the normal curve to determine the precise relationship between a given raw score and its mean requires the calculation of a standard score referred to as z. Once a score is calculated and expressed as z, it can be compared to scores from different groups that possess different characteristics of central tendency and variability. The z score indicates how many standard deviations above or below the mean a given score is located; it is calculated simply by subtracting the mean from the score and dividing the difference by the standard deviation. (Note: The mean must always be subtracted from the score, as the positive or negative sign is necessary to indicate whether the score is above or below the mean.) Using our earlier example of Mrs. Johnson's class in which the mean on a science test was 60 and the standard deviation was 8.29, we could determine Joseph's z score in the following manner:

1. Subtract the mean (60) from Joseph's score (77), yielding a difference of +17.
2. Divide this difference (+17) by the standard deviation (8.29), giving Joseph a z score of +2.05.

Noting the degree to which his grade on the science test had exceeded those of the other students, Joseph was now much happier about his performance.

Figure 3–2.   The Normal Curve

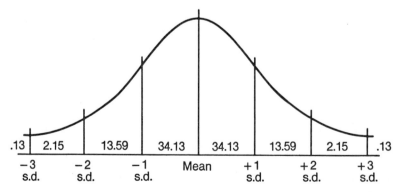

As mentioned earlier, one advantage of the z score is that it permits the direct comparison of performances on tests that have different means and standard deviations. For example, let us imagine that Joseph later took an English test on which he had earned a raw score of 88. On first inspection this would appear to be a much better performance than the 77 that he had received in science. But such a judgment could be premature, depending on the performance of the class as a whole on the English test. If the class average on the English test was 82 and the standard deviation was 5, then Joseph's English test grade, expressed as a z score, would be +1.20, a much lower score (relative to the class average) than the +2.05 that he had earned on the science test.

It is worth noting that the z score is only one of a family of standard scores, all of which are derived from the same concept of comparing the earned score to an average and dividing by the standard deviation. Other standard scores include the T score, the stanine, the deviation IQ score, and the NCE (Normal Curve Equivalent) score. Today every major standardized test of ability or achievement is reported in one or more of these standard score formats.

Correlation

Although many inferences about the population being studied can be drawn from tables and graphs that describe them, it is often important to examine relationships between specific variables in a study. For example, consider a study undertaken by Brad, a gifted eighth-grade athlete, to determine the relationship between grades in mathematics and batting averages. After gathering the two sets of scores, Brad computed what is called a coefficient of correlation—a measure of the degree to which the rise or fall of one score relates to the rise or fall of the other. In essence, Brad was asking, "Does the student who understands mathematics have a better chance at being a successful softball player?"

Since the understanding of the procedure for computing correlation coefficients is predicated upon a background that is usually beyond the pre-college student, and since computer software has placed the determination of statistical analyses such as the Pearson Correlation quickly within our grasp, the method of computing the "Pearson-r" (or correlation coefficient) will not be detailed here. It is essential, however, that the gifted student understand the concept of correlation and be provided with access to statistical analysis software packages, so that this extremely useful analytical tool will be available for use in the investigation of real-life problems.

Tests of Significance

The final method of comparing data that is recommended for use with gifted students is the test of significance. In this type of test, the investigator attempts to determine whether or not there exists a statistically significant difference between the two sets of values. Two examples will be considered.

Case 1

Jeannie was a student in Mrs. Johnson's gifted class. In keeping with her interest in state politics, she decided to poll the 300 sixth-grade students in her school to determine their preferences of the candidates entering the gubernatorial race. In order to test the significance of her findings, Jeannie needed to determine whether or not the trend demonstrated by her fellow students actually was representative of the their city's population in general. She therefore decided to use the chi-square (χ^2) test to analyze the data collected in her poll. (Note: Since the students in one school are not likely to be typical of their city's population, a more accurate sampling would result if Jeannie conducted an informal poll of several hundred adults at the local shopping mall one Saturday morning.)

Case 2

In an experimental study to determine the relative merits of two textbook series, the Greenfield Elementary School administered the same test to its entire student body. To determine the significance of the difference between the mean test scores of those using Textbooks **A** and **B**, a *t*-test was used. This analysis enabled the faculty to select the text series that resulted in the most significant increase in understanding of science concepts.

The Chi-Square (χ^2) Test.   If a researcher wishes to identify a trend that exists in the general population on the basis of a small sample, the chi-square (χ^2) test is a useful statistical procedure. Let us consider the example of Jeannie's project in which she wanted to determine from polling the 300 sixth graders in her school which gubernatorial candidate was likely to receive the greatest number of votes.

1. First Jeannie assumed that the race would be a typical one, with three new candidates running and no unusual circumstances prevailing. The expected number of votes (called fe, for frequency expected) for the three candidates should be equal, or 100 votes each.

2. Jeannie's poll produced the following results:

   Candidate 1: 60 votes
   Candidate 2: 140 votes
   Candidate 3: 100 votes

3. It is obvious that the trend indicated by the sample is in favor of candidate # 2. To determine if this trend was likely to extend to the voters of her city, Jeannie set up Table 3–3, using fo (frequencies observed) as the actual number of votes for each candidate, fe as the number of votes expected (an equal distribution among the three candidates), and ($fo-fe$) as the difference between the two figures.

4. Jeannie's next step was to square the ($fo-fe$) values, divide each by fe, and add the resulting values to find χ^2. In this case, she added 16 + 16 + 0 and derived a sum (χ^2) of 32.

5. Next Jeannie determined the "degrees of freedom," a statistical value that is simply one less than the number of categories. In this case there were three candidates (or categories), thus she worked with 2 degrees of freedom (df). Consulting a table of the critical values of chi-square, she noted that the sum of 32 with 2 degrees of freedom was greater than the highest value for 2 df. She therefore looked at the heading of the last column and found the value .001. This figure revealed that her trend was significant at the .001 level; that is, there was only one chance in 1000 (.001 = 1/1000) that the trend in the student poll could have occurred purely by chance.

Table 3–3. Chi-Square Table

	C1	C2	C3
fo	60	140	100
fe	100	100	100
$fo-fe$	40	40	0
$(fo-fe)^2$	1600	1600	0
$\dfrac{(fo-fe)^2}{fe}$	16	16	0

The t-*test.*   Another test of significance, the *t*-test, is commonly used by researchers to determine whether or not there is a statistically significant difference between two groups of values. Using the means of the two groups, a formula is followed, and a table is used for reaching a conclusion. Because of the complexity of this procedure, and since it is widely available in statistical packages for the computer, the *t*-test is not explained here. However, it is recommended for consideration by the teacher guiding secondary gifted students who have a background in algebra. Further details on the *t*-test and its uses may be found in any elementary statistics text.

PREPARING THE RESEARCH REPORT

Once the student has completed the search for information related to her topic and taken careful notes on any experimental procedures followed, she is ready to compile the written report that will serve as an important part of the final product to be communicated. The final section of this chapter will present an organizational plan for writing a research paper. Regardless of the type of research (descriptive, historical, or experimental) that a student is pursuing, the final written product should take essentially the same format. This plan includes the following sections:

Introduction

The introductory section of the research report sets forth the purpose of the study or the problem to be investigated, the research questions (or hypotheses) to be tested, any assumptions or limitations that might affect the outcome of the study, definitions of terms that the reader must understand in order to interpret the findings correctly, and the organizational plan to be followed in the development of the paper.

Review of the Literature

Having read extensively and taken efficient notes on the previous research that is related to the topic of study, the researcher next writes from these notes an organized summary of the material published in the literature. The review of the literature is an essential component of any investigation, as it presents the findings of researchers who have worked in this area previously and lays a foundation for what is done by the current researcher. A critical factor that should be stressed in writing any literary review is the necessity to give credit (through either in-text citations or reference lists, if not both) to all sources from which information was taken.

Design and Procedures

The third section of the report presents the subjects studied (if any), the instruments used in testing, the procedures followed in experimentation, the types of data gathered, and the statistical analyses performed.

Results and Conclusions

In this section of the report, the researcher presents the findings of the experiments and the conclusions drawn from these results, or (in the case of descriptive or historical research) a new synthesis or interpretation that has not been drawn by earlier researchers. Whereas the review of the literature merely summarizes the work of others, this fourth section enables the researcher to demonstrate the extent to which her work is original. The validity of the conclusions reached is extremely important to the credibility of the research.

Implications and Recommendations

The final section or chapter of the report builds on the results and conclusions but takes the analysis one step further. It is here that the writer extends her findings and conclusions into the future. Essentially the researcher now answers the questions, "What do my findings imply for the future?" and "What do we need to do *now* to improve the situation?" With these final syntheses and recommendations, the text of the report is essentially complete.

References and Appendices

At the end of the report, the researcher includes an alphabetical listing of all references actually used in the writing, using the appropriate format as dictated by the type of report. Following the reference list, a section of appendices may be included if supplementary material (material that is explanatory or complementary in nature but does not fit appropriately into any of the previous sections) is desired. With the conclusion of this section, the research report is complete.

REFERENCES

Renzulli, J. S. (1977). *The Enrichment Triad Model: A guide for developing defensible programs for the gifted and talented.* Mansfield Center, CT: Creative Learning Press.

Renzulli, J. S.; Reis, S. M.; and Smith, L. H. (1981). *The revolving door identification model.* Mansfield Center, CT: Creative Learning Press.

4

Teaching the Future
Perspective

The future doesn't belong to the
fainthearted—It belongs to the brave.
                    Ronald Reagan*

It was January 28, 1986. Commander Dick Scobee, school teacher Christa McCauliffe, and five other members of an excited *Challenger* crew had just lifted off into a blue sky. Suddenly, without warning, a huge fireball engulfed the travelers, and the hopes for this mission were dashed into the ocean. On the evening scheduled for his State of the Union message, President Ronald Reagan spoke briefly to the nation about what these seven lives had signified: peace and hope for the future. "The future doesn't belong to the fainthearted," he said, "it belongs to the brave." It is to these seven brave souls and the families who stood behind them—who support the continued exploration of space and continue to demonstrate their hope for the future—that this chapter is dedicated.

Thinking about the future is not new to mankind. Although the crystal balls and astrological charts have been largely replaced by more sophisticated methods of forecasting, the need to anticipate the future has never been felt more keenly than it has been in modern times. While visiting the United States in 1943, German political scientist Ossip K. Flechtheim coined the term *futurology* to mean an interdisciplinary, scientific study of the future. In the years since this term was first used,

---

*Speech given by President Ronald Reagan, January 28, 1986.

world events have demanded the development of futuristic thinking in scientists, social scientists, educators, astronauts—indeed, the entire human race. On the heels of World War II, the United States Congress in 1950 established the National Science Foundation (NSF) to provide funding for scientific research. Following the launching of *Sputnik* in 1957, a fear of Soviet supremacy motivated the passing of the National Defense in Education Act (NDEA) and the Elementary and Secondary Education Act (ESEA), providing funds for educational programs with emphasis on mathematics, science, and foreign languages. And in 1985, the Congress updated the discarded NDEA with the passage of the Education for Economic Security Act.

For years, science fiction writers and futurists such as H. G. Wells, Buckminster Fuller, Arthur C. Clarke, and Ray Bradbury have influenced society's conversion to futuristic thinking. With the establishment of the National Aeronautics and Space Administration, the World Future Society, and the first "think factory" with its DELPHI technique, and with the publication of futuristic classics such as Toffler's *Future Shock*, a new type of thinking and philosophy entered the scene.

Future oriented writers have reminded us of the obvious fact that we will spend the remainder of our lives in the future. But Toffler (1970) warned of a deeper concern: the anticipation of "future shock"—the result of new cultures being superimposed on the old. Toffler further cautioned that most travelers can return to the culture they left behind, but the victim of future shock cannot. What is the answer to preventing future shock? Toffler defers to Cervantes who, more than three centuries ago, coined that familiar phrase, *fore-warned is fore-armed.*

Since the early days of public education we have recognized the need for schools to prepare their graduates for life. What are the implications of future shock and the relatively new field of futuristics for education? Goodlad said it well: "Other generations believed that they had the luxury of preparing their children to live in a society similar to their own. Ours is the first generation to have achieved the Socratic wisdom of knowing that we do not know the world in which our children will live" (1971, p. 4). Others have pointed out that, although today's students will live most of their lives in the twenty-first century, our educational systems of today remain geared to the needs of the early settlers of this country. With the suicide rate among American youth soaring higher today than it has ever been in the past, much of it no doubt due to a "culture shock" that they face in attempting to reconcile the changing values of their peers and society with the value systems prevailing in their homes, it is incumbent upon the schools— from the earliest preschool years through the highest levels of graduate study—to prepare our students for a future that we cannot adequately describe.

FUTURISTICS AND THE GIFTED

Our Changing Society

No thinking person can doubt that we are living in a rapidly changing world. Toffler (1980) identified three "waves" of civilization. In the first—the agricultural era—life revolved around the nuclear family, with the young learning from the old. The first wave was followed by a second, the industrial revolution, whose vestiges are still present today. We are no longer in an industrial revolution today, however, as the third wave—the wave of technology—has taken over and is rapidly coming to control our society.

Others have spoken of changes that have taken place as our nation strives to rise above the second wave into a "post-industrial" era. Maruyama (cited in Torrance, 1977) pointed out the following shifts of emphasis that are occurring in our society today:

- From homogeneity to heterogeneity
- From standardization to de-standardization
- From competition to interdependence
- From hierarchy to interaction
- From conquering nature to living in harmony with nature
- From material satisfaction to cultural satisfaction
- From efficiency to esthetics and ethics
- From thinking in categories to thinking in social context

Torrance further pointed out that each shift brings about an increasing need for creative, innovative ways of adapting ourselves to change.

Margaret Mead discussed a shift from "post-figurative culture" (the first and second-wave cultures in which the young learned from the old) to "pre-figurative culture" (a third-wave culture that experiences peer teaching and ultimately sees the old learning from the young). Recent research has substantiated Mead's theories, reflecting that the present is increasingly dominated by the future (Torrance and Reynolds, 1978).

The demand for greater creativity is implied again in Terry Newell's prediction that the adult world of today's children will require the fullest development of human potential, the creation of increasingly more diverse careers (most of which do not exist today), and the provision of new opportunities and challenges for personal and societal development through leisure time activities (Torrance, 1980). Torrance further pointed out the increasing need to develop more durable, more functional, more easily assembled products that would last longer and be capable of repair or recycling. These needs, he said, could be met only through an improvement in creativity and problem-solving techniques.

Realistically speaking, we must realize that society cannot adapt to every change that occurs; instead, we must learn to anticipate change so that we can control its direction. Toffler has observed that we must convince our youth that they *can* influence their futures. But he also assigns to educators the responsibility for teaching students to anticipate change so that when today's future arrives it will not be a shock (Toffler, 1972).

According to Cornish (1977), we can define progress as the changes that society wishes to achieve (control of disease and hunger, shelter for the homeless, effective communication and transportation systems, freedom from fear, and the like). He further cautions, however, that progress is accompanied by two problems: First, it is unexpectedly costly, and second, it brings no permanent satisfaction because the satisfaction of old desires merely results in new ones. Overpopulation resulting from the control of disease, unemployment arising from high-tech replacement of manual labor, pollution caused by new modes of transportation, and "rising expectations" caused by satisfaction of our basic needs are all examples of the paradoxes of success. Furthermore, abundance brings about scarcities—problems that appear because the abundant life either causes the supply to diminish or causes the demand to increase. These "scarcities of abundance" include:

1. *Time.* Our lives are too complex; we never find the time to do all that we would like to do.

2. *Recognition.* The identity of self diminishes as abundance increases.

3. *Wisdom.* Decision making is not instilled in today's youth; too much is done for them. (Even their toys work for them!)

4. *Intimacy (Love, Friendship).* A high degree of mobility makes people reticent to establish close and lasting relationships.

5. *Stability (Permanence and Continuity).* Changing and highly mobile career roles, urban renewal, and other signs of 'progress' are displacing our permanence.

6. *Security of Status.* Marital problems and increasingly complex technological changes are causing feelings of insecurity among our populations. Unemployment is rampant at all levels—from maintenance to executive. Ironically the desirable changes in the professional roles of women contribute to this insecurity (Cornish, 1977, pp. 15–18).

The Role of Education

What, then, is the answer? How can we as educators prepare our youth for a changing future filled with paradox? As futurists continue to remind us, we can no longer assume that our future world will be the same as our world of the past. In his prophetic book *Third Wave,* Toffler (1980) discussed the changes that will take place as the "third wave" (or high-tech era) develops, observing that the American educational system—with its emphasis on punctuality, authority, rote and routine, and other characteristics needed for industry—was initially designed to prepare students for the industrial revolution. However, we are no longer in an industrial era. Post-industrial schooling must keep pace with technology!

Numerous authors have decried the conditions prevalent in education today. Holt (1964), for example, charged that the schools actually destroy children's intellectual and creative potentials. Lyon (1971) spoke of the failure of public education and observed that "one-dimensional men cannot teach rounding youngsters how to be properly round" (p. 13). And Leonard (1968) charged that schools are designed to discourage learning. It has long been said that the schools tend toward mediocrity and stifle creative thinking. Miller (1981) cited a report of the United States Department of Commerce which asserted that our educational systems are more effective at "preserving convention than sparking innovation, developing logical rather than conceptual thinking, promoting risk aversion rather than acceptance of change" (p. 15).

If the schools are to prepare our young people to live in a rapidly changing future society, it is essential that our curricula and our ways of implementing them be drastically reformed. Our youth must be trained in coping skills and taught that the future can be molded by careful planning and the application of efficient forecasting, creative thinking, and problem-solving skills. What we need is a curriculum designed to prepare our students for a future that will be radically different and offer totally new challenges from those we are experiencing today.

The Future-Oriented Curriculum

Futuristics may be defined as a field of study whose purpose is "to identify, analyze, and evaluate possible future changes in human life and the world" (Cornish, 1977, p. 258). Futurists, professionals who extrapolate from current trends to forecast future conditions and events, speak of "alternative futures"—an optimistic view implying that many choices are at our command with creative thinking. Simply stated, futuristics enables society to understand and plan for anticipated futures.

Many writers have documented the importance of a "future-focused role image" in the development of socially acceptable personal goals. As research has shown, future-oriented students are higher achievers, and student attitudes can be improved significantly through the study of futuristics. Gifted children must be provided with a positive outlook for the future, without which they will not be able to lead our world in positive directions.

Future Studies and the Gifted

What are the benefits of incorporating futuristics—the study of the future—into the gifted curriculum?

1. It improves the future images of tomorrow's leaders.
2. It provides gifted students with a relevant milieu within which they can practice those skills and abilities that we typically emphasize in gifted education:
   - Higher level cognitive processes
   - Inquiry (problem solving) approach to learning
   - Interdisciplinary thinking
   - Forecasting skills
   - Decision making based on solid American value systems
   - Internal locus of control, self-directedness
   - Intellectual curiosity, love of learning
   - Increased self-confidence
   - Open-ended and divergent thinking, questioning, and problem solving
   - Tolerance for change and ambiguity
   - Teamwork skills
   - Development of a sense of responsibility
   - Creative thinking
   - Leadership development
3. It helps gifted students see the relevance of history, since the study of the past helps us to forecast more accurately the events and conditions of the future.
4. It helps them see that they can control much of their future and learn to cope effectively with that which cannot be changed.
5. The study of the future provides our future leaders with a method of achieving cooperation and understanding among the peoples of the world.
6. Tomorrow's researchers in science and technology will be helped by futuristic studies. The RAND Corporation's development of computer conferencing, a major innovation in communications technology, was motivated by interest in the future.
7. In requiring the use of creative thinking and imagination, the future-oriented curriculum enhances creative potential, by helping students to consider future possibilities which had not been conceived in the past.

Why teach futuristics to the gifted? This century is rapidly drawing to a close. If we are to prepare our future leaders to meet the challenges of a new century, tomorrow will be too late.

Developing a Future-Oriented Curriculum

We have seen that the primary goals of introducing futuristics into the gifted education curriculum are (1) to improve the future images of tomorrow's leaders, (2) to help them learn to use the past as a basis for forecasting the future, (3) to help them recognize that the future is largely within their control, and (4) to develop the skills that are necessary to enable them to cope with those problems that do occur, in order to prevent "future shock."

Current literature is replete with the use of the term *future perspective*. What are the characteristics of the future-oriented person—the person who has a "future perspective"? Cornish suggests the following characteristics, which we would hope to develop in our future leaders through a future-oriented curriculum for gifted students:

1. *Openness to experience.* Futuristic thinkers, according to Cornish, are continuously seeking new information and experimenting with new ideas.
2. *Global outlook.* Futurists avoid provincialism, thinking in terms of a global picture rather than a local picture.
3. *Long-term time perspective.* Futurists continuously study the past and present for clues about the future.
4. *Ecological orientation.* The futurist understands and appreciates the importance of maintaining healthy interrelationships between people and nature.
5. *Broad concern for humanity.* Future-oriented thinkers care about all of humanity—not only our own generation, but those generations of the future who will be here after we have gone.
6. *Rationality.* According to Cornish, "futurists quickly reject notions that lack an adequate scientific or rational basis. They . . . have little time to waste on mystical forecasting."
7. *Pragmatism.* Futurists are concerned with finding solutions to future problems that will work.
8. *Reality of choice.* The futurist is "deeply conscious of the freedom of individuals to make decisions that will have tremendous consequences for good or ill."
9. *Interest in values.* Futurists emphasize the importance of working toward the achievement of happiness for all of humanity.
10. *Optimism.* Future-oriented persons are optimistic about humankind's survival and prosperity in the future.

11. *Sense of purpose.* Futurists have a "sense of mission"; they believe in the importance of what they are doing and know that a future perspective will help to create a better world (Cornish, 1977, pp. 184–186).

Kauffman (1976, p. 30) suggests specific learning objectives that are appropriate for a future-oriented curriculum. Detailed in Table 4–1, these objectives are categorized under six *areas of competence.*

With these purposes and objectives in mind, let us reexamine the four components of the Leadership Training Model and consider their relevance for the futuristic curriculum.

Cognition. Appropriately differentiated curricula for the gifted must be built on a firm base of knowledge in a variety of areas. However, the skills of information retrieval and the presence of a scientific attitude are necessary if the bits and pieces of knowledge learned through the regular curriculum are to be made relevant. It is essential that we train gifted students to be firsthand investigators in their areas of personal interest. An important part of this training is the identification of real-life problems, the development of usable products, and the communication of these products to audiences who have a need for and will use them. As Kauffman (1976) pointed out:

> A democracy cannot possibly function if its citizens are educated to be clever robots. The way to educate children for democracy is to let them do it—that doesn't mean allowing them to practice empty forms, to make pretend decisions or to vote on trivia; it means that they participate in the real decisions that affect them. You learn democracy in school not by defining it or by simulating it but by doing it (p. 35).

Problem Solving. This second component of the Leadership Training Model, is perhaps the area of futuristics about which we hear the most in gifted education. The national Future Problem Solving Program, developed at the University of Georgia in 1975 by Dr. E. Paul Torrance, was designed to foster creative, future-oriented thinking, to strengthen communication and group work skills, to train students in research techniques, and to develop critical and analytical thinking skills (Hoomes, 1984). This futuristic strategy is therefore an essential component of any effective leadership training program for gifted students.

Interpersonal Communication. Of the concepts repeated often in the futuristic literature, one of the most common is that future leaders must be skilled in interpersonal communication. Without the ability to work well with and influence others, a leader cannot be effective. As suggested in the hierarchy of skills listed for this area of the LTM, the development of interpresonal communication skills must include atten-

Table 4–1.   Learning Objectives for a Future-Oriented Curriculum

Access to Information
Reading
Listening and seeing
Direct experiment
Libraries and reference books
Computerized data-retrieval
Data from newspapers, businesses
  government agencies, etc.
Asking experts
Judging experts
Managing information overload

Thinking Clearly
Semantics
Propaganda and common fallacies
Values clarification
Deductive logic
Mathematics
Analytical problem solving
Scientific method
Probability and statistics
Computer programming
General systems
Creative problem solving
Forecasting and prediction

Communicating Effectively
Speaking informally
Public speaking
Voice and body language
Cultural barriers to communication
Formal and informal writing
Grammar, syntax, and style
Drawing, sketching, still pho-
  tography, film making, etc.
Graphic design and layout
Outlines, flow-charts, charts,
  tables, and graphs
Organization and editing
Handwriting, typing, dictating

Understanding Man's Environment
Astronomy, physics, and chemistry
Geology and physical geography
Biology, ecology, and ethology
Genetics, evolution, and population
  dynamics
Fundamentals of modern technology
Applied mechanics, optics, and
  electronics

Understanding Man and Society
Human evolution
Human physiology
Linguistics
Cultural anthropology (including
  history and the humanities)
Psychology and social psychology
Racism, ethnicity, and xenophobia
Government and law (especially
  American constitutional law)
Economics and economic philosophy
Changing occupational patterns
Education and employment
Issues in human survival
Prospects for mankind

Personal Competence
Physical grace and coordination
Survival training and self-defense
Safety, hygiene, nutrition, and sex-
  education
Consumer education and personal
  finance
Creative and performing arts
Basic inter-personal skills
Small group dynamics
Management and administration
Effective citizen participation
Knowledge of best personal learning
  styles and strategies
Mnemonics and other learning aids
Bio-feedback, meditation, mood
  control
Self-knowledge and self-motivation

Source: D. L. Kauffman, Jr., *Teaching the Future: A Guide to Future-Oriented Education*
(Palm Springs, Calif.: ETC Publications). Reprinted with permission.

tion to a realistic and healthy self-concept, concern for others, empathy, and cooperative working skills. All of these goals are stressed in the writings of those who suggest principles for a futuristic curriculum. Interpersonal communication skills are therefore of the greatest importance in the building of healthy future role images in our gifted future leaders.

Decision-Making.   This final component of the LTM is another area that is continuously stressed in the futuristic literature. In a very real sense, decision making is the ultimate goal of the future-oriented curriculum, as it is the skill that will in the final analysis show society the direction in which it must head for survival.

FUTURISTIC TEACHING STRATEGIES

Discussion of the Future

Research has shown that creativity is essential to the effective solution of mankind's problems, and research into what makes creativity possible has documented that knowledge is essential. An understanding of the concepts underlying the study of the future is therefore prerequisite to the effective application of any experientially oriented strategies for classroom use. Toward this end, the following activities are suggested for future-oriented discussions in the gifted classroom.

---

1. Discuss the concept that we create and thus are responsible for our own futures.
2. List as many future-oriented professions, events, publications, films, and so on, as you can (e.g., soothsayers in Shakespearean plays, astrologers who foresaw the coming of Christ, utopian books, the oracle at Delphi).
3. Explore the meaning and possible consequences of culture shock; of future shock.
4. Ask students why the study of futuristics is desirable, and why a positive image of the future is important.
5. Consider the following quotation from historian Arnold Toynbee: "Man's achievement of gaining the mastery over nonhuman nature has been bought at the price of enslaving himself to a new artificial man-made environment." Use the following guidelines to make the discussion more interesting and provocative:
   a. Divide into small groups and proceed as follows: One person presents an opinion about this quotation. The second person then provides confirmation by saying something like, "What I

hear you saying is . . ." and then adds his own thoughts. This procedure continues through the group until all have had an opportunity to present their viewpoints.

   b. Follow this discussion with the question, "How can we preserve our human nature in the advancing technological age?"

6. Ask students to comment on the impact that the computer, the airplane, satellite communications, or other recent innovations or inventions have had on society, on international communication, and on economics.

7. Have students brainstorm unusual uses for an oatmeal box, a cardboard tube, or other common items. Follow this activity with a brainstorming session on potential uses of the computer or other examples of technology.

8. Encourage speculation on future modes of transportation and communication, future sources of energy, schools of the future, future types and contributions of technology, or future careers that do not exist today.

9. Ask students to forecast characteristics of their own city or state in the future.

10. Conduct a discussion about the government's responsibility in the future; consider public health, education, international affairs, and other related issues.

11. Discuss: What future inventions could improve our society? What changes are needed? How can we accomplish them?

12. Ask students to consider what actions they would take if they should become President of the United States:

   a. What new laws would they try to influence?

   b. Whom would they select for their cabinet?

   c. What problems would they address first? What ideas might they consider for solving them?

13. Debate the use of nuclear energy, the prohibition of handguns, and other current controversial issues whose consequences could affect the quality of the future.

14. Reproduce and give to the students the following "Metaphors for 'the Future'" developed by Kauffman (1976). Ask for volunteers to read them aloud to the group, then use the questions that follow for discussion.

(1) The future is a great roller coaster on a moonless night. It exists, twisting ahead of us in the dark, although we can only see each part as we come to it. We can make estimates about where we are headed, and sometimes see around a bend to another section of track, but it doesn't do us any real good because the future is fixed and deter-

mined. We are locked in our seats, and nothing we may know or do will change the course that is laid out for us.

(2)   The future is a mighty river. The great force of history flows inexorably along, carrying us with it. Most of our attempts to change its course are mere pebbles thrown into the river: they cause a momentary splash and a few ripples, but they make no difference. The river's course *can* be changed, but only by natural disasters like earthquakes or landslides, or by massive, concerted human efforts on a similar scale. On the other hand, we are free as individuals to adapt to the course of history either well or poorly. By looking ahead, we can avoid sandbars and whirlpools and pick the best path through any rapids.

(3)   The future is a great ocean. There are many possible destinations, and many different paths to each destination. A good navigator takes advantage of the main currents of change, adapts his course to the capricious winds of chance, keeps a sharp lookout posted, and moves carefully in fog or uncharted waters. If he does these things, he will get safely to his destination (barring a typhoon or other disaster which he can neither predict nor avoid).

(4)   The future is entirely random, a colossal dice game. Every second, millions of things happen which could have happened another way and produced a different future. A bullet is deflected by a twig and kills one man instead of another. A scientist checks a spoiled culture and throws it away, or looks more closely at it and discovers penicillin. A spy at the Watergate removes a piece of tape from a door and gets away safely, or he forgets to remove the tape and changes American political history. Since everything is chance, all we can do is play the game, pray to the gods of fortune, and enjoy what good luck comes our way.

Questions: Which metaphor best describes your idea of the future? Which description is the most "valid" or "realistic"? Is there any way you could prove that one description is "right" and the others are "wrong"? What would be the consequences for society of assuming the truth of one metaphor instead of the others? Would it be more useful to assume one of them, even if it were not more "correct" than the others?

Kauffman cautions:

Try to keep the discussion from degenerating into an argument over the validity of either the first or the fourth view. Each of the four dramatizes (and exaggerates) a useful observation about the future. The first says that much of what we do is determined by our conditioning and our circumstances and not by "free and rational" consideration. The second says that deliberate cultural change is an immensely difficult thing to achieve. The third says that with foresight, flexibility, and determination, we can choose and achieve the future we want. And the fourth reminds us that there is a strong element of chance in everything that happens and a wise person (or society) tries to insure against the bad breaks and take advantage of the good ones.

Most futurists seem to operate most of the time from a perspective that combines the "river" and the "ocean" metaphors. Over the next twenty or thirty years our range of choice is restricted by a set of severe problems which we must cope with, and by forces which have already been set in motion. (For example, a population continues to grow for about seventy years after a stabilized birth rate is reached.) If we survive the next thirty years in reasonably good shape, the range of choices and opportunities will open up considerably as the "river" reaches the "ocean" (pp. 64–65).

The Futures Wheel

The futures wheel is a diagrammatic strategy that begins with one trend as the first level (or the hub) and expands into second-, third-, and fourth-level consequences. This technique may be used to stimulate discussion on the possible consequences of a particular trend or action. In Figure 4–1, the invention of the automobile has been selected as the first-level concern. Branching out from this hub are several second-level concerns that result from the increase of this type of technology. Each of these lower-level concerns then becomes a hub, with related concerns (or consequences) branching out from this new hub, until at least a third or fourth level is reached. The futures wheel can also be used to alert students to the chain reaction or "domino effect" which is caused by current actions, and to make them more keenly aware of the interrelatedness of current trends. After using the automobile, with whose problems students are familiar, have them construct futures wheels beginning with the computer or other modern technological advances and working gradually into anticipated inventions, events, or concerns of the future.

The Relevance Tree

The relevance tree is another schematic that enables us to consider choices, solutions to problems, or sequences of steps for attaining goals. Like the futures wheel, the relevance tree is a networking strategy that relies on the relationships between trends, problems, or steps in a developmental sequence for its core, enabling us to clarify our alternative futures (Cornish, 1977). Two applications might be made of this technique:

1. In considering a variety of choices, a relevance tree might be designed as shown in Figure 4–2.

Figure 4–1. Sample of Futures Wheel

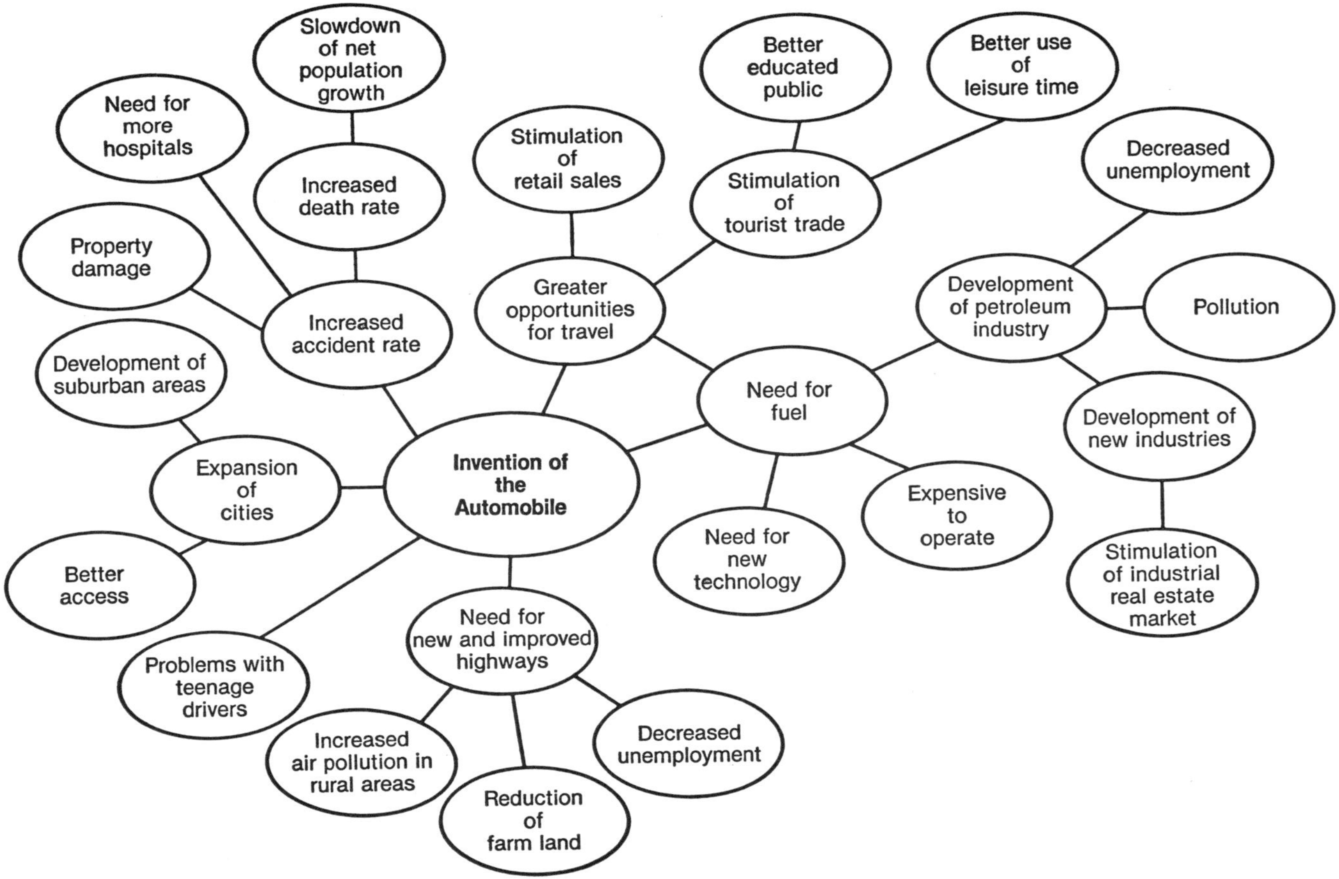

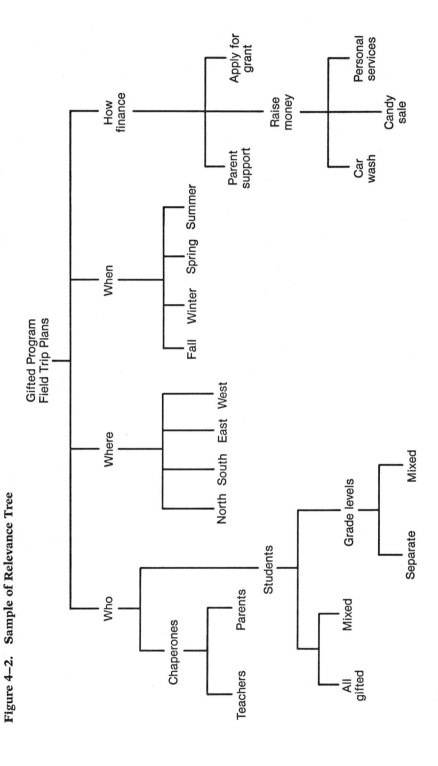

Figure 4–2. Sample of Relevance Tree

2. A second application of the relevance tree might be the development of a plan for implementation of a program, as shown in Figure 4–3.

Trend Extrapolation

Throughout the literature, futurists tell us about the importance of the past in forecasting the future. Trend extrapolation is a strategy that enables us to use events of the past and present, combined with creative thinking, to forecast future trends. While viewing this technique as the simplest way to forecast the future, Cornish (1977) cautions against overgeneralizing, particularly in areas such as biological or technological growth (e.g., projecting human growth on the basis of a child's growth rate during the first five years of life.) Trend extrapolation based on statistical patterns, however, may be used effectively in areas such as business (e.g., forecasting increase or decrease in sales) or social science (e.g., forecasting population growth).

To help students understand trend extrapolation, define the terms *trend, issue, extrapolation, forecast,* and *prediction,* and discuss their implications with students.

Some specific activities in trend extrapolation might include:

1. Ask students to differentiate between *trends* and *issues,* brainstorming examples of each. Ask whether it is possible for trends to conflict (e.g., population growth, which seems to be leveling off in the United States, decreasing in China, increasing in Third World countries). Encourage students to suggest ways in which trends might be recognized and extrapolated (or extended into the future). Ask whether or not (and if so, how) trends can be reversed, thus changing the future. Discuss examples of trends that have been reversed.

2. Ask students to compare and contrast the fortune tellers of early days with the futurists of today.

3. Discuss the etymology of the words *prediction* and *forecast.* Explain that a forecast discusses a future possibility, whereas a prediction discusses a future certainty. Also make it clear that a prediction can be wrong if the person making the prediction lacks a complete understanding of the circumstances; a forecast, on the other hand, can never be wrong, since it is merely an opinion. Share with the students Bundy's criteria for judging the quality of a forecast (cited in Kauffman, 1967):

Figure 4–3. Sample of Relevance Tree

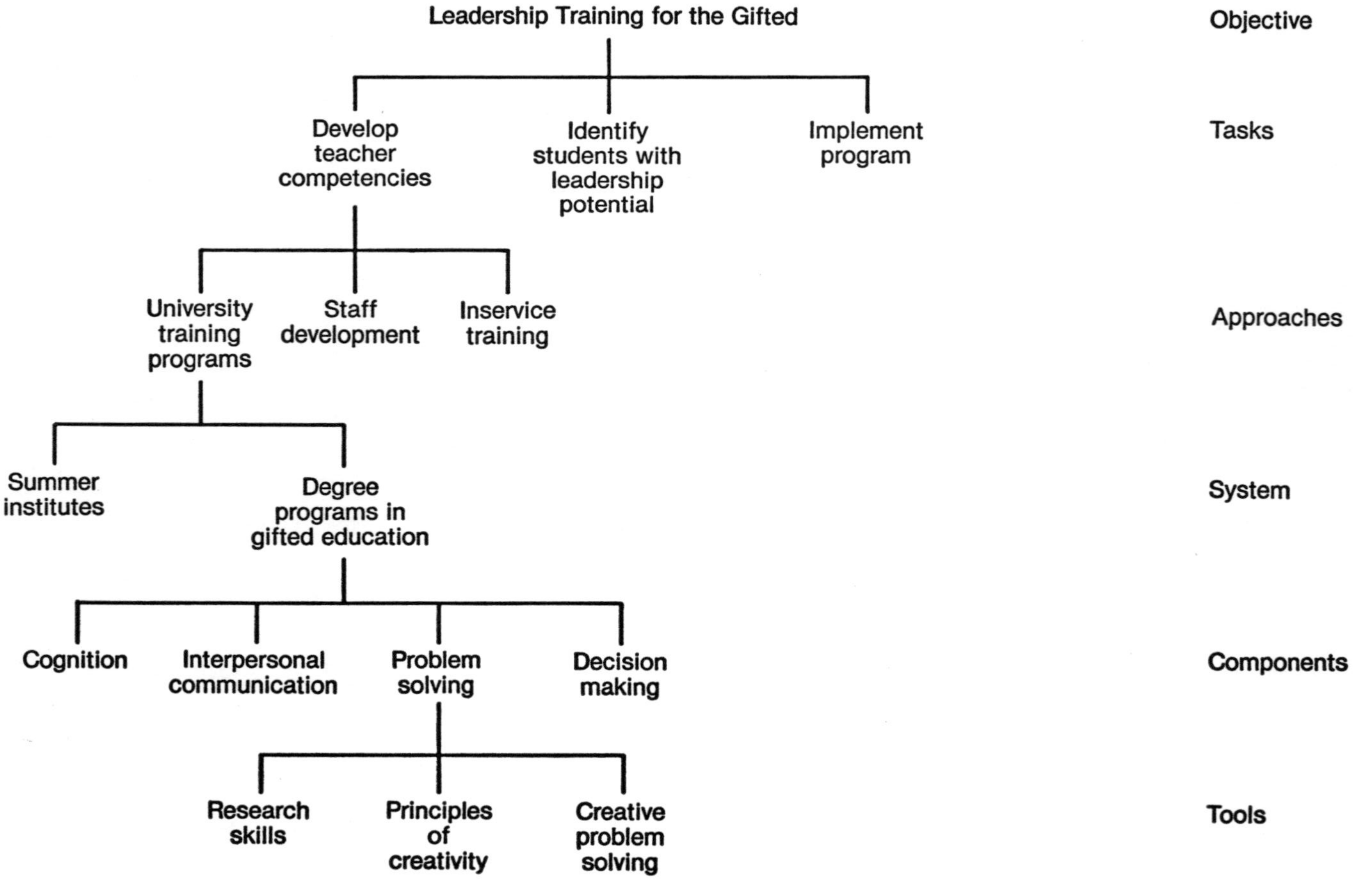

Objective — Leadership Training for the Gifted

Tasks — Develop teacher competencies · Identify students with leadership potential · Implement program

Approaches — University training programs · Summer institutes

System — Staff development · Inservice training · Degree programs in gifted education

Components — Cognition · Interpersonal communication · Problem solving · Decision making

Tools — Research skills · Principles of creativity · Creative problem solving

Clarity (assumptions and time frame are clear)
Plausibility (believable, not in conflict with itself)
Imagination (reflects insight and creativity)
Justification (built on logical rationale)

When the students understand trend extrapolation, the following classroom activities may be used to make this technique more relevant:

---

1. Construct a seven-column "Forecasting Matrix" (see Table 4–2) as follows:
   a. Column One: List current issues, facts, trends (e.g., food shortage in developing countries, decreasing oil revenues in producing states, advances in computer technology and genetic engineering).
   b. Column Two: Project for each of the issues listed in Column One any trends that appear to be resulting.
   c. Column Three: List possible futures that might arise from each apparent trend.
   d. Column Four: List consequences (both good and bad) that might occur as a result of these future events.
   e. Column Five: Mark a "+" for each trend or future consequence that you see as positive (or beneficial) and a "−" for each one that you see as negative (or harmful).
   f. Column Six: Every trend or consequence that you marked "−" suggests changes that must occur to avoid the continuation of negative trends.
   g. Column Seven: List steps that must be taken to enable these changes to come about (Lahe, 1985)
2. Have students identify current events, trends, and forecasts from the local and national news. Classify each trend or forecast as positive or negative. Use future problem-solving techniques to identify ways in which negative trends might be reversed.
3. Examine the current status of technology, and forecast the direction in which it will lead. Consider the computer, various modes of transportation, a variety of energy sources, court decisions, and legislation recently adopted or currently under consideration, as well as research which is currently in progress. Discuss the likelihood and implications of each trend you consider (Epley, 1978).

Table 4–2 Forecasting Matrix

Issues	Resulting Trends	Possible Futures	Consequences of Futures	+ Beneficial − Negative	Changes Needed	Steps Needed to Bring about changes
Decreasing Oil Prices	Decreasing need for workers	Increased unemployment	Increase in poverty and crime	−	(Use creative problem-solving techniques to determine possible solutions/changes needed/steps required)	
Computer Technology	Changing personnel	Obsolete skills	Increased unemployment	−		
World Food Shortage	Increase in death rates	Reduced populations	Lower food needs	+/−		

4. Give each student two sheets of paper. Explain the following instructions:

   a. Draw your life line on the first sheet of paper. Beginning with your early childhood, change your lifeline to reflect the ups and downs of your life to this point.

   b. On the second sheet, begin with your life as it is now and project the future events of your life for the next twenty years. Consider events of your family, your future education and experiences you might have while acquiring this education, your future personal life (marriage, children, home), and the occupation or profession you think you might pursue. Show the problems that might stand in your way as you pursue your future goals, trying after each stumbling block to end up on a positive, upward swing.

   c. Divide into pairs; tell your story to your partner. After you both have shared your stories, discuss the reasons for your future projections.

   d. Write your autobiography, reflecting the "ups and downs" that are shown on your lifeline, and adjusting your future projections as needed to reflect a positive future for your life.

5. Brainstorm recent inventions that have contributed to the improvement of human life. Help students develop criteria for judging the benefits of such inventions. Brainstorm inventions that are (or will be) needed for the future. Divide the class into groups of four to six students each, and give each group a random assortment of "junk" items (cardboard tubes, old eyeglasses, paper clips, rubber bands, cereal boxes, string, clean aluminum cans) as well as paper, colored pencils, and a variety of fasteners (rubber bands, paper clips, glue). Instruct the groups to use their collections to devise "inventions" that might be used to satisfy the needs identified. (Encourage bartering among groups.) Work together as a class to evaluate each "invention" on the basis of the criteria developed previously; award a prize to the group with the highest score.

The Cross-Impact Matrix

Another tool commonly used by futurists is the cross-impact or forced matrix. This technique enables the researcher to identify the relationships between various consequences that affect (or *impact*) each other. A cross-impact matrix lists and forces together trends or issues that are otherwise unrelated, under the assumption that most events/trends *are* somehow connected or related. Essentially, the researcher using this technique asks the question, If Trends A and B occur simultaneously, what will be the result? (See Table 4–3.)

Table 4–3. **Cross-Impact Matrix**

	Energy Shortage	Technology	Unemployment	Economic Recession
Energy Shortage	—			
Technology		—		
Unemployment			—	
Economic Recession				—

Three methods might be used to consider the matrix shown in Table 4–3 and its implications:

1. Ask, "If the energy shortage continues, how will it affect technology?" Write in each box the effect of forcing the two trends together.

2. Ask, "If the energy shortage continues, will it make the current increase in technological development likely to continue?" If the answer is *yes*, place a "+" (or a "++" if emphasis is needed) in the box marking the intersection of the two trends. If the answer is *no*, place a "−" (or a "− −") in the box. After all interactions have been considered, count the number of "+" signs, and subtract the number of "−" signs, in each column.

3. Ask, "If the energy shortage continues, can technological development occur?" In the column mark "P" (for possible) or "I" (for impossible); also list in each column any conditions that would impact this result.

Another application of the cross-impact matrix might be to have a disinterested person or group (another class, another teacher or group of teachers, professionals in areas relevant to the problem under consideration, etc.) look at a list of trends/issues drawn up by the class and to suggest factors that might affect their outcome. The issues or trends might then be listed across the top of the matrix and the impacting factors listed down the left side; each factor could then be matched with each trend/issue and the results assessed and discussed.

The Delphi Technique

The Delphi technique, invented in the late 1950s by Olaf Helmer and Norman Dalkey of the RAND Corporation, is a technique whose purpose is to identify future trends through the polling of experts. The idea of consulting experts is now new; throughout history rulers and presidents have consulted advisory councils, and large corporations could not exist without them. But Delphi differs in that it is a systematic method of leading "experts" into consensus. Simply stated, the steps of the Delphi process are as follows:

1. Select a group of consultants who are willing to participate in the project. The "experts" selected should be competent (preferably recognized) in the field of interest, should be flexible and open-minded, and should be willing and able to revise their thinking in the interest of consensus.

2. Develop a clear, unambiguous set of questions to which the selected panel will respond.

3. Send the survey questionnaire to all participants, inquiring about their perceptions of trends in the area of study. In this first round no panelist should be told the identity or the responses of any other member.

4. Disseminate second, third, and, if necessary, additional rounds of the same questions to all participants. On each of these occasions, provide the panelists with compilations of the group's responses and ask that they reconsider their own responses in an effort to reach consensus. (Extreme viewpoints may be defended at these stages by their authors.)

Having completed the above steps, the final result is consensus, which is recognized as valid because (1) the respondents are chosen for their expertise in their field, and (2) an opinion reached through group study is likely to be more valid than the opinion of one person alone.

In addition to the above guidelines, it should be noted that the Delphi technique cannot be considered a scientific investigation, since the implications drawn from its use are based on opinion rather than substantiated by fact. In spite of its weaknesses, however, Delphi is generally recognized by futurists as a valid and logical method of exploring the future (Cornish, 1977; Kauffman, 1976).

Future Problem Solving

A Creative Problem Solving Approach. A familiar term in many gifted programs of this country is *future problem solving*. Simply stated, future problem solving is a strategy that provides experience in identifying and offering solutions for potential problems of future societies. Based in format on the Osborn-Parnes creative problem solving technique (see Chapter 9 for further details), future problem solving follows five steps: fact finding, problem finding, idea finding, solution finding, and acceptance finding (Noller, Parnes, and Biondi, 1976).

In 1975, Dr. Paul Torrance at the University of Georgia began disseminating to other states and countries the future problem solving program which he had earlier initiated in his own state. Having developed into an annual event, the Future Problem Solving Bowl draws winning teams from around the world to compete with one another in solving the problems of the future. A report of a former future problem-solving student provides a clear rationale for including this strategy in the gifted curriculum:

> After a few weeks in the program, I began to see a change in myself. I was starting to be more open and daring in my thoughts, and I felt I could share my ideas with others without worrying about being ridiculed. Also I realized that other people were starting to open up more too, and this was a great help in making the project more of a success. So, even though I did learn many different pieces of information in my research, I feel that I learned something even more valuable about myself. By becoming more aware of myself, and my mind, and my capabilities, I know now that I have a lot of self potential and that I should use it to achieve whatever goals I set for myself (Torrance and Torrance, 1980, pp. 8–9).

Problem Solving Through Imagery. Another type of problem solving that has been adapted to futuristic studies is creative imagination imagery. Wenger (1980) has used this technique effectively, enabling willing participants to "image" positive futures. This strategy is discussed in detail in Chapter 10 of this text.

What Are Future Problems? In order to become effective problem solvers, gifted students must first be able to identify problems that have meaning for them and with which they can work. It is recommended that students be allowed to select the problems with which they will practice, and that extensive study of the problem status be made before any problem-solving strategy is attempted. The following areas are suggested for consideration:

Government control	Euthanasia
Energy sources	Poverty and famine
Environmental pollution	The changing structure of families
Economic concerns	
The changing role of women	Changing life styles
	Technology

Nuclear energy

Global consciousness

Global communication

Nuclear testing and warfare

The drug culture

Population growth

Terrorism

Stress

Care of the aged

Genetic engineering

Unemployment

Altered states of consciousness

Simulation

Simulation is a strategy that enables participants to explore the possibilities and the future consequences of certain actions, and to gain skill in adjusting behaviors in order to gain a degree of control over the future. Simulation may be compared to the use of models: young children use simulation when they play with stuffed animals, puppets, or dollhouses, or when they play house. Adults use simulation as well: CPR instructors use simulated patients (mannequins) for practice, and flight simulators help pilots in training to experience firsthand the decision-making processes that control thousands of lives every day. Simulation games have become popular—from Chess and Monopoly to war games—all of which provide experiences similar to life but within a totally safe set of circumstances.

Simulation is a particularly appropriate strategy for teaching the future, since we already know exactly what the future holds. Some examples of simulation activities for teaching the future are included in this section; other uses of simulation are discussed in Chapter 6.

A Future City Simulation*

1. Using old maps of your city from founding to the present, transfer their contents to a large grid on newsprint. Color-code this map to indicate changes that have taken place over the years. Have students interview senior citizens about changes they have seen in their lifetimes, visit local museums to view artifacts, historical documents, and so on. Gather and plot on posters or transparencies graphs of population changes, real estate sales, or other economic figures, and other indicators of change that your city has experienced since its founding. Use trend extrapolation and cross-impact matrix techniques to speculate on your city's future.

---

*Adapted from Kauffman (1976) and others.

2. Invite a local architect, civil engineer, planning commission representative, legislator, real estate appraiser, and/or other appropriate visitor to talk with the class regarding current trends in building materials and design, land use, state and federal legislation affecting future cities, and so forth.

3. Using a new color, plot onto your enlarged map the changes you think will have take place in your city 25, 50, or 100 years from now.

4. Imagine your projected city of the future. Consider the following questions:
   a. How do you think your city will be governed?
   b. What type(s) of zoning plans will it have?
   c. What will be the major focus of its economy?
   d. How will your educational system differ from the present system?
   e. What problems and needs are likely to arise?

5. Divide into groups of five to eight members each. Consider the future that you have projected for your city. Think about the problems and needed changes you have identified. Now shift your thinking to the ideal city of the future. Consider these questions:
   a. Where should it be located? (Think divergently: under a dome, under ground, under water? North or south? Near water or mountains?)
   b. What kind of government should it have? Write a charter for your new city. Select the commission that will run it; give your commission a name and decide on a leader. (How will members be selected? How will the leader be selected? Will the leader be a man? A Woman? A Humanoid?) What powers and responsibilities will your commission have? What will be the makeup of your commission? What kinds of laws will your city have? Who will make them? Who will enforce them?

6. Instruct each group to role-play individual members of the governmental commission of its ideal future city. Discuss and make decisions on the following questions:
   a. City design: What will be included? (Consider business, industrial, and residential districts; recreational and health care facilities; schools, cultural facilities; etc.)
   b. Building styles and functions: Will you restrict construction to certain types of buildings? What codes will be required? What types of property/land use will be permitted?
   c. Transportation: What kinds of public transportation will you

offer? Will private transportation still be in use? Will public transportation be accessible to and used by everyone?

d. Economy: How will your economy function? How will government, city improvement, education, recreational programs, and so on, be financed? What will be the mainstay of your city's economy?

e. Laws and ethics: Draw up a bill of rights for your city. What code of ethics will govern your people? Will religion play a major part in your city's life? Do you expect the current ecumenical movement to have an impact on your city's future religious patterns?

f. Leisure time: How long will the work week be? How will people spend their leisure time? What recreational facilities will be used most? What place will athletics or culture have in your society?

g. Will your city have different social classes? Will it be an affluent city?

h. What will be the educational level of your city's population?

i. How will energy use be controlled? What new energy sources will be used?

j. How will the poor and the aged be cared for in your city? Will they be productive? Will welfare still exist?

k. How will police and fire protection in your city differ from the present? How will the crime rate compare to the present?

l. What role will high-tech play in your ideal city?

m. What problems do you anticipate? How will you solve them?

7. Divide into groups, with each student representing a member of a community group (parent, taxpayer, labor union head, school board member, mayor, etc.). Have the "citizens" debate the issues raised in the small groups. Identify a problem that must be solved. Discuss how a decision can be reached.

8. Group together several cities to form a state. (Larger classes can group to form nations.) Discuss the challenges and problems that arise.

The Colonization of Outer Space

The speculation in recent years on the possibility of our planet's being visited by extraterrestrial beings, and our country's exploration of the moon and other planets in our solar system have prompted many books and much discussion about the possibilities of colonizing outer space.

The following questions might be used to stimulate thinking and discussion about the colonization of outer space.*

---

1. What criteria would you use in selecting the first flight crew to visit and live in our first outer space colony?

2. What orders should be given to the first flight crew to another planet? What should they be told to do if they should encounter extraterrestrial beings? Would these policies be changed if they were intelligent beings who could communicate with our visitors? If circumstances did not permit all of the orders to be followed, in what priority order should their orders be considered?

3. How would you feel if you encountered a space ship and beings from another planet? What means would you use to communicate with them? What would be your first message after you developed a mutual communication system?

4. If you were given the responsibility of colonizing another planet with inhabitants of a dying Earth, saving humankind from total extinction, what criteria would you use in selecting those who would represent humanity on the new planet? What items would these people be permitted to take with them on their final voyage?

5. If you were in charge of a new colony to replace a dying Earth, what decisions would you make about the way of life on the new planet? Would you want to make your new home like Earth? If not, what changes would you make to the new planet? To the people exported to live there?

Sociodrama

Another role-playing strategy that is useful in the study of the future is sociodrama. Based on Moreno's (1946) psychodramatic techniques, sociodrama has been identified by Torrance (1975) as an extremely effective method of futuristic problem solving.

Like simulation, sociodrama is not limited to older students; young children engage in futuristic sociodrama when they role-play actors from favorite television shows or "become" the teacher in an imaginary schoolroom. Pointing out that emotional involvement is important to enable the players to break creatively into a future mode of thinking, Torrance suggests a variety of ways for making this technique relevant to the participant.

---

*Adapted from LaConte (1975).

In contrast to Moreno's original technique, the purpose of socio-drama is to use dramatics to work through group or social problems. In futuristic sociodrama, the problem to be dramatized is one that is anticipated on the basis of current trends. The protagonist—the holder of the lead role in the drama—sets the stage and acts out situations related to his own life. Prerequisite to the effective use of this strategy are a complete and open discussion of the problem to be worked on, and a warmup period designed to encourage spontaneity and creative thinking (Torrance, 1975).

Further details on the use of sociodrama in the gifted classroom are included in Chapter 6.

Scenarios, Soliloquies, and Utopias

Kauffman (1976) defines a scenario as "a fictionalized forecast, written from the point of view of a specific future date, looking back over the period between now and then as if it had already happened" (p. 123). Focusing on cause and effect, the scenario presents in story form a sequence of events that might take place between the present and some designated future time. Written in the present tense (as if that future date had arrived), the scenario is a creative method of forecasting future events; by projecting into the future, the writer can draw freely on his imagination without having future possibilities obscured by events of the present or the past. A common method of writing a scenario is to study a selected problem and then select a solution and explore its possible consequences.

Bundy's criteria for a good forecast, listed earlier in this chapter, might be used as well in judging a scenario. They are repeated here with some expansion to demonstrate their application to this new strategy.

1. *Clarity.* The time frame and the assumptions underlying the scenario should be clearly stated.

2. *Plausibility.* The scenario should be believable; if it is not consistent with current thought, arguments should be presented to make it seem possible.

3. *Imagination.* The scenario should reflect creative, imaginative thinking and insight.

4. *Justification.* The rationale for believing that the scenario could happen should be clearly implied within the story (Kauffman, 1976, pp. 68–69).

Cornish (1977) points out three benefits of scenario writing:

> First, it makes us aware of potential problems that might occur if we were to take the proposed action. We can then (1) abandon the

proposed action or (2) prepare to take precautions that will minimize the problems that might result.

Second, the scenario gives us an opportunity to escape from a potentially disastrous action—or to realize a tremendous opportunity. . . .

Third, the scenario can mobilize others—get them involved in assessing a situation and planning action (p. 112).

Like the scenario, the soliloquy presents some future time as if it had already arrived. The soliloquy differs in that it reflects the writer's feelings about what he has accomplished and how these accomplishments fit in with his hopes and dreams.

In keeping with the concept of a utopia as an ideal world or society, the writing of "utopias" simply extends the scenario-writing technique from what might be to what should be. In addition to the benefits of scenario writing mentioned above, the writing of utopias offers further advantages: (1) it encourages students to envision a bright future (helping to develop a positive, "future-focused role image"); (2) it removes restrictions, thus enabling students to apply their creative potential more readily; (3) it causes gifted students to think about the kind of world they would like to live in and the steps they must take as future leaders to bring about the desired changes; and (4) because it is fun, it encourages the study of the future.

When directing students to write scenarios, soliloquies, or utopias, the following steps might be followed:

---

1. Prepare the group for scenario writing through the use of activities such as the following:
   a. Brainstorm things students would like to know about the future.
   b. Brainstorm current occupations that might not exist in the future, or occupations that do not exist (or are rare) today but are likely to exist in the future.
   c. Speculate on possible future uses of the computer or other existing or anticipated technological inventions.
   d. Brainstorm areas of interest in which change is taking place (e.g., genetics, electronics, education). Discuss recent events and current trends in these areas, and forecast future events, discoveries, inventions, and so on, that might be realized fifty years from now.
   e. Write yourself a letter, including changes in yourself, your city/state/nation, or the world, that you would like to see occur over the next five years, your own forecasts about the future, or other things on which you would like to reflect five years from

now. Place your letter in a self-addressed, stamped envelope, and leave it with your teacher. It will not be opened by anyone but you, and it will be mailed to you at the end of five years.

f. Imagine that you are now thirty-five years old. You have completed your education and are now a successful professional in the field of your choice. Describe your life, your family, your job, and what is happening around you (writing in the present tense, as if that future time were now).

g. Remaining in your role at age thirty-five, write a soliloquy about what you have accomplished. Include your feelings, the good that you have done, and your concerns and dreams for the next twenty years. Tell how you have changed since the twentieth century, what changes have occurred in your world, and how you feel about these changes.

h. Brainstorm elements of the society you would like to inhabit in the future. Think of the type of government you would like to be a part of, the educational and religious systems of your society, the economic and social conditions, industry and transportation, food sources, and other considerations that would play important roles in your future life. After brainstorming, discuss changes that would have to be made to acquire this "utopia" (adapted from Didsbury, 1979a and b).

i. Write newspaper headlines of past events, current events, and future-forecasted events.

2. Brainstorm areas of the future that the students might like to explore. Divide the class into groups of four to six students each. Give the following instructions for each group to follow:

a. Select a moderator and a recorder for your group.

b. Narrow the list of areas to one of interest to your group.

c. Brainstorm areas of future life that are related to your topic and that you feel would be appropriate to consider.

d. Brainstorm and record current facts and trends related to your area of interest, events that seem likely to occur in the future if current trends continue, and ideal events or conditions that you would like to have occur. Ask "What if" questions to help elicit consequences of current trends.

e. Decide on a format for your scenario or utopia. It can be anything: a radio broadcast from the future, a trip into a time tunnel, a publicity campaign to draw new residents to a new city or world, a future anthropologist uncovering a lost civilization from the past (i.e., the actual present), a future genealogist researching his ancestors, and so on.

f. Make decisions on the events you wish to include, and develop your final product.

g. After the final product is completed, have each student in the group write a soliloquy reflected personal feelings about his place in the future time described by the group.

3. Have students share their scenarios, utopias, and soliloquies. Discuss the images of the future that were revealed by their writings.

Additional Activities for Teaching the Future Perspective

The following activities, adapted from the writings of Kauffman (1976), LaConte (1975), Flack and Feldhusen (1983), and others, are suggested to enhance the future-focused images of students.

---

1. An extraterrestrial space ship has landed on Earth, and its passengers are threatening to annihilate the human race. You are the only person with whom they will communicate. How will you convince them to spare your fellow human beings?

2. Instruct students to form pairs and sit back to back with their partners. Tell them to attempt to communicate with each other without any spoken or written language. In debriefing, discuss problems they encountered in the activity. Brainstorm ways they might communicate with alien beings who landed on Earth.

3. Teach current events through history. Beginning with a recent event, trace the events that led up to it and the instances in the past of similar or parallel occurrences (e.g., compare the current women's rights movement to events of the American Revolution, the anti-slavery movement, the civil rights movement, etc.).

4. Write science fiction stories based on forecasts of future events. Dramatize the students' best stories.

5. Brainstorm inventions that were once thought impossible ("It'll never fly, Orville!"); study about the impact of such inventions on society.

6. Using synectics (see Chapter 9), invent new types of furniture or machinery, innovative high-tech equipment, new modes of transportation, and so on, for 100 or 200 years hence. Tell their purposes and how they work.

7. Make a time capsule, enclosing in it items that you consider representative of our society today. Imagine that you are a future student, 100 years from now, opening this capsule. How do you

think you would interpret today's society on the basis of your capsule? Write a future "history" or our modern-day culture on the basis of this speculation. "Bury" your capsule in the school library with instructions for it to be opened in 20 years.

8. Create a newspaper that might appear 100 years from now. Include all the typical sections of today's newspapers—news, sports, fashion, business—and add others that might be needed in 100 years.

9. Use the following exercise, developed by Kauffman (1976, p. 70) from the work of Bundy, as a follow-up to other experiences in the study of futuristics or as a pre/postquestionnaire for a futuristics unit.

Beliefs About the Future

Procedure: Distribute the questionnaire to the students and ask them to complete it. (Be sure to tell them it is not a quiz.) Then ask the students to compare their answers and discuss the differences between them. Be cautious about giving your own opinion, even if asked. Usually, it is best to reserve your views until near the end of the discussion of each point, and even then you should make it clear that yours is just another opinion and not the "right" answer. Otherwise the discussion tends to collapse into a session of "guessing-what-teacher-thinks."

A word of warning: question six is a "trick" question—the answer is determined by how you read the question. If "knowledge" is taken to mean "absolute foreknowledge of events" most students will disagree (though some will mention "absolute certainties" such as the movements of the planets). Those who interpret "knowledge" to mean "useful knowledge about possibilities" (such as knowing the chances of filling an inside straight) will generally agree.

What Fundamental Beliefs About the Future Do You Hold?

Here are fifteen statements about the future. Please indicate your opinion of each statement by circling one of the numbers beneath it, according to the following key:

−3=strongly disagree	3=strongly agree
−2=disagree	2=agree
−1=somewhat disagree	1=somewhat agree

0=uncertain

1. From a broad historical viewpoint the human race is moving toward a more desirable future.

   −3   −2   −1   0   1   2   3

2. The future is largely predetermined, at least in all of its important aspects. Individuals, therefore, play out an historically necessary role, i.e., people are swept along by forces over which they have little control.

   −3   −2   −1   0   1   2   3

3. An array of alternative futures, both desirable and undesirable, are open to mankind at any point in time.

   −3   −2   −1   0   1   2   3

4. A prediction is not basically different from a forecast.

   −3   −2   −1   0   1   2   3

5. If one could completely dissect all the forces operating in the present, one could accurately predict the future.

   −3   −2   −1   0   1   2   3

6. It is possible to have knowledge of the future.

   −3   −2   −1   0   1   2   3

7. The most surprising future we can imagine is one in which there are no surprises. It is unreasonable to expect a future in which there are no surprises.

   −3   −2   −1   0   1   2   3

8. Today we can predict outcomes in the social order about as well as we can predict outcomes in the natural order.

   −3   −2   −1   0   1   2   3

9. Generally speaking, the future was more foreseeable for pre-modern man than it is for modern man.

   −3   −2   −1   0   1   2   3

10. Modern approaches to forecasting the future, i.e., attitudes, techniques and beliefs, don't differ basically from approaches used by pre-modern man.

    −3   −2   −1   0   1   2   3

11. The real purpose of futures forecasting is to help us to make better decisions in the present.

    −3   −2   −1   0   1   2   3

12. A useful side effect of futures forecasting is that it helps us to understand the present better.

    −3   −2   −1   0   1   2   3

13. Without forecasting there can be no freedom of choice.

   −3   −2   −1   0   1   2   3

14. How one thinks about the future is intimately connected with how one deals with social and interpersonal relationships.

   −3   −2   −1   0   1   2   3

15. The future 20 years from now is very likely to be completely different from the present.

   −3   −2   −1   0   1   2   3

A FINAL WORD

For our gifted leaders of tomorrow, the study of the future should be the most exciting aspect of the curriculum. Futuristics can encompass all of those skills and experiences that should be incorporated in the curriculum for gifted students—higher level thinking skills, values education, and sociodrama. Using current technology (notably the computer), students can learn to collate and interpret data gathered through Delphi and cross-matrix techniques. Through problem solving, future studies strengthen interpersonal communication skills; through simulation they provide a taste of what the future is likely to be. But futuristics should not be limited to the gifted program. Whether in science, history, mathematics, or reading, the study of the future should be an integral part of the curriculum, be it enrichment or acceleration. For the future belongs to today's students—all of them.

REFERENCES

Allain, V. A. (1979). *Futuristics and education.* Bloomington, IN: Phi Delta Kappa.

Bleedorn, B. D. (1976). Future studies for the gifted. *Gifted Child Quarterly, XX,* 490–496.

Cornish, E. (1977). *The study of the future.* Washington, D.C.: World Future Society.

Didsbury, H. F. (1979a). *Instructor's manual for The Study of the Future.* Washington, D.C.: World Future Society.

Didsbury, H. F. (1979b). *Student handbook for The Study of the Future.* Washington, D.C.: World Future Society.

Epley, T. (1978, May/June). Thinking ahead: Future studies for G/C/T individuals. *G/C/T,* pp. 32–35.

Epley, T. M. (1982). *Models for thinking: Activities to enhance modes of thought*. Ventura, CA: Ventura County Supt. of Schools Office.

Flack, J. D., & Feldhusen, J. F. (1983, March/April). Future studies in the curricular framework of the Purdue Three-Stage Model. *G/C/T*, pp. 2–9.

Goodlad, J. I. (1971). A concept of the "school" in 2000 A.D. *National Elementary Principal, L*(3), 2–4, 86–88.

Guilford, J. P. (1967). *The nature of human intelligence*. New York: McGraw-Hill.

Holt, J. (1964). *How children fail*. New York: Pitman Publishing.

Hoomes, E. W. (1984, March/April). Future problem solving: Preparing students for today and tomorrow. *G/C/T*, pp. 15–18.

Jennings, L., & Cornish, S. (Eds.) (1980). *Education and the future*. Washington, D.C.: World Future Society.

Jones, T. E. (1979, July–August). The futurist movement: A brief history. *World Future Society Bulletin*, pp. 13–26.

Kauffman, D. L., Jr. (1976). *Teaching the future: A guide to future-oriented education*. Palm Springs, CA: ETC Publications.

Kierstead, F., Bowman, J., & Dede, C. (Eds.) (1979). *Educational futures: Sourcebook I*. Washington, D.C.: World Future Society.

LaConte, R. T. (1975). *Teaching tomorrow today: A guide to futuristics*. New York: Bantam Books.

Lahe, L. (1985, Spring). Sharing images of the future: Futuristics and gifted education. *Teaching Exceptional Children*, pp. 177–181.

Leonard, G. B. (1968). *Education and ecstasy*. New York: Delacorte Press, Dell Publishing.

Lewis, C. (1979, March/April). City of the future. *G/C/T*, pp. 21–29.

Lyon, H. C., Jr. (1971). *Learning to feel—Feeling to learn*. Columbus, Ohio: Charles Merrill.

Miller, W. C. (1981). *The third wave and education's futures*. Bloomington, IN: Phi Delta Kappa.

Moreno, J. L. (1946). *Psychodrama. First Volume*. Beacon, NY: Beacon House.

Nasca, D. (1983). Questioning directions for the intellectually gifted. *Gifted Child Quarterly, 27*, 185–188.

Noller, R. B., Parnes, S. J., & Biondi, A. M. (1975). *Creative actionbook: Revised edition of Creative Behavior Workbook*. New York: Charles Scribner's Sons.

Parker, J. (1978, May/June). Future problem solving: Stimulus for tomorrow's leaders. *G/C/T*, pp. 29–31.

Phi Delta Kappa Commission on Schooling for the 21st Century (1984). *Handbook for conducting future studies in education*. Bloomington, IN: Phi Delta Kappa.

Poole, F. R. (1985). The new evolution. *Roeper Review, 7*, 217–220.

Singer, B. D. (1974). The future-focused role-image. In Toffler, A. (Ed.) *Learning for tomorrow: The role of the future in education*. New York: Vintage Books.

Toffler, A. (1970). *Future shock*. New York: Random House.

Toffler, A. (1972, January 17). Education and the super industrial revolution. Excerpts from Kenneth M. Gould Lecture, sponsored by Scholastic Magazines. In Teacher's Edition of *Junior Scholastic*, pp. 3–4.

Toffler, A. (1974). *Learning for tomorrow: The role of the future in education.* New York: Vintage Books.

Toffler, A. (1980). *Third wave.* New York: William Morrow.

Torrance, E. P. (1974). Ways gifted children can study the future. *Gifted Child Quarterly, 18,* 65–71.

Torrance, E. P. (1975). Sociodrama as a creative problem-solving approach to studying the future. *Journal of Creative Behavior, 9,* 183–189.

Torrance E. P. (1976). Students of the future: Their abilities, achievements, and images of the future. *Creative Child and Adult Quarterly, 1,* 76–90.

Torrance, E. P. (1977). Preparing teachers for future educational settings. Paper prepared for the Association of Teacher Educators, Hotel Hilton, Atlanta, GA, February 4, 1977.

Torrance, E. P. (1978). Giftedness in solving future problems. *Journal of Creative Behavior, 12,* 75–86.

Torrance, E. P. (1980). Creativity and futures in education: Retooling. *Education, 100,* 298–311.

Torrance, E. P., & Mourad, S. (1978). Self-directed learning readiness skills of gifted students and their relationship to thinking creatively about the future. *Gifted Child Quarterly, 22,* 180–186.

Torrance, E. P., & Reynolds, C. R. (1978). Images of the future of gifted adolescents: Effects of alienation and specialized cerebral functioning. *Gifted Child Quarterly, 22,* 40–54.

Torrance, E. P., & Torrance, J. P. (1980). *Participating students evaluate the 1979–80 Georgia future problem solving program.* Athens, GA: Georgia Studies of Creative Behavior.

Trischuk, D. L. (1978). *Futuristics for the gifted.* Unpublished paper.

Wenger, W. (1980). *Solving unsolvable world problems.* Gaithersburg, MD: Psychegenics Press.

Section III

AFFECTIVE STRATEGIES

In every child who is born, the potentiality of the human race is born again.
James Agee

Much has been written in recent years about the need to "return to the basics" in our educational systems. Parents and politicians have pressured the schools to leave values and aesthetics to home and church, and to concentrate exclusively on the implanting of knowledge. Yet the educational critics' greatest allies—people like Silberman, Glasser, and Holt—have told us repeatedly that the "basic" curriculum must consist of more than "readin', writin', and rithmetic" if tomorrow's citizens are to reach their potential.

In the early years of the twentieth century, John Dewey stressed the need to educate children for life. With the continuing expansion of the knowledge explosion and the rapid technological changes taking place in society today, we are recognizing more and more the futility of trying to teach children "what they will need to know for the future" and the necessity of providing them with the skills for processing the information of the future and coping with future problems that we cannot currently anticipate. Paramount among those coping skills is the development of affective qualities such as motivation, persistence, and task commitment, as well as attitudes that permit individuals to communicate effectively with their fellow citizens.

The affective domain is the area of education that deals with attitudes and feelings. In the training of gifted students for future leadership roles, it is essential that we integrate the affective with the cognitive (often called the "confluent" approach to education). It is not possible to cover adequately such historic events as the Boston Tea Party and the Emancipation Proclamation, or such concepts as apartheid, genetic engineering, and substance abuse, without allowing students to explore their attitudes, beliefs, and concerns on these questions.

Research has long confirmed the need for intrinsic, rather than extrinsic, motivation. The teaching of conceptual knowledge alone with no relevance for the learner is a meaningless waste of precious classroom time. As Michael Polyanyi has told us, "It is the passion of the scholar that makes for truly great scholarship" (Brown, 1971, p.11).

Along with the current criticisms of the integration of the affective into the cognitive learning of the public schools has come a categorical condemnation of the humanistic philosophy of education. It is unfortunate that humanistic education is semantically linked to the concept of secular humanism, as the humanistic teacher provides the most caring role model possible for her students. Simply defined, humanistic education is an educational philosophy that acknowledges the importance of the individual student's nature and interests, and in which the personal feelings of the student are regarded as equal to (if not above) cognitive learnings (Rubin, 1974). The well-known humanistic psychologist Carl Rogers (1967) proposed that the teacher serve as facilitator rather than director of learning. To facilitate learning, the teacher must be a genuine human being, must be able to interact with students in such a way as to demonstrate human concern, must build a relationship of mutual trust with her students, and must demonstrate empathic understanding in dealing with students. Unless the learner intrinsically senses a need for knowledge, no meaningful learning will take place. And it is the relevance of learning—indeed of all experiences in life—that enables these experiences to lead to self-actualization, or the reaching of one's potential.

Why, then, do we speak of the humanistic philosophy of education as critical for the gifted classroom? First, a review of the definition of giftedness reminds us that gifted children "possess outstanding abilities, are capable of high performance, and require differentiated educational services in order to reach their potential." (Marland, 1972, p. 10). Gifted children, cognitively recognizing their intellectual ability, often have a poor self-concept—perhaps because of a desire for perfection, because of social rejection by age peers, or simply because they are unduly sensitive. Second, gifted children typically possess (and sometimes appear to flaunt) a powerful and fluent vocabulary. In combination with a high energy level, this characteristic can cause gifted children to be impatient with rigid regulations, enforced silence, and relegation to passivity. In the humanistic classroom, students are encouraged to talk, to interact, to question, to debate. Not only do the children have the opportunity to develop their cognitive skills through these interactions, but in this environment they are able to reduce the frustrations caused by the stifled and closed atmosphere of the traditional classroom. Third, children who are truly gifted nearly always possess keen intellectual curiosity. This trait often causes feelings of inadequacy in the conventional teacher who is uncomfortable with her inability to answer all questions posed by the superior students. In the humanistic classroom, gifted children are encouraged to explore on their own, using their most effective and meaningful learning styles, while being given reassurance and guidance by the facilitator. Furthermore, the effective teacher-facilitator is readily able to disclose her own lack of knowledge in a given area (though not as a excuse for not knowing one's subject matter), enabling teacher and student to learn together with the "natural authority" that should exist in any healthy learning environment.

One of the principal aims of the humanistic facilitator is to develop intrinsically self-motivated, self-initiated students who take responsibility for their own learning. An environment in which this type of self-development is encouraged is conducive to the development of the fullest potential of gifted children. Nothing can stifle self-discipline and creativity more quickly than a teacher who can never relinquish control and who feels the necessity to direct all classroom activity at all times.

Finally, gifted children possess an active imagination, a love for discovery, and a creative potential. Because of the subject-centered curriculum of the traditional classroom, these traits are often repressed. The humanistic classroom offers an environment conducive to exploration, discovery, and personal expression—all urgent needs of the gifted.

The Leadership Training Model presents two aspects of affective education that can be used effectively in the classroom and that are essential for leadership development: interpersonal communication (developed through self-awareness and group dynamics activities, covered in Chapter 6 of this book) and decision making (values education and role-playing strategies, covered in Chapters 6 and 7).

REFERENCES

Brown, G. I. (1971). *Human teaching for human learning.* New York: Viking Press.

Krathwohl, D., Bloom, B., & Masia, B. (1964). *Taxonomy of educational objectives. Handbook II: Affective Domain.* New York: David McKay.

Marland, S. P., Jr. (1972). *Education of the gifted and talented: Report to the Congress of the United States by the U.S. Commissioner of Education.* Washington, D.C.: U.S. Government Printing Office.

Rogers, C. R. (1967). Freedom to learn. Columbus, OH: Charles E. Merrill.

Rubin, L. (1974, October). Curriculum, affect, and humanism. *Educational Leadership,* pp. 10–13.

5

Interpersonal Communication

Communication erodes provincialism.
Edmund Gerald Brown, Jr.

One of the primary characteristics of an effective leader is the ability to work with other people. Often gifted students, our future leaders, have difficulty identifying and interacting with their chronological age peers. If a major goal of gifted education is to train the gifted for future leadership roles, then it is essential that we train these students in the communication skills necessary for the development of effective interpersonal relationships.

CONTINUUM OF SKILLS

Current literature in the area of leadership development suggests that the development of effective interpersonal communication skills follows a continuum, beginning with self-awareness. The Leadership Training Model proposes the following steps in this continuum: Self-Realization, Empathy, Cooperation, and Conflict Resolution.

Self-Realization

Maslow's (1959) widely accepted theory that creativity and self-actualization are closely related lends support to the cry for leaders who are mentally healthy, morally strong, and generally self-realized individuals. Research indicates that self-awareness and a healthy self-concept are prerequisite to self-realization or self-actualization. Many types of activities have been developed for this purpose. The use of dyad sharing techniques, the cautious and educated use of interest inventories and sociometric devices, and the application of group counseling techniques and other strategies are effective for developing self-awareness and self-concept. Above all, it is essential that the LTM facilitator be a humanistic educator, demonstrating concern for the individual, valuing students as human beings, and displaying empathic understanding (Rogers, 1967).

Empathy

When self-awareness has been built and the self-concept has been developed to a healthy and realistic level, the individual can begin to be sensitive to others in the group. Sensitivity to the needs of others, and the ability to listen and to recognize the value of other members' contributions to the group product are essential elements in the building of group process skills. Until sensitivity, understanding, and empathy have developed, group cooperation skills will not be possible.

Cooperation

In order for a group leader to elicit cooperation from the members of a group, it is essential that basic communication skills be learned. LTM proposes the inclusion in the gifted curriculum of such basic communication experiences as public speaking, oral interpretation, parliamentary procedure, and debate. Once the potential leader has become skilled in these areas of communication, she is ready to begin the task of working with others. At this point the use of group dynamics activities such as Broken Squares (adapted from Johnson and Johnson, 1975), group projects, simulation, and the like, can help foster a spirit of group cooperation. The ability to work together in a cooperative effort is essential to the development of effective leadership. Also important in the development of group work skills is the teaching of social skills: courtesies, tact, and diplomacy. Finally, the ability to lead demands some understanding of human psychology, including techniques for persuasion and change agentry.

Conflict Resolution

Much has been written in recent years regarding the role of conflict resolution in leadership and interpersonal communication. Filley (1975) suggests several values of conflict in the group process situation:

1. The constructive use of conflict helps to diffuse or prevent more destructive conflicts.

2. Conflict stimulates the creative process through a need for new solutions.

3. The need for group cohesion and cooperation is stimulated by the effort to overcome the conflict.

The use of structured conflict and its resolution through problem solving is an important contribution to the development of interpersonal communication skills and therefore is an essential component of any effective leadership training program.

STRATEGIES FOR DEVELOPING
INTERPERSONAL COMMUNICATION SKILLS

Initial activities in the development of interpersonal communication skills should be aimed at helping the individual to understand self—her preferences, interests, and styles—and then to communicate them to others. Some ways of accomplishing these goals are given here.

Personal Pictures

Instruct each student to create a "picture" of herself. This might be a visual picture (a painting, a mural, a collage, or a three-dimensional model), a verbal picture (an oral description, a role-playing activity such as Charades, or a creative writing), a psychomotor picture (a dance or a song), or any combination of these ideas. These "pictures" may be shared with others, although sharing should not be required in the early stages of self-awareness development.

Boundary Breakers

A boundary breaker is simply a question that is answered by all participants, preferably seated in a circle to allow free interaction. In order to encourage participation and creative responses, the questions must be nonthreatening to the security and psychological safety of all group members. Some boundary breakers that might encourage introspection are:

> If you could be any person, living or dead, real or imaginary, for one week, who would you wish to be?
>
> If you could spend your vacation anywhere in the world, where would you choose to go, and what would you do there?
>
> If you could have any talent that you do not now have, what would it be?

(Be sure the boundary breakers used are open-ended so that no one will feel pressured by them. In this vein, it is usually best not to ask participants to give reasons for their answers; those who wish to do so will probably volunteer this information.) Boundary breakers also may be used to open communication between individual members of the group (e.g., What do you like best about the person sitting on your right?). Because "boundary breaking" is an open-ended strategy, it can also be used quite effectively as a lead-in to the content lesson (e.g., in a unit on the universe, "If you could go into outer space, what would you most like to see?").

Dyad Sharing

After students have begun to improve in self-awareness, the next step in the development of interpersonal communication is to encourage limited disclosure to others. It is important in this step to caution students not to disclose anything to anyone else that makes them uncomfortable or that they would not want the others in the group to know. Dyad sharing can consist of sharing highlights of one's life (e.g., using bell wire to mold a picture of one's lifeline, sharing the "ups and downs" in dyads, and later introducing each other by telling about their lives), sharing the symbolism of the "pictures" developed in the first activity above, and so on. Other types of dyad sharing might include a discussion of a mildly controversial issue (for example, within the context of a lesson), going on a blind trust walk (one partner guiding the other through a series of observations with eyes closed, followed by partners switching roles), and other experiences designed to bring members of the dyads closer together through experiential sharing.

Observation of Others

Instruct students to pair with someone with whom they are not already close friends. Have them observe each other silently for two minutes then turn their backs and change five things about themselves. After turning back around, they should try to identify the five things that were changed. The first pair to succeed in identifying all changes of both partners wins the contest.

Getting Acquainted

Arrange all members of the group in a large circle. Ask the first person to introduce herself by stating her name and sharing something personal that she would like the others to know. The next student repeats the first speaker's name and the information tnat she shared, then introduces himself in the same fashion. The third introduces the first two and then herself, and so on until all members of the group have become acquainted.

Affirmation

One of the most important steps in the development of self-confidence (a necessary prerequisite to the ability to communicate with other) is the acknowledgment of one's self-worth. Activities that encourage group members to affirm the value of an individual's contributions will go a long way toward the fulfillment of this goal. Some effective activities are included here.

I Hear You Saying . . .

Instruct the class to sit in circles of six to eight persons in a group. Introduce a topic with which all are familiar enough to contribute to a discussion (e.g., "What do you think of the use of nuclear power for peacetime use?" "Should gifted students receive grades?") or a maxim or other statement on which to express an opinion (e.g., "The eyes are the windows of the soul."). The first person gives an answer, then the next person affirms the first response and adds her own comments (e.g., "What I hear you saying is . . . . I agree with you that . . . ; however, I really feel that . . . ."). This process continues around the circle until every member of the group has had at least one opportunity to express an opinion. The value of this activity, generally accredited to the counseling techniques of Karkhuff, lies in the affirmation that each member receives as the discussion continues around the circle.

Group Problem Solving

The next activity is designed to build group problem-solving skills by introducing a problem that can be solved only by a cooperative group effort. The teacher's role is provided.

Watson's Dilemma

1. Reproduce the list of clues found in Appendix A (page 328), cutting it into individual clues.
2. Without further introduction, read the following instructions to the class:

   Sherlock Holmes has been called by the Smalltown, USA, Police Department to assist in the solving of a murder. Unfortunately a prior commitment has taken the master detective out of town, and he is not available to help. Because his faithful assistant Watson has worked with him on so many cases, Sherlock has decided to give him a chance to solve a case on his own. Watson, alas, is not so confident in his problem-solving ability. As members of a nationally famous problem-solving team, you have been asked to assist Watson in the solution of the murder.

Before we begin, I would like for you to arrange yourselves in a close circle, ready to work on your assigned task. You may wish to bring pencil and paper with you to the circle for making notes as you work.

3. Allow time for forming the circle, then continue:

Each of you will be given one or more clues that have been uncovered by the Police Department. Your task is to determine the identify of the victim, the murder weapon, the time and place of the murder, the identity of the murderer, and the motive. After I give you your clues, you may organize yourselves in any manner you wish; however, you may *not* get out of your seats, and you may only share your clues verbally. If one of you thinks you have solved the mystery, and you are able to convince the group that your answers are all correct, you may then present your solution to me. At that time I will inform you as to whether or not your answers are all accurate; if they are not all accurate, I will not be able to tell you which ones are incorrect.

4. Pass out the clues. If there are more students than clues, you may wish to form more than one group, giving a complete set of clues to each group and encouraging competition between groups. If there are fewer students than clues, give more than one clue to each person until all clues are distributed. When you are certain that all rules and procedures are clearly understood, instruct the group to begin work. Time the activity (completion will usually range from fifteen to thirty minutes), and encourage analysis of the methods by which the group arrived at a solution. If individual attempts at leadership were stifled, point out that this type of exercise is often called "Recognizing the Value of All Contributions" and is designed to develop group cohesion and cooperation in the problem solving process.

An Exercise in Small Group Cooperation*

The next activity is designed to help students experience firsthand the necessity of cooperation in a group problem-solving situation.

---

* Adapted from the "Broken Squares Exercise" by D. W. Johnson and F. P. Johnson, *Joining Together: Group Theory and Group Skills,* © 1975, p. 325. Adapted by permission of Prentice-Hall, Inc. Englewood Cliffs, New Jersey.

1. Divide the class into groups of six students each, designating one member of each group to serve as observer. Instruct participants to arrange themselves closely around tables, facing one another to facilitate interaction among members of each group. Groups should be separated well to avoid observation across groups. Provide one set of squares for each group; the instructions for making these sets are found on page 114.

2. Tell the group that this activity will help them examine ways in which different members of groups define and prioritize their goals. Inform them that it will consist of completing a group puzzle together, and that the first group to complete its puzzle will be the winner.

3. Instruct observers privately to notice in particular the processes followed by their groups, problems experienced in the completion of the squares, and attitudes (self-help vs. cooperative) displayed by individual members.

4. Distribute to each group one set of envelopes (one envelope for each member of the group). Tell the groups they are to work together to form five squares of the same size—one in front of each group member.

5. Read the following rules aloud:
   a. No talking is allowed during the activity.
   b. You may not communicate, either verbally or nonverbally, that you need or want a piece that another member has.
   c. You may give any or all of your pieces to any other member of your group. However, you may not indicate in any way what can or should be done with it.
   d. You may not throw a puzzle piece into the middle of the table. Pieces may be shared only with individual members.
   e. When you have completed your own square, you still have a responsibility to your group. Remember: The first group to complete five squares of equal size is the winner. However, the only way that you may help another person is to share your puzzle pieces with him. You may never show or tell another person what to do.

6. After one group has completed all five squares (time usually ranges from fifteen to thirty minutes), reveal the patterns that must be followed for successful completion of the exercise. Allow time for groups who did not complete their squares to compare their progress to the correct solutions.

7. Ask observers to share their observations about the groups' completion of their tasks, as previously instructed. Discuss.

Directions for Making Squares

1. Using the patterns in Figure 5–1, cut five squares from one color of construction paper for each set you will need (one set per group of five players). Label the squares as shown, and cut the pieces apart on the indicated lines.

2. You will need five envelopes for each set; label these envelopes **A, B, C, D,** and **E.** Distribute the cut pieces from Step 1 into these envelopes as follows:

Envelope A: One each of pieces i, e, and h.

Envelope B: Three pieces of a.

Envelope C: One piece each of a, c, and j.

Envelope D: One piece of d, and two pieces of f.

Envelope E: One piece each of b, c, and g.

Before placing the cut pieces in the envelopes, erase the pencil marks and replace them with the letter of the envelope in which each piece belongs

---

Figure 5–1. Squares for Exercise in Small Group Instruction

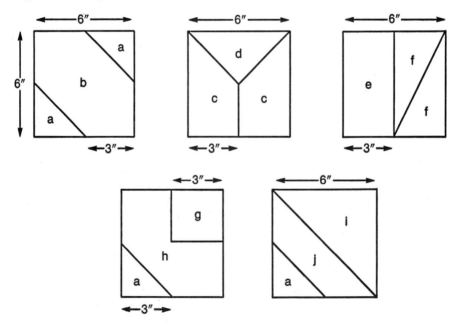

REFERENCES

Filley, A. C. (1975). *Interpersonal conflict resolution.* Glenview, IL: Scott, Foresman & Co.

Johnson, D. W., & Johnson, F. P. (1975). *Joining together: Group theory and group skills.* Englewood Cliffs, NJ: Prentice-Hall.

Maslow, A. H. (1959). Creativity in self-actualizing people. In H. Anderson (Ed.), *Creativity and its cultivation* (pp. 83–95). New York: Harper & Row.

Rogers C. R. (1967). *Freedom to learn.* Columbus, OH: Charles E. Merrill.

6

Role-Playing Strategies

Life is a game that must be played.
Edwin A. Robinson

From the early years of our lives we have all learned to play other roles. The youngest preschool child is engaging in role playing when playing with an imaginary friend, playing school, or dressing up in Mother's old high-heel shoes and furs. Puppet shows and plays from classroom readers provide role-playing experiences for primary and middle-grade children, and secondary students are introduced through their language arts classes to drama of a more serious nature. When we dress like Julius Caesar, a circus clown, or an abstract quality for masquerade parties, we are role playing. And very often, when we attempt to impress others with the selves we would like to be, we are role playing in real life.

Role-playing activities comprise one of the most effective strategies available for the building of group process skills in the gifted classroom. Most notable among these strategies are simulation and sociodrama. Hyman (1974) points out several advantages to the use of these techniques. Applying his assertions to the concept of leadership training in gifted education, the Leadership Training Model offers the following advantages of role playing for the accomplishment of this goal:

1. People learn by doing. Role playing enables students to continue in this method of learning by acting. As Socrates once said, ". . . in teaching children, train them by a kind of game, and you will be able to see more clearly the natural bent of each" (Hyman, 1974, p. 237).

2. Students experience confrontation and conflict resolution through role-playing activities. Much has been written in recent years regarding the role of conflict resolution in leadership and interper-

sonal communication. Filley (1975) suggested that the constructive use of conflict helps prevent more destructive conflicts, that conflict stimulates the creative processes through a need for new solutions, and that the effort to overcome conflict tends to increase group cohesion and cooperation. The use of structured conflict and its resolution through problem solving is therefore an important contribution to the development of interpersonal communication skills and an essential component of any effective leadership training program.

3. Motivation for learning is fostered through active pupil participation and recognition of the relevance of learning for success. Role playing provides these experiences.

4. Through role-playing strategies, particularly simulation and sociodrama, students are given the opportunity to test (in a psychologically safe environment) the possible results of future actions. This advantage allows students to see, as Toffler (1972) deems necessary, that they can change and to some extent control their future destiny.

5. Role-playing activities allow immediate opportunities to apply what has been learned.

6. Simulation and sociodrama encourage the development of advanced thinking skills. Critical thinking is fostered through the analysis of alternative solutions; at the same time, the value of intuitive thinking is seen through confrontations that do not allow time for critical analysis. Decision-making skills are then strengthened in the process.

7. Interpersonal communication skills are built through the need for group cohesion and cooperation. Simulation provides opportunities for practice in this area.

8. Finally, the provision of a debriefing session following the use of role-playing activities fosters the development of evaluation skills.

Two role-playing strategies will be discussed here: simulation and sociodrama. Other examples of role-playing activities are included in Chapter 4 and in the context of the strategies approach to content area teaching (Section V).

SIMULATION

Simulation may be defined simply as an activity that simulates some aspect of real life. In simulation, participants respond as if they were actually part of the action (or interaction) being simulated. Flight simulators and model airplanes are types of simulation, as are games of strategy like Monopoly. The most meaningful types of simulation, however, are often those in which members of a group actually role play (that is, put themselves into the positions of) others. As mentioned earlier, role playing through simulation provides opportunities for participants to try out alternative outcomes in a safe environment. A fine example of the use of simulation to reinforce values in the gifted classroom is described in the following article, written by a young multitalented California actress named Michelle Zeitlin, who was in the tenth grade when she freelanced the article for the *Los Angeles Times*.[1]

A Lesson in Totalitarianism

Editor's Note: Michelle Zeitlin will be entering the 10th grade at Santa Monica, Calif., High School.

By Michelle Zeitlin
Special to *The Los Angeles Times*

"Put your name in the top left-hand corner, with the date underneath. Entitle your paper, 'China Unit.' " Our teacher, Mr. Kramer, pushed back the partition separating his ninth grade history class from that of his team-teaching partner, Mr. Bream. One of the students asked, "Are we all through with the German unit?" No one answered.

Mr. Bream began speaking. "As you know, since President Nixon's 1972 visit to Peking, the United States and the People's Republic of China have begun to establish friendly relations." He paused.

"We have a special surprise for you," Mr. Bream continued. "The State Department has invited the Chinese acrobatic team to visit the United States, and they're going to be here at Lincoln Junior High on Friday." All around the room students began whispering excitedly.

Once we quieted down, Mr. Bream said the Chinese acrobatic team had asked to see a "typical" U.S. junior high classroom, sports program and gym class. What, he asked, did we think that they should see at our school?

"They definitely have to see the noon volleyball games," said a pert blonde who also happens to be an all-star volleyball player.

"Let me interrupt for a moment," Mr. Kramer broke in. "You should be aware that, in the 19th century, Europeans came to China and did great harm to the country. They took spices and silver. The British even hooked the Chinese on opium so that they would trade their valuable silks for the drug.

"Chinese think of Westerners as blond," Mr. Kramer told us, "and the sight of blonds is offensive to them. And so the State Department has asked me to request all blond students to stay away from our classroom on Friday."

---

1. Reprinted with permission of the author, Michelle Zeitlin. From the *Morning Advocate* (Baton Rouge, LA), September 9, 1978, p. 19-A.

Thinking that this was ridiculous, I raised my hand. "Why," I asked, "should we exclude our own classmates just to avoid offending complete strangers?"

"No interruptions, please," Mr. Kramer shot back. "All the kids who don't have blond hair will participate in planning the Chinese visitors' tour of the school. The blonds will go with me now to the library and they'll be given a special assignment."

"Hey, that's not fair," said a girl with tanned skin and curly, sun-bleached hair. "Why should we have to do extra work?"

"Before we go on," said Mr. Bream, ignoring her objection, "raise your hand if you'd like to be part of the tour. Remember, no blonds."

With my dark hair, I certainly was eligible for the privilege. Yet I couldn't bring myself to volunteer.

Taking a long, deep breath, I felt myself begin to sweat. "May I say something to the class?" I asked Mr. Bream, who was already writing down names of volunteers on the board.

I'd been thinking about our recent lessons on Germany and World War II. Coincidentally, the TV Holocaust series was being aired, and almost everyone in our German unit had watched. We even staged a mock Nuremburg trial, in which we convicted Nazi Albert Speer of war crimes.

Now, as I addressed my class about the Chinese visitors, I had the feeling that I was in court all over again. "We just finished studying the Holocaust," I said, "and here we are kicking the blonds out of our class for our own gain. We're behaving just like the Nazis."

"Wait a minute, Michelle," one of my friends said. "Why should we be discourteous to the Chinese just because the blond kids want to stay in class? We wouldn't want the Chinese to insult us if we visited their country."

"How can you say these things?" I asked her. "You're Jewish—you know the Germans exterminated dark-haired Jews just because they didn't like them."

Our teachers, who had always encouraged class discussion, now cut me off. "Look," Mr. Bream said, "Lincoln might never get this honor again."

"All blonds, stand up," Mr. Kramer ordered, "and come with me to the library."

Only two girls and one boy stood. "Come on, brunettes," Mr. Kramer said, "if a blond is sitting next to you, tell that student to stand." One by one the kids began pointing out their classmates.

"This isn't fair," a Mexican-American girl said meekly. Upset and confused, I was embarrassed to raise my hand again, but did so, anyway. The teachers ignored me.

Eventually, 15 blonds had risen to their feet. One of these was a girl who protested bitterly. "I'm not leaving this class," she said. "I don't care if the Chinese don't come."

"Yeah, but we do," reported a brown-haired boy—at which point Mr. Kramer led the blonds out of the room.

Then the rest of us fell silent. "You know, it really isn't fair," one student muttered.

Mr. Bream said, visibly impatient, "Okay, let's settle this once and for all. We'll vote. How many want the Chinese to visit the class and the blonds to be sent away?"

To my chagrin, all but three of my classmates raised their hands.

Then Mr. Kramer told us to cross out the words "China Unit" on top of our papers. "But we haven't written anything yet," I said, puzzled.

"This was only an experiment," Mr. Bream said. "The Chinese athletes aren't coming."

For the past four years, Mr. Bream explained, he and Mr. Kramer had tested their classes in this fashion, swearing each class to secrecy afterward. Amazingly, the vote was always about the same: only one or two (in our case, three) dark-haired dissenters out of 40 or 50 voting not to discriminate against blonds. And, each year, the handful who tried to protest were isolated or stilled by their peers.

Then the two teachers asked us to discuss what had made it so easy to incite totalitarian attitudes, even in Santa Monica.

Until we examined that question, we had not yet completed our German unit.

Another excellent example of a simulation game, published initially by the National Council for the Social Studies, is John D. Gearon's (1966) *War or Peace*.[2]

War or Peace: A Simulation Game

This is a simple international relations game that can be played by ninth-grade classes in world history. Aside from the enjoyment students derive from playing the game, the activity is designed to provide a genuine learning experience. It may be used to introduce or to strengthen several valuable historical insights.

As a model of international relations, for example, the game can be effectively used to point out the condition of international anarchy that has been an important part of the affairs of people and nations throughout history. A fundamental pattern of international relations, the concept of balance of power, may also emerge clearly as a discovery of the students during their playing of the game. Too, international relations terms come to be better understood in classroom action—such terms as foreign policy, crisis, alliance, diplomacy, treaty, neutrality, and peace conference.

The classroom becomes during the game an imaginary world made up of a continent and an island—the arena of interaction of seven sovereign nations. A map of this little world (Figure 1) and a

---

2. Reprinted from *Social Education* with permission of the National Council of the Social Studies.

Figure 1: The Continent and the Island

chart showing the relative war powers of the nations (Figure 2) are all the materials a student needs to play the game. These may be duplicated and given to the students, or they may be drawn on the chalkboard and copied by each student.

The numbers presented in Figure 2 for army and navy do not correspond to numbers of men, regiments, divisions, or ships of war. They are relative figures that express the comparative war powers of the nations. "NMF" stands for National Morale Factor. All nations are equal in NMF, and these NMF points cannot be taken away from the students who make up the original nations.

Once each student has a copy of the map and the chart, three steps are necessary to set up the game.

Figure 2: Relative War Powers of the Nations

Nation	Army	Navy	NMF	Total
Andros	700	600	240	1540
Atweena	1000	0	240	1240
Bismania	800	700	240	1740
Bontus	460	400	240	1100
Egrama	520	400	240	1160
Galbion	500	1000	240	1740
Nurovia	500	500	240	1240

1. Students may be divided into small groups for the game by counting off by sevens. Number 1's are Androsians; number 2's, Atweenans; number 3's, Bismanians; and so on.
2. The map is oriented to the classroom . . . as it appears to the teacher in front of the class . . . [and, with this top view in mind, students] find the relative positions of their nations in the room. [They are aided by nation name-cards on the tables.] Once they have located their respective countries, they may form small circles of chairs as their national headquarters.
3. Their first job, when settled, is to pick a ruler for the nation to serve as chairman of the team and to speak out internationally. The ruler may be either a king or a queen—or perhaps a prime minister or a president. The teacher calls the roll of the nations and each ruler responds, introducing himself in a dignified manner by title, name, and country: "King Alfred of Bismania!" or "Queen Mary of Atweena!" No suggestion is to be given by the teacher as to the ruler's power. Decision making within the nations is to be left entirely to the students who make up the nation-teams.

Before the game begins the students are given some ideas as to the realities of the international power situation as it exists according to the map and the chart. Atweena, a landlocked nation, has no navy, but it does have the most powerful army. Galbion, an island nation, has the largest navy. The two most powerful nations are Bismania and Galbion. The two weakest are Bontus and Egrama. It is a competitive and hostile world and each nation is faced with a different problem in maintaining its power, security, and independence.

The basic rules and pattern of the game should now be explained. In any war the more powerful nation, or alliance of nations, always wins and dictates the terms of the peace settlement. In a war a defeated nation can lose some or all of the power of its army, navy, and its territory on the map to the victorious nation or nations.

Students who belong to a nation that has been wiped out of existence in war and its power and territory lost can continue as a part of the game with their NMF points. They may stay together as a group without nation status to negotiate for the restoration of their independence in return for the use of their NMF points in another war. As a group, they may join another nation with their NMF points. Or, they may go as individual refugees to join other nations, each taking along his equal share of the NMF points.

The game is played in cycles of well-defined phases, and each cycle begins with an international crisis. The basic four phases for the first cycle are: (1) planning foreign policy; (2) negotiations; (3) international declarations; and (4) peace conference. In later cycles additional phases of planning foreign policy, negotiations, or special international conferences may be called for on the request of the rulers of two or more nations.

Crisis. The game begins in the first cycle with a predetermined international crisis. A state of war exists between Nurovia and Atweena. It must be emphasized to the students that neither side is to be considered the aggressor; there is no right or wrong that can be attached to either; and all possibilities for peace have been thoroughly exhausted. The peace and security of every other nation is threatened. Atweena will conquer Nurovia unless Nurovia is able to bargain successfully to bring other nations into the war on her side. Atweena is, therefore, forced to seek allies. Every nation is faced with the decision to enter the war or remain neutral, on whose side to fight, and what kind of bargain to make for joining one side or the other.

Planning Foreign Policy. This first phase of the first cycle should last about five minutes. Each nation goes into secret conference to decide what to do in the crisis, what its long term foreign policy ought to be, and what nations its ambassadors should visit for negotiations. No communication with other nations is permitted during this phase.

Negotiations. In this phase, lasting about ten minutes, rulers are not allowed to leave their countries. National objectives are to be carried out by sending diplomats to confer secretly—and quietly—with the rulers of other nations. Rulers should generally receive only one diplomat at a time, and they have the right to refuse to confer with any nation's diplomats.

International Declarations. Diplomats return to their own countries. Rulers stand. The five nations not originally concerned in the war are asked, in order, to declare themselves. The teacher's question is "War or peace?" If the answer is for war the nation must state whether it is joining Atweena or Nurovia. Nothing else can be stated by the rulers. [The rulers read their declarations from slips they prepare before the teacher begins the questioning.] The teacher totals the powers of the belligerents and announces the results of the war.

Peace Conference. If more than the original two nations were involved in the war, the victorious rulers go to a peace conference to decide what is to be done with the defeated. At the end of a period of from five to ten minutes they must announce whether the defeated are to be wiped out of existence or merely weakened and left alive. The victor, or victors, may revise the map of the world on a chalkboard for all to see, but the changes of national strength need not be given to any nation not involved in the war. Thus ends the first cycle of the game.

    The game continues with an intermediate cycle of three phases. The nations meet for planning their postwar foreign policy, and this action is followed by a phase of negotiations. The rulers then stand for international declarations. They are called in alphabetical order and the question is still "War or peace?" The answer can be "Peace." Or any nation may declare war on any other nation. No nation can commit any other nation in its declaration.

The first declaration of war precipitates a crisis. When this happens the declarations stop and the game goes into a new cycle of phases the same as in the first cycle. This is the pattern of the game from then on.

The game can come to an abrupt end during any time of international declarations if all nations declare for peace. Unfortunately this has never happened in the experience of the writer. If it does happen, perhaps there is real hope for the future of mankind.

One caution should be given with regard to the use of simulation strategies. Preparation and follow-up (or debriefing) are of the utmost importance. The preparation phase should involve explaining all rules and procedures to the group, ascertaining that all participants understand the purpose of the simulation, and so on. (It should be noted that the simulation described by Michelle Zeitlin deliberately omitted this type of preparation. The debriefing phase, however, was extensive.) The follow-up (or debriefing) period should provide opportunities for participants to express their feelings about the activity itself, the feelings that they experienced in their various assigned roles, their reactions to the activities of the simulation, and the like. Finally, the debriefing should encourage participants to explore the interpersonal communication that developed within the groups, and ways in which this type of experience can help to develop group cohesion and build leadership skills. Without these steps, the simulation will revert to a simple game and may, in the case of more emotional types of simulation, cause interaction problems among participants.

SOCIODRAMA

The literature is not clear on the specific origin of the strategy known as sociodrama, but most indications suggest that it developed in the 1950s as an outgrowth of Jacob Moreno's (1946) psychodrama techniques. Essentially sociodrama is a role-playing strategy designed for use in the solution of social problems. Psychodrama, on the other hand, was formulated for the solution of individual psychological problems. In the hands of the untrained practitioner, psychodrama can be harmful to the participants. Sociodrama, however, can be utilized by any skilled teacher, in virtually any classroom setting.

Although the Morenos were perhaps responsible for the initial development of sociodramatic techniques, it was Torrance who contributed the most insight into its use in the educational process. In the early 1970s, Torrance suggested the use of sociodrama for futuristic problem solving. Combining some of Moreno's psychodrama techniques (future projection, Magic Shop, etc.) with basic production techniques such as doubling, role reversal, and the like, Torrance enabled sociodramatic players to identify more thoroughly with their simulated roles. He further suggested that sociodrama is a useful technique for teaching conflict resolution skills through role playing (1975).

An experience from the classroom effectively illustrates the use of sociodrama in the resolution of social problems or conflicts. Working with a group of junior high school students, selected because of their need for training in problem identification and solution, the teacher began by warming up the group through the use of boundary breakers (Chapter 5) and an explanation of the sociodrama techniques that would be used. After leading the students through the identification of their "social atoms" (those persons whose lives revolved around their own), she asked for a volunteer to serve as protagonist. The only criterion for selection was that the volunteer must be able to identify a problem (preferably one of a social or interactive nature) that needed to be solved.

Katrina, a spunky little black girl, was selected, and she promptly identified her classmates who would role play various members of her family. After some practice to set the players appropriately in their roles (such as Katrina correcting her white father in his role by instructing him to "talk like a normal person" rather than using his version of black dialect), the action began. As director, it was the teacher's responsibility to monitor the action, cutting when necessary to insert other production techniques.

After the completion of the sociodrama, all participants had gained valuable insights into their own and their parents' behaviors through this experience. The teacher further expressed a better understanding of several of the students' motivations and behaviors as a result of observing the drama. As a result of incubation following this production, it became obvious that the sociodrama technique has many possible applications, including use in the training of teachers for the gifted classroom.

Although it is not possible in one chapter to give sufficient information for a teacher to use sociodrama effectively in the classroom, there are two aspects of this strategy that might be helpful to the teacher: first, the steps for using sociodrama in problem solving, and second, the major production techniques used in sociodrama.

According to Torrance (1975), the following steps, comparable to the steps of the creative problem solving process, should be followed sequentially in the use of sociodrama for problem solving:

1. *Defining the problem and establishing the conflict.* The leader explains that the group will participate in an unrehearsed skit in an effort to solve some problem of concern to the participants. Recognizing the general area of the problem to be investigated (e.g., getting along with peers, convincing parents of their needs), the director helps students to explore various aspects of the problem situation in an effort to define a specific problem to be solved. Deferring judgment about the possible outcome, the teacher/director helps the group to describe the situation objectively so that a conflict can be clearly defined for dramatization.

2. *Casting characters.* Looking carefully for potential interest, the teacher then selects the protagonists and assists them in appointing the supporting actors who will play the major roles in the drama.

3. *Preparation and warmup.* At this stage the selected cast should be sent out of the room to plan their setting and agree on the direction the action will take. While this planning is taking place, the teacher should instruct the remaining group members (i.e., the audience) to attempt to identify with either one character of the cast or another person with whom the protagonist would have some interaction or relationship with respect to the identified problem. When the cast returns, they should describe the setting and set up any desired props (which should be kept as simple as possible), and the teacher should conduct warm-up activities designed to help them to establish their selected roles.

4. *The action.* As the action begins, the teacher/director utilizes a variety of production techniques to aid the cast in the analysis and solution of the problem. If the action becomes bogged down, or if an actor "falls out of role" (i.e., loses identification with the role she or he is attempting to portray), the director should attempt to encourage the continuance of the action with such questions as, "What would he do next?" or (to a different member of the cast) "What happens next?" If these techniques do not work, the director should cut (stop) the action and use other production techniques (see page 127) to encourage the action to begin again.

5. *Debriefing.* After the sociodrama production has been completed, as in simulation or other types of role playing, the debriefing phase must be utilized. During this stage, guided discussion should be held to help the group redefine the problem or recognize the alternative solutions that have been produced by the sociodrama. At this point, all members of the cast and those in the audience who identifed with related roles should relate to the group their reactions and feelings, as well as their perceptions of the solutions which surfaced from the drama.

Why sociodrama? According to Torrance (1975), research has affirmed that ideational productivity (i.e., creative thinking) occurs more often in varied states of consciousness than in the fully rational state. This finding is supported by stories about Kekule's discovery of the benzene ring, of Mendeleev's dream of the periodic table, and of myriads of musicians who have made discoveries or created productions of major significance as a result of temporary states of incubation and reverie. If such is the case, the projection of oneself into alternative roles would seem to move the player from the cognitive concentration and overwhelming influence of the left hemisphere of the brain into the more creative, open-minded right brain, thus aiding significantly in the solution of problems.

Production Techniques

Torrance (1975) identified a number of production techniques that were developed by Moreno and his associates for use with psychodrama. Those that seem to be most effective and easiest to use with sociodrama as a problem-solving tool are included here.

- *Direct Presentation Technique.* Volunteers act out a problem or conflict related to the problem under study.
- *Soliloquy Technique.* The protagonist turns away from his physical position on stage and expresses his thoughts aloud, as if "thinking aloud" outside of the action.
- *Double Technique.* The double is the "alter ego" of the speaker. For example, if a protagonist is having difficulty with idea production, his "double" may engage in brainstorming with the protagonist, enabling him to resume his original position in the drama. The doubling technique may be compared to the abstract conscience with whom we often "speak" in attempting to solve internal problems.
- *Multiple Double Technique.* Like the double technique, the multiple double offers more than one point of view to the protagonist. The proverbial angel and devil on the shoulders of the speaker would be examples of multiple doubles.
- *Role Reversal Technique.* The reversal of roles is an effective technique for helping an actor to identify more accurately with his role. In the example of Katrina cited earlier, it was necessary to have William (the father) play Katrina and Katrina act the part of the father for a short time so that she might demonstrate for William the accurate portrayal of his role. Another useful application of the role reversal technique is to help members of one culture or point of view to experience the other side of an issue.

(Intercultural simulation games such as Bafá Bafá and Rafá Rafá, published by Simile II, P.O. Box 910, Del Mar, CA 92014, provide excellent extensions of this goal.)

In addition to the above activities, Torrance suggests the use of Yablonsky's Future Projection Technique (1974), Moreno's Magic Shop Technique (1946), Lippitt's High Chair and Empty Chair Techniques (1958), Z. T. Moreno's Dream/Fantasy Technique (1959), and Torrance and Myers' Magic Net Technique (1970). Other techniques can be developed by the skilled and creative teacher after experience has been gained in the basic methods explained above, to help actors in a sociodrama to warm up, to identify with their roles, and to anticipate problem solutions.

As a final word, Torrance (1975) offers the following guidelines for the director of sociodrama:

1. The director should master basic production techniques, as well as techniques for working with audiences, and work into developing his own techniques for use in the types of sociodrama most needed by the students.

2. The action of the sociodrama should move continuously toward a resolution of the identified problem.

3. In the debriefing stage, sociodrama should be evaluated not for its dramatic qualities but rather for its success in fulfilling its initial purpose.

4. The audience should be involved in the conflict and the role playing at all times.

5. Confrontation of the problem should be continuous. Techniques such as fantasy and analogy should be considered to avoid reducing the conflict.

6. The problem selected for sociodrama should be relevant to all members of the cast and to the audience.

7. Warmup is essential for all members of the cast, the audience, and the director.

8. Physical properties and furnishings should be simple, encouraging actors to improvise with commonplace materials and thus fostering creative responses.

REFERENCES

Filley, A. C. (1975). *Interpersonal conflict resolution.* Glenview, IL: Scott, Foresman.

Gearon, J. D. (1966). War or Peace: A simulation game. *Social Education, 30,* 521–522.

Hyman, R. T. (1974). *Ways of teaching* (2nd ed.). New York: J. B. Lippincott.

Lippitt, R. (1958). The auxiliary chair technique. *Group Psychotherapy, 11*, 8–23.

Moreno, J. L. (1946). *Psychodrama, First Volume*. Beacon, NY: Beacon House.

Moreno, Z. T. (1959). A survey of psychodramatic techniques. *Group Psychotherapy, 12*, 5–14.

Toffler, A. (1972, January 17). Alvin Toffler: Study the future. *Junior Scholastic*, Teacher's Edition, 3–4.

Torrance, E. P. (1975). Sociodrama as a creative problem solving approach to studying the future. *Journal of Creative Behavior, 9*, 183–188.

Torrance, E. P., & Myers, R. E. (1970). Creative learning and teaching. New York: Dodd, Mead.

Yablonsky, L. (1974). Future-projection technique. In I. A. Greenberg (Ed.), *Psychodrama: theory and therapy*. New York: Behavioral Publications.

Zeitlin, M. (1978, September 9). A lesson in totalitarianism. *Morning Advocate*, p. 19-A.

7

Decision Making

*Decide not rashly. The decision made can
never be recalled.*

Longfellow

The ability to make intelligent, rational, and responsible decisions is
essential for effective leadership. Effective decision making requires
independence of thinking and action, self-confidence, acceptance of
responsibility, task commitment, and moral strength. What is the role
of the school in the development of these qualities?

THE VALUES ISSUE

Much has been written about the school's responsibility in the moral
development of its students. Rollo May (1982) tells us that "all creativity begins in freedom." If leaders are required to use creative means
of solving society's problems, then leaders must learn to handle
freedom. Without responsibility, freedom results in waste of talent and
delinquency. We are all familiar with the products of misguided,
amoral creativity and leadership; Adolf Hitler was the prime example.
But what of the current plea that moral (or values) education be left
entirely to home and church? Is it indeed possible to educate our future
leaders without some attention to the values issue?

Let us look at the reasoning behind both sides of this issue. The
increase in juvenile crimes of recent years attests to the fact that moral
education left to the home is not enough. On the other side of the coin,
we would certainly agree that it is not the teacher's place to inculcate in
students those personal values by which she conducts her own life.
Adamant objections have been justifiably raised by parents to the
approach that essentially says, "All right, students, close your math
books; it is time for values clarification. Which ones of you would rather

spend your vacation in the woods? in a penny arcade? at a rock concert?" But the point we must make is that cognitive concepts taught without affective integration—without consideration of the values issues involved—are virtually meaningless to the students who absorb them.

Essentially there are two kinds of values: general or societal values and personal (often spiritual) values. The former category consists of those values that are accepted by our democratic society and government—those that all American citizens are expected to uphold. These include respect for the rights of others, honesty, tolerance, and fairness, as well as the obedience of the written law and concern for our earth's environment. Patriotism, courage, and a strong work ethic are important in the building of a healthy citizenry, and skills of diplomacy and courtesy are essential to effective interpersonal communication. Acceptance of those historic documents that are the cornerstone of our liberty—the Declaration of Independence, the Constitution, the Bill of Rights—is essential to the development of effective leadership for our future.

Personal values, on the other hand, are those moral guidelines that cause people to behave differently—the choices that are not governed by law. These are the decisions about religious beliefs and customs, personal health and recreation, self-motivation, and the like, which affect only the individual and not those around her. The responsibility of the teacher is not to indoctrinate students with personal beliefs and values, but rather to encourage students to strengthen their own positive values systems, particularly those governed by the values of society, so that they will live by them. Honesty is a value that is required by society; our laws prevent stealing and our schools prohibit cheating. When the teacher assigns an essay on honesty to a student caught cheating on a test, this teacher is helping the student to strengthen her democratic values to the extent that the student will live her life by them. The presumption that parents can provide the total moral educational needs of students is naive; the child who does not experience values education in all aspects of life will suffer.

Why, then, is moral (or values) education so important in the development of future leadership among our gifted students? First, by their definition, gifted students possess a high intellectual potential, giving them an earlier understanding of societal issues than their chronological age peers. Like the Hitlers of history, without moral guidance in their early years they may lead others in the wrong direction. Second, we know that gifted persons reach higher levels of reasoning at earlier ages. The early acceptance of moral responsibility is therefore essential to guide these students properly.

Realistically, the values issue has not been raised because of teachers encouraging discussion in history class on the problems of apartheid or the moral aspects of the Civil War. Rather, it has come to the forefront as a result of the misguided use of "values clarification" activities out of the context of reality.

How, then, are we to train our future leaders in the skills that will enable them to make (and guide others in making) the right decisions for society? The Leadership Training Model proposes a series of planned experiences designed to develop independence, self-confidence, responsibility, task commitment, and moral strength—the prerequisites of decision-making. The goals of training in the decision-making component of LTM include the development of realistic goals, the ability to organize and implement plans for meeting these goals, and both formative and summative evaluation. Strategies that lend themselves well to the development of decision-making skills include values education, role playing, and counseling. The use of role playing is discussed in some detail in Chapter 6, and the effective use of counseling techniques requires in-depth training. Therefore, only values education will be discussed in this chapter.

Values Education

One important prerequisite of decision-making ability is moral development, particularly the development of a clear values system to guide these decisions. Values education activities enable the facilitator to clarify and strengthen the democratic values brought to the class situation by the individual student. It is important, however, that the facilitator's personal values (e.g., opinions about smoking, life styles, and the like) not be forced upon the students, as a dogmatic attitude will prove to be counterproductive in the development of independent decision-making skills.

What are the responsibilities of the schools in moral education? Raths, Harmon, and Simon (1966) list the following roles of the teacher in values education:

1. Encourage children to make choices freely;
2. Help students discover alternatives when faced with choices;
3. Help children weigh alternatives thoughtfully, reflecting on the consequences of each;
4. Encourage children to consider what values are important to them;
5. Provide opportunities for students to affirm their choices; and
6. Encourage children to act, behave, and live in accordance with their choices.

There are many situations in which the strengthening of democratic values can be integrated into the teaching of cognitive content in the gifted classroom. Some examples of activities are given here.

Language: Assign the reading of *Huckleberry Finn*. Discuss Huck's attitude toward Jim. Have students write a group story with a modern-day version of Huck Finn. Compare the treatment of Jim in Mark Twain's story with the reality of today.

Science: Divide the class into two groups. Have one group role-play a team of geneticists who have just discovered a method of cloning human beings. The other group represents a delegation of citizens opposing the release of this technique. Attempt to place students in groups with views opposite from their own. After the exercise, discuss their feelings, whether or not their opinions have changed, and how they felt about the activity.

Social Studies. Use "The Land of the Spheres" (Appendix A, page 329) as an introduction to a study of the American Revolution, the Civil Rights Movement, apartheid in South Africa, democracy vs. communism, or similar concepts.

REFERENCES

May R. (1982). Decisions that shape us. *Creative Living, 2*(6).

Raths, L. E., Harmon, M., & Simon, S. B. (1966). *Values and teaching: Working with values in the classroom.* Columbus, OH: Charles E. Merrill.

Section IV

CREATIVE
STRATEGIES

Creativity is the key to education in its fullest sense and to the solution of mankind's most serious problems.

J. P. Guilford

The year was 1950; the setting was Guilford's inaugural address as he became president of the influential American Psychological Association. The title of his presentation was "Creativity: Yesterday, Today, and Tomorrow." For the first time in the history of the United States a major figure brought dramatically to the forefront the crying need for psychologists and educators to assign priority to the crucial subject of creativity.

A review of history reveals that failure to apply creative, intelligent methods for solving the problems of mankind is the most expedient road to disaster for a democratic society. The magnificent classical ages of Greece, which have had far-reaching influence even into modern times, collapsed as a result of failure to heed the warnings of the great philosopher Socrates (Torrance, 1962).

In recent years the importance of creativity has been acknowledged by increasing numbers of educators; and yet we find continuing evidence, as charged by writers such as Holt and Silberman, that the schools still destroy children's creative capacities and suppress their natural spontaneity and pleasure in creating.

What is this abstract concept that we call creativity? Where does it come from? Why do we need to encourage it? And how do we go about fostering its development in our students?

THE CONCEPT OF CREATIVITY

Despite the abundance of writing on the subject of creativity, it is apparent that there has been little unification of the theories and definitions that have been advanced. Not too many years ago, creativity was thought of only in terms of product; that is, the creative person was one who could produce what society deemed to be a creative product—(e.g., a beautiful painting, a melodious or moving musical composition, or an inspirational writing). The irony of this approach lies in the fact that talent and creativity are not necessarily equivalent traits; a person can display apparent talent (or skill) without creativity (as in the ability to pick out a melody on the piano or to reproduce an object on paper), and a creative thinker may have no identifiable talent in the traditional sense of the term (e.g., an inventor in the physical science area). More recently, however, researchers have acknowledged two other aspects of creativity: the creative process and the creative personality.

Carl Rogers (1959) defined the creative process as "the emergence in action of a novel relational product, growing out of the uniqueness of the individual on the one hand, and the materials, events, people, or circumstances of his life on the other" (p. 71). Advocating no attempt at moral judgment of the creative product, Rogers pointed out that to be considered historically as creative, such a product must qualify for acceptance by some group at some point in history. Khatena (1978) defined creativity in terms of one's power to break away from a set pattern and develop original ideas, thoughts, or relationships. And Torrance (1977) contributed an additional dimension to the concept of creativity, defining it as "the process of sensing problems or gaps in information, forming ideas or hypotheses, testing and modifying these hypotheses, and communicating the results" (p. 6). Another view of creativity addresses the use of fluency (quantity of ideas), flexibility (variety of ideas), originality (uniqueness), and elaboration (attention to detail). In a recent study on the identification of creative talent, Torrance (1984) isolated thirteen types of responses that point to creativity. These factors are discussed under the section on the creative person.

What is the source of creativity? This question has been debated for many years by researchers, but to date no definitive conclusion has been reached. Gowan (1982) theorized that creativity may have a "transpersonal" source; that is, that it may originate from a source outside of the conscious mind. An alternate way of viewing this theory is that creativity is merely the condition of being psychologically open to "preconscious" sources—sources already within the individual but at a level below the conscious which can be accessed only through techniques such as relaxation, sensory deprivation, imagery, and the like. May (1975, p. 55) defined the unconscious as "the potentialities for awareness or action which the individual cannot or will not actualize" and theorized that these potentialities were the source of what he called "free creativity." And Kubie (1958) contended that only the pre-conscious had the flexibility necessary for creative thinking to take place. Although numerous implications can be found in the literature (especially in the personal anecdotes of working artists) to suggest that the source of creativity is supernatural, most references simply allude to moments of illumination, variously called "eurekas," "ahas," or "satoris." One important criterion for such discoveries to occur seems to be a period of incubation following conscious effort aimed at the solving of a problem. More attention will be given later to the importance of incubation, which has been treated extensively by researchers over the years.

A second hypothesis that relates to the source of creativity is rooted in the widely accepted theory of hemisphericity. This theory, supported by the medical research of neurosurgeons such as Bogen, Sperry, and others, contends that the cerebral cortex of the human brain is divided into two hemispheres, right and left, each of which controls specific functions. The left brain, often called the *linear* or *temporal lobe*, controls the right side of the body in the majority of people. In this hemisphere are based temporal operations such as logic, language, sequential processing, and analytical thinking. Persons with left-hemispheric dominance are thus more efficient in the areas of reading, mathematical computation, and scientific thinking. Conversely, the right hemisphere, which controls the left side of the body in most humans, may be categorized as *spatial* or *holistic*. Persons who are "right brained" tend to be creative and intuitive, to move creatively, to fantasize, and to communicate well noverbally. They are emotional beings who look at the Gestalt and synthesize well, who think analogically, and who appreciate aesthetics. These persons become our artists, our dramatists, our musicians, our dancers; their academic strengths lie in areas such as mathematics concept. If much of the research by these and other investigators is correct, then creative potential is innate in all humans and centered within the right hemispheres of our brains.

If all people are born with creative potential, then why does creativity appear to manifest itself more in some persons than in others? Why is it, as Guilford (1950) pointed out, that only about two people out of every million who have lived since the beginning of recorded history have distinguished themselves for their creative acts? Realistically, we must acknowledge that with respect to all types of potential some persons are born with greater degrees of ability than others. More important, however, is the fact that the left hemisphere of the brain must be almost continuously active during our waking hours in order that we might function in a highly cognitive world. While the right hemisphere activity goes on, it is overlaid most of the time with the cognitive activity of the left brain. And it is only when this conscious cognitive activity is permitted to subside that the creative potential of the right brain can manifest itself (Gowan, Khatena, and Torrance, 1979).

Another aspect of creativity that has been explored for some time is the relationship between creativity and intelligence. Most notable are the classic studies of Getzels and Jackson (1962) and Torrance (1962). Comparing the academic performances of highly creative students with their highly intelligent peers, these investigators found that a "threshold of intelligence" existed at an IQ level of about 120; that is, above this level no significant differences occurred in the academic achievements of the two groups. Guilford (1967) confirmed and expanded these findings, pointing out that persons with low intelligence must be low in creative potential, whereas a wide range of creative performance exists in persons of high intellectual potential.

WHY CREATIVITY?

Why all this talk about creativity? Haven't we been told for many years that creativity, like genius, is closely related to insanity or mental illness? To the contrary! Modern research has proved that the theories of writers such as Lange-Eichbaum (1932) and Lombroso (1891) were far from correct. According to Maslow, who conducted extensive studies of the relationship between creativity and mental health (1968), creative people are the most likely to become self-actualized (or to realize their individual potentials in life). But more specifically why do we want to encourage creative thinking, processing, and production in our gifted students?

First, probably the most universally accepted goal of education is to help students grow to reach their potential. And, according to Arieti (1976), creativity—although not the only type of growth humans can experience—is certainly one of the most important.

Second, creativity has been shown to be positively related to both academic and nonacademic achievement. Various studies have demonstrated the value of creative thinking in that it fosters independent thinking and the ability to cope more effectively with life's problems. Other studies have shown that highly creative students tend to perform at least as well as highly intelligent students in all basic areas of the school curriculum and are more likely than their less creative peers to become creative producers in their adult lives (Bellin, 1967; Cropley, 1972; Getzels and Jackson, 1962; Holland, 1967; MacKinnon, 1978; Sandifer, 1972; Torrance, 1962, 1979). Other researchers have found that the humor that is characteristic of creative persons tends to facilitate incidental learning (Hauck and Thomas, 1972) and that creativity is positively related to interests in literature, music, and other aesthetic experiences (Windholz, 1968).

Section IV of this book addresses more specifically the nature of the creative process and factors that tend to block its realization, common characteristics of the creative person and ways of assessing creative potential, and suggested methods of fostering creativity in the gifted.

REFERENCES

Arieti, S. (1976). *Creativity: The magic synthesis*. New York: Basic Books.

Bellin, A. P. (1968). Creative thinking ability and its relationship to reading comprehension and intelligence of fourth grade pupils (Doctoral dissertation, University of Minnesota). Dissertation Abstracts International, *28*, 2429A. (University Microfilms No. 71–29, 846)

Cropley, A. J. (1972). A five-year longitudinal study of the validity of creativity tests. *Developmental Psychology, 6*, 119–124.

Getzels, J. W., & Jackson, P. W. (1962). *Creativity and intelligence*. New York: John Wiley & Sons.

Gowan, J. C. (1982). *Creativity as a transpersonal source*. Paper presented at the Creative Problem Solving Institute, Buffalo, NY.

Gowan, J. C., Khatena, J., & Torrance, E. P. (Eds.). (1979). *Educating the ablest: A book of readings*. (2nd Ed.). Itasca, IL: F. E. Peacock.

Guilford, J. P. (1950) Creativity. *American Psychologist, 5*, 444–454.

Guilford, J. P. (1967). Creativity: Yesterday, today, and tomorrow. *Journal of Creative Behavior, 1*, 3–14.

Hauck, W. E., & Thomas, J. W. (1972). The relationship of humor to intelligence, creativity, and intentional learning. *Journal of Experimental Education, 40*, 52–55.

Holland, J. M. (1968). Creativity in relation to socioeconomic status, academic achievement, and school, personal, and social adjustment in elementary school children (Doctoral dissertation, University of Tennessee). Dissertation Abstracts, *29*, 147A. (University Microfilms No. 68-9807)

Khatena, J. (1978). *The creatively gifted child*. New York: Vantage Press.

Kubie, L. S. (1958). *Neurotic distortion of the creative process*. Lawrence, KS: University of Kansas Press.

Lange-Eichbaum, W. (1932). *The problem of genius*. New York: MacMillan.

Lombroso, C. (1891). *The man of genius*. London: Charles Scribner's Sons.

MacKinnon, D. W. (1978). *In search of human effectiveness: Identifying and developing creativity*. Buffalo, NY: Creative Education Foundation.

Maslow, A. H. (1968) *Toward a psychology of being*. New York: Van Nostrand Reinhold Co.

May, R. (1975). *The courage to create*. New York: W. W. Norton & Co.

Rogers, C. R. (1959). Toward a theory of creativity. In H. H. Anderson (Ed.), *Creativity and its cultivation* (pp. 69–82). New York: Harper & Row.

Sandifer, P. D. (1973). The relationship between creativity and academic achievement (Doctoral dissertation, University of South Carolina). Dissertation Abstracts International, 34, 214A–215A. (University Microfilms No. 73-16, 316)

Torrance, E. P. (1962). *Guiding creative talent.* Englewood Cliffs, NJ: Prentice-Hall.

Torrance, E. P. (1977). *Creativity in the classroom.* Washington, D. C.: National Education Association.

Torrance, E. P. (1979). Unique needs of the creative child and adult. In A. H. Passow (Ed.), *The gifted and the talented: Their education and development* (pp. 352–371). Chicago: National Society for the Study of Education, 1979.

Torrance, E. P. (1984) Some products of twenty five years of creativity research. *Educational Perspectives, 22*(3), 3–8.

Windholz, G. (1968). The relation of creativity and intelligence constellations to traits of temperament, interest, and value in college students. *Journal of General Psychology, 79,* 291–299.

8

The Essence of Creativity

*Creative intelligence in its various forms and
activities is what makes man.*
                              James Harvey Robinson

We have seen in the preceding introduction that, although much attention has been devoted to the subject of creativity since Guilford's prophetic address in 1950, little agreement has been reached on the definition and nature of this elusive quality. If a surveyor compared definitions of creativity, the responses would likely be stated in terms of the creative product. Having grown up with this concept, we can all identify in our own minds (even if we cannot verbalize to anyone else's satisfaction) those qualities that make a product creative (originality, uniqueness, different perspective). Current literature, however, tends to stray from this age-old concept, speaking more frequently of the creative process and the creative personality. This chapter will address these concepts in an attempt to define creativity more clearly, following these descriptions with a discussion of factors that influence the development of creative potential.

THE CREATIVE PROCESS

As far back as the early twentieth century, creativity was being discussed in the writings of psychologists and educators. Building on the work of the German physicist Helmholtz, Graham Wallas (1926) listed four steps in the creative process: preparation, incubation, illumination, and verification. *Preparation* may be defined as investigation of the problem under study, or the gathering of data relative to the problem; *incubation* is the stage in which the individual consciously breaks away from the problem at hand. After incubation has taken place, *illumination*—or the breakthrough of ideas—occurs. The final stage, *verification,* is somewhat similar to the preparation stage. At this point the individual makes a conscious effort to complete the solution to the problem—critiquing, evaluating, and revising as deemed necessary to prepare for implementation. Other approaches to the sequencing of the creative process (more commonly called the creative problem-solving process) will be examined in depth in Chapter 10.

Incubation and the Creative Process

Much has been written about the importance of incubation. Graham Wallas listed it as a stage in his paradigm of the creative process (described above), and the Leadership Training Model includes it as a necessary step in the problem-solving process. Simply defined, incubation is a period of rest following conscious and determined effort. Numerous examples have been cited in the literature of major breakthroughs in science, the arts, and the humanities, which occurred as a direct result of incubation. Wolfgang Amadeus Mozart, for example, claimed that his most creative ideas came to him when he was alone or when he could not sleep. In the area of science, Friedrich August von Kekule told of an incident that occurred after a lengthy period of laborious effort and resulted in a major scientific discovery:

> I turned my chair to the fire and dozed. Again the atoms were gambolling before my eyes. This time the smaller groups kept modestly in the background. My mental eye, rendered more acute by visions of this kind, could now distinguish larger structures, of manifold conformation; long rows, sometimes more closely fitted together; all twining and twisting in snakelike motion. But look! What was that? One of the snakes had seized hold of its own tail, and the form whirled mockingly before my eyes. As if by a flash of lightning I awoke. . . . Let us learn to dream, gentlemen (cited in Koestler, 1964, p. 118).

Kekule's dream led to his discovery of what Koestler called "one of the cornerstones of modern science": the discovery that the molecules of some organic compounds exist in ringlike structures, like the serpent biting its tail.

Krippner, Dreistadt, and Hubbard (1972) related the following story of the creation of the Periodic Table:

> In 1869, D. I. Mendeleev went to bed exhausted after struggling to conceptualize a way to categorize the elements based upon their atomic weights. He reported, "I saw in a dream a table where all the elements fell into place as required. Awakening, I immediately wrote it down on a piece of paper. Only in one place did a correction later seem necessary." In this manner, Mendeleev's Periodic Table of the Elements was created (p. 218).

Summing up the nature and the importance of incubation, Dewey (1933, p. 284) wrote:

> It is a common experience that after prolonged preoccupation with an intellectual topic, the mind ceases to function readily. It apparently has got into a rut; the "wheels go around" in the head, but they do not turn out any fresh grist. New suggestions cease to occur. The mind is, as the apt expression goes, "fed up." This condition is a warning to turn, as far as conscious attention and reflection are concerned, to something else. Then after the mind has ceased to be intent on the problem, and consciousness has relaxed its strain, a period of incubation sets in. Material rearranges itself; facts and principles fall into place; what was confused becomes bright and clear; the mixed-up becomes orderly, often to such an extent that the problem is essentially solved.

Dewey concluded by pointing out that people often decide, after conscious periods of intense problem-solving effort, to "sleep on it" before completing the task. As a result, they often awake to the realization that the problem has been solved through incubation during sleep. In summary, he defined incubation simply as "one phase of a rhythmic process."

Pointing out the urgent need for creative and intuitive thinking, Torrance and Safter (1986) presented a model developed some twenty years earlier by Torrance. Expanded to address Rollo May's (1975) concept of "suprarational thinking"—a process that goes beyond the rational to bring something new into being, and which Torrance and Safter considered to be "the essence of man's highest ability to think"—this model is designed to enhance incubation and thus to further the creative problem-solving process. The model comprises three stages:

Stage 1: Heightening Anticipation (the warmup stage)

Stage 2: Encountering the Expected and Unexpected and Deepening Expectations

Stage 3: Going Beyond and "Keeping It Going" (follow-up).

The creative teacher can greatly enhance the creative thinking abilities of his gifted charges by using this model throughout the curriculum.

Blocks to the Creative Process

Having investigated the concept of incubation and how it can be encouraged, let us now take a look at another aspect of the creative process: factors that tend to block its realization. Some of these blocks are described below.

1. Lack of time. As we have seen, incubation is a necessary step in the creative process. Time pressures prevent this step from taking place.

2. Lack of self-confidence. Failure to recognize one's own abilities, often due to feelings of inferiority, prohibits a person from taking the risks that must be taken in order to be truly creative.

3. Pseudo-sophistication. The individual who is reluctant to "be a child again" or who lacks a sense of humor has difficulty breaking into a creative mode.

4. Rigidity or convergence of thinking. Flexibility (or divergency) of thinking is essential for the creative process to take place.

5. External locus of control. The individual who relies or places too great a value on the direction or evaluation given by others will have difficulty freeing himself for creativity. Peer pressure and overreliance on authority are among the most common blocks to the creative process.

6. Lack of task commitment. Creativity is hard work; it requires determination and tenacity. A person who lacks task commitment will soon give up the creative endeavor.

7. Conformity. Again schools and industry encourage this block to the creative process. The great creators of civilization have been the nonconformists—those who were not afraid of the "road not taken."

8. Fear of the unknown. Related to the fear of failure, this block prevents the individual from striking out in new directions.

9. Excessive reality orientation. The inability to break away from the real-world orientation will surely prevent a leap into the intuitive world.

10. Inability to incubate. As we have seen, the creative process requires the individual to break away from the problem. The person who cannot get away and relax ("sleep on it") will have great difficult with the creative process.

11. Difficulty in perceiving the real problem. Dewey (1933) said, "A question well put is half answered." Until the problem has been clearly defined, it cannot be creatively solved.

12. Lack of knowledge. Again Dewey (1933) is credited with saying, "We can have facts without thinking, but we cannot have thinking without facts." We have seen earlier that a moderate degree of intelligence is necessary for creativity to be present. Wallas's preparation stage of the creative process is the point at which facts are gathered. Without knowledge, the creative process cannot take place.

13. Inability to go beyond the obvious. In order to be truly creative, one must be able to extrapolate, so to speak, going beyond that which is obvious to all.

14. Overreliance on logic. Torrance and Safter (1986) have told us that the ten rational processes emphasized by the Educational Policies Commission in 1961 are not enough. In fact, they contend, if we had to choose between rational thinking processes and creative/intuitive thinking processes, we would have to choose the latter, which "represent mankind's highest ability to think" (p. 11).

15. Impatience. The anxious, impatient person who has an emotional need to bring quick closure to an issue or a problem will fail to reach a creative solution.

16. Adherence to cultural values/traditions. Cultures that value such qualities as economy and practicality may tend to discourage creative thinking. Cultures in which these qualities are not stressed tend to produce more creative persons.

17. Structure. For creative thinking and production to transpire, a creative environment is essential. Excessive structure blocks the freedom to produce in one's own creative style.

18. Habit. Called "functional fixedness" by Osborn (1963), the habit of doing things one way is difficult to break. By remaining continuously "in a rut," the individual fails to see new ways of doing things. This constitutes a serious block to the creative process.

19. Lack of energy. Incubation, as we have seen, takes place in a state of rest. Fatigue prevents the creative process from being realized.

20. Prejudice or the inability to defer judgment. Osborn (1963) has told us that one of the most important rules of brainstorming is to defer judgment. The person who immediately judges (or prejudges) another person or a product (even one of his own) will have difficulty with the creative process.

21. A "work-play dichotomy." The attitude that work and play must be separated often blocks creativity; those who believe that work is not productive if it is enjoyable will allow themselves few opportunities for creative production.

THE CREATIVE PERSON

Having defined the concept of creativity in several ways, let us look more specifically at the creative individual. This section will consider the characteristics attributed to the creative person.

Prince (1968) maintained that one of the causes of creative blocks is the development of a "censor," which protects the conscious mind from interruptions entering from the unconscious mind via the preconscious. Relating this censor to creative potential, Prince suggested that the creative person is able to bypass the censor, thus using more of his stored or latent potential, following the intuitions or impulses that may arise from beneath the conscious mind.

In his classic study of architects, MacKinnon (1978) identified numerous characteristics of creative persons. He found that one of the most important needs for creative production was a high level of energy. MacKinnon also observed that most highly creative people have above average intelligence and consequently are better able than their less creative counterparts to retain their experiences. They are self-accepting and emotionally stable, have more information at their command, and show clear preferences for the "complex and asymmetrical" (p. 61). The creative architects in his study seemed to have positive self-concepts and assessed themselves as determined, enthusiastic, independent, individualistic, and industrious, as opposed to the less creative subjects, who described themselves as clear thinking, dependable, reliable, responsible, sincere, tolerant, and understanding.

In agreement with other observers, MacKinnon noted that creative individuals possess openness of experience, both in terms of introspection and in relation to the outside world. He suggested that the creative individual is aesthetically inclined, in keeping with his preference for intuitive thinking. MacKinnon's concept of the creative person involved a strong sense of destiny, consonant with Erikson's claim that the creative person has succeeded in establishing his own identity. MacKinnon's studies produced evidence that creative people tend toward task orientation more when independent activity is allowed than when conformity to predetermined standards is required. He further suggested that creative people do not necessarily have fewer problems but rather have more creative ways of coping with and solving them.

Other research has revealed that creative people are more stimulus-free than their less creative peers, that they are self-asserted and energetic, and that they are inclined toward impulsivity and emotional sensitivity. Highly creative individuals often isolate themselves from their peers, causing them to resort to fantasy. And several studies have documented a strong relationship between humor and creativity (Barron, 1957; Getzels and Jackson, 1962; Torrance, 1962).

In discussing his theory of creativity, Rogers (1959) maintained that "the mainspring of creativity appears to be . . . man's tendency to actualize himself, to become his potentialities" (p. 72). He further suggested that "the individual creates primarily because it is satisfying to him, because this behavior is felt to be self-actualizing" (p. 73). Although acknowledging that many eminent persons have been psychologically unhealthy, Maslow (1959) pointed out that "self-actualizing creativeness stresses first the personality rather than its achievements, including such qualities as boldness, courage, freedom, spontaneity, perspicuity, integration, and self-acceptance" (pp. 93–94). Maslow's writings further imply that creative behavior is one of the most ostensible characteristics of self-actualized persons.

Numerous studies have examined the validity of Rogers's and Maslow's theories of self-actualizing creativity. Studies by Parnes (1971) confirmed these views, and Garfield, Cohen, and Roth (1969) found that creative persons are healthier and more self-confident than noncreatives. Kubie (1958) concurred, observing from his studies that neurotic behaviors tend to distort creative ability and production.

In the revision of the scoring methods for the *Torrance Tests of Creative Thinking*, Torrance (1984) identified the following responses that are indicative of creative ability:

1. Emotional Expressiveness (in drawings, titles)
2. Storytelling Articulateness (context, environment)
3. Movement or Action
4. Expressiveness of Titles
5. Synthesis of Incomplete Figures (combination of two or more)
6. Synthesis of Lines or Circles (combination of two or more circles or sets of lines)
7. Unusual Visualization
8. Internal Visualization
9. Extending or Breaking Boundaries
10. Humor (in titles, captions, and drawings)
11. Richness of Imagery
12. Colorfulness of Imagery
13. Fantasy (pp. 25, 34, 44).

Finally, Torrance (1962) analyzed a large number of studies and found certain characteristics that typically differentiate highly creative persons from the less creative. He found that creatives are adventurous, courageous, and risk taking, and that they are stubborn, persistent, and industrious. As a result of their individualistic and introversive nature, they are nonconforming (sometimes even radical), they often prefer solitude, and consequently they are often unpopular with their peers; nonetheless they are emotionally sensitive and temperamental, as well as aware of others, affectionate, and altruistic. Creative persons usually possess high energy levels and tend to be independent in their thinking and judgment. They are self-initiating and self-assertive, intuitive, and curious.

ASSESSING CREATIVE THINKING

For many years researchers have talked about the assessment of the creative potential. Johnson O'Connor, J. P. Guilford, J. C. Flanagan, M. T. Mednick and S. A. Mednick, and C. W. Taylor and R. L. Ellison have developed a variety of tests assessing various aspects of creativity; however, the most widely accepted series of tests for this purpose seems now to be the *Torrance Tests of Creative Thinking* (TTCT), introduced in research edition in 1966. Available in two forms figural and verbal batteries, the TTCT has been used with all ages, from preschool through adult levels. Over 1,000 studies have been conducted using the various forms of these tests, establishing their reliability and their content validity. Recent attempts to confirm the predictive validity of the *Torrance Tests* have shown further that these tests, administered in high school (if not in earlier years), tend to predict creative performance in the later adult years (Torrance, 1976). Other products of Torrance's research in the area of creativity assessment include *Thinking Creatively in Action and Movement,* designed for children three to eight years old, using kinesthetic and behavioral responses as criterion variables: *Thinking Creatively in Sound and Words,* which uses two subtests, *Sounds and Images* and *Onomatopoeia and Images,* to evaluate children from grades 3 to 12 and adults of all ages; and the *Human Information Processing Survey,* a self-report instrument with forms for all ages which analyzes learning and thinking styles in terms of cerebral hemispheric laterality.

Other approaches to the assessment of creativity have utilized checklists and other more subjective measures for identifying the creative person or evaluating the creativity of a variety of products. Besemer and Treffinger (1981) cautioned against the assumption that creative persons and creative products can be evaluated using the same set of criteria and cited Rhodes' analysis that "products are the tangible result of the creative process." Torrance (1984) suggested a third mode of assessing creativity: the examination of the modality strengths, preferred learning styles, and other influential information about the individual (e.g., age, cultural background, socioeconomic status, etc.). For example, the creativity of younger children can be most effectively evaluated through kinesthetic and figural activities (particularly in the case of disadvantaged young children), whereas older children and adults tend to prefer verbal tests. Other factors such as handicapping conditions (visual or auditory problems, learning disabilities, and the like) also affect the individual's preference for (or ability to perform on) tests of all types, and an individual's cerebral hemispheric preference tends to dictate to some degree the kinds of tests on which the most effective measurement can be achieved.

Use of Creativity Tests

Having established that creative potential can be measured, let us now look at ways (and for whom) creativity tests should be used. Torrance (1976) has asked whether we should identify only those who will retain their creativity in spite of the academic and societal efforts to thwart it, or if we should be concerned as well with the individual who has potential that can be realized with the proper environment, guidance, and training. Encouraging the latter approach, Torrance reminded us that those whose creativity is repressed often turn to delinquency, mental illness, or mediocrity. If we agree, then we must find methods of assessing this potential in order that we might encourage its development.

Using Other Types of Evaluation

Viewing the question of creativity from another perspective, Parke and Byrnes (1984) suggested the following guidelines for assessing creativity:

1. Determine the factors associated with creativity that you wish to address.
2. Employ multiple measures to assess the creativity factors chosen.
3. Include performance measures in the assessment package.
4. Provide opportunity for students to display potential as well as performance
5. Consider your assessment schema to determine the types of creative talent it will identify and that which it will not identify.
6. Remember that assessment must be ongoing (p. 217).

The final method of creativity assessment that we shall consider here is the evaluation of the creative product. Jackson and Messick (1965) offered the following criteria for use in recognizing creative products:

1. Uniqueness (difference as determined by both qualitative and quantitative comparisons of the product with others of its type)
2. Appropriateness (how well the product fits the context of the problem, as well as the way in which the parts of the product itself fit together)
3. Transformation (the degree to which the product innovates rather than merely improves on existing forms)
4. Condensation (the worth of the product for pondering or savoring by the viewer)

Discussing the application of their work, these authors stress that the use of any one criterion without a balance involving the other three may result in an invalid evaluation of a product as creative.

Synthesizing over 125 criteria derived from the literature, Besemer and Treffinger (1981, p. 164) proposed the following model for the evaluation of a creative product:

Dimension 1: Novelty (newness of the product in terms of processes, materials, and concepts both in and out of the field, as well as its potential effect on future products)
Criteria: a. Germinal (is likely to suggest additional products)
b. Original (is unusual)
c. Transformational (forces viewers to perceive reality in a different way).
Dimension 2: Resolution (degree to which the product meets the needs of the problem)
Criteria: a. Adequate (answers enough of the situational needs)
b. Appropriate (fits the problem situation)
c. Logical (follows the accepted rules for the discipline)
d. Useful (has clear, practical applications)
e. Valuable (fills a need).
Dimension 3: Elaboration and Synthesis (degree to which the product combines unlike elements into a coherent whole)
Criteria: a. Attractive (commands the attention of the user)
b. Complex (contains elements at one or more levels)
c. Elegant (is expressed in a refined, understated way)
d. Expressive (is easily understandable)
e. Organic (communicates a sense of wholeness)
f. Well-crafted (is developed to its highest possible level for that point in time).

Whatever type of paradigm or instrument we select to evaluate creative potential or performance, the system is not significant in itself. If we do not follow through by doing something with our evaluation results, our efforts will be in vain. Toward this end, Torrance (1976) has suggested the following uses of creativity assessment:

1. For obtaining a more complex understanding of the human mind and personality and their functioning;
2. As a possible basis for individualizing instruction;
3. As a part of the process of guiding mental growth, as an indicator of mental health status, and as a source of clues for remedial or psychotherapeutic programs;
4. As a means of assessing the differential effects of various kinds of experimental programs, new curricular arrangements or materials, organizational arrangements, teaching procedures, and the like; and
5. As indicators of growth potential and future guidance needs (p. 137).

By using creative methods of assessment and evaluation in the classroom, in an effort to reach appropriate goals, the teacher of the gifted will enjoy a wide range of options for enhancing the creative production of her students.

REFERENCES

Barron, F. (1957). Originality in relation to personality and intellect. *Journal of Personality, 25*, 730–742.

Besemer, S. P., & Treffinger, D. J. (1981). Analysis of creative products: Review and synthesis. *Journal of Creative Behavior, 15*, 158–178.

Dewey, J. (1933). *How we think.* Boston: D. C. Heath.

Garfield, S. J., Cohen, H. A., & Roth, R. M. (1969). Creativity and mental health. *Journal of Educational Research, 63*, 147–149.

Getzels, J. W., & Jackson, P. W. (1962). *Creativity and intelligence.* New York: John Wiley & Sons.

Ghiselin, B. (1952). *The creative process: A symposium.* New York: New American Library.

Jackson, P. W., & Messick, S. (1965). The person, the product and the response: Conceptual problems in the assessment of creativity. *Journal of Personality, 33*, 309–329.

Koestler, A. (1964). *The act of creation.* New York: Macmillan.

Krippner, S., Dreistadt, R., & Hubbard, C. C. (1972). The creative person and non-ordinary reality. *Gifted Child Quarterly, 16*, 203–228, 234.

Kubie, L. S. (1958). *Neurotic distortion of the creative process.* Lawrence: University of Kansas Press.

MacKinnon, D. W. (1978). *In search of human effectiveness: Identifying and developing creativity.* Buffalo, NY: Creative Education Foundation.

Maslow, A. H. (1959). Creativity in self-actualizing people. In H. Anderson (Ed.), *Creativity and its cultivation* (pp. 83–95). New York: Harper & Row.

May, R. (1975). *The courage to create.* New York: W. W. Norton & Co.

Osborn, A. F. (1963). *Applied imagination.* New York: Charles Scribner's Sons.

Parke, B. N., & Byrnes, P. (1984). Toward objectifying the measurement of creativity. *Roeper Review, 6*, 216–218.

Parnes, S. J. (1971). Creativity: Developing human potential. *Journal of Creative Behavior, 5*, 19–36.

Prince, G. M. (1968). The operational mechanism of synectics. *Journal of Creative Behavior, 2*, 1–12.

Rogers, C. R. (1959). Toward a theory of creativity. In H. H. Anderson (Ed.), *Creativity and its cultivation* (pp. 69–82). New York: Harper & Row.

Torrance, E. P. (1962). *Guiding creative talent.* Englewood Cliffs, NJ: Prentice-Hall.

Torrance, E. P. (1966). *Torrance tests of creative thinking*. Bensenville, IL: Scholastic Testing Service.

Torrance, E. P. (1974). Norms-technical manual for *Torrance Tests of Creative Thinking*. Lexington, MA: Personnel Press.

Torrance, E. P. (1976). Creativity testing in education. *The Creative Child and Adult Quarterly, 1*(3), 136–148.

Torrance, E. P. (1980). Growing up creatively gifted: A 22-year longitudinal study. *The Creative Child and Adult Quarterly, 5*(3), 148–159.

Torrance, E. P. (1981). Thinking creatively in action and movement. Bensenville, IL: Scholastic Testing Service.

Torrance, E. P. (1981). Testing the creativity of preschool children. In *The faces and forms of creativity*. Ventura, CA: Ventura County Superintendent of Schools Office, 65–80.

Torrance, E. P. (1984). Some products of twenty-five years of creativity research. *Educational Perspectives, 22*(3), 3–8.

Torrance, E. P., & Ball, O. E. (1984). *Torrance Tests of Creative Thinking: Streamlined (revised) manual*. Bensenville, IL: Scholastic Testing Service.

Torrance, E. P., & Safter, H. T. (1986). *Getting students beyond aha*. Buffalo, NY: Bearly Limited.

Wallas, G. (1926). Stages in the creative process. In A. Rothenberg & C. R. Hausman (Eds.), *The creativity question* (pp. 69–73). Durham, NC: Duke University Press.

9

Creative Problem Solving

The message from the moon . . . is that no
problem need any longer be considered
insoluble.
                              Norman Cousins

If a visitor from another planet were to survey teachers of the gifted today, he would probably find that creative problem solving ranks high among the skills that they would recommend for their students. Unfortunately, in spite of the vast amount of literature that has been published on this topic, many teachers do not really understand how to facilitate the problem-solving process.

In his classic work *Applied Imagination*, Alex Osborn listed the following steps of creative problem solving:

1. Fact-Finding
   a. Problem-definition
   b. Preparation
2. Idea-Finding
   a. Idea-production
   b. Idea-development
3. Solution-Finding
   a. Evaluation
   b. Adoption (1963, p. 111)

Since Osborn introduced the concept of creative problem solving (initially intended for use in business and industry rather than education), numerous others have advanced modifications of his initial model. Today probably the most widely accepted model of creative problem solving is the one commonly known as the *Osborn-Parnes* approach, developed by Sidney Parnes (Parnes, Noller, and Biondi, 1976) on the basis of the original Osborn model. The steps in this model are:

1. Fact Finding
2. Problem Finding
3. Idea Finding
4. Solution Finding
5. Acceptance Finding

The Leadership Training Model incorporates elements advanced by Dewey, Torrance, Wallas, and Osborn and Parnes. The steps of this process, which will be discussed in detail in a later section, are:

1. Problem Perception and Definition
2. Incubation
3. Creative Thinking
4. Analysis
5. Evaluation
6. Implementation

BRAINSTORMING

Before we begin a detailed discussion of the creative problem solving process, it is essential that we address the topic of brainstorming—a skill that must be mastered before creative problem solving can be effectively accomplished. Originated by Alex Osborn in the 1930s, brainstorming is simply a technique for producing ideas that lead to the solution of problems. Osborn (1963, p. 156) proposed the following rules for brainstorming sessions:

1. *Criticism is ruled out.* More often stated as "deferring judgment," this rule applies to positive as well as negative criticism. Even the use of positive reinforcement in the brainstorming process can discourage others from exercising their own creative potentials. ("That is a wonderful answer, Chris!" may cause Martha to think, "Well, if that is the kind of answer she wants, that is what I'll give her!" or "I can't possibly be that creative, so I'll just be quiet!") This is not to say that encouragement and evaluation are unnecessary, but rather that this part of the problem-solving process must be deferred to a later stage in order to foster creative thinking.

2. *"Free-wheeling" is welcomed.* Wild, unconventional ideas are strongly encouraged; the more unusual ideas are offered, the better are the chances of obtaining really creative alternative solutions. The moderator should be aware that some types of questions evoke normally unacceptable responses from students, particularly those of preadolescent age groups. If the teacher is

unable to gloss over such responses, a few basic rules such as "anything goes except sex and four-letter words" might control this problem before it occurs. (However, since this type of comment tends to restrict the creativity of the brainstormers, the teacher is encouraged to ignore the few such responses that occur.) "Free-wheeled" ideas are simply the result of flexible thinking.

3. *Quantity is wanted.* The more ideas produced, the better are the chances of finding creative and useful ideas. Quantity, of course, is simply the creative element of fluency.

4. *Combination and improvement are sought.* Osborn suggests "hitch-hiking" (sometimes called "piggybacking") on the ideas of others. As one member of the group throws out an idea, related ideas are spurred in the minds of other members. The group must be encouraged to share these ideas, as they often become the most productive results of the brainstorming process.

Brainstorming is the skill that produces ideas in every stage of the creative problem-solving process. The teacher should provide ample time for students to become proficient in this skill before moving on into the problem-solving stages. Suggestions are provided at the end of this chapter for practice in brainstorming.

CREATIVE PROBLEM SOLVING: THE PROCESS

Problem Perception and Definition

It should be obvious to the reader that it is not possible to solve a problem that has not been perceived. Once a general problem area (e.g., the warming of the earth from the greenhouse effect or an individual's problem with time management) has been identified, the facts of the situation must be explored before any further work can be done. In the classroom, a problem that does not relate directly to the students cannot be solved without background information. Thus, it may be useful to begin by discussing the facts that the students already know about the general problem and then send them out to search for further information. When they reconvene, they can compare notes and learn the background that they need in order to solve the problem.

Once all necessary information has been gathered and shared (preferably written on large tear sheets and posted in the front of the room for all to see), the group should brainstorm consequences that could arise from these facts. At this stage it should be emphasized that consequences are not always negative. For example, consider a practice question, "What would happen if the earth cooled?" One consequence would be that we could no longer complain about being hot, or that people would be less likely to become sunburned. After listing all consequences that might result from the general situation, problems and subproblems should be identified for consideration. When all resulting problems have been listed, the group should review the list to determine the problems that are likely to be the most severe and in greatest need of solution. Here the teacher/moderator must emphasize the importance of specificity in the identification of the problem to be solved. In the example above, a specific problem might address the availability of food for human consumption. Rewording the subject into the form of a question that can then be answered through brainstorming, the group might then state the problem as, "How might we produce enough food for human consumption if the earth cools?" Many writers have pointed out that problem finding is more difficult—and more crucial—than problem solving. Or, as Dewey is said to have observed, "A problem well stated is half solved." With the completion of this stage, the group is ready to move on to the second step of the process.

Incubation

In the previous chapter we examined in depth the role that incubation plays in the creative process. Osborn (1963) recommended that all members of a brainstorming group be provided with a succinct statement of the problem to be addressed at least one day before the brainstorming session is to take place. Since the creative problem-solving process as defined by the Leadership Training Model begins with the identification of the problem, incubation is included as the second step.

Incubation is accomplished simply by getting away from the problem for a period of time. Having identified a specific problem and stated it in a manner conducive to creative attack, the subject is ostensibly dropped until a predetermined future time at which it will be consciously reconsidered. During the incubation period, members of the problem-solving group should resist the temptation to address the problem consciously, devoting their attention to other topics as their "preconscious" mind continues to work on a solution. After at least one day of rest from the identified problem, the group will be ready for the next stage, creative thinking.

Creative Thinking

The third step in the creative problem solving process is the point at which the brainstorming process is applied in its truest sense. At this stage, taking the problem identified in step one, the group brainstorms alternative solutions to the problem. Crucial to the success of this stage is careful adherence to the four rules set out in the preceding section. After providing periods of practice in the brainstorming process, the teacher should reiterate the rules and orient the group to the procedures to be followed. The importance of the physical arrangement of groups has been firmly established through research. If possible, members should be placed in a circle to permit the greatest possible degree of interaction. (If the group is fairly large, it is best to divide into groups of four to six members, to achieve the most efficient idea production.) In order to avoid overlooking good ideas of individual group members, the following procedures are recommended:

1. In order to strengthen the concept of a group effort, a recorder should be appointed for each group. Participants should be instructed to continue calling out ideas until they are recognized and written by the recorder. Other members can then "hitchhike" on the ideas recorded, producing a larger number of possible solutions.

2. The time for the brainstorming process is not agreed upon by all researchers. Parnes (1971) recommends that thirty to forty-five minutes be spent in brainstorming, to allow for delving deeply into the more creative ideas that may not come out in the opening minutes. Others suggest alternating between three-minute brainstorming sessions and five-minute incubation periods. Whatever time period is decided upon, it is wise to stop periodically to examine (and perhaps compare) the ideas of the various groups. Asking the groups to share at each break their two or three wildest/most creative ideas—as well as the number of ideas produced—is an effective method of allowing incubation to take place while motivating creative production through competition. One final word: Although certainly it is unwise to cut off the brainstorming process when worthwhile production is taking place, Parnes recommends that the moderator estimate in advance the amount of time that will be needed. If it appears that lengthy periods will be needed for effective idea production, he suggests that the problem be broken up into smaller, more specific problems that can be handled in a maximum of forty-five minutes.

Analysis

When creative thinking has produced a number of alternative solutions to the identified problem, the contributions of the group must be analyzed and evaluated in order to arrive at the best solution. In this stage, each group recorder reviews the ideas that were produced through brainstorming. At the reading of each idea, the group simply voices (by saying yes or no) its opinion as to whether it might have merit as a solution (or a part of a solution). By this method of elimination, the

group narrows to approximately ten alternatives for serious consideration. At this point the evaluation stage begins.

Evaluation

The evaluation of the alternative solutions is accomplished through the
following steps:

1. Keeping in mind the nature of the problem that is to be solved,
   develop a list of four to six criteria that are appropriate for judging
   the proposed solutions. These criteria might include such factors
   as cost, space needed, availability of the necessary technology,
   ethical considerations, time required for implementation, and so
   on. In the example of the cooling of the earth, cited earlier, all of
   these criteria would be appropriate. In other cases (such as
   problems involving personal relationships), these criteria may be
   irrelevant, and other criteria appropriate to the specific problem
   should be selected.

2. Prepare a matrix, listing the ten or so alternative solutions that
   were isolated in the Analysis stage down the left side. Across the
   top of the matrix, list the criteria on which these alternatives will
   be evaluated.

3. Considering one criterion at a time, evaluate each of the alternative solutions. Again let us use the example of the cooling of the
   earth: "How might we produce food for human consumption if the
   earth cools?" Suppose the criteria were cost, technology, space,
   time, and ethics (as specified above). Taking the first criterion,
   cost, you would go down the column, rating each alternative
   solution as to cost. If you have ten possible solutions, the best one
   would receive a score of 10, and the least acceptable one would
   receive a 1. Therefore you would give a 10 to the least expensive
   (i.e., the best as to cost) and a 1 to the most expensive (the worst as
   to cost). After scoring each alternative with regard to cost, proceed
   to technology, giving a 10 to the one for which we have the most
   accessible technology, a 1 to perhaps the one for which the
   technology is furthest in the future. Continue in this fashion until
   all alternatives have been rated with regard to all criteria, then
   add the scores across each line to arrive at the total rating for each
   solution. A quick glance at the last column will reveal the best
   solution (i.e., the one with the highest score) for the identified
   problem. There are, of course, times when this method does not
   yield a completely clear "best" solution; for example, when a tie
   (or near tie) ensues. In such a case, the next step is to attempt to
   combine those alternatives that received the highest ratings. If this

plan does not accomplish the development of a clearly superior solution, the decision may be made to use two or more solutions, working on planning details for one at a time. With this final step, proceed to the last stage, implementation.

Implementation

In his description of the Enrichment Triad Model, Renzulli (1977) commented about the futility of a basketball team practicing regularly but never playing a game. Similarly, practice in any skill without applying it to reality is essentially a waste of time; so it is with the creative problem solving process. All too often the process is taught in the classroom using practice problems—a worthy cause in the learning process, but a time consumer if there is no extension to real life. The creative problem solving process is much too valuable a tool to be practiced and then placed on the shelf with the classroom games. If not applied to real-life situations, creative problem solving will become just another activity. In order to avoid this waste, LTM proposes that a plan of action be developed and implemented. In this stage, several steps must be followed:

1. **Trouble-Shooting.** Before developing the plan of action, the group should brainstorm to determine potential problems and ways in which implementation could be facilitated. Trouble-shooting will enable participants to work on responses, change-agentry tactics, or different approaches that might make the solution more palatable to opposing parties. Also in this stage the group should consider people who might be involved or who might aid in the implementation of the solution, locations where the solution might be tried, and the like.

2. Sequencing the Action. Next the group should brainstorm those procedures that must be followed in order to implement the solution (i.e., "What are our short-term goals that will lead to the one long-term goal—the solution of the problem?" "What things do we need to do in order to make the solution work?"). Finally, those steps that are decided upon must be sequenced in the proper order, thereby facilitating the action.

3. Setting a Schedule. The final step in Implementation is setting a schedule—adding to the sequenced steps a set of specific dates and times on which the various aspects of the action will be accomplished. With the actual implementation of each step, accompanied by interim (formative) evaluation, the creative problem solving process is complete.

PRACTICE IN CREATIVE PROBLEM SOLVING

The following suggestions are made for training students in the brainstorming process:

1. Beginning with the principle of deferred judgment, suggest a topic with which all are familiar (e.g., unusual uses for a load of clam shells), and practice calling out all ideas that come to mind. Emphasize that the deferral of judgment applies not only to the ideas of others, but to one's own ideas as well. In other words, one should not hesitate to mention an idea just because it is unconventional or may not be an acceptable solution in the long run.

2. When students have become accustomed to deferring judgment, take each of the other rules of brainstorming and conduct simple brainstorming exercises with emphasis on one rule at a time, until all members of the group are deferring judgment, free-wheeling, contributing fluently, and hitchhiking on the ideas of the others. An enjoyable (and productive) final practice problem is to brainstorm names of birds. After five minutes, have each group count their ideas and share their most creative (or wildest) ones. Hearing contributions such as whirlybird and "Red, Red Robin," others will advance beyond their pterodactyls and dodo birds to more divergent ideas such as Admiral Byrd and Meadowlark Lemon, and the creative process will have been advanced.

After the group has become proficient in brainstorming, similar practice can be conducted with each active step of the creative problem-solving process. For example, students can practice identifying consequences with questions such as "What would happen if it snowed in July?" Later the teacher can propose simple problems for "creative thinking" practice, and the process can be carried through gradually to the analysis and evaluation stages. Finally, a simulated problem and solution can be carried through to the implementation stage.

SYNECTICS

Synectics, another type of creative problem solving that has become popular over the last twenty-five years, was originated by W. J. J. Gordon. In synectics, a form of analogy, normally unrelated concepts are forced together to develop novel ideas or approaches. Gordon (1961) identified four types of analogy that are of use in problem solving.

Direct Analogy

The direct analogy objectively compares two concepts that are not actually alike. Similes are simple examples of direct analogy: Carol is as fast as a jackrabbit. A well-known example of the use of direct analogy in problem solving is Alexander Graham Bell's conception of the telephone through comparison with the human ear. Another such story told of Elias Howe's early failures to develop a lock stitch sewing machine, in which he made his needles with the eye in the middle of the shank. Obsessed with his goal, his mind labored day and night to solve the problem. One night he dreamed that he had been captured by a tribe of savages and taken before their king, who commanded him on threat of death to complete his machine at once. Try though he might, the terror-stricken prisoner could not find the missing link that he had sought for so long. In his dream the painted warriors surrounded him and led him away for execution. Suddenly he noticed eye-shaped holes near the ends of his guards' spears, and he realized that he had found the answer: a needle with the eye near the point! When he awoke from his dream, he leaped out of bed and immediately whittled a model of his new needle, with which his experiments came to a successful end (cited in Krippner, Dreistadt, and Hubbard, p. 459).

Personal Analogy

Personal analogy is simply personal identification with a problem—imagining that one is actually a part of the problem—to bring about insights into the nature of the problem itself. Gordon (1961) cited an example of a synectics group attempting to solve a mechanical problem. With each member assigned to role play a part of the mechanism, the group was able to identify more closely with the problem, ultimately arriving at a solution. Students might practice personal analogy by pretending to be blood cells (to understand the circulatory system) or Thomas Jefferson (to understand the concepts put forth in the Declaration of Independence).

Symbolic Analogy

Still more objective than the direct analogy, the symbolic analogy uses symbolism to describe relationships. Once again we may use figures of speech, such as the metaphor, "She is the salt of the earth." In this case, salt is used to symbolize stability, thus the symbolic analogy. As an example, Gordon (1961) cited a group who developed a hydraulic jack through its symbolic comparison to the Indian Rope Trick.

Fantasy Analogy

The fantasy analogy, helpful when conclusions cannot be reached through the more realistic types of analogy, uses a mythical or imaginary approach to problem solving. A common fantasy analogy is the expression "opening Pandora's Box." To describe someone's inconsistent behavior, a person might use the fantasy analogy, "He is a real Jekyll and Hyde!" Referring to Sigmund Freud's theory that creative work must be the fulfillment of a wish, Gordon (1961) suggested the use of fantasy analogy in solving problems. The question is simply posed, "How would we in our wildest fantasies like for this to be done?" After coming up with the wildest ideas possible, analogies are drawn to these fantasies, and a solution is reached.

PRACTICE IN SYNECTICS

Forced Association Techniques

Because the key to the successful use of synectics is to "make the strange familiar" through the forcing together of previously unrelated elements, word associations provide excellent introductory activities for students preparing to learn this method of problem solving. At first most people will give the expected responses: cup–saucer; boy–girl; sleet–snow. As practice is gained, however, the creativity of the responses will improve.

Once these activities have provided practice in the basics of forced association, the teacher can use the following activities to provide practice in the application of the forced-association technique to problem solving.

A Word-Association Problem

Having identified and stated a problem for creative attack, ask a person who is not familiar with the problem to select a word or phrase for you to work with. Use the word or phrase as a stimulus for visualization/imagery. Describe your imagery fantasy aloud, and let others hitchhike to produce ideas related to the problem. For example: An elementary school class identified their group problem as "How might we make our school grounds more attractive?" Given the term *telephone directory* by an outside teacher, they immediately came up with two ideas: (1) Go through the yellow pages to identify people who might help us; and (2) go through the yellow pages looking for pictures that might give us ideas. Hitchhiking on these ideas, the students came up with a list of parents with expertise in a variety of areas related to their problem, and then they launched a search for magazines and other printed materials from which they might come up with ideas for a new school ground plan.

The Electronics Problem

Tell the students that industry has used synectics for many years. Gather from newspapers or magazines examples of foods, pieces of furniture, or household products that combine two or more previously unrelated items (e.g., toothpaste that combines mouthwash with breath fresheners, soap containing hand lotion, peanut butter and jelly mixed in one jar, mixed flavors of ice cream, recliner chairs, bookcase beds, etc.). Make transparencies of these items, and show them to the students as examples of what synectics can do. Next show a transparency containing a matrix with the words *radio, television, stereo, computer, stove, refrigerator, freezer,* and *barbecue grill* written across the top and down the left side. At each intersection of two items, have the students cite current examples that combine two pieces into one and that were not available in the early days of this country (e.g., computerized microwave ovens, refrigerator/freezers, radio/stereo/television consoles, etc.). When they have completed this exercise, divide the class into groups of four to six students. Switching creatively into a new role, tell the students that you are an electronics manufacturer and they are your synectics groups who are responsible for originating new product ideas. Your business has been weak in the last two years, and you must have some new ideas that will build your business. Otherwise, it will be necessary for you to let all but one of the groups go. Instruct each group to create a matrix, listing ten electronic items across the top and down the left side. (Encourage them to use some of the above combinations along with the basic pieces and to use the forced relationships technique to submit ideas for new products which do not exist today.) Only the group producing the greatest number of creative ideas for new, attractive products will retain their jobs. (Of course, if enough creative ideas are produced to rebuild your business, perhaps *all* will be able to stay!)

Practice with Analogies

When this type of "free-wheeling" has become natural, a useful second step would be to practice the formation of analogies by using the techniques of simile and metaphor. As with the word-association exercises, the teacher provides the stimulus, and the students respond. For example, the teacher might say, "as thin as . . ." and the students will respond "a stick" or "a rail" (becoming more imaginative with practice). Although metaphor may be a bit more difficult for the students to understand and work with, it will take them to a somewhat more sophisticated level and help them get into the pattern of creating analogies. After grasping the concept of analogical thinking, the students might enjoy the following activity.

The Armadillo Problem

Tell the students that you are the proprietor of a large exterminating company. A potential client has challenged you to rid his large estate of armadillos which are digging holes under his mansion; if you succeed, you will land a healthy contract for his many properties. The problem is that the client is an avid member of the Society for the Prevention of Cruelty to Animals and does not want to hear any noise from under his house as the creatures are trapped and killed. Tell the class that they are your synectics groups and ask them to use analogies to develop a new and superior trap that will humanely capture and instantaneously kill the invaders. If you have enough students in the class to make four groups of four to six students each, assign a different type of analogy to each group. The following examples suggest ways in which two types of analogy might be used in the solution of this problem:

- Personal Analogy: Have members of the group pretend to be armadillos burrowing under the client's house. Ask them to imagine ways in which they might be caught.
- Direct Analogy: Tell the group to think of living things that trap their prey silently (e.g., praying mantis, Venus flytrap), to consider the ways in which they work, and to design a trap using the same principles.

REFERENCES

Gordon, W. J. J. (1961). *Synectics: The development of creative capacity.* New York: Harper & Brothers.

Khatena, J. (1982). *The educational psychology of the gifted.* New York: Wiley.

Krippner, S., Dreistadt, R., & Hubbard, C. C. (1972). The creative person and non-ordinary reality. *Gifted Child Quarterly, 16,* 459.

Osborn, A. F. (1963). *Applied imagination.* New York: Charles Scribner's Sons.

Parnes, S. J. (1971). Creativity: Developing human potential. *Journal of Creative Behavior, 5,* 19–36.

Parnes, S., Noller, R., & Biondi, A. (1976). *Guide to creative action*. New York: Scribner's.

Renzulli, J. S. (1977). *The Enrichment Triad Model: A guide for developing defensible programs for the gifted and talented*. Wethersfield, CT: Creative Learning Press.

Springfield, L. H. (1986). Synectics: Teaching creative problem solving by making the familiar strange. *G/C/T, 9*(4), 15–19.

10

Fostering Creativity in the Gifted

*Creativity is so delicate a flower that praise
tends to make it bloom while discouragement
often nips it in the bud.*
Alex Osborn

Possibly one of the most exciting findings of recent research in educational psychology has been the discovery that creativity can be taught and that creative teaching makes a difference. Drawing from his extensive research, Torrance concluded that creativity, unlike intelligence, is not a heritable trait. The implications that he drew from these findings suggested that educators have a better chance of improving creative potential than intellectual potential. For many years Torrance and other researchers had theorized that a slump in creativity occurred on a regular basis around the fourth-grade level. In 1968, this phenomenon was documented through longitudinal studies which further revealed that the "fourth-grade slump" could actually be offset through the effective use of technology and materials designed to foster creative potential and motivation (Torrance, 1968, 1976, 1984).

What can the teacher do to maintain or increase the creative potentials of his or her gifted students? Current literature seems to divide the methods for fostering creativity into two categories: providing a creative learning environment and utilizing strategies or activities that tend to encourage creative growth and performance.

THE CREATIVE ENVIRONMENT

Much has been written about the milieu in which education takes place. Although many classroom teachers turn their classrooms into creative environments in which their students may work, others continue to wield the club of authority, stifling whatever creative potential remains. Yet there are many changes that teachers can make—even in the regular classroom—that will help their young charges, from the slowest learners to the most gifted, to exercise their creativity. The following set of guidelines, gleaned from a myriad of writings by creative people, should be of help to the teacher who genuinely wants to teach creatively and to help students be creative.

The Teacher's Attitude

Perhaps the most crucial aspect of the creative environment, regardless of the physical facilities or instructional materials available in the classroom, is the attitude of the teacher. The creative, supportive teacher can do more to foster creativity in students than all the creativity workbooks and games combined. Some specific considerations are:

1. Encourage creative thinking by
   a. accepting and rewarding creative ideas and new ways of doing things
   b. demonstrating that you recognize creative potential
   c. showing students that their ideas have value
   d. welcoming questions and curiosity from students
   e. reminding students to be creative and original
   f. deferring judgment on the creative attempts of students.

2. Provide an open, stimulating, and supportive atmosphere in which children feel free to contribute.
3. Show interest in the areas in which the students are interested.
4. Build a sense of "natural authority"—a state in which mutual respect exists and the teacher and students can share and learn together.
5. Utilize constructive criticism, not just criticism.
6. Model flexibility rather than rigidity and conformity.
7. Help students to develop healthy attitudes about failure—to realize that every failure is a lesson in itself, and that the masters of creativity have failed many times to accomplish their initial goals.
8. Avoid promoting conformity.
9. Learn to laugh at yourself, to admit "I don't know the answer, but I know where we can go to find out, and we'll learn together."
10. Be a humanistic teacher. (See Section III.)

The Teacher as Instructor

No matter how much we talk about the effective teacher of the gifted as a facilitator rather than a director of learning, we must acknowledge that every teacher must play the role of instructor/organizer of learning experiences at some time in his classroom career. How, then, can one encourage creativity in students within this role?

1. Provide opportunities for both individual and small-group work; consider grouping at different times by ability, by interests, or by learning styles.
2. Differentiate and individualize the curriculum in every way possible. Whenever possible use open-ended questions, assignments, and methods of evaluation.
3. Work to develop fluency, flexibility, originality, and elaboration.
4. Expose students to great works of literature and art, to the creative minds of the past, and to the philosophical and ideological bases of our civilization, and encourage students to produce in these vital areas.
5. Provide opportunities for students to develop and exercise responsibility in the classroom. Emphasize that responsibility is essential to freedom.
6. Use provocative, divergent questioning in class discussions. Utilize the inquiry method whenever possible.
7. Allow time for incubation and for the development and sharing of students' creative ideas, discoveries, and products.
8. Stimulate the imagination by providing opportunities for students to anticipate the future.
9. Teach about the creative process—what fosters it, what blocks it, and the steps it takes. Provide instruction and practice in brainstorming, creative thinking, and problem solving.
10. Provide opportunities for students to make choices and decisions. Utilize teacher-pupil planning strategies whenever possible.
11. Encourage the acquisition of knowledge in a variety of fields.
12. Take into consideration the learning styles and interests of individual students when planning curriculum and methods of instruction.
13. Encourage the internalization of concepts rather than simply "teaching" factual knowledge, encouraging independent study and investigation in content areas of student interest.
14. Provide both active and quiet times, free periods as well as guided activity.

15. Provide many types of stimuli, making students sensitive to their environment.

16. Plan warm-up and follow-up activities to facilitate the transition from convergent to divergent experiences.

The Teacher as Facilitator

If the teacher of the gifted is to be truly humanistic, then it is essential that a major part of his role be that of facilitator rather than director of learning. In addition to those facilitative methods of instruction mentioned above, there are several other tasks that the teacher/facilitator should perform regularly to round out this role:

1. Encourage self-initiated learning by providing opportunities for students to pursue their own areas of interest to whatever depth they wish.

2. Provide advanced level resources in students' areas of interest.

3. Expose students to the best available resources—both library resources and other professionals—within the school and the community.

4. Provide mentors who are creative, active practitioners in fields related to students' areas of interest.

INSTRUCTIONAL STRATEGIES FOR FOSTERING CREATIVITY

Creative Imagination Imagery

In recent years the use of imagery as a method of accessing the creative right hemisphere of the brain has become more popular among psychologists, researchers, and teachers of the gifted. It is unfortunate that the hypnogogic state (i.e., the trance-like state through which every human being passes in the process of falling asleep) has been confused with the concept of hallucinations. The paranoia resulting from the wide-spread tales of acid-damaged brains and hallucinogenic nightmares has caused many to think of "altered states of consciousness" as dangerous and even sinful, and to associate any type of other-than-conscious activity with the problems of the drug culture.

Gowan (1978–1979) defined an altered state of consciousness as "any state where the left hemisphere is in abeyance" (p. 141). Research has shown that creative thought and production occur most readily when the cognitive left hemisphere is at rest and the creative right hemisphere can be accessed more easily. Thus it is through an "altered state of consciousness" (by Gowan's definition) that the individual can be most creative.

As Arieti (1976) pointed out, imagery is a common mental function. Images can occur spontaneously, but they occur much more readily if the left hemisphere is at rest. Arieti defined imagery simply as "the process of producing and experiencing images" (p. 37). Although images can be stimulated by desire or need (such as the image of food being stimulated by hunger), he theorized that it might conversely be the image that creates the need (a hope that is fervently espoused by advertising directors!).

In the first chapter of this section, the importance of incubation was documented with evidence that periods of inactivity stimulate one's ability to "image-ine," often giving birth to creative production. Abell (1955) cited a conversation with Johannes Brahms in which the great composer revealed his own creative processes:

> When I feel the urge I begin by appealing directly to my Maker and I first ask Him the three most important questions pertaining to our life here in this world—whence, wherefore, whither? . . . I immediately feel vibrations that thrill my whole being. . . . These are the Spirit illuminating the soul-power within, . . . then I feel capable of drawing inspiration from above, as Beethoven did. . . . Measure by measure, the finished product is revealed to me when I am in those rare, inspired moods.

Continuing, Brahms noted that to receive such inspiration it was necessary to be in a "semi-trance" condition, which he defined as "a condition when the conscious mind is in temporary abeyance and the subconscious is in control," explaining that "it is through the subconscious mind, which is a part of Omnipotence, that the inspiration comes" (p. 6). It is interesting to note that Brahms believed that no more than 2 percent of his contemporaries were divinely inspired.

Again Abell reported on a conversation with Humperdinck in which the composer related from his own diary the comments of Wagner about inspiration:

> I have very definite impressions while in [a] trance-like condition, which is the prerequisite of all true creative effort. I feel that I am one with this vibrating Force, that it is omniscient, and that I can draw upon it to an extent that is limited only by my own capacity to do so (p. 138).

According to Abell, Wagner believed that all men are born with the same ability for divine inspiration, but that circumstances such as heredity, environment, opportunity, and early education can hinder the realization of one's inborn potential. Here, as in the previously cited experiences of Kekule, Mendeleev, and others, we see the relationship between image formation and creativity.

Uses of Imagery. How can the individual use imagery to improve ability, understanding, or quality of life? Practitioners contend that imagery may be used:

1. To develop insight;
2. To gain better control over the autonomic nervous system;
3. To influence future events;
4. To stimulate scientific inquiry and discovery;
5. To increase one's understanding of his world;
6. To improve the self-image and strengthen motivation for self-improvement;
7. To aid in problem solving; and
8. To improve intellectual and creative functioning by increasing the connections between the right and left hemispheres of the brain (Arieti, 1976; Khatena, 1984; Wenger, 1981a).

Stimulating Imagery. If we accept Arieti's (1976) theory that images are totally subjective and therefore can be appreciated only by the one who "sees" them, then we must find a way to bring about images in others. Unfortunately, some people, particularly those who have been unaccustomed to openness and creativity, have difficulty with imagery and must be led into the experience gradually. The following activities may be used to introduce a group to this valuable technique.

Instruct students to select partners with whom they can talk freely. Partners should sit close together so that they can talk quietly without being disturbed by other conversations in the room. When all dyads are properly arranged and spaced out around the room, tell the group that you are going to lead them in an experience through which they will be able to reach into their right brains and be very creative, that they will be guided through a visual experience in their minds, and that they will describe their images to their partners when you give them the signal to begin. Also tell them that you will stop them after five minutes so that they can switch roles, allowing time for students to describe their images to their partners. Tell those who will be observing for the first round that they should watch their partners' facial expressions and the movements of the eyes, which can be seen through their closed eyelids, and that when some moment of illumination appears to occur in the "imager" the observer should ask his partner to describe what came into his mind at that moment. When all are relaxed, quiet, and breathing deeply, read the following instructions slowly and quietly to the group:

With your eyes closed, begin concentrating on your breathing. Breathe very slowly, in and out, in and out . . . [pause] . . . until you are totally relaxed and feeling really good . . . [pause] . . . . Now think of the most magnificent scene in nature that you have ever experienced—a mountain or ocean view, a sunrise, a beautiful garden, a double rainbow—anything that impressed you so much with its beauty that its memory has remained with you. [Pause.] When I tell you to begin, I want those of you who will be imaging first to begin describing this beautiful scene quietly to your partner, in rich, sensory detail—always keeping your eyes closed. As you describe your scene, include every detail possible in your description—colors, sizes and shapes, patterns and textures—everything that you see. Try to make your description so vivid that your partner can "see" it along with you. While you are describing your scene, your partner will be watching your facial expressions and the movements of your eyes and may ask you from time to time what sensory awareness you have just had. Try to be conscious of these times, answering your partner's inquiries to make you more aware of every sensory impression that comes into your mind's eye. I will . . . . [indicate signal—the ringing of a bell, or some other subtle sound—that will mark the end of the first phase of the activity] . . . when you are to stop. Ready? All right, you may begin.

After about five minutes, sound the designated signal and instruct the group to switch roles with their partners. When everyone is settled again—relaxed, with eyes closed and breathing deeply—give the signal to begin again. At the end of five minutes, stop the activity and encourage students to share their impressions and feelings about the activity.

If time elapses between the completion of the above introductory activity and the next experience with guided imagery, begin the next activity with a brief warm-up period similar to the above experience. When the students are ready to begin the next activity, give the following instructions to the group:

For this next activity, I am going to describe some specific things that you are to do in your mental image. As you go through the steps of this activity, both you and your partner should keep your eyes closed. This time each of you will see your own images in the settings that I lay out for you, and you will describe to each other everything that you see. As you go through this "trip down Imagery Lane," keep your eyes closed, even when your partner is speaking. Trying not to interrupt each other, take turns sharing your images aloud, a few sentences at a time. Try not to allow any time to pass when neither of you is describing something that you see. You will continue describing what you see at each phase of your "walk," until I stop you by . . . [indicate what method—such as a call bell—that you will use to signal the stop of each phase of the activity] . . . . With your eyes still closed, you will listen to the next phase and then continue describing your images to each other until you hear the signal again. As you hear each signal, try to stop immediately, so that we can have complete silence in the room for the beginning of the next step.

Note: Wenger (1981a) emphasizes the importance of cautioning participants against attempting to interpret their partners' images. He further suggests that each individual should attempt to interpret the symbolism of his own imaging experience only after it is fully developed through verbal description.

After the above introduction, have the students close their eyes; remind them to relax and begin breathing deeply, with no talking until the activity begins. When all are quiet, relaxed, and ready, continue with the following instructions:

Today we are going to take a trip to a fascinating foreign land—a place we have never heard of before. Each of us will get there in whatever way he or she wishes—some may go by sea, some may fly on a magic flying carpet. Some may get there just by wishing it, and others may ride a flying horse. Whatever way you wish to get to our destination is fine—because our real journey will begin after we all arrive.

Now, with your eyes closed, and with your body relaxed and breathing deeply, take a minute to imagine your trip to the magic land . . . . [Pause for about one minute then continue] . . . When you arrive, you make your way by Magic Land Transportation to the Island Castle, where we are all meeting at the front gate. A beautiful maiden named Esmerelda is waiting to be our tour guide, and as soon as we have all arrived, Esmerelda speaks: [Attempt to change your voice to a soft, magical, and mysterious quality as you become Esmerelda.]

Good morning [afternoon], Ladies and Gentlemen. Welcome to the magic land of Marvella! Today I am going to guide you on a tour of our beautiful royal city. If you will follow me, we will begin our tour.

[At this point you become yourself again, describing the places that Esmerelda takes the group.]

As Esmerelda leads, you follow as if enchanted. The castle gate opens, and inside you see the most beautiful place you have ever seen. As you walk toward the castle, describe to your partners, in the minutest detail possible, exactly what you see there.

[After two minutes, sound the signal, wait for everyone to become perfectly silent, and continue.]

As you approach the castle, the doors open wide, and a lovely princess comes out to greet you. Describe this princess—her hair, her clothing, and what she says to our group about her beautiful land.

[Wait another two minutes, sound the signal, and continue after all are quiet.]

At this point the beautiful princess motions you into the castle. It is the most magnificent building you have ever entered. She tells you to wander freely through the many elegant rooms and halls. Describe to your partner what you see.

[Allow two minutes, sound the signal, and continue.]

Soon Esmerelda rejoins the group and invites you to follow her into the royal gardens. As you walk through the great huge doors leading to the rear section of the castle grounds, the most magnificent gardens you have ever seen come into view. As you walk through the gardens, along winding paths between trees, flowers, and fountains, describe to your partner in great detail everything that you see.

[Allow another three minutes for this description. Then sound the signal and continue.]

Alas, our time in Marvella has come to an end. In your mind's eye, follow Esmerelda back around to the front of the castle and to the gate through which you first entered. Bid a fond farewell to your lovely young guide, transport yourself home, and, when you are ready, rejoin us here in the classroom, refreshed and revitalized from your tour of the most beautiful land in the world.

At this point, give the students a few minutes to talk with their partners about the experience, then encourage them to share their feelings and images with the group. Tell them that imagery trips such as this can be accomplished alone, speaking into a tape recorder and simply allowing the mind to generate all of the images without outside guidance. Remind them of the relaxed feelings that they can achieve from this experience, and suggest that they try these experiences at home and share them with the class.

The use of imagery in the classroom is limited only by the imagination of the teacher. Using the above exercise as a guide, structure your own trips down "Imagery Lane." Two other adaptations of this type of activity are described here.

Activity 1

Before beginning your guided fantasy, arrange the students in pairs and instruct them to think of problems that they would like to have solved. They may be problems of a personal nature (such as how to improve one's self-confidence), world problems (such as hunger), anticipated future problems (such as the heating of the earth from the greenhouse effect), local problems (such as ways to improve the image of a city), anything of concern to the students. Give them a few minutes to decide (with their partners) on the problems they want to solve through imagery. When they have made these decisions, lead them on a "guided tour" through a magic land or a beautiful garden, or over a snow-covered mountain or a jeweled sea. At some point in the experience, lead them to see a window, a boat, a gate, or some other "break-through" which when opened or entered will show them immediately the answer to the problem they are seeking to solve. Have them share with their partners as in the previous activity, describing in the greatest sensory detail everything that they see. After they have arrived at the solutions to their problems, encourage them to share their new awareness with the group. Discuss ways in which these new ideas could be used in real life toward the solving of the problems addressed in the activity.

Activity 2

Before beginning the guided imagery, instruct the students to think of a person they would like to be. This may be a person they know and admire, or an imaginary person who possesses characteristics or talents that they would like to have or who has done things they would like to be able to do. This time have the students image individually, not talking to a partner. Guide them through a sensory experience such as those described above, at which point they will see and become this person that they admire. While they "are" this person, have them do the things that this person does, to get the feeling of what it is like to be able to do these things. After ample time has elapsed in this person, have them return to themselves and picture themselves doing these same types of things. Return them gradually to the present, and have them debrief with a partner. After this time of sharing with one partner with whom they feel free to share openly, encourage them to tell the group any aspect of the experience which they would like to share.*

Additional Activities for Fostering Creativity

---

1. Share with students the following passage from the Pyramid film *Why Man Creates* (reproduced with permission from Pyramid Film & Video):

---

*Adapted from guided-imagery activities developed by Win Wenger (Psychegenics Press, Gaithersburg, Maryland) and presented at the Creative Problem Solving Institute in Buffalo, New York.

Where Do Ideas Come From?

From looking at one thing and seeing another,
From "fooling around"—
Playing with possibilities,
Speculating, changing,
Pushing, pulling, transforming,
And—if you're lucky—
You come up with something
Maybe worth
Saving, using, and counting on.
That's where the game stops,
And the work begins.

Discuss the meaning of this passage. Follow the discussion with time for the students to "fool around"; encourage sharing of the products of this free time.

2. Have students create interesting, unusual pictures using a variety of stimuli (triangles, squares, abstract symbols or designs, combinations of several figures, etc.).

3. Ask students to think of ways to improve a variety of products (e.g., a wagon, a refrigerator, a student desk, a bicycle).

4. Ask "What would happen if . . . ?" questions. As in brainstorming, the wilder questions will stimulate more creative answers. For example, what would happen if:

   a. people could fly?
   b. the winter became warm and the summer became cold?
   c. birds could talk?

5. Brainstorm unusual uses that could be made of

   a. a load of clam shells
   b. old coat hangers
   c. socks with holes in them
   d. cardboard tubes

6. Ask open-ended questions designed to encourage students to break out of their usual modes of thinking or viewing, such as:

   a. What is half of eight?
   (Some students will immediately answer "four"; others may say "zero," picturing the numeral eight cut in half horizontally.)
   b. How many squares do you see?
   (Show the following figure; some will see 16, some 17, some 30 or more. Thirty squares can be found by careful examination: one composed of 4 squares on a side, four of 3 per side, nine of 2 squares, and sixteen single squares. Some creative observers may see the figure as one end of a tunnel, resulting in an infinite number of squares.)

How many squares?

7. Brainstorm (either individually or in groups) any of a variety of listings, such as:
   a. things that are . . . (red, smaller than a bug, shiny)
   b. happy sounds
   c. foods that are fun
   d. things that ripen with age
   e. sights on the ocean
8. Draw from other chapters in this text for ideas of other creative activities, such as:
   a. Generate similes, metaphors, or other figures of speech.
   b. Use morphological analysis to generate story plots for creative writing.
   c. List the attributes of . . . (a tree, a creative picture, a pair of shoes, a chair, a train).

REFERENCES

Abell, A. M. (1955). *Talks with great composers*. New York: Philosophical Library.

Arieti, S. (1976). *Creativity: The magic synthesis*. New York: Basic Books.

Gallagher, J. J. (1985). *Teaching the gifted child.* (3rd Ed.). Boston: Allyn and Bacon.

Gowan, J. C. (1978-1979). Altered states of consciousness: A taxonomy. *Journal of Altered States of Consciousness, 4,* 141–156.

Gowan, J. C. (1979). The role of imagination in the development of the creative individual. In J. C. Gowan, J. Khatena, & E. P. Torrance (Eds.), *Educating the ablest: A book of readings* (pp. 413–428). Itasca, IL: F. E. Peacock.

Holt, J. (1964). *How children fail.* New York: Pitman Publishing.

Khatena, J. (1984). Imagery as function of the individual, environment, and cosmos. In Crabbe, A. B., et al. (Eds.), *New directions in creativity research* (pp. 85–97). Ventura, CA: Ventura County Superintendent of Schools Office.

Torrance, E. P. (1968). A longitudinal examination of the fourth grade slump in creativity. *Gifted Child Quarterly, 12,* 195–199.

Torrance, E. P. (1976). Creativity testing in education. *The Creative Child and Adult Quarterly, 1*(3), 136–148.

Torrance, E. P. (1984) Some products of twenty five years of creativity research. *Educational Perspectives, 22*(3), 3–8.

Wenger, W. (1981a). *An easy way to increase your intelligence.* Gaithersburg, MD: Psychegenics Press.

Wenger, W. (1981b). Creative creativity: Some strategies for developing specific areas of the brain and for working both sides together. *Journal of Creative Behavior, 15,* 77–89.

Section V

A STRATEGIES APPROACH TO CONTENT AREA TEACHING

*What we want is to see the child in pursuit of
knowledge, and not knowledge in pursuit of
the child.*

George Bernard Shaw

In Sections II and III of this book, we considered those strategies that may be grouped into cognitive and affective emphasis; and in Section IV we examined current research about the human brain—notably the theory that different intellectual functions are controlled by the right and left hemispheres of the cerebral cortex. On the other hand, one of the major theses of this book is that, no matter which dichotomy we talk about, perhaps the most important concept in the leadership approach to gifted education is the development of integrated leadership for the future.

The preceding sections have presented a variety of strategies that are widely accepted as appropriate (if not essential) for use with gifted students in our attempts to prepare them for future leadership roles. There are many ways in which gifted students are being served. In the enrichment program, as well as in programs whose primary goal is to accelerate the core curriculum, the strategies presented earlier can be worked with relative ease into the curriculum. In many school districts, however, the total responsibility for providing differentiated educational services to the gifted is assigned to the teacher of the heterogeneously grouped classroom. Regardless of the type of program in which gifted students are served, there are certain principles that should be considered in curriculum planning. These include the following:

1. If integration is a major goal, the subject matter must be correlated whenever possible.

2. If our gifted students are to be the leaders of the future, they must learn, think, and work like leaders. Dewey's premise that the school should provide for the lifetime needs of students is most appropriate here; the school, and particularly the gifted program, should provide opportunities for students to experience leadership roles.

3. Instruction for gifted students must be individualized, keeping in mind both the nature and needs of gifted students in general and the specific needs and interests of the students with whom the teacher is assigned to work. Such individualization must take into consideration:

   a. The accelerated pace at which these students learn and work;
   b. The ability of gifted students to understand and work with problem solving, abstraction, and more complex levels of thought;
   c. The advanced verbal abilities of the gifted, which enable them to work with advanced resources and thus to engage in realistic and meaningful investigation;
   d. The creative abilities of gifted students, which enable them to develop new ways of accomplishing academic as well as lifetime goals and tasks; and
   e. The preference of gifted students for independent learning.

4. All instruction must include enrichment—that is, it must provide exposure to new areas that are not a part of the traditional curriculum as well as opportunities to explore beyond the scope of the regular curriculum in areas of special interest to individual students.

5. The program for the gifted must include deliberate, planned instruction in the skills of rational, logical, and creative thinking.

This final section will present suggestions for integrating these principles, through use of the strategies discussed earlier, into the various subject areas of the core curriculum. The reader is encouraged to "hitchhike" on the ideas presented here, developing new and more creative ways of presenting the traditional content, thus adding a truly differentiated approach to the services provided for the superior student in the regular classroom as well as in the gifted program.

11

Challenging the Gifted Reader

But she didn't talk that much about
"reading for the gifted"!

Some years ago I conducted a staff development workshop entitled "Challenging the Gifted Reader." From the outset I stressed the importance of utilizing an integrated approach to the teaching of language arts to gifted students, and I built on that premise by presenting a variety of strategies designed to build total language proficiency in the gifted. At the end of the workshop, one well-meaning teacher wrote in her evaluation, "But she didn't talk that much about 'reading for the gifted'!" She had totally missed my most important point.

It simply is not enough to "teach reading" to the gifted. Our gifted and creative students should become our leaders and our producers, our orators, our writers, our actors. How can we go about accomplishing this end? First we must integrate our language arts instruction—we must teach much more than "reading for the gifted."

There are many facets of language that should be explored and experienced by our gifted future leaders—whether in the regular language arts class or in the gifted program resource room. The study of language involves literature—not only reading it, but learning to read it critically and creatively, to interpret an author's meanings and to recognize an author's style. It involves writing: poetry, prose, and drama, creative and technical writing, writing for many different purposes. To use language effectively, the student must understand the makeup of language (morphology, orthography, and syntax) and possess a superior repertoire of vocabulary. The leader must be able to use oral language effectively; oral language skills can be developed through choral reading, creative dramatics, and the teaching of basic communication techniques (public speaking, debate, oral interpretation, and persuasive speaking, as well as parliamentary procedure and other specific leadership skills involving oral language usage). If we are to train our gifted students to be creative producers and effective leaders for future generations, we must not separate the language arts into their many small components; we must integrate our language arts instruction.

Why is it so important to use an integrated approach to language education for the gifted? Perhaps the most typical, apparent, and well-known characteristic of gifted persons is a high level of verbal ability. Gifted students typically possess a broad range of knowledge and an extensive vocabulary in a variety of advanced areas. They are often voracious readers with an affinity for advanced material. Their extensive use of their broad vocabulary often creates false impressions among their peers and even teachers who do not understand them. Often a lack of self-confidence, combined with excessive sensitivity and awareness of others, causes these students to reject instructional criticism of their work as totally negative and derogatory. Their critical and abstract thinking abilities enable them to understand cause and effect relationships, to enjoy working at higher levels, and to evaluate people and situations. The gifted are self-directed and self-motivated in their personal areas of interest, and their risk-taking nature allows them to exercise their creative potential in oral and written expression.

Concomitant with these characteristics are problems that can be overcome at least in part by appropriately differentiated, carefully integrated curriculum geared to their special needs. Their love of (and ability for working with) advanced language experiences tends to frustrate gifted students when they are required to conform to a predetermined rate of learning. A considerable proportion of the language arts program for these students should therefore be individualized on the basis of a diagnostic/prescriptive system applied to all areas of their language development. Opportunities should be provided for applying their creative talents through creative writing exercises, oral interpretation, and other activities designed to strengthen oral creativity, and through access to advanced materials and methods of exploration in the language arts areas. In this context, the careful use of positive criticism (rather than simply criticism), along with instruction and practice in proofreading/editing and self-evaluation, will help gifted students to accept instructional feedback as guidance aimed at refining their already efficient verbal skills. It is also important for the teacher to encourage independent work (an escape from routine tasks and continuous direction) and plan for generous amounts of time for group interaction; literature is a particularly effective medium for group discussion and for the development of questioning techniques that foster divergent thinking and responses. Finally, activities based on the higher levels of thinking (using, for example, Bloom's Taxonomy of

Educational Objectives or Guilford's Structure of Intellect model) can help challenge gifted students and strengthen their self-concepts.

THE DIFFERENTIATED READING PROGRAM

Reading Skills for the Gifted

Once I attended a meeting of teachers who were hearing our new district superintendent speak for the first time. The subject was the reading program. After an enlightened presentation, the speaker opened the floor to questions. With bait in hand, I rose and asked, "Do you believe that a child who enters the first grade reading should be required to begin with the pre-primer in order to provide social interaction in the reading groups?" To my delight, the superintendent replied, "Absolutely not!" I grinned broadly, said, "Thank you very much!" and sat down. Immediately a teacher waved her hand frantically, jumped up and cried out, "But they have to have the basic skills!" Of course, I could not agree more. Personally I have seen the sad results of parental pressure on young children who were not yet ready to read; and I have taught learning-disabled gifted children whose problems may well have been caused by an earlier failure to learn the basics of reading. But my point was, and I still believe this strongly, that the child who has already mastered the basic skills will be harmed rather than helped by the approach that requires all children to begin and end their instruction at the same place and time. How, then, can we help these children who teach themselves to read at an early age? One way is to use diagnostic/prescriptive systems to determine their instructional levels and allow—rather, encourage—them to begin there.

Using Criterion-Referenced Tests. At this point in curriculum development, most basal readers are accompanied by criterion-referenced tests. Briefly, a criterion-referenced test (CRT) is an instrument designed to determine the level of skill mastery that a student has achieved from a particular text or section of a text. This type of testing, interpreted in terms of percentage of correct answers rather than from a normative view, allows a teacher to determine which specific skills require further instruction for a student to reach the desired level. The criterion-referenced test provides an excellent tool for diagnosis. To use it for this purpose, the following procedures may be used:

1. Give the early readers the first reading book to complete at their own pace. (To assure control of this procedure, all such reading should be done in class.)
2. Administer criterion-referenced tests as students complete each of the books in the sequence.

3. From the CRT results, determine which if any skills need simple reinforcement, and provide brief one-to-one instruction for each student until mastery is achieved.

4. As mastery is reached on all skills represented in a given reader, proceed to the next level and repeat the above sequence.

5. When students reach their instructional levels (i.e., when they achieve approximately 80 percent comprehension and more guided instruction in reading skills is needed), place them with the appropriate reading groups, preferably with others who have reached this level at roughly the same rate, for regular instruction. Continue to individualize, allowing students to progress at their own rates and using the CRTs at the end of each level to assure mastery of each set of skills.

Specific Skills in Reading.   What are the skills that the gifted students must master early in order to make the best possible use of their advanced verbal abilities? The following skills should be given deliberate attention in the reading program, as they can provide gifted readers with a sense of independence gained from the ability to read and learn with a minimum of instruction. They should therefore be a regular part of the reading instruction provided for these students:

- Recognizing the main idea
- Using context clues to aid in comprehension
- Comprehending inferentially as well as literally
- Reading at an above average rate of speed (and having the ability to vary this rate with the type and purpose of reading)
- Distinguishing fact from fiction
- Following directions
- Understanding and using properly all of the parts of a book, a newspaper, and other types of reading material

In addition to these commonly recognized skills, gifted students should be taught to use a variety of resources (the more familiar ones as well as less common sources such as specialized dictionaries and bibliographies, court and church records, government documents, and the like), and organizational skills such as outlining and note-taking. These latter topics are covered in Chapter 3 under the area of research.*

---

*An excellent system for developing strong language arts skills in the gifted may be found in Mindell and Stracher's "Well-Read" program (cleverly subtitled "Literacy for the Gifted").

Independent Reading.   In addition to the basic reading program, all students, but particularly the gifted, should be given assignments that will provide a variety of reading material and encourage independent reading outside of class. One effective method is to designate three reading contract levels, requiring students to contract for a reasonable number of books in a broad range of categories during the year. Obviously the teacher must exercise careful judgment in approving the contract levels and may wish to correlate them with assessed reading levels, with the understanding that a student could (with the teacher's approval) move to a higher level if substantial progress were made by the middle of the year (or a lower level if the initial contract proved to be overly ambitious).

Another important consideration in the implementation of the reading contract is the defining of parameters within which students may select the books for the fulfillment of their contract requirements. The teacher should provide a list of specific titles in each category that are available in the school library and that are recommended for each level, with the understanding that other approved books may be read for credit. It is advisable to check periodically to be sure that the contract level is appropriate for each student and to employ some method of confirming that the books reported have actually been read. It is not necessary to require a formal report on each book read; perhaps the teacher might select one or two of the books read from each category for the student to report in detail. Teachers are strongly encouraged *not* to require the traditional book report (i.e., read a book and write a summary of it) but rather to use more creative forms of reporting. Some reporting formats that would call on the creativity of the students might include some of the following suggestions.

1. Dress like a character in your book and tell your story.
2. Dress as the author might have dressed. Tell not only the story that you wrote, but also something about your life and what prompted you to write this book.
3. Pretend that you have just completed the writing of this book and are trying to sell it to a publisher. Tell the publisher about the story in the book, and convince her to buy and publish it.
4. Design a cover for your book, using an original illustration that you think best summarizes the main point or moral of the story.
5. Pretend that you are a professional writer. Write a biography of a character in your book.
6. If your book is not illustrated (or if you do not feel the illustrator represented the story well), design a set of illustrations for the book.

7. Write a review of your book for the school newspaper or for any of several magazines that accept student work. (The teacher should share examples of well-written critical reviews as models for this experience.)

8. Pretend that you (the author or a favorite character in the book) are being interviewed by a newspaper columnist or a television talk-show host (represented by a fellow classmate). Discuss your book in the interview.

9. Write or tell an original sequel to the book you have read.

10. Write a scenario (see Chapter 4) representing a day or a week in the future life of a character in your book.

11. Write a one-act play to dramatize the main story in your book. Make puppets and produce the play.

12. Create an animated film based on your book (see Chapter 15).

13. Write an essay telling why you agree (or disagree) with the author or a character in your book. Tell how you would change the story if you were the author.

14. Deliver a campaign speech to help elect your favorite character to an appropriate position in government.

Differentiated Reading Material

As with all areas of gifted education, it is essential that the reading material prescribed for (or accepted from) gifted students be qualitatively different from that which is appropriate for the less capable student. Materials selected for use by the gifted should be at levels consistent with the students' reading levels, should encourage divergent thinking and problem solving, and should require different methods and rates of reading. The newspaper is an excellent source that can be used effectively by gifted students.

Using the Newspaper. Our future leaders must be able to read and interpret the newspaper; therefore, it is a highly appropriate tool to provide for gifted students in the language arts program. Several methods of using the newspaper in the classroom are presented here.

1. Teach about propaganda (or the difference between fact and fiction) through examination of advertisements, editorials, letters to the editor, and the like.

2. Use the newspaper to teach current events, making social studies and science relevant to the students.

3. Have students write newsletters giving information on class projects, accomplishments of individual students, and so on. This method can be used in even the earliest years to help students develop an appreciation and ability for using the newspaper.

4. Encourage students to write their own newspapers in connection with other subjects. In a social studies unit on Ancient History, for example, assign each student a position on the staff of the *Athens Chronicle*—with the assignments made according to students' areas of interest. The sports writer can research sports in the Classical Ages of Greece and Rome, writing about the chariot races; the fashion editor can gather information and write about the dress of the period; and the news writers can report on events of the day. This activity is particularly popular with middle-school students, and the subject matter of the newspaper can be adjusted in accordance with the required topic of the particular grade level—colonial times or American Revolution days for fifth grade American history, ancient Greece/Rome for sixth grade, and so forth. A further extension of this project would be to correlate the literature read in class with the period of history about which the newspaper is being written (e.g., reading *Julius Caesar* along with the writing of the *Roman Chronicle*).

A Creative Reading Approach

The late Paul Witty, international authority in the area of reading, devoted special attention not only to the differentiation of reading instruction for the gifted but also to the need for a "creative reading" approach to reading instruction for all students. According to Witty, creative reading is

> a thinking process in which new ideas are originated, evaluated, and applied. Divergent and varied responses, not right answers, are goals as thinking transpires and conclusions are reached. Finally, the pupil evaluates his conclusions and seeks to extend and use them (1974, p. 15).

Witty further laid out the following characteristics of the creative reading approach:

1. It requires active responses that go beyond the literal meaning or the answers found in textbooks.

2. Emphasis is on higher level responses and thinking.

3. It resembles creative thinking in that it helps the reader gain new insights by evaluating hypotheses and reaching conclusions.

4. It goes beyond facts and considers their meanings, implications, and usefulness.

5. It is the highest level of reading—even higher than critical reading.

How can the teacher encourage creative reading in gifted students? The following characteristics of creative readers may be of help to the teacher who wishes to formulate student objectives designed to foster creative reading in the gifted classroom:

- They achieve intrinsic satisfaction from reading.
- They can distinguish between fact and opinion and often draw conclusions that differ from those of the author.
- They empathize with characters in the stories they read, sometimes imagining themselves in the story or speculating about what they would have done differently in a character's place.
- They analyze the behaviors of the characters and the reasons for the inclusion of these behaviors in the story.
- They add original ideas to the stories they read.
- They use reading to build and stimulate more creative use of their vocabulary.
- They evaluate the story in light of their own experiences.
- They demonstrate self-confidence in their own opinions and in their interpretations of the author's meanings.
- They visualize the plots, characters, and events of the story.
- They tend to go beyond the literal meanings of a story, analyzing the author's purposes and raising questions that are not addressed in the story itself.
- They are able to transfer what is read to other situations or problems, assimilating new information into schemata already developed from previous readings and other experiences.
- They gain new insights from thinking creatively during the reading process.
- They make predictions about future events in the story.
- They develop other versions of the story—new beginnings, new endings, new characters, new events.
- They express themselves creatively and elaborate when relating or discussing a story.
- They gain motivation for original writing from what is read.

Literature for the Gifted

From the earliest years of their reading experience, all children, but especially the gifted ones, should be exposed to good quality reading material. Like the arts and other branches of the humanities, literature should be selected carefully and offered with skill and enthusiasm. To be appreciated for its values (which are many), literature must be *enjoyed*. Kauffman (1976) came right to the point with these comments:

> Out of the whole broad sweep of human art and culture, most of our schools concentrate almost exclusively on one tiny sliver: critically approved writings in English during the last 400 years. Even these are taken almost entirely out of cultural context and taught instead with the intent of inculcating a particularly artificial set of esthetic standards. To devote up to a quarter of the secondary curriculum to the likes of *Ivanhoe* or (shudder!) *The Last of the Mohicans* is folly, especially as the principal effect on adult Americans seems to be to give them a distaste for books and a particular dislike of "literary classics."

Drawing a parallel with art, Kauffman further suggested that, if used properly, literature can be "a special kind of window onto other people's lives and feelings" (p. 31). How, then, are we to achieve this lofty goal in our literature program? First we must select the best literature for our students to read, and then we must present and explore it through the most exciting, creative, and fulfilling approaches we can develop.

Selecting Literature for the Gifted. There are many approaches to the selection of literature for the gifted. Whereas literature textbooks typically govern the selection of readings in secondary English, the most common approach to selecting reading materials for elementary students of all ability levels is probably the use of award lists. Although it is commonly assumed that books earning the Newbery, Caldecott, and other coveted awards are the "best" reading available for all children, Baskin and Harris (1980) caution against overreliance on this approach. According to these authors, the selection of books for the gifted should be based on both their intrinsic and their extrinsic qualities. That is, they should be evaluated not only with regard to their internal characteristics (style, structure, content, and reading level) but also in the light of their ability to elicit intellectual and divergent responses from their readers—those types of responses about which we spoke in connection with of creative reading. According to Baskin and Harris, literary works for gifted students should:

1. Leave the reader with as many questions as answers;
2. Include juggled time sequences, a variety of narrators, and unusual speech patterns, requiring added concentration from the reader;
3. Be open-ended, leaving problem resolution to the reader;
4. Help to build problem-solving skills and develop productive thinking; and

5. Provide role models for building character, effort, and intellectual curiosity.

What of the "great" literature? William Bennett, former chairman of the National Endowment for the Humanities and more recently the United States Secretary of Education, surveyed 325 journalists, teachers, business officials, and parents, and compiled from their responses the following list of authors and their literary works in the humanities which all American students should be expected to study (Bennett, 1984):

1. Shakespeare (particularly *Macbeth* and *Hamlet*)
2. American Historical Documents (particularly the **Declaration of Independence, the Constitution, and the Gettysburg Address**)
3. Twain (*Huckleberry Finn*)
4. The Bible
5. Homer (*Odyssey, Iliad*)
6. Dickens (*Great Expectations, Tale of Two Cities*)
7. Plato (*The Republic*)
8. Steinbeck (*Grapes of Wrath*)
9. Hawthorne (*Scarlet Letter*)
10. Sophocles (*Oedipus*)
11. Melville (*Moby Dick*)
12. Orwell (*1984*)
13. Thoreau (*Walden*)
14. Frost (poems)
15. Whitman (*Leaves of Grass*)
16. Fitzgerald (*The Great Gatsby*)
17. Chaucer (*The Canterbury Tales*)
18. Marx (*Communist Manifesto*)
19. Aristotle (*Politics*)
20. Dickinson (poems)
21. Dostoevsky (*Crime and Punishment*)
22. Faulkner (various works)
23. Salinger (*Catcher in the Rye*)
24. de Tocqueville (*Democracy in America*)
25. Austen (*Pride and Prejudice*)
26. Emerson (essays and poems)
27. Machiavelli (*The Prince*)

28. Milton (*Paradise Lost*)

29. Tolstoy (*War and Peace*)

30. Virgil (*Aeneid*)

A Differentiated Approach to Teaching Literature. Literature can be taught in many ways. One school of thought is to teach the major works of a given author, whereas another approach concentrates on a period of history. Some texts group literary works by nationality; others use genre to organize the content of a course. Whichever method of presentation the teacher selects, it is once again important to remember that qualitative differentiation is a major goal of programming for the gifted. It is also necessary to incorporate into the program an integration of the various areas of language development. With these goals in mind, the following approach to the teaching of literature is suggested:

1. Regardless of the age of the students, read aloud to them often, using the best available examples of the type of literature you are introducing. (Also remember when selecting the "best" to select examples that students can enjoy, varying the styles and types of material and the methods of presentation to hold student interest.) Follow these readings with discussion.

2. Use a variety of activities to introduce each selection to be read (present relevant background information, using media, artifacts, guest speakers, or other resources that will make it more interesting; go over unfamiliar vocabulary words whose meanings will not be apparent from context clues; suggest questions to explore in reading; give examples of the author's style; etc.).

3. After students have read the assignment, divide them into small groups for follow-up discussion. In junior or senior high school, it may be rewarding to train volunteers (if not all students) in the formulation of discussion questions, perhaps following the Junior Great Books approach, which is discussed in the next section of this chapter. In such a case, students could be paired for planning after reading the material to be discussed, and the selection of discussion leaders could be made on a rotating but random basis. When this approach is followed, the teacher should serve as facilitator—circulating, observing, and coaching as the small-group discussions take place.

4. Following the whole-class or small-group discussions of the material read, activities such as the following may be used to culminate the experience:

   a. Role-play a drama or improvise a sequel to a story, using creative dramatics.

b. View a stage or television drama and write a critical review of it.
c. Write original poetry, prose, or drama as motivated by the material read.

Discussing What Is Read: The Junior Great Books Approach. *   The Great Books Foundation, formed in 1947, is a private, nonprofit educational corporation. The Foundation publishes nineteen series of books (for adults and for grades 2 through 12) and conducts training sessions for leaders of discussion groups.

The Junior Great Books Program prescribes specific readings for students from the second grade through high school. Using a unique method known as "shared inquiry," trained discussion leaders work with groups of students in an effort to lend new insights to some of the outstanding literary works of the world. Because it is a qualitatively different approach to the teaching of literature, JGB is extremely well suited for use with gifted readers. (The Foundation recommends the program for students who read at grade level or above.)

According to the Junior Great Books system, there are three types of questions that a person can ask about a story: factual, evaluative, and interpretive questions. *Factual questions* are simply those that can be answered directly from information supplied in the story. They are totally convergent, that is, there is no doubt about their correct answer. An example of this type of question, using the familiar "Jack and the Beanstalk" as a model, might be, "How many times did Jack go up the beanstalk?" Since the story clearly discusses Jack's first, second, and third trips, there is no room for debate in determining the answer to this question. *Evaluative questions* are those that can be answered in terms of the reader's own experience, that is, the reader answers from the perspective of her own background and attitudes. Using our same fairy tale, an evaluative question might be, "If you had been Jack, would you have gone up the beanstalk the third time?" This type of question requires knowledge of the story, but the reader need not refer to the story in responding. *Interpretive questions* are used most often in JGB discussions. An example might be: "Why did Jack go up the beanstalk the third time?" This question requires divergent thinking—the type of thinking we most often encourage in our gifted students. Here, however, the response must be developed using both the reader's intuitive powers and information from the story. In fact, one of the requirements of the JGB discussion is that the answers to interpretive questions must be

---

*The material in this section is reproduced in part from the instructional manuals of the Junior Great Books Program, with the permission of the Great Books Foundation, 40 East Huron Street, Chicago, IL 60611 (1-800-222-5870).

supported by evidence from the story (although the answers are not clearly stated in the story itself).

When using Junior Great Books, a teacher plans clusters of questions for group discussion. A cluster consists of a basic question and several related interpretive questions. The program gives the following guidelines for the formulation of basic questions:

1. Basic questions should always be of the interpretive type.
2. They should be specific and clearly worded, stating what the problem is and what the leader cannot answer about the problem.
3. The leader should have a legitimate doubt, as well as a genuine concern, about the answer to any basic question.
4. Each question must be discussable on the basis of the story/book itself.

Basic questions are used as the focus for discussion of the story that has been read by the group. After the leader has presented a basic question, she asks follow-up questions for any or all of the following purposes:

1. To explore the implications of the basic question
2. To require a participant to support a response
3. To correct factual errors
4. To elicit additional opinions or responses
5. To encourage discussion/debate about a response
6. To clarify a statement
7. To develop the most important idea in a response
8. To encourage a participant to examine his or her response
9. To return a discussion to the reading

The key to successful use of the Junior Great Books approach is training. The Great Books Foundation offers both beginning and advanced workshops; the teacher of the gifted is strongly encouraged to attend these sessions, as this approach to the study of literature is one of the finest available today.

Enriching the Literature Program: Drama in the Classroom.   One of the most effective and rewarding methods of teaching and enhancing the study of literature is the use of drama in the classroom. As a part of an ESEA Title III program administered jointly by the Connecticut State Department of Education and the American Shakespeare Festival Theatre, Mary Hunter Wolf and Victor B. Miller developed an experientially based system for teaching drama to secondary students. Since gifted students in the middle and upper elementary grades are often excited by the study of sophisticated dramatic literature, this approach can also be extended downward and used as a motivating device in either academic or enrichment programs for the gifted. In *New Approaches to Teaching Shakespeare,* Wolf and Miller (n.d.) presented activities for involving students (and helping them to "live" the various roles and stories) in *Twelfth Night, Romeo and Juliet, King Lear, Julius Caesar,* and *Hamlet.* With the permission and encouragement of the authors, their approach to teaching *Julius Caesar* (perhaps Shakespeare's most popular play among young people) is reproduced here.

Julius Caesar

In the work of the Center for Theatre Techniques in Education we have found that the use of theatre games and improvisations are essential to helping the student understand the interaction of drama. A booklet, *Theatre's Different Demands,** published by the Theatre under a Title III grant, will supply more of the theoretical basis for this approach. To help students and teachers get "off the page" and "into the action" the following suggestions should be of use:

Julius Caesar explores four main ideas—the nature of politics, the struggle for power, motives which inspire personal choice of a course of action and the power of persuasion. Four interesting men are involved in acting our attitudes around these ideas—Caesar, Brutus, Cassius and Antony along with a late starter in the play, Octavius.

If the class room is physically flexible, divide the class in three groups each to plan without the knowledge of the other group a new arrangement for the room. Group One has a few friends in Group Two known to each other; Group Three has no friends in either group but has a secret control over specified people in Groups One and Two. Each group presents its plan and tries to influence the others to accept it using the specially known relationships to assist them in winning the adoption of their plan.

Combine the class in couples. Assign to each partner a special task to convince the other to carry out. For example, one partner is to persuade the other to take his coat off and put it on backwards; the other is to convince the first to improve his handwriting by immediate practise. They may pursue their objectives simultaneously and use any means except physical violence. Let as many couples as you wish try out their persuasive powers while an assigned group of critics watches.

---

*For further details on this and other existing and forthcoming publications in this area, teachers are encouraged to contact the Center for Theatre Techniques in Education, 800 Dixwell Avenue (P.O. Box 6213), Hamden, CT 06517.

After critics discuss with their actors, the entire class should discuss what worked and what did not—was it a matter of personalities and/or techniques—did the nature of the problem or the nature of the people involved change the techniques?

In many ways Caesar deals with humans behaving in the manner in which they are treated. Cassius' Caesar (Cassius' mental and spoken image) is not in many senses the Caesar that Caesar is in reality. But, ironically, for us, for Brutus, and for other conspirators, Caesar becomes the person he is treated as. One of the best ways to get at this idea is to play *Who Am I*? The class decides what kind of person they would like to create while one of its members is outside the room. The "it" is then asked back and treated as if he were the new imaginary character. As he begins to pick up clues as to his character, he should behave accordingly, without saying out loud things like "Oh, I get it, I'm a grouch." Nor should the other students focus on giving him hints. Rather they should all just be at a place, doing some activity, treating the grouch the way they might normally treat someone like that. In terms of Caesar, you might suggest they treat the "it" as if he is all-powerful, yet dangerous, crafty and ambitious. The discussion afterwards can center then on how it felt to be treated this way and what behavior it elicited from the "Caesar" figure. Did he begin to get worse than they had originally imagined? How did they respond to him once he knew and behaved accordingly?

A special adaptation of the *Asking and Rejecting* game can open up the areas of power and jealousy that move much of the play. Students are paired off; one is the asker, one the rejector. The asker is to ask for something real or imagined that he has lent the rejector; the rejector is to turn him down no matter what. The asker has to keep trying to find new ways of getting back his possession. The individual "scenes" may then be restaged for the entire class. The emotions, the dynamics of the scenes parallel in a real sense the feelings that surround Caesar. He has been given power, love, and admiration. Now that he has achieved this eminence, many of those who, in fear, have given over their own power, want it back.

The whole area of the supernatural lends itself to creative exploration by students and teachers. The visions of Act I in the night's storm can be the subjects for painting, creating an environment, making a sound and light show.

There are many ways in which scenes can be improvised around the subject of loyalty, split loyalties, and so on. Students can make lists of common split-loyalties they run up against and work out scenes that concern themselves with these dilemmas. An easier way to get at this subject might be to adapt the *Letter of Apology* game [reproduced below] and have each student write a letter to a friend or relative he has had to be "against" in a question of contrasting loyalties. The discussion may then focus upon what it feels like to be in Brutus' and Caesar's positions respectively.

The Letter of Apology Game*

Ask each student to write a note of apology to anyone for anything, real or imagined. Ask each student to read his letter aloud. Choose one student and ask him to bring his letter to the front of the class. Place two chairs back to back and have him sit in one and another student in the other. The second student is to be the recipient of the apology.

Set the Scene: The first student has decided not to write after all—he's going to apologize by phone. Advise him to obtain the forgiveness of the second student whom you advise to make certain that the apologizer has really earned that forgiveness. They now improvise the phone call based on the information contained in the original letter. (If the letter was to Mr. Jones, the second student now plays Mr. Jones.) When the call is finished, reset the scene: The apologizer has decided not to write, not to phone, but to apologize in person at the recipient's home, as if there had been no phone call. They improvise the scene face to face with the same goals. Repeat the process with other letters and actors.

Sample Question: What changes happened between the letter and the confrontation? What new information did we learn that wasn't contained in the original letter? What did we learn about the two characters in the scene? How did we learn it? What kinds of things did they say or do to each other that made them react most strongly? What did the way they sat or moved say about them as people in the situation?

Basic Objectives: To find the inner or emotional life of the letter/script; to experience the action-reaction-action of human interaction as it is reflected in the acting process; to introduce the student audience to all the nonverbal elements which help us understand character and the nature of the effect of these elements on feelings; to introduce the student performers to how their emotions were affected by these elements; to create scenes; to play an objective: "I want forgiveness"; to provide theatre pieces for a discussion of theatre; to introduce students to a different kind of in-class work.

---

*Reproduced with the permission of the authors. Wolf, M. H., & Miller, V. B. *Theatre's different demands: An approach to the classroom teaching of plays.* Hamden, CT: The Center for Theatre Techniques in Education.

THE FORMAL STUDY OF LANGUAGE

Unlike reading, which most commonly begins in school, the learning of language begins at birth. Parents, siblings, friends, and the media (particularly television) all influence the quality of language development that takes place in the early years. The formal study of language begins in the primary grades of school; it is here that we hope to refine the skills that children have learned during their earlier years.

The formal language curriculum from the first grade through college comprises many components. Perhaps the three most important aspects of language that are studied in school are morphology, defined by the *American Heritage Dictionary* as the study of word formation, including the inflection, derivation, and compounding of words; orthography (the correct spelling of words); and syntax, the skill of putting words together to form concepts and generalizations. It is also important to utilize a variety of methods for expanding the vocabulary of gifted students as one's comprehension and use of words impacts his or her degree of success in the three areas defined above.

Morphology: Inflection, Derivation, and Compounding

The teacher who taught me English in junior high school had a system teachers today would do well to emulate. Not satisfied with the published texts, she developed her own eclectic approach to the teaching of language. We also had a Grammar Club, and everyone in the class belonged. If a fellow student caught us in a grammatical error, we were fined a penny. Would that grammar were taught that way these days! In high school I was fortunate to have another language expert in each of my four years of English. When I took Advanced Grammar in my first year of college, I realized that our school system had taught us in our twelve years most of the English grammar there was to know!

Our gifted students, tomorrow's leaders, must learn to use the English language like scholars. If they are to be scholars, there are certain essentials that must be learned. The following skills should form the skeleton of the formal language program.

Inflection. With respect to language, inflection simply refers to the changes that words undergo as they are made ready for use in combination with other words. Inflection includes the conjugation of verbs and the parsing of nouns (changes in mood, voice, tense, number, gender, and case). It also includes the analysis of phrases, clauses, and sentences by part of speech and usage or by diagramming. Gifted students should be familiar with all of these changes which make our language what it is, in order to avoid those errors that are common even among teachers today—pronouns without antecedents, lack of agreement, split infinitives, and the like.

Derivation and Compounding.   One of the most efficient ways in which students can be taught to build broad and effective vocabularies is through the study of etymology—or the origins of words. Twenty years ago, the study of foreign language in the secondary school was required (or at least strongly encouraged through a limitation of elective courses). Unfortunately, foreign language study at the pre-college level has diminished significantly in recent years. Because many of our modern English words originated from Latin or Greek, the study of these ancient languages—or any of the other languages derived from them—strengthens the student's understanding about the makeup of our own language. The *World Book Dictionary* offers a marvelous segment on the derivations of words in the front of its first volume. (Another excellent source of this information is Crocetti's (1987) preparation manual for the Graduate Record Examination.) By teaching all of the prefixes, suffixes, and combining forms, their meanings, and the ways in which words are compounded using these word parts, a teacher can greatly enhance her students' vocabulary potential. Today's gifted students may not have the command of English that they need, but their repertoires can be greatly increased through the study of etymology. This, then, should be one of the major focuses of the language program for gifted students.

Orthography: The Spelling of Words

Simply defined, orthography is spelling. The spelling texts of today's schools, like those of fifty years ago, present lists of words for student memorization. Although no thinking educator can argue against the learning of certain essential English words, and admittedly the methodology of practice has advanced significantly since the days of "Write each word fifty times," there is little room in the traditional spelling lesson for consideration of individual differences. However, like all other aspects of the language arts program for the gifted, the spelling program must be differentiated in order to meet the needs of our brighter students. How can the teacher individualize the teaching of spelling? The following system, field-tested at several levels, works well both in the regular classroom and in the gifted program.

Monday: The teacher administers a pretest consisting of all words in the spelling text lesson for the week (requiring students above the third grade to take their tests in ink for security purposes). Students exchange papers and score the pretests in color as the teacher calls out the correct spelling of each word. The papers are returned to their owners, and students are assigned to two groups for the week: Group One (those missing no more than five of the words on the pretest) and Group Two (those missing more than five words on the pretest). The teacher collects all papers for rechecking, returning them the next day with any necessary corrections; no grades are given at the pretest stage.

Tuesday: All students develop their individual lists from a variety of sources (see details below), with Group Two students including words provided by the teacher that relate to (and thus will help in learning) those on the original list. Each student then writes a sentence demonstrating the correct usage of the word (looking up the definition of any word with which she is not familiar). Finally, the teacher collects all lists to check for correct spelling, to assure that incorrectly spelled words will not be studied.

Wednesday and Thursday: The teacher returns the checked and corrected lists and sentences to the students, pointing out errors in word spellings or usage in sentences. Students spend the remainder of these two days working with their partners on activities designed to strengthen their command of the words on their lists, preparing for Friday's test.

Friday: All students take spelling tests (using ink above the third grade), alternating with their partners to administer tests on the individualized lists. All tests are collected by the teacher for grading and returned on the following Monday.

Making Individual Lists: There are numerous sources from which the better students may develop their individualized spelling lists. Some of these sources might include:

1. All words missed on the pretest for the week (out of a text list of twenty words, this source would include a maximum of five words for Group One students)
2. All words misspelled on the previous Friday's spelling test
3. All words misspelled on tests and written work in other subjects during the preceding week
4. Any words for which the student has recognized a special need
5. Words selected from other sources such as the vocabulary section of the *World Book Dictionary*, manuals such as *Spelling Made Simple*, graded spelling lists, terminology from fields of interest to the student, and the like.

In addition to the obvious benefits of individualized instruction, there are several advantages to the use of this type of system:

1. Students are motivated to learn the text list in advance of the pretest, giving them more freedom and a sense of achievement.
2. Additional motivation is gained through the earning of credit for learning words that they feel they need to know.

3. A broader vocabulary base is built through the use of various sources and the writing of sentences which demonstrate comprehension of the words selected.

4. All students are given weekly opportunities for placement in the top group, reducing the resentment toward the gifted which often occurs among their less able classmates.

5. The opportunity to work with partners increases opportunities for interaction and encourages the development of self-disciplined study. (In order to derive the greatest benefit from the partnership arrangement, it is wise to develop some type of rotational system to preclude students' working with the same partner each week.)

Syntax: Putting Words Together

It is most unfortunate that the diagramming of sentences is one of the most unpopular techniques of learning the English language. Presented appropriately by the creative teacher, diagramming can be viewed by students as a type of game—not at all unlike the working of a variety of puzzles.

Although the exact format of sentence diagramming has varied over the years, the basic technique is still the same. A sentence is simply divided by means of a group of lines into clauses and then into subject, predicate, direct object or predicate nominative/adjective, and modifying words and phrases. Once the procedures have been mastered, diagramming can be of great benefit in the analysis and synthesis of sentence structure. One method of diagramming is illustrated below:

Sentence: History has demonstrated the power of praise.

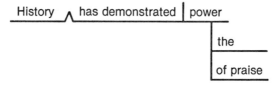

A more complex example:

Sentence: When the war ended, millions of people had lost their lives.

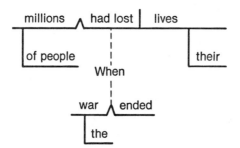

Additional information on sentence diagramming can be found in any good English language textbook; the teacher is strongly encouraged to utilize this excellent strategy for helping gifted students to understand their own language more thoroughly.

Another important aspect of syntax is the ability to recognize the various parts of speech and their usage in written language. Since it is not possible to include a complete discussion of the parts of speech here, the teacher is encouraged to consult a basic grammar manual for a review of these elements of our language.

Vocabulary Development

Material for vocabulary enrichment can be found in many places. A good newspaper is an excellent source, particularly editorials written by columnists such as James J. Kilpatrick and William Buckley, who consistently demonstrate a superior command of the English language. Students can be assigned to read selected sections of the daily newspaper and to select one new word each day to add to their repertoires. Each word should be written on a separate card along with the dictionary definition, the sentence in which the writer used it, and an original sentence in which the student demonstrates understanding of the word and its meaning. If partners exchange their vocabulary cards daily, a new vocabulary of over 300 words can be amassed during a given year.

Another method of increasing one's vocabulary is the study of word relationships—notably synonyms and antonyms. By encouraging the use of the thesaurus for editing and improving students' writing, a teacher can help greatly in the building of broad and effective vocabularies among the gifted. Other associations that can help students to internalize meanings might involve the pairing of descriptive words with well-known persons who exemplify the characteristics or concepts expressed (e.g., Albert Schweitzer as an exemplary humanitarian, or Abraham Lincoln as the great emancipator) or with inanimate objects that the words appropriately describe (e.g., a massive boulder, a roaring fire).

In decoding or studying new vocabulary, the learner should first examine each word, determining whether or not it contains any familiar prefixes (*pre-*, *in-*, *mono-*, *equi-*), suffixes (*-ment*, *-able*, *-some*, *-ist*), or combining forms/roots (*astr*, *annu*, *fin*, *loc*). The word *infinity*, for example, is composed of the prefix *in-* (meaning not), the combining form or root word *fin* (end), and the suffix *-ity* (state of being). Taking this word apart, the student with a command of the prefixes, suffixes, and combining forms might recognize it to mean "a state of notending" (or "without end"). Looking next at the definition of the word, the student should write a sentence that clearly illustrates its correct usage.

THE COMMUNICATIONS PROGRAM

Perhaps the most important ability a leader must possess in order to be effective in leading others is the ability to communicate. The skill of interpersonal communication has been discussed in Chapter 5 of this text. Other aspects of communication that should be addressed in the language arts program include the balanced use of questions, the development of oral communication skills, and the practice of good listening skills.

Questioning Techniques

Earlier in this chapter the types of questions used by the Junior Great Books Program—factual, evaluative, and interpretive—were discussed. In this section we will look at another way of classifying questions: convergent and divergent.

In his classic paradigm of the human intellect, Guilford (1967) presented two types of thinking (or intellectual operations): convergent and divergent production. Based on the Latin words *con* (together) + *verge* (turn), *converge* literally means "to turn together" or to focus on a specific, predetermined response. Convergent production/thinking is thus the production of responses that are expected, or that conform to a predetermined pattern, and a convergent question is one that presupposes one right answer or family of answers. An example of a convergent question might be, "Who are the most likely presidential candidates for the next election?" The term *diverge*, on the other hand, is derived from the Latin words meaning to turn away, or to go in different directions. A divergent response is thus one that is out of the ordinary, not expected; and a divergent question is one that allows many possible responses. A divergent question in the same vein as the above example might be, "Who might be potential candidates for the next gubernatorial election?"

Traditionally schools have trained students to be convergent thinkers. Instead of encouraging them to seek many alternatives, the educational system has concentrated on factual information—the concept of one right answer. In preparing our gifted students for leadership, we must train them to think divergently. The leaders of the future must be able to identify a variety of options and directions if they are to lead our world out of its problems.

Just as teachers must learn to use divergent questioning and thinking in their classrooms, we must teach our gifted students to do the same. Students must be taught to question unsubstantiated information, to seek many possibilities when solving problems of all types. It is therefore important for teachers to help these students to understand the difference between convergent and divergent thinking, recognizing that each has a place in intellectual endeavor but breaking away from the convergent patterns that have been established over the many years of schooling.

Oral Communication Strategies

From the earliest years of school, students should be encouraged and given frequent opportunities to speak before groups. In the preschool years, the familiar "Show and Tell" not only gives children the chance to share their interests and to enjoy the "limelight" for a brief period but also provides them with practice in oral communication skills. (The clever teacher in the upper grades might find a way to expand on this primary strategy, giving older gifted students chances to share as well.) As children mature and progress through the grades, teachers should provide frequent opportunities for practice, as oral communication is an essential skill for effective leadership.

Within the language arts program, as well as in classes in the content areas (science, social studies, mathematics, health), all students should be called on regularly to share their readings, their areas of interest, and their knowledge gained from their studies. Although formal instruction in the art of public speaking is traditionally postponed until the secondary school, there are numerous ways in which the elementary school student can build oral communication skills within the language arts program and other areas of the curriculum. Some of these include:

1. Delivery of "campaign speeches" in connection with local, school, or simulated elections
2. Use of parliamentary procedure in school organizations
3. Practice of extemporaneous speaking through the use of imaginative topics (e.g., "Where does the light go when the light goes out?")
4. Organizing in debates on topics of current interest (e.g., the use of nuclear power, the legalization of marijuana, the relative merits of two political candidates)
5. Practice of oral interpretation (e.g., reading aloud a variety of examples of poetry, such as James Whitcomb Riley's "The Bear Story" or "Little Orphant Annie")
6. Use of choral reading
7. Regular practice of creative dramatics (improvisation) in the classroom.

The latter strategy, creative dramatics, involves actors in the improvisational development of a script simultaneously with the acting. In other words, the players "invent" the action as the drama progresses, with no prepared script to dictate their cues, lines, or movements. Creative dramatics is a most appropriate activity for the language arts program, as this technique has been shown to improve reading skills, and it motivates interest in the drama—a most valuable form of literature. Probably the best and most consulted volume in the area of creative dramatics is Viola Spolin's *Improvisation for the Theater: A Handbook of Teaching and Directing Techniques* (1963). Spolin believes that spontaneity brings about personal freedom, and she suggests seven "aspects of spontaneity":

1. *Games.* Spolin says that games provide an integrated experience— a "total self in a total environment"—that frees the player "to explore, adventure, and face all dangers he meets unafraid" (p. 6).

2. *Approval/Disapproval.* This aspect plays a part in spontaneity in that the need for judgment in a really free person no longer exists. Moving away from the concept of the teacher as authority, then, is an essential part of achieving spontaneity or personal freedom.

3. *Group Expression.* In theater, expression by the group takes precedence over individual triumph. As Spolin says, the actor who "steals the show" is a thief!

4. *Audience.* According to Spolin, if all who are involved in theater are striving for personal freedom, each member of the audience must as well be involved in personal experience. The importance of the audience cannot be overemphasized.

5. *Theater Techniques.* Spolin believes "When the actor knows 'in his bones' there are many ways to do and say one thing, techniques will come (as they must) from his total self. For it is by direct, dynamic awareness of an acting experience that experiencing and techniques are spontaneously wedded, freeing the student for the flowing, endless pattern of stage behavior. Theater games do this" (p. 14).

6. *Carrying the Learning Process into Daily Life.* Spolin observes that the world provides the material that makes up the theater, and that the actor will be able to grow artistically only on recognizing himself within that world.

7. *Physicalization.* The final aspect of spontaneity is what Spolin calls "physicalization," or the involvement of the actor/student in a personal concrete experience—one that enables the individual to communicate directly with her audience. This may be the aspect of spontaneity that is closest to the concept of improvisation, as improvisational theater involves few (if any) props or costumes, and the actor must create reality out of nothing.

Spolin's manual presents a comprehensive workshop plan for training student actors in theater, beginning with simple orientation activities and working through such techniques and concepts as the environment (immediate, general, and larger), acting with the whole body, movement on stage, refining awareness, technical effects, developing materials, character and emotion, rehearsal and performance, and post-mortem consideration of special problems. Inasmuch as the present text cannot include the degree of details that is needed for the thorough preparation of the student actor, the reader is referred to Spolin's manual for a step-by-step guide to the use of creative dramatics in the classroom.

Developing Listening Skills

The final aspect of communication that should be addressed is an area that has long been ignored in schools—the skill of listening. Listening has been defined in a variety of ways; however, most researchers would agree that it involves more than the efficient use of the hearing mechanism (that is, we can hear with our ears while not listening with our minds). Listening, then, might be best defined as a process by which sound is transformed into meaning within the mind. Why should listening occupy a portion of our time and attention within the language arts program? First, listening is the first of the language skills to develop in infancy, and thus it is sometimes referred to as the primary language skill. Second, it is apparent that efficiency in the other language skills—speaking, reading, and writing—increases in direct proportion to listening ability. Listening ability is prerequisite to the skills of phonetic analysis and auditory discrimination, as well as an essential part of interpersonal communication (Lundsteen, 1976; Donoghue, 1979).

Research has shown that listening skills can be improved by instruction, particularly if this instruction is integrated into the overall educational program for reinforcement through practical application. It is therefore incumbent on every teacher to plan instruction in every subject area, as well as in enrichment classes, to include practice in (and motivation for) the development of this most significant area of language facility. In gifted education, the development of effective listening skills is even more important, as gifted children frequently tend to monopolize conversation. Furthermore, the ability to listen and attend to the contributions of others is an essential skill for leadership.

How can the teacher foster effective listening skills in the gifted? The following guidelines may serve as the basis of a plan for incorporating listening skills practice into curriculum for the gifted:

1. Serve as a role model. Listen to students, encourage divergent responses and input, act on their ideas, and empathize when they share problems and concerns.

2. Discuss with the students the characteristics of a good listener. Help them to establish their own standards for listening.

3. Precede oral activities with introductions or background information that will help students know what to listen for (the purpose of listening) and how to listen (the process of listening). Encourage them to take notes on what is heard by recording main ideas from the presentation.

4. Make the environment conducive to good listening. Use relaxation and/or imagery activities before listening activities; minimize distractions, and present material that will be of interest to the students. Take into consideration the students' level of sophistication, and provide opportunities for interaction between teacher (or speaker) and students, as well as between and among students.

The following activities may be used within either academic or enrichment classes to strengthen listening skills in the various areas of the curriculum.

---

1. Use choral reading, or have students perform dramas, either memorizing brief sections or reading from printed scripts. The necessity to listen for one's cue will strengthen listening skills.

2. Limit the number of times that directions are given or that each word is dictated on a spelling test. Knowing that information will not be repeated will motivate the student to listen.

3. Divide the class into small groups. Have them discuss literary selections read in English class, oral presentations made by other students, or controversial subjects.

4. Teach the art of storytelling, and encourage students to tell stories to the class. Follow each such episode with a question period.

5. Take the students outdoors for observation. After comparing their lists of things observed, point out the need to observe with all of the senses. Instruct them to observe again, this time listing sounds, odors, and so on.

6. Provide practice in following oral directions; exercises that require observation of a specific sequence will be of greatest help. Gradually increase the number of steps in the sequence, to increase retention of directions.

7. Present themes that appear as variations in musical compositions. Play the compositions through without interruption, instructing students to raise their hands or otherwise indicate when they hear the theme.

8. Have students create art (any medium) to represent a piece of music played in class, a poem read by the teacher, a sound heard on the playground, and so on.

9. Play recordings containing a variety of sounds (rustling of leaves, ringing of bells, whistling of a train, crackling of a fire, crumpling of paper, etc.). Have students list the sounds they heard, and award a prize to the one who arrives at the greatest number of correct answers. (This activity can also be included in a learning center for individual work.)

10. Read good literature (prose, poetry, drama) to the class. Provide in advance a list of questions to which the answers may be determined from the reading; or have the students listen for specific writing techniques such as anachronism, hyperbole, alliteration, metaphor, simile, and so on.

11. Encourage the development of critical listening skills through exercises in distinguishing between fact and propaganda in advertising or between relevant and irrelevant facts in a discussion; by having students evaluate dramatic performances in a television drama; or by listening for bias in political speeches.

THE WRITING PROGRAM

Types of Writing

Expository writing is simply writing that provides information about or an explanation of a topic. There are many types of expository writing that can provide practice for students from the elementary grades through high school. Two good examples are:

1. Technical Writing: Using the terminology appropriate to a particular field of endeavor, the technical writer provides information about a specific area of interest.

2. Editorial Writing: Editorial writing presents the author's viewpoint about a given issue. Newspaper editorials and essays are typical examples of this type of expository writing.

Unlike expository writing (or exposition), creative writing is descriptive and is valued for its style more than for the information provided. Usually creative writing originates from the writer's imagination rather than from an outside source of information.

There are numerous sources of subject matter for both expository and creative writing. Some of the more popular products that might be selected as writing goals in teaching gifted students are:

1. Articles for newspaper or journal, based on topics on interest to the student

2. Poetry or creative stories written for periodicals that accept student work

3. Writings grouped by subject (e.g., a creative essay on some aspect of nature)

4. Use of story starters and endings

5. The morphological approach to story plotting (see end of this chapter).

Building Basic Writing Skills

A major goal in any language program for the gifted is for students to produce writing for consumption by others. However, they must first have a thorough command of the basic skills of writing. The following skills must be addressed individually and deliberately within the integrated language arts program.

Using Phrases, Clauses, and Sentences.   Along with the building of vocabulary and the ability to classify words according to part of speech and usage, students should learn to write and to distinguish between and among phrases, clauses, and sentences of all kinds. They must understand that phrases are groups of words that neither contain subject and predicate nor express a complete thought; they must also be able to recognize the different types of phrases—noun, verb, or prepositional—and their uses in sentences. The types of clauses (independent and subordinate) as well as their uses (e.g., adverbial) should also be learned. Until these elements have been mastered, the writing of effective, well-balanced sentences cannot be achieved. Finally, the classification of sentences (declarative, interrogative, imperative, or exclamatory, as well as simple, compound, complex, or compound complex) must be understood. Until the art of sentence writing has been conquered, it is not possible to write a well-organized paragraph—the backbone of any composition.

Writing Good Paragraphs.   Once the art of sentence writing has been mastered, the students can begin to learn the skill of paragraph organization. Most writers agree on three elements that comprise a well-written paragraph: unity (one and only one topic discussed throughout the paragraph, usually related to a topic sentence); coherence (tying together sentences in the paragraph with conjunctions or phrases to enable the reader to move from one sentence to another without breaking the trend of thought); and emphasis (a gradual progression of details elaborating on the main topic of the paragraph, leading up to and culminating in the most significant point to be made). Although these elements should be taught and emphasized in the teaching of paragraphing skills, it is perhaps more important that the teaching of paragraph writing be placed within the context of the writing program in general. Without an incentive for learning and an opportunity for applying these skills, much of what is learned will be lost when the need arises. For this reason, the methodology for teaching paragraph writing is deferred to the suggested sequence for the writing program, which follows this discussion.

Summarizing and Paraphrasing. As a sixth-grade science teacher, I once required each student to prepare a booklet in connection with a unit on astronomy. One of my more memorable occurrences was the grading of a section of a student's booklet in which he discussed the history of space travel. As I read the student's unusually well-organized, well-written treatise on the subject, I encountered the sentence, "The astronaut in the picture above is placing the American Flag on the surface of the Moon." Needless to say, neither picture nor astronaut was present.

In spite of our emphasis on the evils and the inherent dangers of plagiarism, students from elementary school through graduate school will continue to copy from encyclopedias, journals, and any other source they can find. Regardless of the students' ages, the reason is usually the same—they have never learned the skills of summarizing and paraphrasing. Like notetaking and outlining, these skills must be deliberately taught, and opportunities must be provided for practice. Further details will be covered in the section that follows.

Strategies for Teaching Writing

Cowan (1983) suggested that there are really only three stages to the writing process: creating what is to be said, shaping the writing for delivery to the reader, and completing the writing (or editing and rewriting). The following sequence provides a beginning for the teacher who wishes to help students to accomplish these purposes.

---

1. After teaching and providing practice in the writing of phrases, clauses, and sentences, explain about topic sentences. Provide practice in paragraph writing by using the following activities:
   a. Using an overhead transparency, project a well-written paragraph from which the topic sentence has been removed. Ask one student to read the paragraph aloud. Have students identify the main idea of the paragraph, starting with several options from which to choose and working gradually to stating the main idea in sentence form. Project the paragraph again, and help the class compose a topic sentence that effectively sets the

stage for the remainder of the paragraph. Repeat this procedure, using paragraphs that are unrelated to each other, until the quality of the topic sentences has begun to improve.

b. Distribute to each student a page containing two or three paragraphs on familiar topics with their topic sentences omitted (all paragraphs should be different and each one should have a number). Ask the students to write, on a separate sheet of paper, a topic sentence for each paragraph (numbering each topic sentence to agree with the paragraph it represents). Have students exchange topic sentence sheets with their neighbors and develop paragraphs of two to four sentences based on the new topic sentences. Direct the students to compare their paragraphs with those on which the topic sentences were written. Using several paragraphs as examples, discuss this activity.

c. Distribute to all students a brief article consisting of five to seven well-written paragraphs with their topic sentences omitted. Have them write a topic sentence for each of these paragraphs and then combine these ideas into one paragraph summarizing the article, adding a topic sentence that sets the tone of the summary. Have several students read, compare, and discuss their summary paragraphs.

d. Read short passages aloud to the class; after each such reading, have students write in their own words what they heard. Begin with sentences and progress gradually to paragraphs. Follow this procedure with brief lectures on which students take notes in their own words and write paraphrased accounts of the lecture material. Finally, provide the class with identical copies of various articles and instruct them to rewrite the articles in their own words. Encourage students to share their versions to demonstrate the many different ways of wording the same idea.

e. To illustrate the concept of unity, distribute paragraphs into which sentences that are not directly related to the topic sentence have been inserted. Instruct them to identify and delete these sentences. Discuss.

f. Point out examples of words that link sentences together to assure coherence (e.g., *moreover, nonetheless, either/or, inasmuch as, consequently*). Using a good film (see Chapter 15 for ideas), have students take notes on words and phrases that are used to link sentences together into a coherent pattern of thought. Distribute paragraphs from which the linking words have been removed; have students supply conjunctions or phrases, linking the sentences together to form a coherent paragraph.

g. Project a topic sentence about a subject with which the students are all familiar. Have them brainstorm facts about this topic and then turn these facts into short sentences. Demonstrate methods of combining short sentences into better, more complex sentences. Then help them select their most significant sentences on the appointed topic, combining them into about five succinct, well-written sentences and numbering them in order of their significance for the topic. Next instruct them to combine these sentences into a coherent paragraph which builds from the least significant to the most significant point. Compare the paragraphs, and repeat the process until sufficient practice has been provided.

h. Provide an outline of ideas on a given topic. Each main heading (Roman numeral) should indicate the main idea of a paragraph, and the subheads (capital letters) should provide the "meat" on which the topic will be developed. Instruct students to write topic sentences for the subheads, arranging them in logical order and tying them together into coherent paragraphs.

i. Distribute a short article (approximately four to six paragraphs) that discusses a topic with which the students are familiar (or at least have sufficient background to understand). Instruct the students to read the article and summarize it in one paragraph (i.e., one sentence to represent each paragraph in the article). Discuss this method of summarizing.

2. Provide practice in topic expansion. The futures wheel format presented in Chapter 4 provides a convenient method of expanding a topic for discussion. Simply have the students select a topic, use it as the hub of their wheel, and branch out by means of the "spokes" into subtopics that can be discussed.

3. Provide frequent opportunities for writing practice, using the following strategies as a beginning:

a. Set aside a regular time, at least once each week, for a free writing period. During this time students should select a topic, expand it using the method suggested above, brainstorming in small groups, or other strategies for producing ideas, and write for five to ten minutes without interruption. During this period they should not stop for any reason, as spelling, grammar, and other technicalities will not be considered for this exercise. No grading of this work should be done, as the purpose of the activity is to encourage free expression and a flow of ideas.

b. Encourage the writing of journals in one or more classes. This type of journal can serve several purposes. In addition to (indeed, often more important than) the provision of writing practice, the journal can provide gifted students the opportunity to share with the teacher valuable insights into their own problems, concerns, and triumphs. Journals can confide, "Would you please elaborate on the reasons why drug use is so dangerous?" or "Please have a talk with Jennifer; she is depressed this week, and I am worried about her." or "I'm so excited—I finally conquered the Base 2 system!" A multipurpose strategy, the journal can be an invaluable aid to the teacher who wishes to know the students better.

c. Whether you are the English teacher for a given group or you simply have the students one day each week for academic enrichment, plan some formal writing activity at least once each month (and preferably once each week, particularly if you have the total responsibility for the group's language instruction). This assignment can be as varied as the types of writing— an essay one time for submission to the local newspaper's essay contest, or a class contest for the submission of the best short story or poem to a periodical that publishes children's work. (The editorial page of the local newspaper can provide a good variety of topics.) And by all means do not overlook the exciting possibilities of having the class create and produce its own publication—a journal of nonfiction articles, a book of poetry, or an anthology of Shakespeare plays rewritten in story form for younger children. The possibilities for enjoyable projects that will bring students to love writing are endless.

d. Use subjective testing methods, allowing students to synthesize their learnings and transfer factual information to the application level. This method not only fosters higher levels of thinking in the students but provides excellent writing practice as well. (When this method of testing is used for subjects other than English—and even when testing nongrammatical aspects of English such as literature—encourage the students to use the dictionary and/or the thesaurus to avoid spelling errors and improve the quality of their written expression.)

Proofreading and Editing. One of the most important skills that must be acquired by a writer is the ability to proofread and edit. Because it is often difficult to see problems in one's own writing, this skill is not easily acquired. Some suggestions for teaching these skills are given here.

---

1. Encourage students to "think like an editor/publisher"; remind them that even the best writers must submit their work to editors,

who make corrections/suggestions for the improvement of the writing. Instill in them an appreciation of the importance of proofreading their own work before submitting it to anyone else.

2. Teach the basic proofreader's marks (e.g., symbols to insert a word, to begin a new paragraph, etc.), and provide typed, double-spaced passages for students to edit.

3. Have students work in pairs, editing each other's work.

4. Provide "noncreative" writings for students to improve. (A sub-standard small town newspaper can offer good material for this purpose.) Train them in the use of the thesaurus to substitute more interesting words for underlined words in the passages provided.

5. Provide practice in editing and proofreading by critiquing each other's work. This can be done in small groups, with students exchanging within their groups and helping each other, or the teacher can assign each student's paper a number, then collect and redistribute all papers anonymously for editing. (One approach to preserving anonymity is to have each student use his or her mother's first and maiden name as a pseudonym. In this way the teacher can keep a running evaluation on student progress while guaranteeing that grades will not be influenced by spelling, grammar, and other formalities used [or not used] in creative writing.) In any case, the students should be encouraged to proofread and improve their own work (using the thesaurus whenever possible) before submitting it to an "editor."

6. After students have completed creative writings of their own, have them follow one step at a time to improve their work: first proofread for errors; then use the thesaurus in an attempt to make the expression more descriptive and interesting.

Teaching Poetry Writing to Students. Poetry is like music—no one will ever hear or read all of it. It is also like music in another curious way—students often claim not to like it, although they have rarely given it a chance. The creative teacher has the power to teach children of all ages not only to love poetry written by others but also to create their own poetry as an extension of their own selves, their own emotions. Since many teachers have never attempted to write poetry themselves, the following suggestions are made for beginning a unit in this delightful type of creative writing.

---

1. Read good poetry to your students. Include not only classics such as Poe's *Annabel Lee* and Thoreau's *Walden,* but the more modern

works of Shel Silverstein and other popular living poets as well. Encourage students to bring in poetry that they like for sharing with the class.

2. Provide background information when this information is relevant and interesting; do not force students to listen to biographical data on every poet whose work you will share. Present information on how various types of poetry originated and what their patterns are (e.g., haiku, three-line nature poetry originally written by Japanese suitors to their lady loves, consists of seven lines with a specific pattern: five syllables on the first line, seven on the second, and five on the third).

3. Bring in authors or poets—either through their writing or in person as guest speakers. Include people who are known for accomplishments other than poetry writing (e.g., Abraham Lincoln) as well as ordinary people who write poetry simply for their own enjoyment.

4. Write poetry together as a class; write the class poem on the chalkboard or overhead transparency as it is created, and have the students copy it for themselves.

5. Provide the first line of a poem, and have the students complete the poem. If you are working on rhyming poetry, first brainstorm words that rhyme with the last word of your first line, to give them a start. If you are working on free verse, no such preparation will be necessary. (Note: While the students write their poetry, the teacher should write poetry of her own to share after the students have read theirs.)

6. Examine as a class the styles and techniques used by popular poets. Have students emulate these poets to provide a variety of writing experience on which to base their own styles.

7. Provide time and motivation for students to write poetry; encourage them to express themselves through poetry and to retain what they write in journals and personal diaries.

As evidenced by the many "everyday people" who indulge in poetry writing as therapy, as hobbies, even for sharing with others, this form of literature can contribute greatly to personal freedom and self-expression. It is therefore a marvelous tool for teachers of the gifted (or any other students!) to use to foster creative thinking and writing in their students.

Publishing Student Work

Many publications accept student work. Teachers are encouraged to secure information from these sources regarding their procedures for submission of original work, and to take advantage of the many opportunities to publish the work of the good writers in their classes. Nothing is more satisfying and motivating for students (or, for that matter, for adults) than seeing their work in print!

The following listing suggests several publications that encourage the submission of student writing. Teachers are encouraged to contact these sources for further details. (For best service, enclose a self-addressed, stamped envelope when making inquiries.)

American Newspaper Carrier, P.O. Box 15300, Winston-Salem, NC 27103

Boy's Life, 1325 Walnut Hill Lane, Irving, TX 75062

Creative Kids, P.O. Box 6448, Mobile, Al 36660

Child Life, Children's Digest, Children's Playmate, Humpty Dumpty's Magazine, Jack & Jill, and Turtle Magazine for Preschool Kids, 1100 Waterway Blvd., Box 567, Indianapolis, IN 46206

Ebony Jr., 820 South Michigan Avenue, Chicago, IL 60605

Highlights for Children, 803 Church Street, Honesdale, PA 18531

Microkids: The Magazine for Kids who Love Computers, 133 Fifth Avenue, New York, NY 10003

Scholastic Scope, 50 West 44th Street, New York, NY 10036

Seventeen, 850 Third Avenue, New York, NY 10022

Stone Soup, The Magazine By Children, The Children's Art Foundation, Box 83, Santa Cruz, CA 95063

Teen, 8490 Sunset Blvd., Los Angeles, CA 90069

OTHER IDEAS FOR ENHANCING LANGUAGE ARTS INSTRUCTION

1. Utilize film as a central stimulus for creative writing or art. Suggestions for using two excellent examples, *The Stonecutter* and *Why Man Creates*, are detailed in Chapter 15.
2. Have students read elementary versions of a well-known play such as Shakespeare's *The Merchant of Venice*. Two such versions useful for the elementary gifted classroom are included in *Shake Hands with Shakespeare* and *The Enchanted Island*, inexpensive paperback books published by Scholastic Services. Using these two references (the first providing elementary level scripts and the second giving narrative summaries of the plays), have students write, cast, and produce their own version of the original dramas. Older students can research the more memorable and well-known passages from the original play and include some of these passages in Shakespeare's own language. (Another approach is to rewrite a

Shakespearean drama, or major parts of it, in modern vernacular, using modern problems, scenes, and characters that parallel the original play.)

3. Use Lewis Carroll's delightful fantasy poem "Jabberwocky" (from *Through a Looking Glass*) as an enjoyable way to practice identifying the parts of speech and their usage in sentences. ("Jabberwocky" is a nonsense poem; have students analyze the entire poem as to part of speech, diagram the sentences, etc.)

4. Teach the morphological approach to story plotting, which Fran Stryker (Shallcross, 1981) developed and used in the creation of hundreds of different plots for his famous movie serial, *The Lone Ranger*. To use this strategy, prepare a matrix as shown below:

Characters	Goals	Obstacles	Outcomes

Proceed as follows:

a. Column One: Brainstorm and list in this column all of the possible characters around whom a story plot might revolve. They can be any types of characters you wish (e.g., Joe Palooka, Bambi, a cyclops, a herd of cattle, a stuffed elephant).

b. Column Two: Covering up and disregarding your responses in Column One, brainstorm and list in Column Two all of the goals that a character might wish to achieve in life (for example, fame, riches, freedom).

c. Column Three: Again disregarding your previous responses, list here all of the obstacles that might prevent characters from reaching their goals in life (an accident, a lost key, being arrested, going bankrupt).

d. Column Four: Covering the first three columns, brainstorm and list in this column all the story outcomes that you can think of (e.g., they lived happily ever after, death, won the sweepstakes).

e. Call on a student to give the last four digits of his or her telephone number (or social security number). Using the first digit, count down to that number response in Column One, and circle it (in other words, if the first digit called out by the student is 5, circle the fifth response in the first column). Continue in like manner until you have circled one response in each column. Develop a plot based on the combination of these four elements—character, goal, obstacle, and result (Shallcross, 1981).

REFERENCES

Barbe, W. B., & Myers, R. M. (1971). Developing listening ability in children. In S. Duker (Ed.), *Teaching listening in the elementary school: Readings* (pp. 31–33). Metuchen, NJ: Scarecrow Press.

Baskin, B. H., & Harris, K. H. (1980). *Books for the gifted child.* New York: R. R. Bowker.

Beery, A. (1971). Listening activities in the elementary school. In S. Duker (Ed.), *Teaching listening in the elementary school: Readings* (pp. 31–33). Metuchen, NJ: Scarecrow Press.

Bennett, W. (1984, September 5). Important works in the humanities for students. *Education Week, 4*(1), L29.

Bergman, F. L. (1982). *The English teacher's handbook: An ideabook for middle and secondary schools* (2nd ed.). Boston: Allyn and Bacon.

Canfield, R. (1971). Approaches to listening improvement. In S. Duker (Ed.), *Teaching listening in the elementary school: Readings* (pp. 31–33). Metuchen, NJ: Scarecrow Press.

Casebeer, B. (1981). *Using the right/left brain: An auditory imagery program.* Novato, CA: Academic Therapy Publications.

Coleman, D. R. (1983). Effects of the use of a writing scale by gifted primary students. *Gifted Child Quarterly, 27,* 114–121.

Cornett, C. E., & Cornett, C. F. (1980). *Bibliotherapy: The right book at the right time.* Bloomington, IN: Phi Delta Kappa.

Cowan, E. (1983). *Writing: Brief edition.* Glenview, IL: Scott, Foresman.

Crocetti, G. (1987). *The Graduate Record Exam: General (Aptitude) Test* (2nd ed.). New York: Arco Publishing.

Donoghue, M. R. (1979). *The child and the English language arts.* Dubuque, IA: William C. Brown.

Frasier, M. M., & McCannon, C. (1981). Using bibliotherapy with gifted children. *Gifted Child Quarterly, 25,* 81–85.

Guilford, J. P. (1967). *The nature of human intelligence.* New York: McGraw-Hill.

Isaacs, A. F. (1963). Should the gifted preschool child be taught to read? *Gifted Child Quarterly, 5,* 72–77.

Kauffman, D. L., Jr. (1976). *Teaching the future: A guide to future-oriented education.* Palm Springs, CA: ETC Publications.

Lundsteen, S. (1976). *Children learn to communicate.* Englewood Cliffs, NJ: Prentice-Hall.

Martin, C. E., & Cramond, B. (1984). A checklist for assessing and developing creative reading. *G/C/T, 32,* 22–24.

Master, D. L. (1983). Writing and the gifted child. *Gifted Child Quarterly, 27,* 162–168.

Mindell, P., & Stracher, D. (1980). Assessing reading and writing of the gifted: The warp and woof of the language program. *Gifted Child Quarterly, 24,* 72–80.

Polette, N., & Hamlin, M. (1980). *Exploring books with gifted children.* Littleton, CO: Libraries Unlimited.

San Diego City Schools (No Date). Teaching appreciative, attentive and analytical listening. In S. Duker (Ed.), *Teaching, listening in the elementary school: Readings* (pp. 31–33). Metuchen, NJ: Scarecrow Press.

Shallcross, D. (1981). *Teaching creative behavior.* Englewood Cliffs, NJ: Prentice-Hall.

Smith, J. A. (1967). *Creative teaching of reading and literature in the elementary school.* Boston: Allyn and Bacon.

Spolin, V. (1963). *Improvisation for the theater: A handbook of teaching and directing techniques.* Evanston, IL: Northwestern University Press.

Witty, P. (1974). Rationale for fostering creative reading in the gifted and the creative. In M. Labuda (Ed.), *Creative reading for gifted learners: A design for excellence* (pp. 8–24). Newark, DE: International Reading Association.

Wolf, M. H., & Miller, V. B. (No date). *Theatre's different demands: An approach to the classroom teaching of plays.* Stratford, CT: Connecticut State Department of Education and The American Shakespeare Festival Theatre.

Wolf, M. H., & Miller, V. B. (No date). *New approaches to teaching Shakespeare: Twelfth Night, Romeo and Juliet, King Lear, Julius Caesar, Hamlet.* Stratford, CT: Center for Theatre Techniques in education.

12

Mathematics Education in the Gifted Classroom

Problem solving must be the focus of school mathematics in the 1980s. . . . Performance in problem solving will measure the effectiveness of our personal and national possession of mathematical competence.
The National Council of Teachers of Mathematics

A survey of the literature in the area of mathematics education, or a conversation with any mathematics educator who keeps in touch with current trends, will reveal a strong emphasis on problem solving as the most essential mathematics skill for tomorrow's leaders. Certainly no thinking person can discount the need for computational skills, but the solving of real-life problems is the most important use of the mathematics that is taught throughout the school years. It is unfortunate that today's mathematics curricula, like so many other areas, still retain vestiges of Industrial Revolution teaching. Perhaps mathematics is the area in which the Third Wave should begin, since the technological society is centered around the use of a mathematically based tool—the computer.

In most areas of the country, mathematics programs for the gifted consist largely of providing more problems to work or simply allowing those individuals to progress at their own pace through the same material as the average math students. Because of the scarcity of mathematically proficient teachers in most elementary (and even many secondary) schools, few gifted students have access to teachers who can take them as far as they can and should go in the sequence of mathematical learnings. The more-of-the-same approach is clearly not enough.

What approaches should be taken in teaching mathematics to gifted students? What skills should be emphasized, and how should they be practiced? What content should be included in the mathematics curriculum to enable students to see the relevance of what they are learning? Does the use of calculators in the classroom cause students to be incompetent in basic computation skills? What place should computers have in the gifted program? These and other questions will be explored in this chapter.

DIFFERENTIATING THE MATHEMATICS CURRICULUM FOR THE GIFTED

In mathematics, as in all other areas of the curriculum, there are specific principles that should be considered in planning learning experiences for the gifted. These principles, designed to provide integrated instruction not only in mathematics computation but in concept and application as well, must take into consideration the characteristics of gifted people which distinguish them from their less able peers. It is important to recognize that it is rare for any student to be equally gifted in all subject areas; therefore, the mathematics curriculum must be even further differentiated for those students who are specifically gifted in mathematics.

Gifted students learn more readily than their less able peers and retain what they learn, easily transferring these concepts to new challenges. They are able to recognize patterns and relationships, and to draw valid conclusions from the results of their experimentation. Their ability to think in an open-ended, logical, and abstract manner enables them to solve more complex problems and to generate new problems out of their solutions. Gifted students are intellectually curious and welcome new challenges that stimulate higher levels of thinking. Considering these characteristics, the mathematics program for the gifted should be based on the following principles:

1. Mathematics is developmental in nature; it is not possible to skip the basic concepts and proceed directly to the more advanced areas. The teaching of the basic mathematics skills therefore must progress sequentially. The mathematics curriculum for the gifted, however, should compact the concepts and skills, allowing students to progress at their own pace.

2. The mathematics curriculum for all students must involve meaningful practice (not simply rote memory and repetitive drill) in the skills taught. The curriculum for the gifted student should be

individualized, with practice exercises progressing quickly to realistic, more sophisticated problems.

3. Whenever possible, mathematics instruction for the gifted should utilize the terminology of the discipline (e.g., avoid "take away" even with young children).

4. As a major life skill, mathematics should pervade the entire curriculum. Exercises using mathematics should be purposefully included in science (metric conversions in measurement), in social studies (map study using scale, or use of graphs), in language arts (learning the vocabulary of mathematics), and even in physical education (e.g., measurement of body functions or scorekeeping).

5. Any teaching of a new skill should be accompanied by instruction designed to help the student understand the logic behind the skill (e.g., multiplication as repeat addition). Without conceptual understanding, there will be little if any transfer of the skills learned to the solving of real problems.

6. The ability of gifted people to think in abstract terms enables them to solve more complex problems and to perform mathematical tasks mentally at earlier ages. As early as possible, gifted students should be given the tools of "short-cut" mathematics and taught other techniques that will increase their efficiency in mental computation and problem solving.

7. All methods of problem solving have common elements; working with many types of problems will strengthen the student's ability to solve the real problems of everyday life. The mathematics curriculum for the gifted should expose students to logic (inductive and deductive reasoning, as well as the logic of philosophy and mathematics), creative problem solving, and the scientific method.

8. The mathematics curriculum for the gifted should emphasize the higher levels of thinking—logical thinking and reasoning, analysis and synthesis, evaluation and decision making—as well as the scientific method of problem solving (discovery/inquiry in mathematics, gathering and analysis of data, etc.).

9. The "basics" of mathematics education, especially for the gifted student, should encompass not only computational skills but also problem solving, everyday applications of mathematics, estimation skills enabling the individual to recognize obvious errors in problem solving results, geometry, measurement, use of graphics (tables, charts, graphs), use of probability for prediction, and skill in using calculators and computers (NCTM, 1980).

ENRICHING THE MATHEMATICS CURRICULUM
FOR THE GIFTED

If we believe that gifted students must be provided with differentiated educational opportunities in order to "realize their contribution to self and society" (Marland, 1972, p. 10), then we must enrich the curriculum for these students from the earliest grades throughout their school years. Perhaps the most essential principle on which to base mathematics curriculum for the gifted is that they must be taught individually and allowed to progress through the prescribed curriculum at their own pace. Regardless of the structure within which the individualized instruction is delivered, there are several ways in which mathematics enrichment can be built into the program:

1. A diagnostic-prescriptive system, such as that suggested for the teaching of reading to gifted students (Chapter 11), may be adapted to the mathematics program, enabling each student to work at his or her own pace.

2. As basic concepts and skills are mastered, more sophisticated and realistic problems applying the concepts learned can be provided for practice.

3. When students have mastered all concepts and skills in the prescribed curriculum for the year, explore other aspects of mathematics that are not a part of the regular curriculum in higher grades (e.g., tesselations, probabilities).

4. Use mathematics-related topics (e.g., statistical research, number theory) in the gifted resource room to enrich the students' mathematical backgrounds without repeating basic topics covered in the regular curriculum.

Any (or a combination) of the above approaches can be used or adapted in schools or districts that do not permit students to move on to concepts or skills that are traditionally covered in higher grades. The ideal situation, of course, would be to permit gifted students to begin each year's mathematics instruction at the level they reached the previous year. Bartkovich and George (1980) suggest the following course sequence for students gifted in mathematics:

Algebra I	Trigonometry
Algebra II	Analytic Geometry
Algebra III	Calculus
Geometry	

In any case, there are many opportunities for enriching the mathematics curriculum for gifted students, whether or not acceleration is feasible. Some methods or topics that might be considered are presented in this section.

Problem Solving in Mathematics

In *An Agenda for Action: Recommendations for School Mathematics of the 1980s*, the National Council of Teachers of Mathematics (NCTM) recommended that problem solving be made the major focus of school mathematics for this decade. Pointing out that this skill involves much more than the typical word problems found in traditional texts, the NCTM suggested that educators give attention to the following aspects of problem solving:

- Application of mathematics to solving real-world problems
- Methods of gathering, organizing, and interpreting information; drawing and testing inferences from data; and communicating results
- Use of problem-solving capacities of computers to extend traditional problem-solving approaches and to implement new strategies of interaction and simulation
- Use of imagery, visualization, and spatial concepts

The report further called attention to the characteristics of a scientific attitude that have been noted in previous chapters of this text (intellectual curiosity, openmindedness, and willingness to take risks, to question, to make intelligent guesses, to experiment) as prerequisite to effective problem solving.

With respect to the education of our gifted youth, the NCTM recommends that programs be based on sequential enrichment experiences providing problem-solving training and practice, rather than on mere acceleration.

The Creative Education Foundation, sponsor of the internationally known Creative Problem Solving Institute, has developed a number of materials relating the Osborn-Parnes creative problem-solving approach to specific areas. In a booklet entitled *Creative Problem Solving in Mathematics* (Noller, Heintz, and Blaeuer, 1978), the authors define creative problem solving (as applied to mathematics) as follows:

> By CREATIVE . . . we mean looking at a problem in a new way . . . from one . . . or more perspectives . . . or points of view . . . looking for some new angles . . . at least for you . . . the one who is searching for the solution.
>
> By PROBLEM . . . we mean any situation . . . involving such elements as number . . . shape . . . pattern . . . equation . . . proof . . . etc. . . . . that can be investigated . . . using methods and analyses peculiar to mathematics.

> By SOLVING . . . we mean finding . . . or describing . . . ways to answer . . . or satisfy . . . the requirements . . . or restrictions . . . set by the problem.

Encouraging people to look at the world (and at mathematical problems) from a different perspective, the authors continue by saying, "we are talking about APPROACHING IN NEW WAYS . . . the usual types of mathematical problems that we are quite familiar with. This involves a PROCESS . . . a method . . . a format . . . for helping us . . . to be better mathematical problem solvers" (p. 9). Pointing out that most people solve mathematical problems in convergent ways, these authors challenge the reader to keep an open mind—to use divergent methods of problem solving. Why is this approach particularly suited to working with gifted students? First, we know that mathematics teachers typically require their students to work problems in the traditional manner; often it is immaterial that the answer is correct, if the method used to derive it was not exactly as explained in the text. If we are to encourage divergent thinking, flexibility, and inventiveness in our gifted students, we must permit them to explore different methods of solving problems. Second, creativity and creative problem solving are strategies that are commonly identified with gifted education. For these reasons, the CPSM (Creative Problem Solving in Mathematics) method is most appropriate for enriching the mathematics skills of our gifted students.

For many years I have presented workshops on creativity. In one of my favorite activities I project a transparency that looks like Figure 12–1 and I ask the audience to count the squares silently and then share their answers. Since many of the people who attend these sessions have some knowledge of creativity, it is rare now to have anyone answer the expected sixteen. Those who are new to creativity may find a seventeenth (the large perimeter square) and stop; most will find between twenty and thirty. By counting every combination of 1×1 (sixteen squares), 2×2 (nine squares), 3×3 (four squares), and 4×4 squares (one square), or by using mathematical progression formulas, one can reach the number of thirty squares. When a student of mine once found those thirty plus one more, I asked her to go to the screen and show us the thirty-first one. With a large smile, she approached the front of the room and pointed confidently to the word "squares" in the heading at the top of my transparency. Until recently, this had been my most creative response. Then a colleague attending my convention session on "Fostering Creativity in the Home" suggested a very large number (which I have since forgotten). When I asked him to explain, he reported that he regularly used the same technique and that one of his students had seen the figure as three-dimensional, counting all of the squares that would have existed in such a cube. Now, *this* was divergent thinking!

To solve problems creatively in mathematics, Bartalo (1983) suggests the use of methods similar to those used in solving other types

Figure 12–1   How many squares?

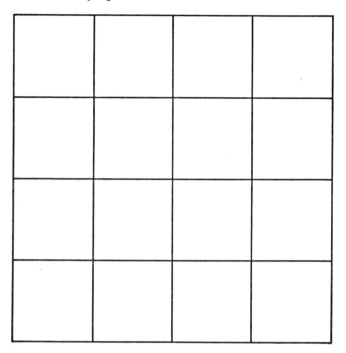

of problems. Adapting LTM's creative problem-solving approach to mathematics, the teacher should simply select word problems that might be solved in different ways, then take gifted students through the process of creative problem solving: Problem Perception and Definition (gathering all of the data and determining exactly what the problem is that must be solved), Creative Thinking (finding different ways of solving the problem), Analysis (determining the most efficient way of solving the problem), Evaluation (solving the problem), and Implementation (verifying the solution by applying it to different uses). Let your gifted students take it from there—the sky is the limit!

Tesselations

Tesselations are simply geometric patterns that completely cover a surface with no gaps between figures and no overlapping. A figure that fits this description is said to tesselate a plane. A tesselation is regular if it uses only one type of regular polygon (such as a rhombus or an equilateral triangle); if a tesselation uses two or more types of regular polygons, it is semiregular. In either type of tesselation, polygons must be arranged edge to edge. Examples of regular and semiregular tesselations are shown in Figure 12–2.

Figure 12–2

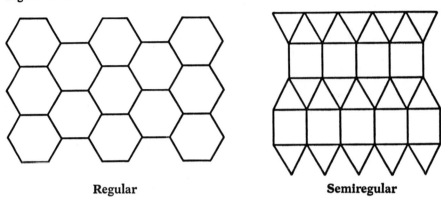

Regular	Semiregular

It is important to note that not every type of regular polygon will tesselate. In order to tesselate, a polygon must be able to be arranged edge to edge with other polygons of the same type, with no gaps or overlapping. An equilateral triangle, a square, and a regular hexagon will tesselate, but some other regular polygons (such as octagons) will not. To determine whether or not a regular polygon will tesselate, simply let s represent the number of sides and divide $2s$ by $s-2$. If the result is a whole number (no decimals and no remainders), the polygon will tesselate.

Tesselations are found in art; for example, M. C. Escher, known for his unique style, made wide use of the technique in his woodcuts, lithographs, and engravings. Their use, however, is widely recommended for the enhancement of mathematics teaching, as they help students become confortable with geometric figures. Thus, tesselations provide an excellent tool for the academic enrichment of gifted students.

Probability and Statistics

In Chapter 3, the use of statistics in research was presented as an important tool for gifted students to master. Basic concepts of statistics are also closely related to mathematics, however, and their introduction within the mathematics curriculum could well precede their application for research purposes. Since this topic is treated rather thoroughly in the research chapter, the techniques will not be discussed here. However, a specific area of statistics that commonly interests gifted students—probability—will be presented as an additional topic for mathematics enrichment.

Games of chance (probability) are well known to today's students, as afternoon television abounds with game shows. Players of board games such as Monopoly and Backgammon rely largely on chance for winning, and newscasters regularly report winners of the lottery—a game of chance often operated by state governments for producing revenue. Even in academic testing, probability enters into the discussion when older students speculate on their likelihood of success resulting from the guess factor on standardized tests. Nonetheless, despite the interest that students have demonstrated in the area of probability, little attention has been given to this topic in the mathematics curriculum.

To teach probability, first demonstrate that there are 36 possible combinations of dice throws (computed by multiplying 6 spots by 6 spots): 1–1, 1–2, 2–1, 1–3, 3–1, 1–4, 4–1, 1–5, 5–1, 1–6, 6–1, 2–2, 2–3, 3–2, 2–4, 4–2, 2–5, 5–2, 2–6, 6–2, 3–3, 3–4, 4–3, 3–5, 5–3, 3–6, 6–3, 4–4, 4–5, 5–4, 4–6, 6–4, 5–5, 5–6, 6–5, 6–6. Next have students generate the probability of throwing each of the possible combinations of spots. (The probability of throwing a one is 0/36, since no die face is blank; a two can be thrown only one way, with each die having one spot, thus the probability of throwing a two is 1/36; the probability of throwing a three is 2/36, since a three can be obtained only two ways: by a one on the first die and a two on the second, or by the reverse; and so on.) Then have students throw dice 36 times, recording the number of spots appearing on each throw. Help the students to see the number of times each combination appears, and connect this information into the above probabilities.

Other activities with probability might include dealing cards into various sizes of hands (e.g., 10 for gin rummy, 13 for bridge, 5 for poker) and computing the probability (or "odds") of any player's being dealt all four suits, all four aces, or all black cards. Students might also enjoy recording and analyzing tosses of a coin, the frequency of left-handers in each grade in your school, the number of public address system announcements made by the principal each day, and so on. The possibilities for probability are innumerable!

Estimation

Estimation skills are used every day in life. Students use estimation when they figure the distances they ride their bicycles, when they calculate the time they have left to play before Mother comes home, or when they decide on the hour that they can meet at the park after completing their Saturday morning chores. The bowler must estimate the angle that the ball must take to eliminate a spare, and the game-show contestant must estimate just how hard to spin the wheel to avoid the "Lose one turn" slot. The wise shopper makes estimates to determine which size of detergent is the better buy, and we have all seen the familiar "How many beans are in this jar?" contest. In spite of the frequent need for estimation ability, however, this skill is rarely included as a regular part of the mathematics curriculum.

There are many ways in which estimation power can be achieved; some examples of estimation exercises are presented here.

---

1. Estimate which of several jars of different sizes will hold the largest volume of water.
2. By counting windows, doors, floor tiles, tables, desks, or other familiar items of standard size, estimate the size of a room or a building.
3. Estimate the height of a tree, a telephone pole, or a fence by comparing it to your own height.
4. Estimate the price of a $69.99 bicycle on sale for 20 percent off.
5. Use sampling methods to estimate the number of words in an essay, the number of polka dots on a shirt, the number of sheets in a stack of paper, and so on.
6. Estimate the square root of 88 by recognizing that it will be between the square root of 81 (9) and the square root of 100 (10).
7. Estimate the product of 2,895 ×4.103 (round 2,895 to 3,000, and multiply by 4).

The Metric System

Some years ago, it was recommended that the United States convert from our English system of measurement to the metric system which is used by most of the world. Although some frenzied efforts were made to teach metrics in the schools, and the use of metrics is still accorded some attention in mathematics texts, many teachers have not yet become comfortable with the metric system themselves! Nonetheless, many materials are available for this purpose. And, since the idea of mathematics enrichment for the gifted implies the provision of differentiated curriculum, the metric system is an ideal place to begin. To explain metric measurement to students, follow these steps:

---

1. Obtain one meter stick for each two students in the class. To instill the concept of metric size in the students' minds, have them measure everything they can find, using meters, centimeters, and

millimeters. Conduct similar activities using liters and milliliters, grams and kilograms, Celsius and Fahrenheit, and so on.

2. Teach students the rough equivalents of the metric system and the English system (a liter is a little more than a quart; a meter is a little longer than a yard; there are approximately 2.5 cm in an inch).

3. Teach the basic terminology of the metric system, using etymology wherever possible to help students make associations and thus retain more effectively what they have learned (e.g., *centi-* as a Latin prefix meaning 100th, *deci-* meaning 10th, etc.).

4. Help students discover the concepts—not simply memorize the facts—related to equivalencies within the metric system (milliliters=cubic centimeters; 10 mm = 10/1000, or 1/100, of a meter, or 1 centimeter; etc.).

5. Use metrics for classroom measurements, particularly in connection with science demonstrations and experiments, whenever possible. Relate the metric system to our own decimal system, which is also based on intervals of ten.

Combinations and Permutations

In considering the probability of any given event actually occurring, it is often necessary to know how many different events are possible. To determine the path that might have been taken by a lost child, for example, it would be helpful to know how many different paths (or combinations of paths) he could have followed. In preparing a strategy for defensive play in a football game, a coach may need to know how many different plays might be developed from combining the various steps of these plays in different ways. To determine the total number of different events that might occur in any situation, we compute combinations or permutations. Combinations simply consider the number of groupings into which the elements can be placed; combinations have no regard for sequence. For example, if six students are to be divided into pairs, and neither member of a pair will be "first in line," then we use the combination method. In this case, we can group the students AB, AC, AD, AE, AF, BC, BD, BE, BF, CD, CE, CF, DE, DF, or EF—fifteen possible combinations. If, on the other hand, each member of a pair will perform some task, and the one to perform first will have an advantage over the other, then sequence may be significant. In such a case, we could have AB, or BA, AC or CA, AD or DA, etc., for twice the number of sequenced pairs. We refer to this type of grouping as permutation.

In working with only a few individuals, it is a simple matter to figure and count the number of possible combinations (or permutations) that can be made. If the numbers are large, however, the problem can take an inordinate amount of time to solve by the above method. For this reason, mathematicians have developed formulas for figuring combinations and permutations. The formula for a combination is:

$$C(n,r) = \frac{n!}{r! \, (n-2) \, !}$$

Applying this formula to our above example, C would represent the number of possible combinations, n would represent the total number of students (6), and r would represent the number of students in each grouping (2). The ! represents "factorial"—the product obtained by multiplying a given number by every number below it, down to 1. Thus $n!$ in this case would be 6! or $6 \times 5 \times 4 \times 3 \times 2 \times 1$. Substituting our given values for n and r in the above formula, and cancelling like numbers in the numerator and denominator to reduce to the lowest terms, we have:

$$C(6,2) = \frac{6!}{2!(4)!} = \frac{\overset{3}{6} \times 5 \times 4 \times 3 \times 2 \times 1}{2 \times 1 \times 4 \times 3 \times 2 \times 1} = \frac{15}{1} = 15$$

If in the above example we wished to determine the number of possible permutations, we would use the following formula:

$$P(n,r) = \frac{n!}{(n-4)!}$$

and would solve it like this:

$$P(6,2) = \frac{6!}{4!} = \frac{6 \times 5 \times 4 \times 3 \times 2 \times 1}{4 \times 3 \times 2 \times 1} = \frac{30}{1} = 30$$

Thus we can see that there would be 30 possible pairings if sequence were important; these sequenced pairings would be called permutations.

To provide practice in combinations and permutations, present the students with the following problems.

------

1. You have won first place in a contest for selling the largest number of tickets to your school's band concert. Your prize is four tickets to an upcoming concert of your favorite rock group. No one else in your family is interested in going, and you must decide which three of your twelve closest friends you will invite. How many possible combinations must you consider?

2. What is the total number of combinations of the first ten letters of the alphabet taken two at a time?

3. You have just moved to a new city, and it is the first day of school. To help the class get acquainted right away, the teacher instructs everyone to introduce himself to everyone else. Each introduction is to take exactly three minutes. Your new class has twenty students. How many different introduction will you exchange? How long will it take for the entire class to complete the process?

4. Your parents are taking you out for pizza to celebrate your birthday. There are fifteen different toppings, from which you can select any three. You also will be asked to specify the order in which you want your toppings to be arranged. How many different choices can you make? (Hint: Sequence is important here!)

5. There are twenty-five words on your spelling list for this week. Assuming all the words would fit and make sense in any order, how many five-word sentences would be possible with these words?

6. Your school's swimming team has thirty members. The pool in which your competitions are held can be divided into seven lanes. How many *different* starting groups can be made from your team?

7. You are playing a game that uses dice to determine the number of moves made at each turn. One of the dice is blue, and the other is red. How many different combinations (permutations) can be thrown?

8. There are fifty-two playing cards in a deck. How many different hands are possible in a game in which each player is dealt ten cards?

9. How many other ideas can you think of for using combinations and permutations?

Numeration Systems

Another mathematics topic that provides an excellent stimulus for enrichment is the study of different numeration systems. Although today's students have grown up using the decimal (or base ten) system, few of them really understand how it works. The use of other bases contributes immeasurably to the internalization of our own numeration system and therefore suggests another excellent enrichment component for the mathematics curriculum for gifted students.

In addition to the use of other bases to help in the understanding of our own decimal system, this area of mathematics can be used to strengthen students' understanding of computers (the binary, or base two, system) and metrics (based on multiples of ten). It can also be used to teach Roman numerals (including performing of the basic mathematical functions using this system); in keeping with our goal of integrated education, the use of Roman numerals could be correlated as well with the study of ancient history, adding still another depth to the enrichment of the mathematics curriculum. Still another use of other numeration systems is the teaching of exponentials ($1=10^0$, $10=10^1$, $100=10^2$; $2^0=1$, $2^1=2$, $2^2=4$, etc.).

Mental Math

A final area of mathematics enrichment that provides an excellent source of material for the gifted student who has mastered the regular curriculum is what we might call "mental math." Not really a discipline of mathematics in itself, this skill simply encompasses many of the "tricks of the trade" that we have learned while growing up. Unfortunately, although some of the more common "tricks" (e.g., multiplying or dividing by ten or one hundred) are regularly taught by mathematics teachers, there are many more such techniques that have been ignored and that would greatly enhance the mental efficiency of our gifted students with respect to mathematics. Some of these techniques are included here.

Finger Mathematics.   Finger mathematics has traditionally been outlawed by teachers who recognized that reliance on the fingers for calculating could discourage children from learning the basic arithmetical facts and operations. When the basics have been mastered, however, the use of finger mathematics—any of several systems that enable students to perform mental calculations with the use of their fingers—can add significantly to the mathematical efficiency of our gifted students. Chisanbop, a Korean method of performing mathematical calculations, uses the fingers in much the same way that the ancient Chinese abacus used beads. This and other methods of finger calculation are presented in numerous publications.

Short-Cut Multiplication and Division.   There are many ways in which students can be taught to multiply or divide mentally when large numbers are involved. Some of these methods include:

1. Multiplying or dividing by multiples of ten: Move the decimal point one place to the right or left for each zero in the number by which you are multiplying or dividing.
2. Multiplying by other numbers, using the various properties of mathematics, such as:
   a. To multiply by nine, add a zero to multiply by ten and then subtract the original number.

b. To multiply by 15, add a zero to multiply by ten and then add one-half of that number.
c. To multiply by 25, add two zeros to multiply by 100 and then divide that number by 4.
d. To multiply $3.95 by 5, raise the $3.95 to $4.00, multiply by 5, and subtract 25 cents (5 × .05).
e. To estimate the discounted price of a $499 item on sale for 40 percent off, round the $499 up to $500, mentally remove the two zeros (i.e., take 1 percent of $500), and multiply the resulting figure (5) by 60 (since the sale price will be 60 percent of the original). Subtract 60 cents to find the exact price.

3. Dividing by 25: Multiply by 4 (double that number twice) then divide by 100 (move the decimal point two places to the left).

4. Dividing by 500: Divide by 5 and then move the decimal point two places to the left.

5. Squaring a number ending in 5: The last two digits of the product will be 25; the beginning of the product can be found by multiplying the original first digit(s) by the next largest number. For example, to square 125, multiply 12 × 13. Using short-cut multiplication, multiply 12 × 10 then add (12 × 3), for a product of 156. Add 25 at the end; the product is 15625.

Other Strategies for "Gifted Mathematics"

In addition to the above strategies, there are many other topic areas that can be explored with or by gifted students in the mathematics classroom. Some of these might include the history of mathematics, topology, and the use of mathematically oriented games and puzzles. There are various sources from which teachers may secure such materials; some examples are: Cuisenaire Rods, geo boards, games of strategy (Chess, Mastermind, Backgammon), and games commonly used in academic competitions (e.g., Wff-n-Proof, On-Sets, and Equations).

TECHNOLOGY IN THE
MATHEMATICS CLASSROOM

If the gifted students in today's classrooms are to be the leaders of tomorrow's society, they must possess the concepts and the skills necessary to utilize the most modern technologies available. In its 1980 report, the National Council of Teachers of Mathematics recommended that the use of calculators and computers be "integrated into the core mathematics curriculum . . . [and] used in imaginative ways for exploring, discovering, and developing mathematical concepts and not merely for checking computational values or for drill and practice." It further stated that courses in computer literacy, as well as regular access to calculators and computers, be made a part of every student's general education. Unfortunately, philosophical discord has prevented these recommendations from being implemented as widely and as rapidly as the NCTM would have liked.

The Calculator Controversy

Ever since the hand-held calculator became widely and inexpensively available, a debate has raged between mathematicians and classroom teachers regarding the use of calculators in the mathematics classroom (especially at the elementary level). Those who oppose their use believe that children who use calculators in class will come to rely on them rather than building mathematical concepts and facts in their own minds. Certainly no one can argue that the memorization and internalization of certain basic "math facts" is essential for our lives today, as we will not always have calculators at our fingertips. But what about their use by people who have mastered the basics of arithmetic?

In its 1980 yearbook, the NCTM recommended that school mathematics programs use calculators at all grade levels. On the basis of a study on the effects of calculator use in the elementary grades, Bartalo (1983) concluded that the greatest value in the use of calculators is that it prevents students from worrying about computational accuracy and thus frees them to concentrate on more complex techniques of problem solving. Acknowledging that it is essential for elementary school children to learn the mathematics concepts and facts and develop efficient computational skills, Bartalo nonetheless points out that they must learn to apply these skills and concepts to practical usage.

Hembree (1986) correlated the findings of seventy-nine reports, transforming all experimental results into a common form and conducting analyses to determine the effects of calculator use on the achievement levels and attitudes of students of all levels. His studies demonstrated that the use of calculators improved mathematics skills in both computation and problem solving for students (especially low- and high-ability students) in all grades except the fourth grade. He further found that calculator use during testing produced much higher achievement than manual calculation, again in both computation and problem solving. Finally, this study showed that the use of calculators at all grade levels improved the attitudes and self-concepts of the students with respect to mathematics. (Hembree did, however, emphasize that calculators offered advantages only when students understood the concepts that were involved.)

Garman (1984) found that calculator use makes students conscious of the order of the operations, encourages them to follow directions more closely, helps them learn mathematical terminology more readily, provides opportunities for them to practice their algebra skills in enjoyable ways, helps them internalize the meanings of written algebraic expressions, and challenges them to delve into the reasons why algorithms work.

Having established the advantage of calculator use at all levels of education, let us now explore ways in which they may be employed in the classroom. Some possibilities are:

1. Use calculators to provide immediate feedback on class assignments. The teacher can easily develop an adaptation of programmed learning, in which students can work problems and immediately check their answers while the method chosen is fresh in their minds. In this way, they can learn to diagnose their own areas of difficulty and reinforce correct methods of solving problems.

2. Teach skills of estimation and have students check their estimates on calculators just as they check their manual computations. (Estimation skills can be sharpened if they will estimate prior to computing, then check both the estimation and the computation; this procedure will also encourage students to watch for and recognize significant errors in calculator solutions caused by careless keyboarding.)

3. Allow students to use calculators to perform higher level computations than they are able to perform manually (e.g., computing standard deviations, working with large numbers, etc.). This experience will permit them to work with more advanced concepts, providing motivation for the learning of the computational skill at a later date.

4. Use programmable calculators to teach the basics and the uses of computer programming.

Computers in Gifted Education

In the years when many of today's teachers were going through school, the computer was an intimidating, large, and unwieldy room full of equipment, accessible only to the largest and wealthiest corporations and universities. Little did we know that in a relatively few years this incredibly clever device could be made available to the youngest child in the smallest class of the least progressive school district! Although computers were used by the Soviets with gifted students in the 1950s, it was not until 1963 that the National Science Foundation formally introduced the microcomputer into the gifted classrooms of this country (Suppes, 1977). Since that time, this marvelous tool has become standard equipment in many gifted programs (and even in many regular classrooms), and its uses have become virtually unlimited in our attempts to provide relevant and challenging experiences for our gifted students of all ages.

According to Overall et al. (1981), the computer is "the ultimate individualized learning tool, because it can go in any direction, at any pace and to whatever depth the child wants to take it" (p. 43). Seeing the use of computers as one of the highest priorities for gifted education, Dover (1983) points to various studies that have demonstrated the following benefits of computer education:

1. Computer experience builds thinking and learning skills, particularly abstract and logical thinking.
2. Work with computers helps to develop problem-finding, as well as problem-solving, skills.
3. Students learn to develop conceptual models from programming experience.
4. Computer success builds self-confidence and positive attitudes toward learning.
5. Curiosity and exploratory behaviors are stimulated by computer programming experience.
6. The necessity for accuracy in programming helps students recognize that important lessons can be learned from failure.
7. Gifted underachievers are stimulated through computer work, building positive attitudes about learning.
8. Computer studies strengthen interpersonal communication skills through the sharing of enjoyable and challenging experiences.
9. Networking provides access to broad bases of data as well as to peers, consultants, and businesses or agencies that can serve as valuable sources of information.
10. Skills learned through computer practice are readily transferred by gifted students to other subject areas.
11. Computer use makes students more conscious of their spelling, punctuation, and other common errors that may cause problems in the efficient writing or execution of programs.

How can computers be most effectively used in gifted education? Many writers emphasize the importance of the hands-on experience: allowing the gifted students extensive access to computer use (as opposed to watching teachers demonstrate their use). Generally it is recommended that students work on computers in pairs—not only to stimulate interest but also to encourage peer teaching through team work. There are many ways in which computers can be used throughout the school years: for solving complex mathematical problems, for analyzing statistical data, for developing visual models, and for writing music or poetry. Since not every teacher has access to classroom computers (or, for that matter, the knowledge or skills necessary for operating them), the most efficient method of instructing students in computer use is to have one or two teachers in the school with expertise in computer programming to teach this area of the curriculum to all students. Even with such an arrangement, however, there are foundational skills that the classroom teacher with a minimum of computer training can develop in preparation for the more advanced instruction. The following steps can be accomplished by any teacher:

1. Provide instruction and practice within a variety of contexts in logical thinking and problem solving.
2. Talk about the computer as a marvelous tool of technology, but make it clear that computers are only as efficient as the humans who operate them. Talk about the tongue-in-cheek term "GIGO" ("Garbage In, Garbage Out").
3. Help students build elementary flow-charting skills by working on sequencing, using syllogisms, futures wheels, and relevance trees.
4. Use computer terminology regularly in the classroom (e.g., refer to lectures as input sessions, student responses as output).
5. Show students many examples of computer graphics, statistical computations performed by computers, and other products that the computer provides for modern society.

CORRELATING MATHEMATICS WITH OTHER SUBJECTS

Of all of the subjects of today's elementary and secondary schools, language arts and mathematics are the most in demand and thus are the easiest to correlate or integrate with other subject areas. There are many ways in which mathematics can be used in conjunction with other subjects; a few ideas are shared here, with the hope that the inventive teacher will hitchhike on these and invent dozens of ways in which the concepts learned in math class may be reinforced throughout the curriculum. As in every other area, the possibilities are limited only by the creativity of the teacher.

1. Have students plan field trips or role-play travel agents. Planning a trip requires multiple uses of mathematics (e.g., interpreting distances from mileage scales on maps, budgeting for expenses, calculating travel times between cities, etc.).
2. In a unit on architecture, have students use the metric system to draw plans to scale.

3. In teaching the scientific principles of aerodynamics, have students build model rockets, calculating the launch angle necessary to effect a landing on a specific target.

4. To aid in teaching latitude and longitude, have students track hurricane paths on maps.

5. Use mathematics to teach the concept of perspective in art.

6. Teach statistical procedures in the context of a research project in any subject area.

7. Relate mathematical concepts in economics to a course on the free enterprise system of the United States.

8. In science laboratory exercises (or in calculating distances on maps, or even measuring paper for classroom bulletin boards), use the metric system for all measurements.

9. Use tesselations to develop new designs in art.

10. Use origami to reinforce geometric shapes.

REFERENCES

Bartalo, D. B. (1983). Calculators and problem-solving instruction: They were made for each other. *Arithmetic Teacher, 76,* 18–21.

Bartkovich, K. G., & George, W. C. (1980). *Teaching the gifted and talented in the mathematics classroom.* Washington, D.C.: National Education Association.

Burns, M. (1975). *The I Hate Mathematics Book.* Boston: Little, Brown.

Dover, A. (1983). Computers and the gifted: Past, present, and future. *Gifted Child Quarterly, 27,* 81–85.

Garman, B. (1984). The calculator, math magic, and algebra. *Mathematics Teacher, 77,* 448–449.

Hembree, R. (1986, September). Research gives calculators a green light. Arithmetic Teacher, *79,* 18–21.

Hersberger, J. & Wheatley, G. (1980). A proposed model for a gifted elementary school mathematics program. *Gifted Child Quarterly, 24,* 37–40.

Marland, S. P. (1972). *Education of the Gifted and Talented.* Report to the Congress of the United States by the U. S. Commissioner of Education. Washington, D.C.: U. S. Government Printing Office.

National Council of Teachers of Mathematics (1980). *An agenda for action: Recommendations for school mathematics of the 1980s.* Reston, VA: NCTM.

Nay, F. (1981, November/December). Computer Challenge: The Henry Taitt story. *G/C/T,* pp. 48–50.

Noller, R. B., Heintz, R. E., & Blaeuer, D. A. (1978). *Creative problem solving in mathematics.* Buffalo, NY: D.O.K.

Overall, T., Lola, P., Murphy, K., Dafoe, M. M., Housey, J., & Leventhal, S. (1981). Learning with Logo at the Lamplighter School. *Microcomputing, 5*(9), 42–47.

Suppes, P. (1977). The future of computers in education. In *Computers in the learning society: Hearings before the Subcommittee on Domestic and International Scientific Planning, Analysis and Cooperation of the Committee on Science and Technology* (Report No. 47) (pp. 548–569). Washington, D.C.. U.S. Government Printing Office.

Tucker, B. F. (1982). Providing for the mathematically gifted child in the regular elementary classroom. *Roeper Review, 4,* 11–12.

Vance, J. H. (1983, September). The mathematically talented student revisited. *Arithmetic Teacher, 76,* 22–25.

Wavrik, J. J. (1980). Mathematics education for the gifted elementary school student. *Gifted Child Quarterly, 24,* 169–173.

Wheatley, G. H. (1983). A mathematics curriculum for the gifted and talented. *Gifted Child Quarterly, 27,* 77–90.

Wiburg, K., & Rader, B. (1984, January). Computers are elementary. *Arithmetic Teacher, 31,* 18–22.

13

An Inquiry Approach to Science and Social Studies

Our scientific lead depends on . . . the ability of our educational system . . . to find and encourage scientific talent.
General Omar Bradley

It is regrettable that many educational systems do not recognize the importance of identifying and encouraging scientific talent. Science and social studies—the subjects in which students with scientific talent excel, and that are essential preparation for future leadership—unfortunately are seen by many as the lowest priorities in the school curriculum.

Several years ago I was called to a neighboring school district to advise a principal as to what could be done to inject some motivation and interest into his junior high school science program. "Our science classes are nothing but reading classes," he lamented, "and we need to find a way to make science exciting for the students!" When I looked over the science classrooms, I began to see why. In addition to the common problem of having too many students per teacher, the classrooms were filled with individual student desk/chairs—row after row of them. There were no work surfaces, no demonstration centers, and no place to display project work. It was no wonder that the teachers did little more than read from the textbook!

Recent reports by educational commissions studying the needs of United States schools and the university programs that train their teachers have pinpointed several deficiencies that exacerbate the problems caused by inadequate facilities. Ironically we have a "Catch

22" situation: The schools do not offer adequate science programs because they do not have well-trained teachers to staff them; students do not want to take science in high school because they found it boring in elementary school (because teachers didn't really teach science); and the colleges do not place high priority on science because it is not in great demand in the schools. What does all of this have to do with gifted education?

If our gifted students are to be our future leaders, they must be prepared to deal effectively with technology and to be productive members of society. The discoveries and inventions that will keep our society in touch with the Third Wave will be products of the natural, applied, and social sciences. They will be discovered and invented by our bright graduates who have the creative imagination and the potential to apply their learnings to the molding of the future. It is not enough to have our gifted students learn the sciences and the social sciences through reading alone—they must learn to apply their skills to solving the problems of these important areas. Unless we give them experiences of value beginning in the early grades, our gifted students will be won over to other areas, and our scientific superiority will be lost to other nations in the future.

Science and social science have many characteristics in common. Primary among these is the methodology of their research procedures. The scientific method of problem solving, commonly called the inquiry approach, was discussed in Chapter 3 of this text. The purpose of this chapter is to present characteristics of the inquiry approach to science and social science (or social studies) education and to demonstrate ways in which this method can be used to motivate interest in these vital areas among our gifted students.

THE INQUIRY TEACHER

No matter now elaborate the laboratory, how enlightening the textbooks, how small the classes, or how bright the students, the key to successful implementation of any inquiry science (or social science) program is the teacher. Teachers who motivate their gifted students to use the scientific method of problem solving and to enter scientific professions typically display the following characteristics:

1. They prepare themselves exceptionally well in the subject matter they teach.
2. They encourage the use of creative and divergent methods of thinking and problem solving.
3. They provide persistent but gentle encouragement to their students.

4. They enjoy working with students and are dedicated to remaining in education.

5. They provide excellent role models for their students, who often see them as parent images.

6. They develop mutual respect and trust with their students.

7. They relate well to students, listening carefully to and empathizing with their problems, but they demand high standards of scholastic achievement and personal conduct.

8. They use questions more often than lectures.

9. They utilize teacher-pupil planning, basing lessons frequently on the inquiries, needs, and interests of the students.

10. They allow wait-time for students to respond to questions and convert incorrect responses into learning experiences.

11. They suggest problems for students to investigate and answer students' questions with additional challenges rather than simple answers, thus stimulating intellectual curiosity and helping students make discoveries for themselves.

12. They motivate their students to value intrinsic, rather than extrinsic, rewards for their efforts.

13. They utilize small group work, encouraging interaction between and among students.

14. They provide classroom environments that are conducive to divergent production.

15. They model flexibility and open-mindedness.

16. They teach the inquiry method to students and encourage the development and significant application of efficient research and problem-solving skills.

17. They serve as facilitators, rather than directors, of learning, providing technical instruction and assistance as well as a variety of sophisticated resources.

18. They encourage students to be self-initiated learners and to think for themselves.

19. They recognize and acknowledge the value of all contributions, encouraging all students to participate in class discussions and activities.

20. They foster critical thinking rather than blind acceptance of factual information.

21. They evaluate student achievement on the basis of demonstrated progress and behavioral change rather than on convergent written tests alone.

How can a teacher determine if her method of teaching fits the pattern of inquiry? Using the preceding list of characteristics as a guide, the teacher can become more inquiry-oriented, particularly in the science or social science class. Simply consider the frequency with which you use each of the strategies described, and award yourself three points for each one you use on a regular basis, two points for each one you use occasionally, and one point for each one you rarely use. A total score of 55 or above indicates that you are indeed an inquiry teacher; 45–54 is excellent, and 40–45 indicates that you are making an attempt at becoming more inquiry-oriented. If your score is below 40, take another look at your teaching; work on the development of inquiry techniques, and evaluate yourself again in six weeks!

INQUIRY EDUCATION FOR THE GIFTED

In the Enrichment Triad Model, one of few curriculum models designed specifically for gifted programming, Renzulli (1977) emphasized the need to teach gifted students the research methods employed by professionals in the various fields of endeavor. Inquiry is the problem-solving approach employed by professionals in the natural, applied, and social sciences. Getzels, Sternberg, and others have stressed the importance of problem finding in inquiry training. Although it is fairly obvious that the identification of the problem to be solved must precede any productive attempts at arriving at a solution, problem finding is probably the most difficult step in the process.

In the early grades, inquiry teaching is preceded by the "discovery" approach. Since young children are not able to identify significant problems to be solved, it is necessary for the teacher to provide simple problems for practice. An example of the discovery approach is shown here.

Place a collection of arthropods on the table. Ask the students a divergent question such as, "What do all of these arthropods have in common?" Encourage the children to examine the various specimens and make observations about what they see (e.g., all arthropods have exoskeletons). Then have them divide the specimens by class (arachnids, insects, etc.) and identify the specific characteristics by which each group is classified.

As children mature in their problem-solving abilities, they can be challenged to develop classification systems for various types of life (trees, insects, etc.). These experiences will help greatly in preparing them for the more sophisticated and abstract skills required for truly scientific problem solving.

When students have reached the middle grades, they should be encouraged on a regular basis to identify problems that can be solved in the context of the units of study. In addition to this method of building problem-finding skills, Sternberg (1982) has suggested that students examine major discoveries resulting from scientific research and use inductive reasoning to determine the problems which led to these discoveries and their significance in the particular discipline of science (or social science).

AN INQUIRY LESSON

The popular NASA Moon Survival Task provides an excellent example of the use of inquiry in science. Procedures for its use are given here.

With little introduction, distribute the NASA Moon Survival Task* exercise and instruct students to complete the exercise individually. Then divide the class into groups of four to six students each to compare their answers and arrive at consensus for presentation to the class.

Part One: The NASA Moon Survival Task

You are in a space crew originally scheduled to rendezvous with a mother ship on the lighted surface of the moon. Unfortunately, mechanical difficulties have forced your ship to crash-land at a spot some 100 miles from the rendezvous point. The rough landing damaged much of the equipment aboard. Since you must reach the mother ship in order to survive, the group must select the most critical items to take on the 100-mile trip. Below are listed the 15 items left intact after landing. Your task is to rank them in terms of their importance to your crew in its attempt to reach the rendezvous point. Place a "1" by the most important item, a "2" by the second most important, and so on.

_____ A. Box of matches

_____ B. Food concentrate

_____ C. 50 feet of nylon rope

_____ D. Parachute silk

---

*The NASA Moon Survival Task is adapted from its original version with the permission of its author, Dr. Jay Hall, of Teleometrics International, 1755 Woodstead Court, The Woodlands, Texas 77380 (713-367-0060).

_____ E. Portable heating unit

_____ F. Two .45 caliber pistols

_____ G. One case dehydrated milk

_____ H. Two 100-pound tanks of oxygen

_____ I. Map of the moon's constellations

_____ J. Life raft

_____ K. Magnetic compass

_____ L. 5 gallons of water

_____ M. Signal flares

_____ N. First-aid kit with injection needles

_____ O. Solar-powered FM receiver-transmitter

When all groups have completed the task, allow them to share their group ratings and explain the reasons for their responses. Then present the answers contributed by the Manned Spacecraft Center of NASA in Houston, Texas (see Appendix B), and discuss.

After completing the moon simulation, make note of those science concepts that need reinforcement. For example, any individual or group who did not rank oxygen and water as 1 and 2, respectively, may need information on the lack of these substances on the moon and/or on their essential nature for survival; others may need information on gravity, radiation, or other concepts related to space travel. Taking one concept at a time, generate problems whose solutions might help the learner understand the concept under study. Select one problem for attack and develop an inquiry lesson designed to strengthen students' comprehension of the necessary information. A sample lesson of this type is offered below (adapted from McGavack and LaSalle, 1971).

Concept: Need for oxygen in outer space.

Problem: Must astronauts traveling in space take a similar environment with them?

Materials Needed: Three jars with tight covers, aquarium plants, snails, and water

Procedures:

1. Fill the three bottles with aquarium water. Place plants in Jar A, snails in Jar B, and some of each in Jar C. Add more water until both jars overflow.

2. Cover the jars tightly and leave them at room temperature in an moderately lighted room for a few days. Instruct students to observe them periodically, making notes about what is observed.

3. After three to five days, discuss students' observations using questions such as:

   a. Are all of the original organisms still living? What is the condition of each? How can you explain the observed conditions?

   b. How could we relate these jars to conditions that might be present in a manned space capsule?

   c. What conditions would need to be present in a manned space capsule? Why?

4. Discuss the meaning of a "closed ecological system" and the environmental adjustments which are actually made in a manned space craft.

SCIENCE AND SOCIAL STUDIES FAIRS

Academic fairs have been a part of the American educational system for many years. Those devoted to science and social studies have prevailed, primarily because these are the two major content areas in the school curriculum that lend themselves best to project work. Although science and social studies fairs may not receive the recognition that they deserve in the educational program, it is estimated that over one million student projects are undertaken each year in science and/or engineering alone, and that fairs exist in one form or another in more than twenty countries outside of the United States (Sherburne, 1985). Furthermore, it appears that students in gifted programs are given more opportunities to participate in social studies and science fairs than are those in regular education. Why are fairs so popular among teachers and students—particularly in gifted education?

1. They stimulate in our future leaders an active interest in the natural and social sciences.

2. They serve as valuable educational experiences through exposure to knowledgeable professionals who serve as judges.

3. They strengthen interpersonal communication skills by providing students with a forum for meeting the public and discussing topics with which they have become familiar.

4. They offer opportunities for students to apply the research and problem-solving skills they have learned.

5. They foster a spirit of fair competition as students work to develop superior projects.

6. They award public recognition to talented and conscientious students for work well done.

In the early days of the science fair, projects were categorized primarily in the areas of biological, physical, or earth science. In recent years, however, fairs have become more sophisticated in keeping with the technological advances of the Third Wave. Today's science fairs typically offer competition in thirteen areas: behavioral and social sciences, biochemistry, botany, chemistry, earth and space sciences, engineering, environmental sciences, mathematics, computers, medicine and health, microbiology, physics, and zoology. Similarly, social studies fairs categorize projects into the various disciplines of social science: history, geography, economics, sociology, anthropology, psychology, and political science. Although the volcanoes and simple descriptive projects of the earlier fairs still appear in the school fairs of lower elementary schools or among less studious contestants whose teachers have not taken the time to provide inquiry-oriented guidance, the older and more able students typically present projects of a more sophisticated nature. At a recent Louisiana state fair, for example, the following projects earned top awards for their creators:

Stonehengessing: The Evolution of the Gravestone

Economic Consequences of Terrorism in the Middle East

Hyperactivity: Is There a Treatment of Choice?

Donor Organs: Why They Reject. The Molecular Basis of Specific Antigens

Quantitative Determination of Alcohol Content of Selected Beverages by the Use of Gas Chromotography

The Effects of Bimodular Versus Unimodular Stimulation in a CO_2 Laser System

The Teacher's Role

Participation in a science or social studies fair provides valuable experience in the research methodology that is an inherent part of the gifted program. It is therefore a totally appropriate activity for either the accelerated science or social studies class or the gifted resource room. As in most other areas of gifted education, the teacher's role is primarily that of facilitator. The importance of this role should not be underestimated, as the preparation of projects for science and social studies fairs offers a unique opportunity for the teacher to provide individualized instruction and to evaluate the student's grasp of the methodologies learned. It is the teacher's responsibility to assist the student in selecting a topic, locating appropriate resources and gathering the necessary data, conducting relevant experiments, evaluating results and drawing conclusions, writing a report on the project, developing the physical display, and preparing an impressive oral presentation that displays the student's ability to answer anticipated questions about the findings of her research.

Selecting a Topic.   The first responsibility of the teacher/facilitator in preparing students for science or social studies fairs is to help with the selection of a topic. Although the student should have the final say about her topic, the proposed investigations should be encouraged only if the following questions can all be answered in the affirmative:

1. Is the topic one that is not commonly found in fairs at this level?
2. Can the general topic area be narrowed to a specific project that involves the investigation of a research question?
3. Is there sufficient information available on the topic at a level that the student can understand?
4. Does the student possess the prerequisite skills needed to understand the necessary background information and to conduct the experiments required for the investigation of the problem?

Once the topic has been approved, the student must study background material in order to become thoroughly familiar with the topic and with the related research that has been done to date, and to obtain an overview from which to narrow to a specific research question for investigation. This narrowing process may consist of several steps such as those presented below:

1. Beginning with environmental science, a student might decide to investigate the prevalence and causes of acid rain, finally narrowing the problem to "What atmospheric factors affect the acidity level of precipitation in different areas of the state?"
2. In the area of life sciences, a student might narrow first to biology (as opposed to microbiology), then to zoology, and finally to herpetology (the study of reptiles and amphibians). Even within the area of herpetology the student can continue to narrow the focus—perhaps first to reptiles, and within this group to turtles—before isolating a specific problem for investigation.
3. In the area of social studies, a student interested in economics might wish to investigate implications of an oil import tax on the United States economy or on the petroleum industry itself.

Facilitating the Research. As soon as the student has isolated an approved problem for investigation, it is wise for the teacher to request a formal proposal (or prospectus) describing the student's plan for the development of the project. Usually a prospectus should include the category (or general topic area) of the project, the statement of the problem to be investigated, the hypotheses to be tested, a brief description of the data to be gathered and the procedures to be followed, and a sketch (with materials list) of the exhibit for the fair with a list of materials required for the project. Once this proposal has been approved by the teacher (with the flexibility to make approved changes that become necessary as the project progresses), the steps of the Scientific Method of Problem Solving (see Chapter 3) should be followed under the teacher's watchful eye. At this stage it is important for the teacher to provide instruction in the process and to suggest guidelines concerning procedures for keeping citations of all materials used, taking notes, organizing the report, planning and carrying out experiments, and maintaining observation records.

One of the most valuable aspects of science and social studies fair participation is the opportunity that it affords the teacher for supervising students in the process of research. Unfortunately, the amount of time required for preparation of a winning project often discourages teachers from requiring their students to develop fair projects. Since virtually all subject areas can support research in either science or social science, the teacher of the gifted can well justify the time spent on fair projects. The teacher is encouraged to require participation in at least one fair a year for all gifted students (and perhaps for less capable students as well), and to require that the projects be developed within the classroom. There are several advantages to having the work done only in the classroom: First, the teacher who personally supervises the project work assures that the students do all of their own work and receive accurate (but not inequitable or excessive) assistance while proceeding through the investigation. Second, since the gifted classroom is typically well supplied, the students have greater access to needed materials and equipment at school than they would have at home. Third, classroom production allows the teacher to evaluate students on a continuous basis, helping them to locate appropriate resources and providing individualized instruction as needed. Participation in science and social studies fairs thus offers valuable educational experiences and should be made a regular part of the gifted program curriculum.

Writing the Research Report. Although fairs rarely require more in writing than a brief abstract, the preparation of a good research report provides valuable experience for the student and should be required by the teacher, especially if course credit is to be given for the project. This report should present all of the stages through which the student progressed in the preparation of his project, as well as a concise but thorough treatise on the topic itself. The teacher should work with the student in an effort to anticipate questions that judges or visitors might ask and to be sure that these questions can be answered intelligently and resourcefully. (Students might role play judges and quiz each other in preparation for the fairs.) The report should be typed and well organized with title page, table of contents, and abstract; it should present the statement of the problem (and/or purpose of the project), the hypotheses, a journal with details of the procedures followed, the results obtained, and the conclusions reached. Pictures of the experimental segments of the project, if not presented in the exhibit, should be interspersed within the written report. Finally, an accurate list of references consulted in the preparation of the project, recorded in approved citation form, should be included.

Preparing the Exhibit.   The exhibit that the student must prepare for the science or social studies fair should have three major components: a backboard (usually a triptych, which is a three-fold board containing photographs or drawings of intermediate stages of the project development, graphs, and charts reflecting changes observed intermittently throughout the investigation, and the like); a physical display (a new product developed; a display of collected specimens, classified as to genus and species; two groups of plants on which controlled experiments have been conducted; etc.); and a written report. Before making the assignment, the teacher should determine the regulations that will govern the dimensions of the display; nothing could be more dejecting to a conscientious student than to work for several months on a project and then have it disqualified because of an excessively large exhibit.

In supervising the preparation of the display, the teacher should provide guidelines by which the students can work. The following elements should be considered:

1. Size. After ascertaining that the planned display will adhere to regulations, the teacher should help the student decide on a proportionate size that catches the eye but does not overpower the observer.
2. Color. Two or three conservative and compatible colors are generally more dramatic and appealing than either one irridescent color or a barrage of bright colors. The object is to appeal, not to blind!
3. Neatness. The display should have a finished look about it. There should be some type of attractive border around each section of the triptych, all lettering should be consistent in size and type style, and *nothing* should be written by hand. Pictures, graphs, and other

visuals should be neatly trimmed (with no jagged or unparallel edges) and mounted before attaching them to the board; the size of each such item should be proportionate to the sheet on which it is mounted. Any print that is to be read by a judge should be of a legible size, color, and intensity, and wording should be as brief and concise as possible for quick and easy reading.

4. Accuracy. When the student presents the prospectus, including the initial drawing of the board that will focus the exhibit, the teacher should immediately check for accuracy of terminology, spelling, and factual information. Nothing is so disconcerting to a judge than a misspelled word on the triptych of an otherwise appealing project! If a student's display contains inaccuracies, the judge is likely to disqualify the project.

Preparing the Oral Presentation. When the student has completed the investigation and has developed the physical exhibit to a logical conclusion, the final step in preparing for the fair is the preparation of the oral presentation. Because of the varied circumstances under which science and social studies fairs are held, the time the judges will allow for each student's oral presentation may vary from two to ten minutes. Therefore, the teacher should determine early in the process exactly how much time the student will be allowed to speak on her topic. Having prepared a written report containing both background information and the details of the project investigation, the student will have ample material from which to select comments for the oral presentation. Depending on the amount of time that will be allotted for this presentation, the student should present briefly the major principles or background information on which the project was based (including information about closely related topics or current events) and then spend the remaining time covering the procedures followed and the conclusions reached. It is best if notes are not used for the oral presentation; however, a "canned" speech tends to signal judges that the information presented is memorized rather than understood. It is also wise to anticipate and prepare responses for the types of questions the judges are likely to ask. In the final analysis, it is probably the student's knowledge and understanding of the topic that makes the greatest impression. The preparation of the oral presentation, although one of the last steps in the completion of the project, is therefore an extremely important part of a successful project.

Evaluating Science and Social Studies Projects. Usually science fair projects are judged on the basis of five criteria: scientific thought, creative ability, thoroughness, skill, and clarity. (Social studies fairs often use the same basic criteria, although development and interpretation of the idea and effectiveness of the presentation sometimes take the place of scientific thought and thoroughness.) Although these criteria are not uniformly adopted, they are all appropriate factors to consider when evaluating or judging science or social studies fairs. They are treated below in some detail, in order that the teacher may utilize them more meaningfully in working with students.

1. Scientific thought. This criterion is designed to determine the degree to which the student followed the scientific method of problem solving; typically it is assigned 30–40 percent of the total score. Questions that a teacher or judge might ask in arriving at this score are:
   a. Is the problem concisely stated, with a clear purpose? Is it specific enough to allow a logical and significant solution to be reached?
   b. Is there evidence of critical, scientific thinking? Did the student follow a planned and logical procedure in the investigation of the problem? Were the variables clearly defined and accurately tested? Were data and/or specimens collected and organized in an appropriate and orderly fashion?
   c. Was an adequate review of the related literature evidenced by the student's knowledge of relevant information? Were the presenter's sources valid and supported by scientific evidence (as opposed to articles written by nonauthoritative authors in popular magazines, newspapers, etc.)?
   d. Were the conclusions supported by the data and the experiments involved in the investigation? Has the solution been tested for workability? Is it economically feasible, acceptable, and usable?

2. Creative ability. The creative ability criterion, like creativity itself, involves primarily the degree to which the project reflects original thought (including new or improved methods of expressing or communicating ideas), planning, or applications on the part of the presenter. It is here that the score will be affected by apparent outside help (topic provided by a teacher, method of investigation suggested by parent's occupation, etc.). This criterion usually receives 20–30 percent of the total score.

3. Thoroughness. Earning 15–20 percent of the total score, thoroughness is a judgment of the extent to which the student has accomplished the original purpose of the project and demonstrated the principles on which the project was based. It also considers the student's understanding of the principles involved, the comprehensiveness of the data gathered, and the procedures followed.

4. Skill. This criterion judges the degree to which the student possesses the skills necessary to conduct scientific research in the area of the project: observational skills, technical or design skills,

and computational skills. It also considers the sources of supplies and equipment used in the investigation. Skill typically accounts for 10–15 percent of the total score.

5. Clarity. Clarity, usually assigned about 10 percent of the total score, relates to the student's concepts and discussion of the project (including again the presenter's understanding of the principles underlying the project). A high score on this criterion might also reflect an exhibit that has dramatic value (catches and holds the attention) but is not gimmicky in the visual presentation.

The Young Gifted Child and Fairs.   Teachers of young gifted children may find themselves torn with regard to the place of science and social studies fairs in their programs. Whereas these children are undoubtedly capable of much greater sophistication than their less able peers, they lack the skills needed to research and present a topic with any degree of efficiency. It should be noted, however, that the foundations for research that are offered in the early years are prerequisites for the firsthand investigations that are conducted by older students. It also is the responsibility of the lower elementary teacher to provide young children with ample opportunity to read about topics of personal interest and to share with their peers what they have learned from these readings. By the time they reach the third grade, students should be able to develop simple projects with posters and even very elementary science experiments (or descriptive social studies projects accompanied by models made of clay or other art materials) for presentation to parents, other primary teachers, or older gifted students serving as "judges." These experiences can be invaluable in the early years of school, as they lay firm foundation for later projects of greater significance.

LEARNING CENTERS

The term *learning center* has been used and abused for many years by well-meaning teachers. A learning center is simply an area of the classroom that has been set aside for independent student activity in a particular area of study. Unfortunately, this useful tool, which can help a teacher individualize instruction and encourage independent study among the brighter students, often becomes simply a file for ditto sheets and an escape from responsibility for the less conscientious teacher. In this section we will explore several types and adaptations of learning centers and suggest ways in which they can be used to encourage independent study and individualization in the content areas with gifted students.

Interest Development Centers.   In the presentation of his Enrichment Triad Model, Renzulli (1977) promotes the use of "interest development centers"—centers focused on specific topics of student interest. Unlike the typical learning center, these centers provide process rather than content information (e.g., "how-to" books that will teach a student to conduct research in the manner used by professionals in the field, rather than simply information about the topic itself). Interest Development Centers are most appropriate for the gifted classroom, particularly in conjunction with studies of the content areas such as science and social studies, as they foster the use of the inquiry method, which is the kernel of research in these important areas.

Discovery Boxes.   The use of "things-to-do boxes" has been suggested by Sisk (1976) to complement the presentation of a central stimulus such as a book or a film. Another application of this strategy is the discovery box. Similar to the things-to-do box, the discovery box is simply a large container that provides the materials needed for experiential learning based on a specific topic in science or social studies. The box itself may be decorated in keeping with the topic (e.g., made in the shape of a volcano, covered with pictures of King Tut's treasures, decorated like a "mad scientist"). Its contents could include any items that might foster interest in the topic—costumes or music of another country, insect-collecting equipment, microscopes, star maps, simulation games on environmental protection, and the like. Useful for children of all ages, discovery boxes provide enrichment for students who complete their work early in the regular classroom or for "free-time exploration" within the gifted resource room.

Classroom Learning Stations.   Perhaps the most common use of the learning center concept is the classroom learning station. Such a center, set up on a table along the wall or in a back corner, might include a triptych and a variety of materials/equipment with guidelines for activity development. An example of this type of center might be designed to enrich a social studies unit on Japan. Backed by a triptych, bulletin board, or wall display showing pictures of the countryside, of Mount Fuji, or of Japanese customs, this center might contain books and films, recipes and utensils for cooking Japanese food, chopsticks and instructions for using them, a kimono and Japanese slippers, an abacus, a selection of Japanese games, the filmstrip and/or book entitled *The Stonecutter* (see Chapter 15), or any of a myriad of other possible items.

Mini-Labs.   A final adaptation of the learning center that sparks an interest in learning, helps to provide for individual differences, and fosters independent study, is the mini-lab—an area of the classroom that is designated for use as a laboratory. The mini-lab may rotate among a variety of topics (insects, the Acadian culture, motion, human behavior) or offer a continuing variety of activities in a specific discipline of science (herpetology, paleontology) or social science (economics, history). For example, a science mini-lab in chemistry could offer chemicals that can be safely combined for interesting results, such as sodium chloride (table salt), white vinegar (acetic acid), chalk (calcium carbonate), baking soda (sodium bicarbonate), and/or charcoal (carbon). A supply of books detailing safe experiments from which elementary students might work should also be included, along with strictly enforced regulations specifying that chemistry experiments may *not* be conducted except under the direct supervision of the teacher and requiring that students follow specified methods of inquiry in working in the labs.

ENRICHMENT ACTIVITIES FOR THE SCIENCES AND SOCIAL SCIENCES

This chapter has addressed specific ways in which the teacher of the gifted can train students and offer opportunities for rewarding research in the sciences and the social sciences. Whether gifted students are served in resource rooms, accelerated academic programs, or the regular classroom, there are many other ways in which the teacher can offer differentiated opportunities to enrich the educational opportunities of these students. Some suggested activities are included below.

1. Use a plastic "bubble" to simulate unfamiliar environments such as the sea or outer space. To make the bubble, fold and tape together layers of clear plastic film (4–6 mil thickness) to form a "room" of the desired size. Connect one corner of the "room" to an electric fan by means of a large plastic tube, and turn on the fan. The bubble will inflate, creating space for several students to enter. Use the film as a rear projection (back-lit) screen to project slides or motion films, conduct a guided fantasy, and/or play appropriate music to create the desired atmospheric effects. The bubble may be used to stimulate creativity for writing or other activities that will be enhanced by the perception of alternate environments.

2. Set up science mini-labs in conjunction with units of study on rocks and minerals (test for hardness, mineral content, etc.), nongreen plants (grow fungi or nonpathogenic microorganisms), electricity (provide materials for making batteries or electromagnets, for lighting fluorescent tubes with static electricity), and so on.

3. Encourage students to organize a Future Scientists/Anthropologists/Economists/Geologists Club. Club activities might include weekend or after-school field trips to places of interest (bird sanctuaries, Indian reservations, petroleum refineries, hospitals, archaeological excavation sites, U.S. Mint, etc.), hosting of guest speakers from the local scientific community, or presentation to other classes in the school of student research projects or debates on controversial issues (e.g., genetic engineering, socialized medicine).

4. Have students replicate famous inventions that have become common or essential in our everyday lives (e.g., the electric light bulb). Use synectics to invent new types of consumer products. Employ creative problem solving to analyze their usefulness, to test their efficiency or their workability, and so forth.

5. Make a classroom planetarium for use in the study of astronomy.

6. Develop and maintain a class file of science and social studies fair projects (revised copies of the initial proposals, with results and conclusions added, would be appropriate) for use by future students.

7. Start a Bird-Watching Club. Take weekend birding trips to nearby sanctuaries, wooded or coastal areas, and other locations known to be habitats of a variety of wild birds. Catalog all birds sighted and encourage new classes to add to the file.

8. Set up a mentoring or internship program for students interested in careers related to science or social science.

9. Organize a science/anthropology/state history museum. Include pictures or specimens of native plants, trees, insects, birds, or other wild life; an operating weather station using instruments made by the students; obsolete scientific equipment donated by a local university or laboratory; archaeological artifacts; baskets or art work made by a local Indian tribe; and so on.

10. Have students plan a future colony that might be developed in outer space. Using the procedures discussed in Chapter 4 for writing utopias, design the ideal government, economic structure, or educational system. Try to anticipate the types of problems the inhabitants of such a colony might have that do not exist on earth today. Use futuristic problem-solving methods to find ways of averting (or solving) these problems.

11. Conduct a guided imagery activity in which students imagine themselves in a time machine, going back to any period in history that they would like to see (or to a specific period that they are preparing to study). Lead them to "image" the modes of dress, the customs, the economics and government, the schools, and so on, as

they travel in their time machine. Bring them back to modern civilization, and have them write and/or share what they "saw" on their travels.

12. Teach history through its relationship to the past. For example, use events and attitudes that exist today (apartheid, arms control, religious wars) and trace them back to the early days of the United States or the Old World. Examine the ways in which modern times are alike and different from the periods before the students were born.

13. Select an event from recent history that would in the distant past have seemed impossible for our country (the assassinations of President Kennedy, his brother, Martin Luther King, and others; the resignation of President Nixon over the Watergate issue; the exploration of outer space). Using the future tense, write an "outrageous prediction" of one or more of these events. Then examine current affairs that appear to be similar to events that have preceded tragic or shocking events of the past, and forecast events that might occur in the near future (adapted from Kauffman, 1976).

14. Instruct students to interview their parents, grandparents, and/or other older family members of friends. Tell them to explore what life was like when these people were the students' age—considering school, entertainment, finances, drugs and other temptations or problems of the day, social customs, and the like. They should then examine the changes that have taken place between then and now and, considering the current status of the above topics and others of interest, write scenarios predicting how life is likely to be fifty years from now if conditions and trends continue as they are now.

15. Have students gather data on population shifts that have occurred in the United States within the last twenty years. Consider particularly the increases that have occurred in the immigration of Asian families, the growth of Hispanic populations in all areas of the country, the changing roles of minorities and women in political, educational, business, and social leadership, and so on. Tell them to make forecasts about the impact that these changes will have on our government and society within the next twenty to fifty years.

16. Discuss the economic bases and other factors that contribute to the business/industry/cultural growth of various successful areas of the country. Compare this information to parallel factors regarding your own area. Ask students how your city might use their successes to improve life in your own area.

17. Instruct students to collect information (geographic, historic, demographic) on their city that would be of interest to persons

who are considering relocation to your area of the country. Write to tourist agencies and Chambers of Commerce in other growing and popular areas of the country to request brochures, statistical data sheets, and the like. Using these materials as a guide, develop promotional literature to encourage others to move in to your area.

18. Conduct a simulated archaeological "dig." Divide the class into two groups, each representing a foreign culture in a specified era (past, present, or future). Using the utopia format discussed in Chapter 4, have students plan the details of their respective cultures—government, education, economic, and the like. On the basis of their plans, have each group develop and bury in boxes of sand "artifacts" and "relics" they might leave behind if their civilization were suddenly annihilated by a cloud of poisonous gas. Have each group "excavate" the civilization of the other and attempt through examination of what they find to reconstruct information about the other culture.*

19. Develop simulations in which students "re-live" events of history—the Boston Tea Party, the drive for women's suffrage, Lincoln's fight to emancipate the slaves—as introductory activities prior to the study of current rebellions and Civil Rights issues.

REFERENCES

Adler, M. J. (1984). *The Paideia Program.* New York: Macmillan.

Brandwein, P. (1981). *The gifted child as future scientist.* Ventura, CA: Office of the Ventura County Superintendent of Schools. Originally published by Harcourt Brace Jovanovich, 1955.

Epley, T. (1978, May/June). Thinking ahead: Future studies for G/C/T individuals. *G/C/T,* 32–35.

Isaacs, A. F. (1970). What to do when you discover a child is gifted and is interested in science. *Gifted Child Quarterly, 14,* 259–263.

Kauffman, D. L., Jr. (1976). *Teaching the future: A guide to future-oriented education.* Palm Springs, CA: ETC Publications.

Long, S. M. (1982). *Using the census as a creative teaching resource* (Phi Delta Kappa Fastback #184). Bloomington, IN: Phi Delta Kappa.

McGavack, J., Jr., & LaSalle, D. P. (1971). *Crystals, insects, and unknown objects: A creative approach to the teaching of science to intermediate school children.* New York: John Day Company.

---

*This activity is based on "Dig 2," a simulation game developed by Jerry Lipetzky and offered along with other excellent simulations by Interact, Box 997, Lakeside, CA 92040 (619-448-1474).

Muir, S. P. (1980). Social sciencing: Social studies for gifted adolescents. *Clearing House, 53*(7), 323–327.

Renzulli, J. S. (1977). *The Enrichment Triad Model: A guide for developing defensible programs for the gifted and talented.* Mansfield, CT: Creative Learning Press.

Sherburne, E. G., Jr. (1985). *Judging guide: 36th International Science and Engineering Fair.* Washington, DC: Science Service.

Sisk, D. (1976). *Teaching gifted children.* Reston, VA: The Association for the Gifted.

Sternberg, R. J. (1982). Teaching scientific thinking to gifted children. *Roeper Review, 4,* 4–6.

14

The Arts in Gifted Education

When art reaches that point when it can be
called creative, it is the expression of the life
of man. It is philosphy. It is depth.
                    John H. Waddell

Often hailed as a major impetus to the development of programs in the United States for the academically gifted, the Soviet launch of Sputnik in 1957 also began a frenzied drive for excellence in education at all levels. The methods for reaching this goal have been variously interpreted by zealots and educators, yet no panacea has been found. Largely as a result of the efforts of the Council for Basic Education, a push for a "back-to-basics" approach has caused many well-meaning parents and educators to overlook the importance of a broad, enriched education in favor of limiting the curriculum to "reading, writing, and 'rithmetic" and setting aside those elements that they sometimes view as frills— notably, the arts. Ironically, research now seems to indicate that the addition of art, music, and dramatics (particularly creative dramatics) to the curriculum actually improves performance in academic areas.

INCORPORATING THE ARTS
IN GIFTED EDUCATION

In spite of the arguments advanced by back-to-basics advocates, the research of the past twenty years or so has produced increasing evidence that the arts are in fact basic education rather than frills. Why should we include the arts in gifted education?

1. The study of art and music contribute to the development of creativity (and hence to scientific discovery and invention, which

are creative products) through access to right hemisphere imagery (Gowan, 1984).

2. Like the intellectually or creatively gifted student, the talented student often remains incognito in the regular classroom—through the masking of art abilities that make the student feel "different," because of the inability of the untrained teacher to recognize artistic talent, or because the lack of opportunity to create art stifles the innate abilities of the student. Curriculum in the arts, like all curriculum for gifted/creative/talented students, must be differentiated; such a curriculum encourages the student to be different in valued ways without being considered "elitist." Failure to identify and foster giftedness in the arts contributes to a growing national decline in cultural strength (Clark and Zimmerman, 1984; Waddell, 1960).

3. Experiences in the arts offer socially acceptable methods of self-expression and foster the development of healthy self-concepts (Krippner and Blickenstaff, 1970; Williams, 1977).

4. The arts are seen as basic academic subjects by the College Board, which included the arts in a listing of six areas in which all students who expect to attend college should be prepared. Developed by the College Board's test development and academic advisory committees and its Council on Academic Affairs, the arts statement contended that the arts "challenge and extend human experience." It continued by saying, "The actual practice of the arts can engage the imagination, foster flexible ways of thinking, develop disciplined effort, and build self-confidence. Appreciation of the arts is integral to the understanding of other cultures sought in the study of history, foreign language, and social sciences" (Dorn, 1984).

5. The arts foster self-confidence, concentration, motivation for learning, observation, abstract thinking, and problem analysis (Szekely, 1981).

6. The introduction of the arts into the curriculum improves academic performance in those areas that back-to-basics advocates consider essential—mathematics, reading, science, and others (Williams, 1977). Furthermore, the use of creative dramatics has been shown to improve scores on reading achievement tests.

7. Research has documented that superior artistic performance cannot be attained without both above average intelligence and specific training in the arts. Furthermore, artistic potential exists in varying degrees in many young people. Thus, the inclusion of arts education in any curriculum for gifted students is essential to encourage the development of the full scope of their abilities (Clark and Zimmerman, 1984).

Perhaps a rationale for including a planned program in the arts as a part of any curriculum for gifted students is best synthesized by Eisner, who observed:

> Since the arts as well as the sciences constitute one of the major realms through which meaning is acquired and expressed, they are in no sense peripheral to the educational enterprise. If education seeks to help men come to know, and if the arts provide one of the basic avenues to knowledge, the arts should constitute one of the fundamental realms of general education for all students (1966, p. 496).

CHARACTERISTICS OF PERSONS TALENTED IN THE ARTS

Although numerous studies have been conducted to identify the characteristics that are most typical of intellectually and creatively gifted students, the research into the talented student seems to be somewhat limited. In spite of this apparent deficiency, however, the existing research has been of a quality that allows reasonable generalizations regarding characteristics of artistically talented persons. For our purposes, these traits will be classified into three categories: cognitive abilities, affective traits, and creative competencies.

Cognitive Abilities

Although the characteristics of the talented are not usually viewed in terms of cognitive abilities, there seems to be agreement among researchers that above average ability is essential for significant artistic production to take place. Bloom (1985) in particular has noted that most talented individuals have a facility for learning rapidly, especially in those talent areas in which they have previously mastered the prerequisite skills and concepts. Other cognitive skills that are typical of artistically talented persons include a keen sense of observation, the ability to recall visual detail (analysis) as well as an overall picture (synthesis), and skills of organization.

Affective Traits

Several affective qualities seem to be possessed by persons talented in the arts. Among these, perhaps the most apparent is an intense interest in one or more art areas. This interest spawns a high degree of motivation which is manifested in eagerness to express ideas using the favored medium (visual art, music, theater, or dance) and frequent reversion to artistic endeavor for leisure time activities. Also present are: self-confidence and willingness (often eagerness) to share ideas and products; tendency to identify personally with both one's subject matter and the medium used; high but realistic standards for self-evaluation; and sensitivity/sensibility toward movement, content, and environment (with each artist being most sensitive to the elements of her particular art—the musician or dancer to rhythm or sound, the visual artist to form, line, color, and texture).

Creative Competencies

Finally, and certainly one of the most (if not *the* most) significant, is the group of traits that might be classified as creative competencies. It is interesting to note that most of these abilities fit easily into the four basic components of creativity that have been cited for many years by Guilford, Torrance, Williams, and countless others: fluency, flexibility, originality, and elaboration. Grouped under these four "umbrella" abilities or skills, these traits are:

1. Fluency
   a. Expressiveness
   b. Spontaneous flow of ideas
   c. Lengthy periods spent on problem finding and solution
2. Flexibility
   a. Tendency to experiment freely with a variety of ideas and subjects, media, materials, and techniques
   b. Facility for solving problems using nontraditional methods
   c. Aptitude for viewing/approaching art from a different perspective
   d. Tolerance of ambiguity and conflict
   e. Ability to adapt from one situation or medium to another
3. Originality
   a. High degree of imagination; ability to image clearly
   b. Freedom from stimuli
   c. Tendency to experiment with problem finding as opposed to adopting preconceived problem situations
4. Elaboration
   a. Use of many elements
   b. Facility for piggybacking/hitchhiking on (as opposed to copying) the ideas of others

Other creative traits that characterize the talented individual are openness (keeping an open mind with regard to new experiences and new ideas, as well as resisting closure—often causing the artist to feel that a work of art can never be "completed" or that a problem can never be completely solved), ability to effect structure and balance in art, and a futuristic perspective—including plans for future endeavors and projection to future careers in the arts, often involving the assumption of leadership roles within the areas of interest. (It should be noted here that talent can exist without creativity.)

ART TEACHERS FOR THE GIFTED

The characteristics of art teachers who are successful in the teaching of gifted and talented students are similar to those traits that are necessary for all teachers who work with gifted students. Some adaptations should be made, however, when considering persons who will be given the responsibility of training gifted and talented students in the arts. Perhaps the most important criteria for selecting art teachers for gifted programs are the following:

1. A humanistic philosophy of education. The teacher assigned to work with gifted students in the arts must espouse the humanistic philosophy of education. This teacher displays a good sense of humor and is not afraid to show that he cares about and values students as human beings. He shares his ideas and work with students while showing a sincere interest in the students' ideas and work, encouraging and motivating them to derive pleasure in their own endeavors. The humanistic art teacher encourages self-initiated, independent learning and considers as a major goal to facilitate each student's drive to reach his own individual potential.

2. High level of personal ability. To be successful in working with gifted students, the teacher must possess above average (if not superior) intellectual ability, must be well-read, and must demonstrate a broad scope of knowledge in his own field as well as in a wide range of other subject areas.

3. Flexibility. One of the most important characteristics of a successful teacher of the gifted is flexibility. The teacher must be able to use a variety of teaching styles and to individualize with students who prefer any of a wide range of learning styles. He must model and encourage tolerance—indeed, appreciation—for a variety of styles and schools of visual or performing art and must use creative teaching methods to encourage creativity and originality in students.

4. Personal Involvement with the Arts. Last, but by no means least important, the successful teacher in any art area must be personally involved with at least one (and preferably more than one) of

the various art media. Once again, as in all areas of gifted education, the ability to emphathize with one's students is an essential quality for the teacher.

A Model for Certifying Teachers of the Talented

In 1975, the Louisiana Legislature enacted a state law that required the provision of special programs for both academically gifted and artistically talented students from ages three through twenty-one. In response to this mandate, Louisiana's Board of Elementary and Secondary Education in 1982 adopted standards for the identification of these two groups and for the certification of teachers for working with them. Unfortunately, few states or school systems offer (much less mandate) programs for the talented. In 1983, the Teacher Certification Sub-committee of the NAGC Professional Development Institute proposed a model for certification of talent program teachers. Based largely on the Louisiana standards, this model is presented below as an excellent synthesis of the professional credentials that might be used in the selection of teachers of the talented (Karnes and Parker, 1983).

CERTIFICATION FOR TEACHERS OF THE FINE AND PERFORMING ARTS

OPTION ONE.   Certification for teachers of the fine and performing arts may be incorporated into Model A through the nine-hour content block. [Note: Model A, certification requirements for teachers of the academically gifted, requires a master's degree including or in addition to at least 12 semester hours in gifted education, one graduate course in research procedures, 9 semester hours in an approved content area, and a university-supervised practicum.] In such a case, graduate program coordinators would have the responsibility of guiding students in the selection of appropriate course work to support the anticipated teaching role.

OPTION TWO.   Certification for persons with demonstrated records of achievement in the fine and performing arts may be earned as follows:

There must be substantive evidence of artistic and/or creative accomplishment over an extended period of time.

There must be evidence of professional recognition in the arts area for which certification is sought.

Qualification of an individual in the above areas must be judged by a committee of three recognized experts in the area to be credentialed, appointed by the State Department of Education.

DIFFERENTIATING THE ARTS
FOR GIFTED STUDENTS

Earlier in this chapter a rationale was presented for the incorporation of arts instruction into programs for the gifted. One of the prime arguments for this inclusion lies in the need to differentiate the arts curriculum. Clark and Zimmerman (1984) suggested that Robert Frost's classic poem, *The Road Not Taken*, is an appropriate metaphor for the education of students who are talented in the arts. As these authors so aptly asked,

> How many gifted and talented young people have opted to take the road less traveled by? It is easier to lead all students down the same path than to provide alternative roads that are less traveled. . . . Artistically talented students are a unique school population that deserve opportunities to take optional routes that will make a difference, not only to themselves but to society (p. 165).

The provision of qualitatively differentiated instruction is probably the most essential goal in developing curricula for gifted programs. Designed to meet the unique needs of gifted students, differentiated programming involves individualization, acceleration, and enrichment of the curriculum through the use of strategies, materials, and administrative arrangements that are not appropriate for those of less than gifted potential and thus are qualitatively different from those found in the traditional school program. Since the arts are frequently omitted from (or at best accorded only minimal attention in) the regular school program, the provision of any instruction in the arts is often considered to be qualitatively different, regardless of the ways in which the instruction is presented. Unfortunately, this misguided philosophy causes many gifted and talented students to miss out on challenging experiences that could greatly enrich their academic experiences and their lives.

The most common format of gifted programs in the United States, especially at the elementary level, is the pull-out enrichment program. Frequently enrichment program facilitators are professionally qualified for teaching the gifted but lack specialized training for the teaching of art, music, or drama. Similarly, many well-qualified art, music, and drama teachers have gifted students in their regular classes, but few possess a real understanding about the unique needs of the gifted or the strategies that are specifically appropriate for serving these needs. What is needed, then, is a method of differentiating instruction in the arts for students of all ages which can be used either by the gifted program teacher with no background in the arts or by the art/music/drama teacher with gifted students in the regular classroom.

Differentiation in arts instruction should follow essentially the same general principles as in other areas of the curriculum for gifted students. Applied specifically to the arts, several considerations should be remembered:

1. Contrary to common practice, the arts program for gifted students should be individualized. This principle does not imply that there should never be whole-group or small-group instruction, but rather it demands that the teacher acknowledge, understand, and allow for the development of each gifted student's individual abilities, encouraging each potential artist to self-expression in accordance with his own styles and interests.

2. The classroom environment should be open, warm, and flexible, allowing students to feel free to use their imaginations in the application of the principles of art that are learned from the instructor.

3. Students should be offered a breadth and depth of experience in order that they may identify with the materials they use, understanding all of the nuances of color or tone, the possibilities for coordinating and combining media, and the ways in which these learnings can be transferred to other contexts.

4. Regardless of the art form being studied, students should be encouraged—indeed, trained—to keep records of their work. To the visual artist, a record may be a sketchbook or a portfolio; to the music student, it may be a notebook of musical themes or original passages that spring from the subconscious during periods of rest or even other classes. These records, possibly accompanied by (or later added to) journals expressing their feelings about their work and the emotions that were present when it was being produced, can be of inestimable value in the artist's later years and should be a major part of the habits that are engrained in all art students from the early days of the program.

Clark and Zimmerman (1984) have suggested that, in order to be differentiated or different from the traditional arts program, the instruction of students talented in art should be centered around a problem-solving approach rather than based on the distinctions among the various media. The Leadership Training Model, detailed in previous chapters, presents six steps that must be followed for the effective solution of a problem: problem perception and definition, incubation, creative thinking, analysis, evaluation, and implementation. Problem finding, which incorporates the perception and definition of the problem—the first step in LTM's creative problem-solving approach—has been addressed by numerous researchers. John Dewey is perhaps most often cited for his observation that "A problem well stated is half solved."

Problem Solving in the Arts

Until recent years, little thought was given to the concept of problem solving in the arts. However, art, music, dance, and drama are essentially products of problem solving by their creators. In a significant study on the process of problem solving in art, Getzels and Csikszentmihalyi (1976) documented the importance of "problem finding," the process of determining the problem to be solved or the goal to be sought. In this study, artist-subjects were brought to a studio and, after a brief period of orientation, presented with a collection of objects commonly used as subject matter for still-life paintings. In each case, the subject was instructed to study these objects and to decide which ones would be used for his composition. Although it was suggested that it might be best to limit the time spent on the development of the product, each artist was allowed to take as much time as needed. As the artist worked, a recorder made detailed notes on every movement and procedure followed, in an attempt to analyze the thinking processes by which each worked. After all subjects had been tested in this manner, the creativity of each product was evaluated by a panel of experts. In analyzing the results of the study, the investigators found that those who had spent more time studying the objects and deciding on the approach that would be taken—the problem-finding stage—had achieved the most creative products.

The production of art—whether visual, musical, or dramatic art—is essentially a problem-solving process. As such, it must follow essentially the same steps as problem solving in any other area. Having identified a problem (or established a goal) and set it aside for a period of incubation, the artist begins the creative thinking process. It is during this stage that many different techniques, media, and materials are considered. After analyzing and evaluating the various alternatives, the artist implements the solution by using the selected processes and materials to complete the final product. Because the alternatives produced in this stage determine to a large extent the success that will be achieved in the final product, let us explore several approaches that the artist might consider.

Art as Analogy.   Analogy is simply an expression of similarity between two objects or ideas, often unrelated in the literal sense. Gordon (1961) proposed the use of analogy in a problem-solving method which he called *synectics*—the forcing together of previously unrelated elements. He identified four types of analogy that might be used in this manner: direct analogy, personal analogy, symbolic analogy, and fantasy analogy. Since these concepts are detailed in Chapter 10, the discussion here will be limited to the ways in which these four analogies might be used to solve problems in art. (A most useful manual for the use of analogy in art is Roukes' *Art Synectics*, listed in the reference section following this chapter.)

Direct Analogy. Direct analogy makes a specific comparison between two elements. In Chapter 10, this approach was used in designing an animal trap based on the principles by which predatory animals trap their prey. In the arts, direct analogy can be used to determine a way in which a likeness might be portrayed. A realistic sculpture might be seen as a simplistic use of direct analogy, in that it is made to look as much as possible like the object it is meant to represent. Other examples of the use of direct analogy in art are the animal topiaries seen at Walt Disney World; the use of musical passages from *Carnival of the Animals* or *Peter and the Wolf*, which mimic the sounds and characteristics of animals; or the use of the Colosseum of Ancient Rome as a model for modern domed stadiums.

Personal Analogy. Metaphor can be used effectively to illustrate personal analogy; in modern vernacular a dolt is often referred to as a turkey, a genius as a brain. In literature, animals frequently are used to portray concepts and foibles of human personality (e.g., the swan in *Swan Lake)*. An excellent example of personal analogy in art is Saul Bass's depiction in his classic film, *Why Man Creates*, of a vacuous personality. (An elderly woman is pictured at a cocktail party mouthing trivia about her moral upbringing; the action stops abruptly, her head opens, and a voice echoes out of her empty head.)

Symbolic Analogy. Symbolic analogy uses symbols to represent ideas. In art, symbolism is commonly used to portray concepts (e.g., the eyes as "the windows of the soul"; angel and devil as the forces of good and evil; and so on). Symbolism is also used frequently in design for theater, as well as in visual art and modern dance.

Fantasy Analogy. In using fantasy analogy the individual simply fantasizes a solution to a problem and then works toward it. In art, the fantasy analogy may be illustrated as a stairway to heaven, a magic kingdom, and so on.

In his creative work entitled *Art Synectics*, Roukes (1982) suggested one other analogy that does not fit directly into the four types suggested by Gordon: the "synaesthetic" analogy. Roukes observes that this type of analogy combines different perceptions (i.e., sensory perceptions are transformed from one mode to another). Examples of the synaesthetic analogy might be the concept of a blood-curdling scream, a rotten smell, or a full-bodied wine. Artists engaged in commercial advertising often attempt to appeal through the sense of sight to the taste of the individual, as in a taste-tempting dessert or a relaxing glass of wine. A musician may portray the sound of the sea (as in Debussy's *La Mer*), or a painter might attempt to depict sound through "feeling" in paint—as did one of my former students when she created a composition which she entitled "Horns Blowing." Roukes talks further about "paradoxical analogies" in art—images combined in an illogical manner which then must be reconciled through the viewer's emotions (p. 8). Two such visual paradoxes are a magnificent old church in Boston, flanked and almost overshadowed by a lofty, ultra-modern glass building; and the serene beauty of majestic mountains surrounding Las Vegas, largely masked by the raucous and gaudy casinos on "The Strip." These scenes would make excellent subject matter for an artist desiring to portray the paradoxes of modern life.

Another method of creative problem solving in art might use the acronym SCAMPER technique developed by Robert Eberle to facilitate the use of Osborn's (1963, p. 26) checklist for enhancing creative thinking. Several examples for applying this technique to artistic problem solving are suggested below.

Substitute: Substitute a different instrument in a musical composition to change the emotional impact communicated to the listener (e.g., portray sadness with a guitar rather than a violin); substitute an unusual visual medium to convey a different attitude to the viewer (e.g., use sculpture rather than paint to portray the coldness of death); substitute a man for a woman in a familiar dramatic role; substitute new words with a conflicting message set to a familiar tune.

Combine: Use two alter-egos or multiple doubles in drama to help a character think through two sides of a problem or a role; combine two songs into a paradoxical medley or round (e.g., the Confederacy's "Dixie" with the Union's "Battle Hymn of the Republic"); combine contrasting visual art media to create an original effect.

Adapt: Adapt a song originated as hard rock to another style or interpretation (as in "Hey, Jude," originally performed by The Beatles, later adapted to melodic instrumentation); set poetry to music to create an original song (e.g., the musical *Cats*, based on *Old Possum's Book of Practical Cats* by T. S. Eliot); adapt an old story to a modern setting (e.g., the musical play *Joseph and the Amazing Technicolor Dream Coat*).

Modify, Magnify, or Minify: Modify the tempo, meter, or rhythm of a musical composition, or use pallet knives rather than paint brushes to create a different effect or emotion in a painting; create a human sculpture larger than life to depict a specific personality, power, or other abstract trait, or magnify a piece of music by making it longer, louder, or faster; minify a song by using only a guitar rather than an orchestra or chorus as background.

Put to other uses: Use interpretive dance to depict other art forms, to portray emotion, or to represent an abstract concept; use various art media as backdrops for creative dramatics; use music during an art class to foster relaxation and creative thinking.

Eliminate: Eliminate characters or events in a dramatic production to change the course of action and the climax of the story.

Reverse: Introduce a musical composition with a style normally used as an ending; reverse roles in a stage play or sociodrama; or use artistic symbols to portray the opposite of their stereotypic concept (e.g., an angry dove as war).

CONTENT OF THE ARTS PROGRAM
FOR THE GIFTED

In the development of a comprehensive arts program, the taxonomy developed by Bloom (1956) offers an appropriate foundation for curriculum development. In the arts, there are indeed three domains: cognitive, affective, and psychomotor. Dealing with intellectual learnings, the cognitive domain in an arts program should include historical background and underlying principles, concepts, and methodology. The affective domain is involved in the development of aesthetic appreciation and the ability to evaluate "good" art. The psychomotor domain is the area in which a product is created—the application of the skills and techniques learned through the cognitive segment of the program combined with the appreciation developed in the affective. For our purposes, let us look at the arts program from three perspectives: understanding the arts (cognitive domain); appreciating and evaluating the arts (affective domain); and creating and communicating art (psychomotor domain).

Understanding the Arts

Regardless of its subject matter, any educational program must begin with factual information. Dewey has been quoted as saying, "We can have facts without thinking, but we cannot have thinking without facts!" Eisner (1966) further cited Dewey's contention that in order to produce a work of "genuine art" one must possess more intelligence than would be needed to accomplish the "so-called thinking that goes on among those who pride themselves on being 'intellectuals'." It is Eisner's belief that "artistic activity is among the most sophisticated and highly complex modes of cognitive functioning of which men are capable" (pp. 493–494). The cognitive segment of the arts program should include the concepts to be learned—the historical and theoretical perspectives, or the history and elements of each of the arts.

A Historical Background: The Development of the Arts.   In any arts program an essential element must be a study of the historical background of the particular medium, and this information is essential for any educated person. A survey of art history should begin with the cave paintings of prehistoric man and proceed through the pyramids of ancient Greece, the Parthenon of ancient Rome, the Taj Mahal and great cathedrals of the Middle Ages, and the Renaissance sculptures, paintings, and frescoes of Van Eyck, Donatello, Michelangelo, Rembrandt, and da Vinci. The Neoclassicists and Romanticists of the eighteenth and nineteenth centuries should be explored, followed by the Realists and the great Impressionists such as Renoir, Degas, Monet, and Van Gogh. And the course would not be complete if twentieth century artists such as Matisse, Picasso, and Mondrian, as well as the more recent Pollock, Miró, and Rauschenberg, were not included.

In order to develop a thorough knowledge of art history, a program must examine the major figures, works, and styles—including their significance for the particular art form and their impact on (or relationship to) the society of their day. It should also address the interrelationships between and among the various art forms and styles, as well as their relationships to other disciplines (particularly history and philosophy).

Musical history might begin with the harps, trumpets, and cymbals cited in Biblical literature and the pentatonic scales of the early Chinese, and continue through the plainsong and Gregorian chants of the Middle Ages and the secular madrigals of the Renaissance. Following an examination of the Baroque period, in which elaborate and emotional compositions gave way to opera and oratorio, our survey should take a close look at Bach and the Classical composers (Handel, Haydn, Mozart) in the eighteenth century, and the Romantics (Beethoven, Chopin) and Nationalists (Bizet, Wagner, Verdi, Tchaikovsky) of the nineteenth century. Finally, a study of the twentieth century should explore Prokofiev, Strauss, and others of the early 1900s as well as more modern composers such as Copeland.

Although we cannot define exactly when drama originated as an art, it can be assumed that almost every civilization in written history has had some form of dramatic art. Since Aristotle's early work—notably his *Poetics*—has been cited as an exemplary analysis of the drama, it would seem logical to begin any survey of this art form with the tragedies and comedies of ancient Greece and Rome. Following the miracle and morality plays of the tenth through the fifteenth centuries, sixteenth century Elizabethan drama developed rapidly in England, while professional acting companies were established in France, and Spain experienced its "Golden Age" of drama. In the 1600s, while such dramatists as Dryden in England and Corneille and Moliere in France entered the scene, Italian drama saw the rise of opera and the commedia, and Spanish drama declined. Voltaire and Goethe dominated the eighteenth century, and in the late 1800s melodrama, Romanticism, and opera gave way to Realism and Naturalism. Finally, twentieth century writers such as Tennessee Williams and Arthur Miller must be examined, as they bring to the scene a totally new and modern perspective of the drama.

Having explored each of the arts from a historical perspective, a second cognitive aspect that must be included for a complete survey of the arts is theory. Most artists would agree that art theory is second in importance to art production, and that theories of art are developed on the basis of created art, rather than theory before practice as in most other disciplines. Furthermore, most people do not engage in artistic experience for the cognitive learnings that will result. Nonetheless, theoretical background must be explored in any area if talent is to be efficiently and fully developed. Thus, it is the premise of this chapter that a sophisticated cognitive component incorporating both historical and theoretical perspectives must be included in any arts program for gifted and talented students.

A Theoretical Background: The Elements of Art.   Basic to the production and appreciation of any type of art is an understanding of the theory behind the medium. In visual art, the content of the program must include the basic elements of design—color, texture, line, shape, space, and value. In teaching about these elements, numerous examples from the masters should be used to illustrate the various options available to the artist. Georgia O'Keefe's work provides an excellent illustration of color, whereas Van Gogh is a master at texture. Jackson Pollock might be used to illustrate line, and Picasso's work shown for a taste of shape. Mondrian's use of space and Rembrandt's contrasts of value could provide excellent examples of the final two elements.

The elements that make up music may be categorized in two ways: the sound that music makes and the language by which it is communicated. A basic element of physical science, sound may be classified according to pitch (high or low), intensity (loud or soft), duration (long or short), and quality (the difference in the "tonal color" according to the instrument or voice producing it). Of these elements, one of the most essential to good music is duration—the factor that controls rhythm and tempo (or time). Still another consideration (perhaps secondary but nonetheless crucial to the production of "good" music) is harmony—the way in which different tones fit together to produce pleasant sounds or melodies.

The language of music involves the reading of music as written for a given instrument or voice. To read music, one must possess an understanding of musical notation (how the notes are written on the staff) and symbolism (flats and sharps, key and time signatures, different types of notes), as well as an understanding of the terminology that is unique to music.

In the brief discussion of the historical perspective, it was noted that Aristotle's *Poetics* served as a basis for much of our knowledge background on drama. Considering the tragedy as the major form of drama, Aristotle identified six essential elements that have since been cited by many modern writers as the basic elements of the drama: Spectacle, Fable, Characters, Diction, Thought, and Melody. The Fable (or Plot), or the action in the story being enacted, was considered by Aristotle to be the end or purpose of the drama and therefore its most essential element. Second in importance came the Characters, followed by Thought (the ability to put across the appropriate ideas). The fourth element, Diction, was simply the way in which the characters expressed their thoughts; Melody was considered to be an important element in the Tragedy of Aristotle's day, although this component has been largely omitted in the drama of modern times. The final element, the Spectacle (which Aristotle considered to be the least artistic of the six), was simply the appearance of the actors on stage. These six, then, with the possible exception of Melody, are still considered to be the basics of drama.

In addition to Aristotle's elements of drama, the dramatist should be familiar with the concept of drama as a collaborative art—one which incorporates all other types of art rather than simply the acting. The theater production involves many contributors—playwright, director, actor, designers, and architect. All are significant in the production of a drama, and an effective drama program must introduce the student to each of these essential roles. Finally, the drama student should be introduced to the various forms and types of drama (farce, melodrama, tragedy, and the like) that can be found in any good dramatics manual.

Appreciating and Evaluating the Arts

The second major component of the differentiated arts program, the segment that falls within the affective domain, involves the development of aesthetic appreciation and the ability to recognize "good" art. Perhaps it should first be observed that one need not "like" every work of art (every painting or sculpture, every drama, every type of music) to appreciate the manifestation of talent. However, this ability does demand another quality that is characteristic of the creative person: open-mindedness. Therefore, although the development of a "feeling" for what is good in art is essential to aesthetic appreciation, some degree of cognitive understanding must also be built into the program.

Citing Goethe's ideas about the three functions of art—"entertainment, edification, and exaltation of the human spirit"—Archer (1978) suggested that art "deals with man's relationships with himself, his fellowmen, and his existence. Much of the world's greatest art depicts the magnificence of the human spirit, especially when faced with adversity" (p. 9). This perspective, then, strengthens our concept that the affective is an essential component of any comprehensive program in the arts.

Again citing Goethe, Archer (1978) pointed out three simple questions that can serve as guidelines for evaluating all types of art:

1. What was the artist trying to do?
2. How well did he do it?
3. Was it worth doing? (p. 49)

Using these three criteria, any person with a modicum of training in the historical background and principles of the various art forms should be able to develop basic skills of art criticism.

Creating and Communicating Art

Having established a historical and theoretical background in the arts, the teacher is ready to begin art instruction. For the teacher who is untrained in the arts, this segment of the program may be the most difficult. It is essential, however, that the classroom production of crafts not be allowed to substitute for the production of fine art. It is not possible to develop in this chapter a complete sequence for instruction in the three major art areas; however, many manuals are available to assist the teacher in the achievement of this goal. The most efficient (and effective) method of teaching art skills may be a team-teaching arrangement in which visual art, music, speech, and English teachers cooperate to share their various talents with the students. In this context it should be noted that the role of the gifted program teacher, trained to serve the needs of the gifted through differentiated instruction, is paramount in the success of such an arrangement. Serving as facilitator and coordinator of the team teaching plan, this teacher has the ultimate responsibility for (1) assuring that the instruction that takes place in each area is indeed qualitatively different from the approaches that are used in the regular art, music, drama, and English classes; and (2) facilitating the application of the techniques learned in such classes through the creation and communication of appropriate products in all of the art areas within the gifted program structure. For it is ultimately in the creation and communication of art that the value of the entire program becomes evident and begins to affect the student's life.

SUGGESTED ACTIVITIES FOR
THE ARTS PROGRAM

The nature of art is such that the pursuit of a "cookbook" approach to curriculum development would obviate the very creativity that must be inherent in the type of program proposed herein. Nonetheless, some examples of strategies that could foster the necessary understandings and appreciations should be helpful to the teacher who cannot proceed directly into the development of a total program. The following activities are offered as only a beginning; the extent to which students might be exposed to the various art forms is limited only by the creativity of the teacher.

1. Following the lead of Getzels and Csikszentmihalyi (1976), lay out at random a generous variety of objects of the type that might be used in still life painting (fruit, dried or fresh flowers, musical instruments, books, artifacts, and anything else that might stimulate ideas for an unusual composition). Be sure that there are enough objects for each student to select several. Instruct a few students at a time to go to the display and examine, feel, smell, and otherwise explore the objects that interest them. Encourage them to select a few items, take them back to their individual work places, and compose an arrangement to reproduce. The medium need not be painting, it can be sculpture or even a musical composition. Other art forms might be used (e.g., collage). At the end of the project, have students compare and discuss the different media that were explored through the activity.

2. Show the film *Why Man Creates*, turning off the projector immediately after the historical sequence. Have students list as many events from the sequence as they can recall, and compare until all of the major events have been listed. Instruct them to make their own sequential lists of significant events in history and to represent them in some type of art form which, while not literal in interpretation, represents them symbolically (in a fashion similar to the filmed sequence).

3. Role play abstract qualities in nature—trees blowing in the wind, spider webs sparkling with frozen rain; instruct students to move to music to represent these various concepts, then portray them symbolically in some form of visual art.

4. Take a field trip to a scenic area, then write about it in haiku on return to the classroom. Illustrate the poetry that has been written.

5. Design visual compositions or musical passages to deliver messages about societal conflicts, controversial issues, or similar concepts.

6. Portray through various art forms the types of contrast that are discussed earlier in this chapter (e.g., an ultra-modern building looming large in the background of a magnificent old church; mankind's most inhuman creations flanked by God's most beautiful; etc.).

7. Using the old familiar composition *Peter and the Wolf* as a model, set a fairy tale, a drama, or an original story to music.

8. Use Stryker's Morphological Analysis system (see page 216) to stimulate ideas for visual art, music, or drama. Use forced relationships (Gordon's synectics) to generate new ideas to represent in art form. (If these ideas are opposites or conflict in some way, the result may be even more interesting.)

9. Use audiovisual media (tapes, slides, films) to teach about the history of the various arts.

10. Hold an art festival; have each student research a selected artist, period or style of art, and so on. (See page 324 for further details on ways to develop this project.)

Other excellent examples may be found in Roukes' (1982) *Art Synectics,* Edwards' (1979) *Drawing on the Right Side of the Brain,* Spolin's (1963) *Improvisation for the Theatre,* and other such materials. Use these and other activities to stimulate your own imagination and develop extensions that will encourage students to create their own methods of exploring the arts.

INTEGRATING THE ARTS
INTO THE CURRICULUM

A major concept in the philosophy of the Leadership Training Model is the importance of integration in the curriculum for gifted and talented students. Although this chapter has previously set forth a strong rationale for formal (as well as informal) instruction in the arts as a regular part of gifted curriculum, many of the potential benefits of art instruction would be missed if the arts were not integrated as well into every other subject of the regular curriculum. The schools are encouraged to develop and offer interdisciplinary courses that integrate the various art forms with a variety of humanities areas. Realizing, however, that such courses are rarely available outside of the gifted program itself, the remainder of this chapter will propose activities by which the arts may be integrated into, or correlated with, the various content areas of the core curriculum.

The Arts and the Study of Language

1. Integrate drama as a literary form with drama as an art form (e.g., act out Shakespearean dramas studied as literature; see Chapter 11 for specific ideas).
2. Research the concept of negative space in various art media (e.g., pauses in music, blank space or reverse print in visual art, or open space in sculpture).
3. Collect examples of metaphor that can be represented visually in art, comparing the figure of speech to its visual representations (e.g., an antique light fixture compared to a cluster of bell-shaped flowers; a ballet dancer compared to a blossoming tree).
4. Illustrate an original poem or story through painting, mime, or melody, or write poetry based on a musical composition or painting.
5. Use choral reading to build both language and music skills.
6. Develop creative dramatics skills through oral interpretation of poetry that students might enjoy, such as James Whitcomb Riley's *The Bear Story (That Alex 'ist Made Up His Own Se'f)*.

Mathematics and the Arts

1. Use computer graphics to illustrate an original poem.
2. Make a study of the geometric shapes that can be found within paintings of the great masters.
3. Create interesting designs using tesselations; vary designs as to color, texture, and space.
4. Compare fractions to meter signature in music; compare musical patterns to mathematical sequences.
5. Use Cuisenaire rods or other manipulative materials to develop a three-dimensional design that simultaneously demonstrates a mathematical concept.
6. Study the invention of mathematical theorems (e.g., Jacques Hadamard, *A Study of Invention in the Mathematical Field*) and compare the imagery to the work of visual artists.
7. Use creative dramatics to teach basic algebra by drawing a number line on the floor and moving through the parts of the problem.

Integrating the Arts with the Sciences

1. Draw an analogy between the way the human ear picks up sounds and transmits them to the brain (biology) and the way in which a musical instrument transmits different tones (physics).
2. Compare the concepts of color in light and color in paint. Hold jars of colored water up to a window to demonstrate the blending of various colors in light. (Point out that the absence of color is black in light but white in paint, etc.)
3. Make a pinhole camera (camera obscura). Explore the principles by which photography operates, and use the camera to make creative compositions from nature.

Social Studies and the Arts

1. Use the musical composition *Pictures at an Exhibition* (Moussorgsky) and the paintings on which it was based it to enrich a social studies lesson on the Soviet Union.
2. Teach native dances, music, art history and styles, in connection with a social studies unit on a given country.
3. Use the film *The Stonecutter* to illustrate elements of the Japanese culture (pentatonic scale, costumes, customs, and the like).
4. Make puppets and produce a show to present the folklore of a country to younger children.
5. Encourage students to live the concept of free enterprise by helping them develop small businesses (e.g., silk-screening shirts, making arts/crafts for a Christmas bazaar, etc.).

The Arts in Health and Physical Education

1. Use creative dramatics or sociodrama to help students work through their concerns about drug use.
2. Conduct art activities before and after various types of exercise to test the degree to which exercise frees the mind to create.
3. Develop an animated film to teach younger children about the dangers of talking with strangers, traffic safety, current problems of drug abuse, and so on.
4. Write a song to teach children about some part or function of the body (a familiar example is the "bone song").
5. Choreograph dance steps for a musical production.
6. Use interpretive dance to tell a story.

REFERENCES

Archer, S. M. (1978). *How theatre happens.* New York: Macmillan.

Bloom, B. S. (Ed.) (1956). *Taxonomy of educational objectives: The classification of educational goals.* New York: David McKay.

Bloom, B. S. (1985). Generalizations about talent development. In B. S. Bloom (Ed.), *Developing talent in young people* (pp. 507–549). New York: Ballantine Books.

Burton, J. M. (1984, July). Abstracts and chronicles of our time: The arts in adolescent development. *Art Education,* 32–35.

Cane, F. (1936). The gifted child in art. *Journal of Educational Sociology, 10*(2), 67–73.

Clark, B. (1983). *Growing up gifted.* Columbus, Ohio: Merrill.

Clark, G., & Zimmerman, E. (1984). *Educating artistically talented students.* Syracuse, NY: Syracuse University Press.

Dorn, C. M. (1984, July). The arts as academic education. *Art Education,* 16–19.

Ecker, D. W. (1963). The artistic process as qualitative problem solving. *Journal of Aesthetic and Art Criticism, XXI,* 283–297.

Edwards, B. (1979). *Drawing on the right side of the brain.* Los Angeles: J. P. Tarcher.

Eisner, E. (1966). Arts curricula for the gifted. *Teachers College Record, 67,* 492–501.

Gallagher, J. (1985). *Teaching the gifted child* (3rd ed.). Boston: Allyn and Bacon.

Getzels, J. W., & Csikszentmihalyi, M. (1976). *The creative vision: A longitudinal study of problem finding in art.* New York: John Wiley & Sons.

Gordon, W. J. J. (1961). *Synectics.* New York: Harper and Row.

Gowan, J. C. (1984). Art and music as stimulants to right hemisphere imagery and creativity. In Crabbe, A. B., et al. (Eds.), *New directions in creativity research.* Ventura, CA: Ventura County Supt. of Schools Office.

Greene, L. B. (1953). Creative art teaching and the gifted high school student. *California Journal of Secondary Education, 28*(4), 197–202.

Hickok, D., & Smith, J. A. (1974). *Creative teaching of music in the elementary school.* Boston: Allyn and Bacon.

Janson, H. W. (1966). *History of art.* Englewood Cliffs, NJ: Prentice-Hall.

Karnes, F. A., & Parker, J. P. (1983). Teacher certification in gifted education: The state of the art and considerations for the future. *Roeper Review, 6,* 18–19.

Khatena, J. (1979). The nurture of imagery in the visual and performing arts. *Gifted Child Quarterly, 23,* 735–747.

Krippner, S., & Blickenstaff, R. (1970). The development of self-concept as part of an arts workshop for the gifted. *Gifted Child Quarterly, 14,* 163–166.

Lowenfeld, V., & Brittain, W. L. (1965). *Creative and mental growth.* New York: Macmillan.

Madeja, S. S. (Ed.) (1983). *Gifted and talented in art education.* Reston, VA: National Art Education Association.

McHose, A. I. (1951). *Basic principles of the techniques of 18th and 19th century composition.* New York: Appleton-Century Crofts.

Moyers, B. (1984). *Curriculum guide for creativity with Bill Moyers.* Fort Lauderdale, FL: School Board of Broward County.

National Assessment of Educational Progress (1981). *Procedural handbook: 1978–1979 art assessment.* Denver: Educational Commission of the States.

Osborn, A. (1963). *Applied imagination.* New York: Charles Scribner's Sons.

Renzulli, J., Smith, L., White, A., Callahan, C., & Hartman, R. (1976). *Scales for rating the behavioral characteristics of superior students.* Mansfield Center, CT: Creative Learning Press.

Ritson, J. E., & Smith, J. A. (1975). *Creative teaching of art in the elementary school.* Boston: Allyn and Bacon.

Roukes, N. (1982). *Art synectics.* Worcester, MA: Davis Publications.

Spolin, V. (1963). *Improvisation for the theater: A handbook of teaching and directing techniques.* Evanston, IL: Northwestern University Press.

Szekely, G. (1981). The artist and the child—A model program for the artistically gifted. *Gifted Child Quarterly, 25,* 67–72.

Waddell, J. H. (1960). The way of art for the gifted child. *Studies in Art Education, 2,* 66–71.

Williams, R. M. (1977). Why children should draw: The surprising link between art and learning. *Saturday Review,* pp. 11–16.

Wilson, B., & Wilson, M. (1976). Visual narrative and the artistically gifted. *Gifted Child Quarterly, 20,* 432–447.

Ziegfeld, E. (Ed.) (1961). *Art for the academically talented student in the secondary school.* Washington, DC: NEA/NAEA.

15

Media in Gifted Education

A film is a petrified fountain of thought.
Jean Cocteau

Over the years, numerous publications have addressed the values of using audiovisual media (radio, television, tapes, and films) in all levels of education. In an empirical study of second grade reading instruction, Witty and Fitzwater (1953) found that the use of films in conjunction with related readers produced the following advantages over the traditional use of basal readers and other supplementary materials:

1. Pupils experienced greater gains in reading level during the experimental phase than during the control period.
2. More independent reading was done (particularly in areas related to the films) during the experimental than during the control phase.
3. Motivation, interest, and attention spans were greater during the experimental phase than during the control period, particularly with respect to the brighter pupils.
4. The films served as concrete experiences for the children, helping them grasp concepts more readily than with the use of traditional methods.
5. Group discussions improved with the use of films, encouraging more pupils to enjoy and retell the stories that they read and helping the usually solitary children to socialize more readily.
6. The pupils experienced greater general language growth during the experimental period, including the ability to express themselves more distinctly, more accurately, and more effectively.

7. The improvement in vocabulary comprehension, especially in areas that used the same terminology as the films, transferred to the reading of other materials.

In spite of the obvious advantages of using audiovisual media in connection with various subject areas, little attention has been given to the specific values of media use in gifted education. Recognizing the need to explore the possibilities offered by audiovisuals for the gifted classroom, a colleague and I collaborated in a two-year series of articles entitled "A Picture is Worth a Thousand Words" (Parker and Kreamer, 1982–1984). For this series, we previewed a large number of films in a search for examples of media that could be used effectively in the gifted classroom. As we explored, we found that the films we considered most creative and most effective for lesson stimuli were those that were either animated, nonverbal, or both. This discovery has suggested two methods of using media in the gifted classroom: teaching gifted students to use film either as a self-contained art form or in connection with their own independent studies in areas of personal interest, and using film as a central stimulus on which to build a lesson or a unit.

TEACHING GIFTED STUDENTS TO USE FILM

Film Animation*

With the introduction of existing-light (XL) Super-8 photographic film and equipment, the technique of film animation became easily accessible to students of all ages. Once students have been instructed in the technique—either as part of a unit on media or photography, or through individualized instruction—it may be explored simply as a graphic art form or used as a supplement to creative writing or other class activities (e.g., writing a creative story and using film animation to develop a narrated film, or preparing an animated film and then writing a narration to accompany it; illustrating an oral presentation of a topic researched by the student; etc.). A suggested plan for teaching film animation to gifted students is detailed below.

---

1. Begin with a brief historical background of the use of film. (The Time-Life series on photography provides an excellent reference

---

*A significant portion of the section on film animation represents the author's adaptation of instructional materials prepared by Jim Rogers, a teacher in the Lafayette, Louisiana, Gifted Program, and Chris Nelson, Coordinator of Gifted Programs for the State of Georgia. Their permission to use their material and their assistance in developing this section of the media chapter are gratefully acknowledged.

for this purpose.) Then proceed to activities designed to help the students understand film and how it works to produce motion pictures.

a. Show the students a strip of Super-8 movie film, explaining that it is divided into individual squares which, when projected in rapid succession, gives the illusion of movement.

b. Use a zoetrope to demonstrate the principles involved in motion picture projection. A simple nineteenth-century toy, the zoetrope can be made using a turntable or lazy Susan and a wide strip of stiff paper (oak tag or heavy construction paper works well). Cut the paper approximately four inches wide and about two inches longer than the circumference of the turntable. Cut about ten vertical slits, approximately one inch in length, at about one-half inch from the top edge of the strip. Overlap and fasten the ends to make a large cylinder, and place it on the turntable (see Figure 15–1).

c. Explain the mathematical aspect of filming, and encourage students to do their own figuring whenever possible. They should be told that each roll of Super-8 film is fifty feet in length, and that fifty feet of film, projected at eighteen frames per second, will last about three minutes. At the rate of three clicks of the shutter release (and thus three frames) per scene, six scenes (or scene variations) will take only one second to view. If each student prepares a ten-second film, eighteen short

Figure 15–1

films can be included on each fifty-foot roll. (Note: If parents desire copies of their children's films, they can be easily converted to videocassettes, with the parents providing their own tapes.) Film animation is therefore a very cost-effective method for use in the gifted classroom.

2. Talk about stories; ask the students what every story must have (beginning, middle, and end). Using Stryker's Morphological Analysis (see page 216) or other brainstorming activity, lead the students to develop simple story lines with a beginning, a middle, and an end. Have them make story boards to represent their stories pictorially as described below:

   a. Cut a second strip of stiff paper the same length as the first strip and two inches in width; divide this strip into ten squares (or one for each vertical slit). In the first square, print the title of the story to be filmed. In the second square place the appropriate credits (Producer, Director, etc.); and in the last square write "The End," to indicate that the film has ended. In the other squares, sketch a series of pictures to tell the story; each "frame" should depict a movement (and a more advanced stage of action) from the previous position (see Figure 15–2).

   b. Overlap and glue the ends of the prepared story board so that the pictures in the frames face the center of the loop. Fit this strip inside of the zoetrope. To create the illusion of movement and help the students understand the concept of film animation, simply turn the table rapidly as they look through the slits at the moving story board (see Figure 15–3).

3. Once students understand the concept of animation, use one or more animated films (such as *Wind*, or *Changes, Changes*, or others suggested in the later sections of this chapter) to help them grasp the concept of what can be accomplished through the use of this technique. (With older students, the teacher may wish to use films on animation such as *The Light Fantastic, The Handy Dandy Do-It-Yourself Animation Film*, or *The Yellow Ball Workshop*.)

4. Now you are ready to begin making a film. (At this point you may wish to arrange the students in teams of two, so that one can

Figure 15–2

Figure 15–3

handle the movement of the scenes and the other can do the filming.) For the best effect, students should draw story boards illustrating the action that they wish to have take place in the film. (Note: Although the story board is often the key to a successful film, it is important for the students to understand that the "frames" of the story board need not be elaborately drawn, since it is only a plan for the actual organization of the film itself.) In this step, interest will be held more effectively if each frame shows a significant change in action from the previous one (see Figure 15–4).

5. When the story board has been approved by the teacher, instruct the students to begin by drawing or cutting out letters for the title and credits, which will be shown at the beginning of the film (the credits may be shown at the end if preferred). Next they draw on

Figure 15–4

colored construction paper, sketch on white paper and color with one or more appropriate media, or select from coloring books, magazines, or other publications the figures that will be included in the films (e.g., the sun, a tree, people or animals, buildings). The students then cut out these figures and set them aside for use in the filming.

6. In preparation for filming the planned sequence, follow these steps:

   a. Assemble the following equipment and supplies:
      Super-8 movie camera with through-the-lens viewfinder, single-frame exposure feature, and cable release (also desirable, but not essential, are a fast lens for use with existing-light (XL) film, a zoom lens, a macro-focus, and/or an auto-exposure feature)
      Tripod (need not be elaborate or heavy-duty)
      Film—ASA 160, Tungsten balanced (one roll for each movie to be made)
      Large sheet of background material (white or any appropriate background color which reflects light, at least the size of poster board)
      Cut-out letters and characters to be used in telling the story

   b. Have students place the background material on a flat surface and arrange the letters for the first title frame on this background. Set up the tripod above the background, in a position that will permit the students to look *down* through the viewfinder without disturbing the mounted camera.

   c. Load the film into the camera, attach the remote cable release, and mount the camera on the tripod with the viewfinder aimed downward toward the background setting. The setup, now ready for filming, will look like Figure 15–5.

   d. Check to be sure that the camera is focused so that the first frame can be seen through the viewfinder.

   e. Instruct (and closely supervise) students in the filming process, as described below:
      Using the cable release, film the title frame by pressing the release button ten times. (With a little imagination, even this introductory material can be made interesting; for instance, add one letter for each frame, use letters that give a three-dimensional effect, and so on.)
      Arrange the initial scene on the appropriate background and film, using twelve clicks of the release button (ten for primary children) for this scene only, to allow the viewer time to acclimate to the action.
      Change the scene, either by removing the old scene and replacing it with a new one or by making some slight adjustment in the last scene (1/4″ is effective) to depict movement.

Figure 15–5

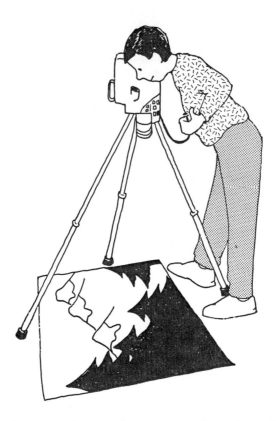

Film the second scene by pressing the release button two or three times.

Repeat the last two steps (using two to three exposures between each two scene changes) until the last scene has been filmed.

Note: Be sure to save a few frames at the end of the film for a final message ("The End," or something more creative).

When the final frame has been completed, remove the film, have it developed, and your animated film is complete!

In addition to the above discussion, which presents a simple method of teaching and using film animation in the gifted classroom, this strategy can be expanded for more advanced studies. Techniques such as editing and splicing can be taught to the older students (local photographers are often eager to share their knowledge with interested students), and even young students can develop sound tracks for recording on cassette and playing back along with the showing of their films. Film animation is a highly versatile tool, and its uses are limited only by the imagination of the teacher and students who work with it.

Before leaving the subject of animation, it should be noted here that computer graphics has introduced an entirely new world to this art form. Several of the popular microcomputers that are commonly used in gifted programs now offer animation software (unfortunately the use of a "mouse" is required for this type of drawing). Whereas computer graphics is best managed by older students, this technique offers exciting new possibilities for the future of animation as an art.

Video

The advent in recent years of the videocassette recorder (VCR) has contributed significantly to the classroom usefulness of audiovisual media. Video is used for filming classroom projects (including science or social studies fair presentations for self-evaluation or judging), as well as for regular instruction. It is becoming a preferred medium in the classroom, as its rewinding ("instant replay") and counting functions enable a presenter to locate and replay one or more preselected sections easily, and the structure of the cassette eliminates many of the headaches that the use of other types of films have caused in the past for teachers (burned film, burned projector bulbs, damaged films, and the like). In keeping with "Third Wave" technology, increasing numbers of school districts are providing video equipment for their schools—especially for gifted programs—and students are being taught not only to use the systems for playing prerecorded videocassettes for instructional purposes, but to do their own classroom filming as well. Perhaps the most attractive advantages of video are that films of all types are widely available in this less expensive and more durable format, and that reusable tapes are readily available at nominal cost for classroom use.

USING FILM AS A CENTRAL STIMULUS

Paraphrasing Clifton Fadiman, Sisk (1976) pointed out the need for utilizing "models of high thought and feeling" in the education of the gifted. The use of the central stimulus technique was heralded by Sisk as an excellent and appropriate vehicle for presenting such models as Fadiman had proposed, helping to make the gifted feel "buoyed up by the noble stream of Western civilization of which we are a part." In a column co-authored with colleague Jean Kreamer for *G/C/T* (1982–1984), several methods of using film as a central stimulus in the gifted classroom were addressed. These included curriculum development (e.g., using film to introduce a discussion of intercultural relationships), subject matter enrichment (such as several films suggested for motivating interest in specific topics of science), personal development (e.g., films designed to stimulate values discussions or to set the stage for a group counseling session), and creativity development (notably, several outstanding films that might be used as stimuli for creative writing or other activities designed to foster creativity in the gifted).

In the section that follows, excerpts from the film review columns are presented; however, the teacher is strongly encouraged to use these suggestions only as springboards to other ideas. The films that are discussed here are among the very best—their usefulness is limited only by the imagination of the teacher.

FILMS FOR USE IN GIFTED EDUCATION*

Why Man Creates

On rare occasion there appears a creative endeavor that withstands the test of time. "A true work of art" it may well be termed—a classic, a masterpiece. Created by Saul Bass and distributed by Pyramid Film & Video, *Why Man Creates* is such a film. In its treatment of the subject of creativity and the underlying reasons why man does create, as well as in film-making technique and in content, this unusual film is indeed a masterpiece.

Why Man Creates is divided into eight segments of varying length, focus, and technique, each segment serving somewhat as a chapter in a book. "The Edifice," an historic overview of the world man has created for himself, is entirely animated. Using humor and irony, this segment explores almost in a fleeting glance man's entire political, scientific, sociological, cultural, and philosophical history, ending with a view of today's rapid technological explosion. The second segment, "Fooling Around: Sometimes Ideas Start That Way," is a series of takeoffs on where and how ideas may appear. In "The Process," an eccentric artist's avant-garde sculpture is analogized with quotations from Edison, Einstein, and Hemingway, all of whom were at times considered eccentric. "The Judgment" symbolizes the shooting down of ideas and creations as society judges the artist's work. In "The Parable," another example of clever symbolism, a nonconformist ping-pong ball is exiled amidst a sea of conformist balls. Its mysterious disappearance leaves the viewer with a wide range of interpretations, provoking thought about the impact of nonconformism on society. "A Digression" uses a subtly humorous conversation between two animated snails to depict

*Major sections of the film reviews in this chapter are excerpted or adapted from a column entitled "A Picture Is Worth a Thousand Words: Film in Gifted Education," published in *G/C/T* (1982–1984). The author gratefully acknowledges the permission of her co-author, Dr. Jean T. Kreamer (Director of the University Media Center, University of Southwestern Louisiana, Lafayette, LA), and *The Gifted Child Today* (formerly *G/C/T*), P.O. Box 6448, Mobile, Al 36660, to reprint the materials used herein.

the abrupt death of a creative idea; and "The Search" demonstrates the necessity of long-term commitment in many creative endeavors. The last segment, entitled "The Mark," is an attempt to summarize the concept of creativity—the commonalities and the diversities of creative people. Whereas this film does not attempt to judge society and its often scathing reaction to creative ideas, *Why Man Creates* ends with a hopeful and elegant statement praising the uniqueness and potential of the individual.

Using *Why Man Creates* in Gifted Education

Why Man Creates is one of those rare films that improves with every showing. View it again and again, and show it to your students *at least twice!* Following are suggestions for its use in the development of creative thinking/production:

Before Viewing:

1. Talk about the creative process:
   a. What is creativity? the creative process? the creative person? the creative product?
   b. What is different about the creative person?
   c. What makes a product creative?
   d. What factors block the creative process? (See page 143.)
2. Encourage students to share their experiences with the creative process:
   a. What did they create?
   b. What emotions did they feel in the process?
3. Pose value questions such as:
   a. What do *you* value in art? What does *society* value in art?
   b. Is society's approval important? Why or why not?
   c. If you were an artist, what kind of art would you like to create? (Encourage discussion of various styles of art, music, etc.)
4. Ask, "How many of you think you have creative potential?" Have students list and then share creative things they have done and/or would like to do.
5. Tell students they are going to see a film entitled *Why Man Creates.*
   a. Ask, "If you were going to produce a film with this title, what kinds of scenes would you include?"
   b. Ask, "Why do *you* think man creates?" (Write class answers on a transparency for comparison after viewing the film.)

During First Viewing:

1. Indicate to the students that you will show the first segment of the film and then will ask them to list all the people or events they can remember from it. Show the introduction and "The Edifice."

   a. Have students list in chronological order everything they can remember.

   b. Have one student read her list, while others check theirs. Have others share additional events until all are covered. Show a transparency listing everything in this historical sequence, allowing different students to conjecture about the symbolism as each event, discovery, invention, person, or period is mentioned. Have students count their responses then compare to see who has the longest correct list.

   c. Discuss the overall symbolism of "The Edifice."

2. Ask, "How do ideas start?" Discuss.

   a. Show "Fooling Around."

   b. Ask for examples of situations in which "fooling around" results (or might result) in creative production.

3. Show "The Process." Allow students to share their impressions of the artist's work and predict what society's reactions might be.

4. Show "The Judgment."

   a. Compare the segment to their impressions.

   b. Discuss symbolism of "The Process" and "The Judgment."

5. Show "A Parable."

   a. Encourage students to speculate on the message of this segment.

   b. Ask, "Did the ball remind you of any person, thing, event, or story character?" (Lead into discussion of *Jonathan Livingston Seagull.*)

   c. Ask, "What happened to the ball?" (Use this question as a boundary breaker, and/or have students write creative stories about the ball's fate.)

   d. Read Thoreau's famous quotation from *Walden Pond:* "If a man does not keep pace with his companions, perhaps it is because he hears a different drummer. Let him step to the music which he hears, however measured or far away." Discuss its meaning, and its relationship to the story of the ball.

6. Show "A Digression."

   a. Use a transparency containing the snail's dialogue. ("Have you ever thought that radical ideas threaten institutions then become institutions and in turn reject radical ideas which threaten institutions?" "No." "Gee—for a minute I thought I had something!") Be sure that the students understand the meanings of the terms.

b. Rewind this segment and show it again.

c. Ask what the significance of "A Digression" is. Attempt to lead students to discover that creative ideas are often suppressed.

7. Show "The Search." Stop the film and explore the message imparted by this section. Remind the students that a lack of time is a factor that blocks the creative process, since most creative endeavors take time to accomplish.

8. Tell students that the last section ties it all together in a final attempt to answer the question "why man creates." Show the remainder of the film.

After First Viewing:

1. Ask questions to stimulate thinking, such as:

a. What if the ball had come back?

b. What if the second snail had given a different answer? (What kind of answer would have encouraged the first snail? How does this lesson relate to human relations and interpersonal communication?)

c. What if the artist's work had been conventional? (How would the people have reacted?)

d. What if the artist's work had been simply ignored by the people? Would he have liked that kind of reaction better than the one he received? Why or why not?

2. Conduct a group dynamics activity to help students understand about feelings.

a. Label each person in a group with a direction (unknown to the one wearing it) such as "Ignore me," "Flatter me," "Agree with me," "Laugh at me," and so on. With the group members so labeled, have them discuss an issue, a plan, a saying, and the like.

b. After the discussion (with each group member reacting appropriately to the comments of the others) allow the students to look at their labels. Encourage them to share how they felt after being ignored, flattered, ridiculed, and so on, and how these behaviors affected their own participation in the discussion.

3. Explore the affective reactions induced in students by the film, using such questions as:

a. Is creativity always good? Is learning always good? (Ask for examples of creativity and leadership ability that turned away from the good; for example, the creativity of a carefully planned murder, the leadership of Adolf Hitler, etc.)

b. What examples did you observe in the film of:

Beauty? (Encourage consideration of poetic passages and free thinking as well as visual aesthetics.)

Emotion? (Consider each segment; for instance, the Greek slaves in "The Edifice" attempting to achieve rule of and by the people.)

Creativity being squelched?

Figures of speech or other literary techniques (irony, metaphore, hyperbole, symbolism)?

c. How do you feel about failure? What *is* failure? Is failure always bad? What about scientific failure? (Can a scientific experiment fail? Why or why not?)

d. Are you more of a conformist or a nonconformist? Explain.

4. Arrange opportunities for students to have contact with creative producers and thinkers. Young children can benefit from contact with other students who are creative; visiting speakers (artists, musicians, writers, inventors); field trips to galleries, laboratories, concerts; interviews (e.g., what most influenced their creative development?); mentorships or internships; and the like.

5. Show the film through without interruption. Encourage students to plan and begin work on a creative product or a creative skill that they would like to learn or improve. Encourage them to keep journals, portfolios, or other records of their progress.

Balablok

One of the most important skills that gifted students will need for successfully undertaking leadership roles in society is the ability to communicate effectively with others. Although only eight minutes long, essentially nonverbal, and totally animated, *Balablok* deals directly with the subject of interpersonal conflict and offers a wide diversity of instructional uses for the gifted classroom. Using animated geometric shapes speaking in staccato, nonsensical syllables, this novel film symbolically relates a story of the problems arising from differences between cultures, and ways in which these problems are often solved.

Balablok can be used as an introduction to a discussion or simulation dealing with intercultural relationships, particularly the antiquated concept of the United States of America as a "melting pot" of old-world cultures. It also can be used effectively with older students in conjunction with studies of the nature of power and war. More specifically, it can be shown as a springboard for open discussion in a study of Adolf Hitler and the Nazi movement. Two other films that might be used successfully after *Balablok* are *Hitler–Anatomy of a Dictatorship* (Learning Corporation of America, twenty-three minutes, 1969) and *The Last Nazi* (Learning Corporation of America, seventy-two minutes, 1977). The former is a straightforward documentary film comprised in part of World War II footage; the latter—an interview with Albert Speer, architect and Master of Armaments for Adolf Hitler—also contains unusual documentary film footage. *Balablok* sets an ideal stage for these films; however, showing the three consecutively could be overwhelming to viewers, as the impact of moving images complemented by sound is the most powerful instructional medium available to teachers.

Using *Balablok* in Gifted Education

Some specific suggestions for using *Balablok* in the gifted classroom might include the following:

Before Viewing:

Consider using this film without an introduction. Simply tell students that it is an animated film with at least one moral, and encourage them to look for symbolism and messages portrayed by the film.

After Viewing:

1. Ask the following question as a boundary breaker: "If you could come back after death as a person of another culture/race/ nationality, which culture would you choose?" Encourage students to share their reasons if they wish.
2. Compare and contrast the "melting pot" concept with that of pluralism. (The "melting pot" concept suggests that all cultures blend together to form one integrated society. In a pluralistic society, on the other hand, numerous distinct cultures coexist within one nation, with each retaining its own integrity.) Explore these concepts further through such questions as:
   a. Is this assimilation usually peacefully accomplished? Is it always desirable?
   b. In the settlement of many nations, including the United States, the "melting pot" theory has been noted. What does the

"melting pot" concept imply? Do you think cultural compromise has occurred in our country?

3. Explain that the results of the "melting pot" spawned a movement toward pluralism, which itself is being questioned in modern times.

   a. Explore the etymology of the term *pluralism*, relating its meaning to current society.

   b. Encourage discussion of the advantages and disadvantages of pluralism (e.g., the sharing of cultural strengths; the use of nonstandard language or behavior in standard situations, etc.).

4. Have students name examples of conflicts in early and modern history that have been caused by cultural differences.

5. Discuss the symbolic meaning of the film.

6. Follow the film with optional writing activities such as essays on pluralism, coexistence, or similar topics; creative stories or poetry on related topics; editorials urging greater cooperation among cultures; and so on.

7. Conduct values activities designed to stimulate serious and productive thinking about intercultural relationships.

8. Use simulation gaming to provide vicarious experiences in intercultural relationships. Two such games that have been used effectively are Rafá Rafá and Bafá Bafá. Both of these games are cross-cultural simulations. The former, published in 1976, takes a little less time and may be used with younger students; the latter, published in 1977, requires approximately two hours to complete and is more effective with older students. (Both are published by SIMILE II, P.O. Box 910, Del Mar, CA 92014.)

A Drop of Water

This film uses innovative camera techniques, cleverly matching action with music and color. Following a drop of water as it makes its way from a sparkling mountain rainshower to the sea, this spectacular film creatively highlights the water cycle. Only fourteen minutes in length, *A Drop of Water* holds the interest of its viewers through photographic vignettes accompanied by a variety of appropriate musical selections ranging from classics to rock, revealing nature's vast use of our water resources. Winner of the coveted Cine Golden Eagle Award in 1973, this delightful film clearly conveys its message through the passage, "In each drop of water is born the seed of life itself; for all living things are nourished by the passing stream."

Using *A Drop of Water* in Gifted Education

Before Viewing:

1. Trace a hypothetical drop of water through the steps of the water cycle (or perhaps lead students through a guided fantasy in which they imagine themselves as drops of water in the water cycle).

2. Have students write creative stories that might be told by a drop of water describing its journey through the water cycle. (The imagery activity suggested above would be an excellent stimulus for this type of writing.)

3. Brainstorm ways in which nature (man, animals, plants) uses water.

After Viewing:

1. Encourage participation among more reticent or less verbal students by asking:
   a. Describe in one word what feelings you experienced while viewing this film.
   b. Using a different one-word response, tell what you heard in the film.

2. Use the film as a stimulus for art and music activities.
   a. Have students illustrate the water cycle creatively.
   b. Encourage students to write or arrange musical sequences to accompany various scenes (consider using the film without sound for this purpose.)
   c. Have students make collages from colored tissue paper (or other materials), illustrating the journey of a drop of water or their feelings while viewing the film.

3. Expand on the earlier brainstorming activity by describing in detail the interdependence of nature and the importance of water to humans, plants, and animals.

4. Discuss renewable versus nonrenewable natural resources. Ask "Is water a renewable resource?" Discuss.

5. Lead students to discuss our responsibility in conserving our water and other natural resources. Consider wilderness areas that have been changed by humans (e.g., the Everglades in Florida, the Atchafalaya Basin in Louisiana), other natural resources that are dwindling (e.g., petroleum), and the like.

6. Encourage students to do creative writings about rain or about use/abuse of our natural resources.

7. Use the film in photography classes (or with younger students in gifted resource rooms who have an interest in photography and filming) as a stimulus for various techniques of live photography, color, action, music, and other elements of filming.

8. Call to students' attention the wide variety of flora displayed in the film. View the film again, using it as a stimulus for discussing and comparing botanical specimens.

The Periodic Table

The Periodic Table, a twenty-four-minute color film, unveils Mendeleev's marvelous scientific contribution in an original and interesting presentation. The common attributes of the rows (periods) and columns (groups) of elements are discussed in a readily understood manner, interspersed with an interesting blend of historical film clips, animation, live photography, and special effects, to compare the elements and their uses. This excellent film won the 1981 Blue Ribbon Award, Science Division, of the American Film Festival.

Using *The Periodic Table* in Gifted Education

Before Viewing:

. Simply introduce the film, telling students that this is an introduction to chemistry and Mendeleev's Period Table of the Elements, but that it is presented in an unusual manner.

Suggest that they watch/listen for:
1. The progression in which Mendeleev made his discoveries
. The uses of the various elements
  Ways of organizing the elements into the table
  Importance of chemical formulas
  Unusual techniques used in the film to enhance its lesson

During Viewing:

the historical film clips and the significance of Mende-
overies in regard to each of these events in history (e.g., the
the Hindenburg, the use of chlorine gas in World War I).

After Viewing:

students understand the difficulties Mendeleev may have
ced in organizing the periodic table, do this activity:

ach student a matrix containing five one-inch squares on

    b. Instruct students to draw five Xs in the small squares such that there are no two Xs on any row, column, or diagonal.

    c. Examine a current chart of the periodic table, noting similarities shown in the film.

    d. Discuss the difficulty of doing this type of puzzle, and relate it to Mendeleev's problems with the Periodic Table.

2. Help students understand the difficulties experienced by inventors, creative artists, and others who attempt to have their innovative ideas accepted.

    a. Encourage students to read biographies of great scientists, stories about their great scientific discoveries, and the like. Guide them in drawing parallels among these people and their work.

    b. Conduct group dynamics activities designed to encourage students to recognize the value of all contributions (see activity entitled "Watson's Dilemma" on page 111). Help them see that "far-out" ideas sometimes prove to be great ideas.

    c. Use imagery as a problem-solving tool; introduce this activity by sharing with the students the information on page 142 regarding Mendeleev's discovery of the Periodic Table in a dream.

Patrick

"The music soars within the little lark, and the lark soars." Elizabeth Barrett Browning never saw *Patrick*, but its author Quentin Blake might well have been inspired by the beauty of Browning's thoughts. Viewed literally, *Patrick* is simply a short, nonverbal tale of a lanky youth who buys an ancient fiddle from a junkman and "infuses every leaf and creature in the countryside with vibrant color and vigorous movement." Described by other reviewers as a "lyrical portrait of music and its effect on the spirit," *Patrick* similarly infuses in its viewers an emphatic realization of the significant role of music in life, exemplifying the concept that music is an international language and the "gladness of the world." Winner of the Gold Medal at the Atlanta International Film Feltival and the Chris Bronze Plaque at the Columbus Film Festival, this remarkably brief but refreshingly delightful film has much potential for fostering creativity in the gifted/creative child.

Using *Patrick* in Gifted Education

Before Viewing:

1. Ask students how they feel about music. Encourage expressions that recognize the impact music has on the emotions.

2. Play a variety of types of music for the class. Ask students to move to the music, demonstrating in their moves the emotions evoked by each type of music. Encourage them to share their observations and feelings.

3. Play the sound track of *Patrick* without projecting the film. Ask students how this type of music makes them feel.

4. Ask if any of the students know the story of *The Pied Piper of Hamlin*. Encouage someone to share the story. Tell them they will see a film about another young man who enticed others to follow him.

After Viewing:

1. Encourage discussion of the film, using divergent questions such as:

   a. Did Patrick know what he was looking for when he went to the market?

   b. Why do you think he wanted the fiddle? Do you think he had ever played before? Why or why not?

   c. Why did the children, the animals, and the old couple follow Patrick?

   d. Where do you think they went in the end of the film?

   e. Why did the colors change as Patrick approached with his music?

2. Follow the film with a variety of creative activities, such as:

   a. Have students do creative writings (e.g., a sound track for *Patrick*; poetry about music or color).

   b. Using the sound track of *Patrick* without projection, have students move and/or act in accordance with their feelings about the music.

Wind

An unusually stimulating animated film, *Wind* uses rich pastels and deep cool greens and blues to show a happy, carefree child who is caught up in a gust of wind and transported into a world of his own imagination. Typical of small boys, our freckled-face cherub bounds happily in the wind, encountering clouds, dandelion seeds, sailboats, and kites. As he runs and explores, he becomes giddy, losing all concern for reality and experiencing a total fantasy world while blowing with the wind. Totally nonverbal except for the child's gurgling laughter and the shrill "voice" of the wind, this enchanting film offers many possibilities for encouraging creativity in the classroom. The image action in this film is rapid, changing often from one concept to another—much as a very windy day could rapidly change a landscape into quickly divergent patterns. It is the viewer's imagination that creates the action in this delightful sequence, giving a very real sensation of the wind itself during the brief span of the film.

Using *Wind* in Gifted Education

Before Viewing:

1. Encourage students to share their own experiences and feelings from being in the wind. (If the film is shown on a windy day, and if conditions permit, take the students out into the wind for a brief time before beginning this discussion.)
2. Play the sound track of *Wind* without projecting the picture. Have students move with the sound, draw pictures that they feel would be appropriate, or perform other activities to go along with the sound track.
3. Tell students that they are going to see a film called *Wind*, and ask how an artist might portray the wind. Compare their ideas to the film title.

After Viewing:

1. Discuss the animation and sound techniques used to portray the concept of wind.
2. Have students write poetry (especially nature forms such as haiku) about the wind, or fiction stories about the little boy in the film.
3. Use the film as a springboard to a science lesson on wind and weather.
4. Ask how other artists (musical composers, painters) have captured the concept of wind.
5. Share with students examples of music, poetry, prose, sculpture, dance, and other art forms that represent wind or its ethereal qualities.
6. Have students express their feelings about wind through creative movement activities.
7. Ask questions such as:
   a. Did the little boy like the wind? How could you tell?
   b. Did he want the wind to stop? Why? Are there any types of activity (playing football, riding a bicycle, reading) that you don't like to have to stop?
8. Explore the scientific nature of wind—both as a force and as a condition of weather. Encourage interested students to do further research, and report to the class, on the causes and effects of wind.

9. Ask students if they have ever imagined seeing pictures in the clouds. If weather permits, take the class outdoors to look for cloud pictures. Tell them that the ancient peoples imagined many things in nature, such as men in the sky (e.g., the constellation of Orion the Hunter), the sun as a god, and so on. Ask what other kinds of imaginary pictures they might find in nature.

10. Conduct a guided fantasy, leading the students through an experience on a windy day. After the activity, encourage them to share their feelings. Follow this activity with a guided fantasy that tends to relax them more than the heavy wind. Have them compare their reactions to the two activities.

11. Offer several options for creative activities the students might enjoy as a follow-up to *Wind*, such as:

    a. Write a creative story about the little boy in the film, including as many items as they can remember that the little boy imagined in the sky.
    b. Write a poem about the wind or other aspects of nature.
    c. Write a script to accompany the film, a children's book based on the film, or other types of creative writing.
    d. Draw a picture of wind. (Ask why this task is so difficult.)

Note: Some of the above activities are adapted from suggestions in a teacher's guide provided with the film.

Earthly Beings

A 1982 release by filmmaker Chuck Eyler, *Earthly Beings*, offers a unique combination of science-oriented content with creative animation, music, and concept. *Earthly Beings* can be many films when viewed on different levels. In the words of the filmmaker, this film builds human bodies from nature with musical images. Various earth elements assemble in the form of two walking human beings, viewed from a somewhat dramatically abstract perspective. This creative film was inspired by a quotation from T. H. Walkins' book *John Muir's America:* "Can't you see what I'm trying to tell you? You're earthly beings. You're a part of this world—not something that walks about in it without connection. . . . You're a rock, a flower, the wind, the rain, this thunderstorm!"

Using *Earthly Beings* in Gifted Education

Before Viewing:

1. Explore possible meanings or interpretations of the title.
2. Share the Walkins quotation (above) with the students. Encourage speculation about the content of the film.

3. Consider favorite quotations, personalities, or events that might inspire creative endeavors. Encourage students to share inspirational experiences from their own lives.
4. Discuss the oft-debated question, "Does art imitate life, or does life imitate art?"

After Viewing:

1. Discuss the symbolism of the film and its title.
2. Use the film as a stimulus for science lessons on evolution, symbiosis, or the human body.
3. Brainstorm ways in which computer graphics might be used to illustrate a concept.
4. Compare this film to *Wind*, particularly in light of the use of vivid color and sharp images in *Earthly Beings* versus the water-color effect and pastel softness of *Wind*.
5. Discuss the emotional impact of music.
6. Encourage students to share their reactions to the sound track of the film. Ask students, "Do you consider this sound track "music"? Why or why not?
7. Read to the students the filmmaker's description of *Earthly Beings*: " . . . earth, air, water, and fire play their parts in building two walking human bodies who becomes ideas of the mind." Ask students for their reactions to this statement.

The Dot and the Line

The Dot and the Line, a fascinating precursor to modern color graphics, is a whimsical animated film featuring three geometric characters in a romantic triangle. The story of a flighty little dot who is captivated by an unkempt, disorganized, squiggly line, the film imaginatively portrays the metamorphosis of her greatest fan from a straight and unbending line into a creative and versatile acrobat with whom Miss Dot immediately falls madly in love. Though somewhat melodramatic in plot, *The Dot and the Line* appeals to audiences of all ages and can be used to motivate interest in mathematics, computer graphics, and creativity.

Using The Dot and the Line in Gifted Education

Before Viewing:

1. Explore the concept of balance—balance in nature, in government, in personality, in learning style, in interpersonal relationships.

    a. Discuss the characteristics of productive groups and their need for different perspectives (e.g., conservative and liberal, divergent and convergent).

    b. Explore different roles (both occupational and avocational) that people assume in life. Compare occupations that are considered more traditional (accountants, engineers) with those that are viewed as creative (architects, musicians). Ask students if traditional roles in life could be improved through the addition of flexibility and imagination.

2. Compare this film to the book *Flat Land*; discuss the similarities and the symbolic implications to the two stories for societies.

After Viewing:

Examine the symbolism of the dot and the two lines, and the roles they represent in life.

1. Consider the reasons why the dot was at first enchanted by the undisciplined line.

2. Keeping in mind the previous discussion on balance, ask students to speculate on the moral of the story and the implications it might have for creative thinking and production.

The Stonecutter

The fable, a concise narrative, is a mirror of the traditional wisdom of man. The fable presents a cautionary point in short and often subtle ways. *The Stonecutter* is just such a tale, told in a seemingly simple mode. Briefly, it is an ancient Japanese tale of envy and greed. Tasaku, the stonecutter, dissatisfied with his lot in life, is changed on demand into a prince, then into the sun, a cloud, and finally a gigantic mountain. To be especially noted is the semi-abstract and impressionistic illustrative style of the film. In full color, it tells a vivid visual tale. The mood of *The Stonecutter* is set through the haunting soundtrack featuring the narrator complemented by quiet accompaniment of a koto, a Japanese zither with thirteen silk strings. Listen carefully for the ending; it is not to be missed or glossed over.

    Gerald McDermott, winner of the Blue Ribbon at the 1970 American Film Festival for the film version of *Anasi the Spider* and the Caldecott Medal for his book *Arrow to the Sun* (1974), is the producer of *The Stonecutter*. In addition to the book and film of the same title, McDermott narrates a sound filmstrip entitled *Evolution of a Graphic Concept: The Stonecutter*. Basically, this filmstrip compares the parallels and nonparallels between the book and the film. In the filmstrip, author-filmmaker McDermott makes reference to the artistic and aesthetic design of the book and the 16mm film in their various stages, showing ways in which the actual design of the book and film are different. Using his own designs, illustrations, sketches, and storyboards, he traces the evolution of a concept into a concrete illustration/book/film. An interesting revelation of the graphic symbols that unify his book unfolds in the filmstrip, showing the fluidity of the artist's concept. Through this story, help students to recognize the tremendous amount of research that must be conducted in order to effect an authentic production of this type (in this case, research on the fables and folktales, literature, and illustrative modes of ancient Japan).

As one views *Evolution of a Graphic Concept: The Stonecutter*, it becomes obvious that great time and talent were required and expended in making *The Stonecutter*. Appreciation of the book and film is sharpened through the viewing of this filmstrip. Further, the filmstrip will add immensely to the viewer's appreciation of the artist as a communicator.

Using *The Stonecutter* in the Gifted Classroom

Before Viewing:

1. Ask the students how many thought at some time in their lives that they might like to be someone or something different.
   a. After a show of hands, ask the following boundary breaker question, to be answered by each person in the group: "If you could be anyone or anything you wanted to be, what or whom would you choose?"
   b. Compare the students' answers, exploring underlying reasons that might have motivated them (e.g., a desire for power, altruism, popularity, personal fulfillment, greed, etc.).
2. Have the students write "If I were . . ." stories, speculating on consequences that might result from their being changed to whatever they suggested in the boundary breaker. Encourage students to share their ideas with the class.
3. Briefly discuss different forms of folklore: folk tales, legends, myths, tall tales, fairy tales, fables, and so on, comparing and contrasting their characteristics.
   a. Ask for examples of fables, such as those of Aesop, that have morals or messages in their stories.
   b. Talk about ways in which the reader can infer the moral of a story.
   c. Ask, "Do any of these folklore forms have practical reasons for their existence?"
4. Tell the students they will see a filmed story of a stonecutter in ancient times who was always wishing he could be something different. Encourage the students to look for a moral to the story

and to listen carefully for a surprising ending and speculate on its meaning.

5. Show the film through without interruption.

After Viewing:

1. Ask the students what type of folk literature *The Stonecutter* is, giving reasons for their answers. Ask if the story has a moral.

   a. Have the students write the moral they think was intended by the author of the story, supporting each idea (or each different moral proposed) with evidence from the film.

   b. Compare and discuss the different ideas presented.

2. Ask why the author might have selected a stonecutter as the main character of the story.

   a. Lead students to recognize the symbolism of the permanence and strength of stone.

   b. Encourage students to suggest other examples of this concept (e.g., the Ten Commandments, the obelisks, etc.).

3. Invite students to do creative writings (e.g., proverbs, maxims, syllogisms, fables).

4. For grades 4–6: Encourage students to read books with similar form, morals, and so on, such as the following:

   a. *Aesop's Fables* (1967). Translated by V. S. Vernon Jones, illustrated by Arthur Rackham. New York: Watts.

   b. Marcia Brown (1961). *Once a Mouse.* New York: Scribner.

   c. Geoffrey Chaucer (1958). *Chanticleer and the Fox.* Adapted and illustrated by Barbara Clooney. New York: T. Crowell.

   d. Jean de LaFontaine (1977). *The Frogs Who Wanted a King.* Illustrated by Margot Zemach. New York: Four Winds.

5. For grades 7–12: Follow film and discussion with opportunities for realistic goal setting, career discussion, future projection, and the like. Show the filmstrip *Evolution of a Graphic Concept: The Stonecutter.*

6. Discuss the similarities and differences between the book and the film.

7. Identify examples of symbolism used in the film and discussed by McDermott in the filmstrip.

   a. Encourage students to hitchhike (as in the brainstorming process) on McDermott's explanations of symbolism in the film, adding their own interpretations.

   b. Explore other uses of symbolism in such areas as history, art, literature, music, picture books, culture, and so on.

8. Introduce the concept of the film as a visual figure of speech.

   a. Compare visual symbolism, as used in the film, to figurative language (e.g., metaphor, allusion, analogy).

   b. Explore literary techniques employed symbolically in the film (e.g., irony and allegory).

9. McDermott describes the basic theme of *The Stonecutter* as "The lonely journey of self-transformation." Examine the concept of self-transformation through such questions as:

   a. What self-transformations occur in human life (e.g., birth, self-actualization, sainthood)?

   b. Is self-transformation limited to the human condition?

   c. What other examples of self-transformation can you suggest (e.g., evolution, metamorphosis, examples in literature, science, the arts)?

   d. In what way is *The Stonecutter* an example of self-transformation? Why does McDermott consider Tasaku's self-transformation "a lonely journey?"?

10. McDermott observed that, in an attempt to embody the emotional impact of a story, its visual representation often must change drastically before the final version is developed. He mentions three states through which the product passes on the road to actualization: the sketching of the original concept, the development of a color dummy or mockup, and the creation of the final conceptualization.

   a. Allude to parallels between the creation of a film and the publication of a book, exploring such questions as:

     Is it easier to write a book or illustrate a film? Why?

     Which was the better representation of Tasaku's "lonely journey to self-transformation": the book or the film? Why?

     Which do you think McDermott produced first: the book or the film? Give reasons for your answer. (*Note to the teacher:* The film was produced first.)

     How did McDermott achieve the flow of action and ideas within the film? Within the book?

   b. Refer to McDermott's comments in the filmstrip about the influences of his childhood and his parents on his work. Encourage students to reveal factors in their lives which have influenced their own creative products.

   c. Invite a guest speaker to discuss techniques of animation, or show films that demonstrate the making of animated films. Have students produce an animated film based on a creatively illustrated book of their choice or on an original story.

11. Have students create their own picture books, animated films, or other media, using collage.

   a. Repeat McDermott's comment that "In the film, motion and music generated the excitement. On the printed page, I had to rely on active composition and vibrant color to provide the excitement."

   Have the book *The Stonecutter* available as well as other examples of McDermott's work such as *Anansi the Spider* and *Arrow to the Sun* (all available in both book and filmstrip form). Have students compare his various works, noting elements that are typical of his style.

   Provide opportunities for students to study the works of various artists, writers, and musicians (e.g., Maurice Sendak, Beatrix Potter, Pablo Picasso, Aaron Copeland) to discern the "signature" (visual, verbal, and tonal stylistic characteristics) of each. Discuss the concepts of "active composition" and "vibrant color." Have students brainstorm words and colors that connote action. Combine the action words into phrases, working into the creation of written passages that reflect McDermott's manipulation of concepts. Using various art media, experiment with color to develop a visual composition which creates excitement.

   b. Investigate the characteristics of traditional Japanese art and music.

   Invite a guest artist to discuss and demonstrate Oriental water color techniques.
   Have students develop projects in the Oriental art style.
   Study the history of the pentatonic scale developed by the Chinese and its influence on Japanese music.

   c. Discuss collage as an art form. Provide materials for students to develop collage compositions incorporating McDermott's methods as revealed in the filmstrip. Encourage the use of many textures, colors, shades, and shapes.

   d. Show the last section of the filmstrip in which McDermott points out Tasaku "in the folds of the mountain." Instruct students to watch for this segment and for the "surprise ending" in the second showing of the film.

12. Show the film a second time to tie together the concepts developed through the viewing of the filmstrip.

   a. If, in the previous discussion, no student mentioned the ending of the film (the sound of the stonecutter cutting away at the mountain), ask the class what the surprise ending was.

   b. Ask the class why the narrator said, "The mountain trembled." If no student gives an appropriate answer, or if it is apparent that some of the viewers missed the ending, show the end of the film again.

   c. Lead into a discussion of the ending and its significance.

   d. Encourage students to discuss its meaning for their lives.

   e. Ask, "Who do you think was the stonecutter who chipped away the mountain in the last scene?" Discuss implications of student responses.

   f. Ask, "What would you have done in Tasaku's place?" Discuss.

13. Conduct a guided imagery activity in which students close their eyes and imagine themselves to be the person suggested in the boundary breaker. Encourage them to share their feelings while "in role" (preferable with partners). After bringing them back to their real selves, encourage discussion of their feelings about "being" the other person and about the things that they did while "in role."

All Summer in a Day

"On a planet other than Earth, at a time other than the present, a group of children attend school under the constant pelting of rain. It is a planet where the sun shines only once every nine years and today the children wait in anticipation for this one brief, exciting moment. Only one of them, Margot, has a recollection of the sun. Her family has been a late exile from Earth, and she recalls her days in Ohio and the warmth and glory of sunshine."

This is the setting of a Ray Bradbury short story, *All Summer in a Day*, a science fiction gem. The plot involves a conflict between Margot and her jealous classmate, William. His hatred builds and, when the sun does appear, William tricks Margot into entering a storage room, in which he locks her. Margot is left alone in this dark room while the other children cavort outdoors, enjoying their brief moment in the sun. This event results in a tale of contrasting emotions: jealousy, spite, loneliness, joy, ecstacy, remorse, and forgiveness.

The film is hauntingly beautiful, the mood set by the colors— predominantly grays and blues. Its pacing reflects the monotony of a long rainy day, rapidly changing into a colorful kaleidoscopic whirlwind when the sun and flowers finally emerge. Despite the starkly range of emotions presented, the film is about forgiveness without being didactic.

Using *All Summer in a Day* in the Gifted Classroom

All Summer in a Day is an unusual film; although some types of discussion and activities spring naturally from its use, we would avoid dulling its emotional impact through excessive introduction or follow-up. Nonetheless, the following suggestions are offered for the use of this provocative film in the guidance and counseling of gifted students.

Before Viewing:

1. Ask questions such as:
   a. What would you do if you had to live without rain, without sunshine during the day, without darkness at night?
   b. How would you organize your day/night?
   c. How would this change in your environment affect your life?
2. Ask, "Have you ever had an idea that no one else would accept?"
   a. Encourage students to share their experiences, their feelings at the time, and the ways in which they handled the rejection of their peers, parents, or teachers.
   b. Ask students to think of other persons in history whose ideas were not accepted (e.g., Galileo, Einstein, Edison, the Wright Brothers, Aristotle, Jesus), reminding them that many famous people have suffered at the hands of their contemporary skeptics).

After Viewing:

Have students write in a single sentence why William was so jealous of Margot. Encourage them to share their answers. Ask what Margot could have done to avoid the jealousy that William felt and the ridicule to which she was subjected.

At Some Later Time:

1. Ask why Margot and her family had left Earth and moved to this dismal planet (Answer: Because of overcrowding). Have students brainstorm the conditions/consequences that could have resulted from the overcrowding of Earth. Use this discussion as a springboard for a future problem-solving exercise on overpopulation.
2. Have students imagine Margot's feelings which prompted her to create the model of her home in Ohio.
   a. Ask, "If *you* moved to another planet, what would be *your* fondest memory of home?" Explore the feelings students would have if they were forced to leave their homes.
   b. Considering the grade level of the students, select one or more familiar stories in which people were forced to leave their homes, and discuss (possibly role play) the feelings they might

have had (e.g., *Fiddler on the Roof, The Day After, The Expulsion of the Acadians, The Exodus, The Wizard of Oz*).

c. Encourage students to depict their "fondest memory of home" through some type of art (diorama, drawing, painting, music, etc.).

3. To bring students back to reality and away from sadness, conduct a guided fantasy in which they are guided into imagery of a particularly wonderful time in their lives. Encourage sharing by those who wish to do so (keeping in mind that students should never be coerced or required to reveal personal feelings if they do not so desire).

4. Ask students to recall the gaiety experienced by the children in the film during the brief period the sun was out (gathering flowers, running and playing). Ask them how the weather affects their emotions. Have them create some type of art work to illustrate a sunset, a flower blooming, or other happy thoughts of nature.

5. Use the story of *All Summer in a Day* to initiate group counseling discussions about similar problems that are experienced by gifted students (e.g., rejection, jealousy, loneliness, ridicule).

Related Media

All Summer in a Day brings to mind several other media that might be used in a related context. One popular production is Carl Sagan's *Cosmos*. A spectacular series of science films, aired on television in 1983 and effectively represented in a publication of the same name, *Cosmos* offers several examples of people in history who were "prophets before their time" and thus were rejected by their contemporaries. *Cosmos*, a series of thirteen sixty-minute color films, is available from Films, Inc., 5547 N. Ravenswood, Chicago, IL 60640-9979.

There are many other films that offer futuristic themes and thus might be used as follow-up to *All Summer in a Day*. Because of the variety of impacts imposed by films of this nature, the teacher is reminded of the importance of previewing all films, and planning appropriate introductory and follow-up activities, before using them in any classroom. A few such films are:

Future Shock (1972). Contemporary/McGraw-Hill. Color, 42 minutes. 16mm and video.

Legacy: A Very Short History of Natural Resources (1979). Billy Budd Films. Color, 5 minutes. 16mm.

The Ugly Little Boy (1976). Learning Corporation of America. Color, 26 minutes. 16mm and video.

Several books that treat futuristic or science fiction themes and thus might be useful as sequels to *All Summer in a Day* include:

Bradbury, R. (1974). *The Martian Chronicles*. Bantam.

Bradbury, R. (1970). *S Is for Space*. Bantam.

Cogswell, T. R. (1963). *The Wall Around the World*. Pyramid Publications.

Del Rey, L. (1962). *The Eleventh Commandment*. Regency.

Gilman, R. A. (1968). *The Rebel of Rhada*. Ace Books.

White, J. (1974). *The Dream of Milennium*. Ballantine.

These science fiction books are highly recommended for older readers, specifically the young adult. Each title deals with a topic similar to areas addressed in the film.

Changes, Changes

Wooden blocks, that most basic of children's toys, are the major components for the innovative nonverbal book-turned-film, *Changes, Changes*. The book, written by Pat Hutchins, has been widely acclaimed for its clever originality; the film is an animated version of the book, faithfully reproduced.

Changes, Changes features two wooden dolls who rearrange wooden building blocks in a variety of configurations to accommodate solutions to problems that seem to keep occurring. When the house of the wooden dolls catches fire, this ingenious little couple contrives a fire engine from these same wooden blocks to put out the blaze, but this creates a flood! Step by step, the couple resourcefully rearrange their wooden blocks into a boat, then a truck and a train, finally rebuilding their wooden house.

Changes, Changes presents a series of potential catastrophies to the stiff wooden couple. In a creative response to each situation, they use the same basic wooden blocks to construct progressively more elaborate solutions to their problems. The action is fast-paced and complemented by a clipped xylophone musical background. The musical timbre is actually that of wood.

This is a wholly satisfying tale completing a full, happy circle of events.

Using *Changes, Changes* in Gifted Education

A marvelous example of improvisation, *Changes, Changes* can be used to introduce or motivate creative activities. Some suggestions for using the film for creativity development follow.

Before Viewing:

1. Discuss the role of change in society and in our lives. Ask:
   a. Is change good or bad? Why?
   b. What examples of change in society have you observed?
   c. Are changes in one's life always predictable? If not, how can we prepare for them?

2. Play the "Add-On Game": Ask, "What would you do if . . . (e.g., you built a house and it caught on fire? your key broke in the lock and you couldn't get into your house?)" Student #1 begins, telling the first thing she would do. The second student adds on to the first student's story, and so on. Encourage students to respond divergently rather than conventionally.

3. Ask students if they have ever heard the expression, "When life gives you lemons, make lemonade." Encourage students to speculate on the meaning of this expression.

4. Introduce the word *improvisation*. Ask students if they have ever had to improvise anything, and encourage them to give examples. Have the class brainstorm materials they might appropriately use for improvisation in the classroom. (For example, sixth graders might use paper towel tubes to make model rockets; older students might replenish the sodium chloride supply in their classroom chemistry center from a grocery store salt box; young children might make doll furniture or other toys from oatmeal boxes, match boxes, or other common household items).

After Viewing:

1. Ask students to speculate on the moral of the story.
   a. Discuss the implications of the film for life.
   b. Explain what a maxim is, how maxims are used, and what are some common ones found in reading, television programming, and the like.
   c. Refer again to the maxim, "When life gives you lemons, make lemonade." Ask how this maxim reflects the moral of the story portrayed in the film.
   d. Encourage students to contribute ideas of ways in which people might use the advice given in the above maxim.
   e. Have students write maxims that might be appropriate to express the moral of the film. Then have them write others that might apply to their lives and the lives of others their age.

2. Show the students the book on which the film was based.
   a. Discuss the quality of the film's reproduction—its faithfulness to the original story, and so on.

    b. Ask, "If you were the filmmaker doing *Changes, Changes*, what would you change about the film? Why?"

3. Ask the students for examples of improvisation in society and in nature. Encourage discussion of renewable resources (including such unusual topics as the starfish's ability to regenerate a broken arm); explore the idea of recycling paper and tin cans.

Don't

The lyric passage of the monarch butterfly is strikingly told in *Don't*. Beginning with its birth, this film shows the delicate metamorphic process from caterpillar to butterfly as well as the journey from country to city. The tension of this perilous flight is felt from the first frame as the butterfly encounters its various adversaries. Throughout the film the butterfly faces serious dangers from a railroad train to a ferocious-looking praying mantis, and finally man himself, all threatening his glorious freedom.

Essentially this is a science film; however, from the beginning it strays from the expected documentary-style film. *Don't* is nonverbal, having virtually no spoken narrative. There is one dramatic exception to this totally nonverbal concept, and even it might elude the passive viewer/listener. *Don't* enjoys a unique soundtrack, quite unexpectedly mixing everyday sounds with music composed by Frederick Chopin—as lovely and lilting as the monarch butterfly itself. Sound is ingeniously used in pacing the action of the film. While at times music is used to imply the grace of the butterfly, rhythmic sounds—more like tapping—convey the action of other bugs in a sequence vividly describing the cannibalistic nature of insects and the implication that the monarch, too, does often fall prey to others of its kind.

All of this film is composed of live-action photography, shot in stunning, clear color. From the viewer's perspective, *Don't* is well-paced, presenting a lively set of events in rapid succession; where the grace of the monarch is emphasized, however, the film takes on an elegant, slower pace. Creative camera angles, unexpected at times, blend a filming technique that dramatically moves various objects within the depth of field into and out of focus. Another unexpected technical surprise is the multifaceted lens used to simulate the view the monarch has of its world—or a "bug's-eye-view" of its surroundings.

Utilizing a dignified treatment of subject while maintaining the integrity of its technical creation, *Don't* enjoys exemplary continuity, making it difficult for the viewers to discern whether they are watching the same one or many monarchs. Simply, *Don't* is a visual short story, blending sequentially the events in the life of a single small creature—one of the nature's most beautiful—the monarch butterfly.

Using *Don't* in Gifted Education

This is a film that is intrinsically beautiful and needs little or no introduction. Also, it should be viewed *in toto* without interruption for explanations, questions, or comments. *Don't* should be followed by activities, not introduced by them.

After Viewing:

1. Use *Don't* as an introduction for:
   a. A lesson on butterflies, insects, nature, ecology, or symbiosis
   b. A values discussion on our responsibility to/for the environment, the beauty of everyday things, our encroachment on nature, and the contribution of each tiny element of nature
   c. A lesson on Chopin's music
   d. Any of a variety of creative writing activities

2. With no prior discussion, have students write their thoughts/impressions of the film. Instruct them to write continuously, never lifting their pencils from the page, for a specified period of time (usually not exceeding five minutes).
   a. From their continuous writing, have student isolate three to five ideas, developing them into any of various forms of creative writing (poetry, stories, essays, etc.).
   b. Encourage (never require!) student to share their thoughts and writing with the class.

3. Present a variety of recorded music to the class.
   a. Brainstorm examples of sequences from nature which might be suggested by the various forms.
   b. Have students write (or draw) their thoughts (or pictures) suggested by the various musical selections.
   c. Ask students to cite examples of musical compositions in which the composer attempted to simulate the "music of nature" (e.g., *La Mer, The Flight of the Bumble Bee, The Grand Canyon Suite*).

4. Requiring evidence from the film to support their responses, ask questions about the symbolism of the film, such as:
   a. What do you think was the filmmaker's major focus in this film?
   b. Why do you think the butterfly is shown in two distinct environments (the country and the city)?
   c. What was the significance of the title?
   d. What effect are the pastoral scenes intended to convey?
   e. Would it have mattered if the child had *not* shouted, "Don't!" to prevent the father from killing the butterfly?

f. How is the butterfly used in modern symbolism (e.g., religion, art)? Could there be any connection between this concept and the filmmaker's choice of the butterfly to convey his message?

5. Discuss techniques used in the film.

   a. Ask, "How were literary techniques (e.g., suspense, tone) used in the film?"
   b. Compare the lyrical quality of the scenes and the music to various art forms (e.g., poetry, sculpture, music, etc.)
   c. Consider the special effect of time-lapse photography and its contribution to films of this type. Discuss ways in which other special effects can affect the impact of a film or other medium of communication.

Extender Activities:

1. Language Arts:

   a. Brainstorm other words in the English language that can convey the same sense of urgency as "Don't!" conveyed in this film (e.g., "Fire!" "Charge!" "Help!"). Encourage students to conceptualize other examples from life that might be portrayed/dramatized as the butterfly was in this film (and perhaps use these ideas as stimuli for creative writing).
   b. Share with the class a variety of literary works in which poets, essayists, and other creative writers have referred to butterflies as "flying gems," "winged flowers," and other such beautiful and imaginative names.
   c. Have students suggest other colorful names for butterflies. Ask, "If butterflies are 'flying gems' and 'winged flowers,' what might we call people?" Extend this activity to other forms of nature, exploring various analogies and figures of speech and their uses in writing.

2. Science:

   a. To motivate additional reading by the students, ask questions such as:

      How does the life cycle of the butterfly compare to that of other insects? Why do scientists say the butterfly undergoes a "complete metamorphosis"?
      Where does the monarch lay its eggs? Why?
      Do monarch butterflies hibernate or migrate? Why? Where do they spend the winter?

   b. Explore with the class the Batesian Theory of Protective Mimicry. Is the monarch/viceroy likeness a true example of mimicry in nature? Can a lower form of life will itself to be like another creature? What do modern scientists suggest about the concept of mimicry?

c. Have interested students do further reading and share their findings with the class. Suggest articles such as those in *National Geographic Magazine* (see reference list).

d. Encourage students to investigate other scientific facts (and fantasies) about butterflies in general and the monarch in particular. Then show the film again to explore new meanings.

In summary, the use of media in any type of education adds a most effective component to teaching. In media, students encounter vicariously many experiences that they could not otherwise come to know. Used creatively, with carefully planned preparatory and culminating discussions and activities, media can provide valuable enrichment to any curriculum or topic. The films reviewed herein are but a sampling of the wealth that is available in the field. Teachers are encouraged to search on their own, looking for those that enable the students to reach out to new horizons. From the use of media students can gain much, as it gives students the chance to experience the old proverb, "I do, and I understand."

REFERENCES

Books and Articles

Parker, J. P., & Kreamer, J. T. A picture is worth a thousand words: Film in gifted education. Column in *G/C/T*, consisting of the following subtitles in the indicated issues:

Oldies but goodies: Why Man Creates. Issue #24, Sept./Oct. 1982, 29–33.
Curriculum Development: Balablok. Issue #25, Nov./Dec. 1982, 30–31.
Creative science teaching through film. Issue #26, Jan./Feb. 1983, 38–39.
Encouraging creativity: Changes, Changes. Issue #27, Mar./Apr. 1983, 46.
Personal development: The Stonecutter. Issue #28, May/June 1983, 35–37.
The beauty of science: Don't! Issue #29, Sept./Oct. 1983, 47–48.
Color graphics: A place in the curriculum. Issue #30, Nov./Dec. 1983, 22–23.
Counseling: All Summer in a Day. Issue #31, Jan./Feb. 1984, 35–37.
Encouraging creativity: Patrick and Wind. Issue #32, Mar./Apr. 1984, 42–43.

Sisk, D. (1976). *Teaching gifted children.* Tampa: University of South Florida.

Urquhart, F. A. (1976, August). Found at last: The monarch's winter home. *National Geographic Magazine*, 160–173.

Witty, P., & Fitzwater, J. P. (1953). An experiment with films, film-readers, and the magnetic sound track projector. *Elementary English, 30*, 232–241.

Zahl, P. A. (1963, April). Mystery of the Monarch Butterfly. *National Geographic Magazine*, 588–598.

Films

All Summer in a Day. 1982. 16mm, 25 minutes, color. Produced by Learning Corporation of America, 1350 Avenue of the Americas, New York, NY 10019.

Balablok. 1974. 16mm, 8 minutes, color. Produced by National Film Board of Canada. Distributed by Encyclopedia Britannica Educational Corporation, 425 N. Michigan Avenue, Chicago, IL 60611.

Changes, Changes. 1972. 16mm, 6 minutes, color. Produced by Weston Woods, Weston, CT 06883.

Don't. 1974. 16mm, 19 minutes, color. Produced by Robin Lehman; distributed by Phoenix Films, Inc., 470 Park Avenue South, New York, NY 10016.

The Dot and the Line. 1965. 16mm, 9 minutes color. Distributed by Films, Inc., 733 Green Bay Road, Wilmette, IL 60091.

A Drop of Water. 1970. 16mm, 12 minutes, color. Produced and distributed by Barr Films, P.O. Box 5667, Pasadena, Ca 91007. Currently out of print; some copies may be available from the publisher or through film libraries.

Earthly Beings. 1981. 16mm, 8 minutes, color. Distributed by Heaping Teaspoon Animation, 4002 19th Street, San Francisco, CA 94114.

Patrick. 1973. 16mm, 7 minutes, color. Produced by Quentin Blake, distributed by Weston Woods, Weston, CT 06883.

The Periodic Table. 1980. 16mm, 24 minutes, color. Distributed by Media Guild, 118 S. Acacia Avenue, Box 881, Solana Beach, Ca 92075.

The Stonecutter. 1965. 16mm, 6 minutes, color. Also available as color sound filmstrip. Produced by Gerald McDermott, distributed by Weston Woods Studio, Weston, CT 06883. Sound Filmstrips: *The Stonecutter* (#SF178C); *Evolution of a Graphic Concept* (#SF454C); Combination package (2 sound filmstrips, #SF455C). Book: Hard cover (#HB178); Paperback (#PB178).

Why Man Creates. 1968. 16mm, 25 minutes, color. Produced by Saul Bass and Associates for Kaiser Aluminum and Chemical Company. Distributed by Pyramid Films, Box 1048, Santa Monica, CA 90406-1048.

Wind. 1973. 16mm, 10 minutes, color. Produced by Ron Tunis, distributed by Learning Corporation of America, 1350 Avenue of the Americas, New York, NY 10019.

16

Unit Teaching: Tying It All Together

You can teach a student a lesson for a day;
but if you can teach him to learn by creating
curiosity, he will continue the learning
process as long as he lives.
                                        Clay P. Bedford

With the pressure of "back-to-basics" and "excellence in education" weighing heavily on school administrators, an increasing amount of effort has been made in recent years to teach content-oriented subject matter (as opposed to the fun-and-games approach) to gifted students. With this change has come a resurgence in the use of unit teaching. Although new teachers often consider unit writing to be a difficult (or at best tedious) chore, the development of a comprehensive unit can greatly facilitate a teacher's organization and contribute significantly to the quality of the material and methods incorporated in teaching.

A unit is simply an organizational plan for teaching a particular topic. Essentially there are two types of units: the resource unit, which presents copious amounts of information and numerous options for strategies, activities, and materials that will contribute to the teaching of the topic; and the teaching unit, which includes only the material that will be taught and the strategies and materials that will be used during the designated period over which the topic coverage will take place. The resource unit is invaluable in that it enables a teacher to combine materials from many sources into one extremely useful and flexible tool from which lesson plans may be formulated. A teaching unit, on the other hand, represents careful planning to include for each day's lesson exactly the right amount of material for coverage during the prescribed period. Whichever type of unit is selected, the components are essentially the same:

I. Goals (general goals to be met through the unit)

II. Content (factual information to be taught)

III. Procedures (strategies/activities, sequenced for use)

IV. Materials needed (teacher and student books, equipment, instruments, software and supplies—with annotations wherever possible for future reference)

V. Evaluation and follow-up (evaluation of pupil progress, evaluation of instruction, assignments)

The ways in which these components may be arranged are quite flexible; some teachers follow conventional plans whereas others prefer to make more creative adaptations. It is also extremely helpful to include—perhaps in a unit appendix—source notations on all "borrowed" material (often needed later, when this information has become "cold") as well as copies of all transparencies, tests, handouts, bulletin board or learning center designs, examinations with scoring keys, and other materials to be used during the unit.

The first step in developing a unit for any purpose is the selection of a topic. For teachers who are responsible for core curriculum and who have gifted students in their classrooms, the selection of the topic is less flexible. Nonetheless, many creative adaptations can be made in any subject area, incorporating the required textbook as the foundation for the content to be taught and the minimum procedures to be followed. The gifted students in the classroom can and should be given differentiated experiences, from individualized assignments to specially grouped activities, providing later opportunities for them to share their extended experiences with both their regular classmates and their gifted program peers. To provide for the needs of the gifted, the regular classroom teacher must embellish the material provided in the text, encouraging the gifted students to develop much of their own curriculum through research and the incorporation of skills and talents gained independently or through the gifted program.

An effective and popular approach to unit writing in gifted education is the use of one or more curriculum models as the foundation of a unit. Again, the way in which the selected model is used is left entirely to the teacher; however, examples are given below to demonstrate ways in which units might be based on any of several models that can be appropriately used in developing curriculum for the gifted:

Method One: Organizing the procedures section under the various components of the selected model.

MODEL I: The Leadership Training Model (Parker)
  Cognition:
    Exploration
      Possible field trips

Appropriate guest speakers
Suggested learning centers
Selected bibliography
Specialization
   Interest inventories
   Methods of focusing the topic
Investigative Skill Training
   Research skills
   Statistical procedures
   Selecting resources
Research
   Related topics for research
   Appropriate resources
   Suggested products and outlets for communication
Problem Solving
   Practice in problem solving steps
   Practice problems: Futuristics and personal problems
   Problem solving applied to leadership
Interpersonal Communication
   Self-awareness activities
   Group dynamics experiences
   Conflict resolution through simulation
Decision Making
   Activities designed to strengthen democratic values
   Simulation activities
   Group counseling sessions

MODEL II: Enrichment Triad Model (Renzulli)
   Type I Enrichment: General Exploratory Activities
      Activity I.   Objectives
                  Procedures and Resources
   Type II Enrichment: Group Training Activities
      Activity I.   Objectives
                  Procedures and Resources
   Type III Enrichment: Investigations of Real Problems
      Possible investigations
      Possible resources
      Possible products
      Possible audiences

MODEL III: Taxonomy of Educational Objectives (Bloom, Krathwohl, and others)
   Level I.   Knowledge
      Activity I.   Objectives
                  Procedures

MODEL IV: Structure of Intellect (Guilford)
  Cognition:
    Objectives
    Procedures
  Memory:
    Objectives
    Procedures

MODEL V: Multiple Talents Model (Taylor)
  Academic Talent:
    Objectives
    Procedures

MODEL VI: Model for Implementing Cognitive-Affective Behaviors in the Classroom (Williams)
  Lesson 1:
    Lesson Objectives
    Curriculum Area
    Teacher Strategies #___ _____
                #___ _____

The above examples simply provide formats in which curricular activities can be organized under the headings of the various models. This approach may be of greatest value to the newly trained teacher who has not yet become accustomed to developing balanced curriculum for use with gifted students.

Method Two: The second approach to the use of models in planning unit activities is simply to list the procedures to be followed (or the activities to be used), classifying each different activity as to the component of the model into which it fits (e.g., noting in parentheses after the description of the activity whether it is an Exploration activity or helps to develop Interpersonal Communication skills). The advantage of this type of organization is that it enables the teacher to build in balance (e.g., assuring that the higher levels of thinking are emphasized rather than simple cognition activities) while working within the teacher's own preferred style of teaching.

In the gifted enrichment program, the units written by one teacher should be contributed to a data bank and shared with other teachers, taking care to plan scope and sequence and thus preclude any student's receiving the same instruction in more than one class. The selection of the subject matter for the unit in the enrichment class typically is left up to the teacher (or a committee of teachers), but the activities and content are usually left to the individual teacher to develop and enrich. The following courses, offered in recent years in the University of Southwestern Louisiana's summer Academic Enrichment Program, should provide a variety of ideas from which a teacher may select units to be taught. (Grade levels follow the course titles.)

Paper Plate Pets (K–2).   Learn the characteristics, habitats, and living environments of twelve domestic animals. We will make "pets" from paper plates and construction paper, learning about a new pet every day and making that pet in our art project.

Terrific and Scientific (1–2).   Let's explore the wonders of our world through experimentation, inquiry, and investigation. We will try to discover why things in science behave as they do. I wonder; do you?

Dream a Drama (1–3).   Let your imagination soar, and learn to express yourself through the magic of drama. Take part in games, plays, puppet shows, and much, much more.

Magicalculations (2–4).   Learn how to operate a calculator and use it as a springboard to further discoveries. Mathematical concepts will be introduced through challenging games and problem solving situations. Students will even write jokes and solve mysteries using push-button mathematics. Let your fingers do the walking over the calculator.

Pond Life (3–5).   Explore pond life through the microscope. Learn to identify living microscopic plants and animals, aquatic insects, and fishes. Pond ecology, including a food web, habitats, and succession, will be discussed.

Junior Geologist (3–5).   Find out how to identify common rocks and minerals using real geology techniques. The course will include lab activities and field trips to develop your rock hound skills.

What Are My Chances? (4–5).   What are your chances of being invited to two birthday parties in one day? How many times could you tap your foot in thirty seconds? If you'd like to test theories and have lots of fun, chances are excellent you'll be a big winner in this class.

The Writer in You (4–6).   Discover the writer within yourself through language games, films, records, and visits from published authors. Creative writing activities will include poetry, short fiction, and drama.

Drawing on the Right Side of the Brain (5–7).   Can you draw? Would you like to know how? This course will teach the basics of drawing and/or improving existing skills. We will experiment with different media while concentrating on developing right-brain (creative) functions.

Wheeling and Dealing in Financial Markets (7–10).   Learn how to read and understand the *Wall Street Journal* and financial statements, and research a publicly owned company. Investments such as stocks, bonds, money markets, and mutual fund will be discussed, and we will visit a brokerage firm.

In closing this chapter and concluding this book, I am reminded of one of the most memorable experiences of my years in the gifted classroom. Since it served as the culminating activity of a unit, it seems to be an appropriate way in which to close.

For several weeks our fifth and sixth grade classes had been studying art history. We had shared many delightful experiences: viewing examples of all visual art media from Louisiana's superb slide library, attending a lecture at the university in preparation for a visit to the King Tut exhibit at the New Orleans Museum of Art, enjoying a visiting speaker from the docent staff at our local art museum, experimenting with a wide variety of art media, and creating our own methods of expressing our ideas. Together, the students and I decided to culminate the unit with an art festival. Structured somewhat like a science or social studies fair, the festival required each student to research an artist of his choice and to prepare an exhibit for presentation in an assigned space for viewing by judges, parents, and other invited guests. But it was here that the resemblance to any usual type of exhibit ended. There were no set requirements as to the form the exhibit could take; as facilitator, I simply suggested several options as stimuli and then considered each proposal submitted. One student who did not consider himself "artistic" did a reproduction of a famous work by his chosen artist; several others created original compositions in the styles of the artists they had decided to represent. Awards were made for the most original exhibit, the costume most typical of the artist, the composition most similar to the artist's own style, and whatever else seemed appropriate for the projects exhibited.

The students were ecstatic. Having been heavily involved in the unit, they experienced no difficulty in selecting their favorite artists. As they delved into their explorations, the excitement grew. By the time Festival Day arrived, all were ready—brimming with new-found knowledge to share with our guests, and proud of the tremendous efforts that they had made in the development of their extremely fine projects. Needless to say, the festival was a success, and all agreed that we would remember the experience for a long time. The most exciting event, however, was Billy's story.

Billy had selected Will Hinds, a local artist whose incredibly realistic style of portraying nature (woods, pastures, and swamps) had taken hold and mushroomed in a relatively short period of time. Through a mutual friend, the artist was invited to visit the class as a resource person. Unfortunately, he declined. However, on learning of the reason for the request, he asked about Billy. Happily for everyone, our artist surprised Billy with a telephone call to his home one evening and shared beautifully intimate glimpses of his painting—how he loved to go to the country and paint icicles dripping off wagons, and the like—and sent him autographed brochures of his work (including his unlisted telephone number and an invitation to "call anytime you would like to talk to me"—as long as Billy did not share it with anyone else). The excitement that this youngster felt was the highlight of the unit (and indeed a highlight of Billy's life that, now in his twenties, he still recalls as a special memory of his childhood). This experience illustrates only one of the infinite possibilities that a unit on the arts can hold.

In summary, the use of unit teaching holds countless potential for differentiating the curriculum for gifted students. It also provides fuel for the district or the teacher who must justify what happens in the gifted classroom in order to keep a program in existence. The unit can provide the very best balance possible for the gifted—a balance of goals (cognitive, affective, and psychomotor), exposure to sophisticated topics, materials, and processes that are not available in the traditional school program, and a meaningful context in which to utilize the many strategies that are especially appropriate for gifted students. Unit teaching encourages a variety of teaching strategies and styles while encouraging students to progress at their own rates and pursue their own preferred styles of learning. It provides opportunities for small group work, for whole class instruction, and for individualized, independent experiences. If a single approach to teaching the gifted were required, the unit approach would offer the greatest flexibility while providing methods of meeting all reasonable criteria set by administrators, school boards, parents, and—yes—even back-to-basics advocates. It therefore seems fitting that the unit approach should provide the synthesis for all that has gone before—a most appropriate method of incorporating appropriate instructional strategies into the education of the gifted.

REFERENCES

Guilford, J. P. (1967). *The nature of human intelligence.* New York: McGraw-Hill.

Parker, J. P. (1983, September/October). The Leadership Training Model. *G/C/T*, pp. 8–13.

Peter, L. J. (1980). *Peter's quotations: Ideas for our time.* New York: Bantam Books.

Renzulli, J. S. (1977). *The Enrichment Triad Model: A guide for developing defensible programs for the gifted and talented.* Wethersfield, CT: Creative Learning Press.

Taylor, C. W. (1978). How many types of giftedness can your program tolerate? *Journal of Creative Behavior, 12,* 39–51.

Williams, F. E. (1970). *Classroom ideas for encouraging thinking and feeling.* Buffalo: D.O.K.

Appendix A:
Activities for Use
in the Gifted Classroom

Note: The activities on the following pages may be reproduced as needed for nonprofit classroom or workshop use without specific permission. Written permission of the publisher *must* be obtained when they are to be used in workshops from which the presenter will earn remuneration. When any of these activities are used (whether with or without written permission of the publisher), the following credit line printed at the end of each section must be included on all copies distributed to participants: "Copyright © 1989 by Allyn and Bacon, Inc. From *Instructional Strategies for Teaching the Gifted* by Jeanette Plauché Parker."

THE NEW LONDON PROBLEM

The New London School District has five high schools: PS 1, 2, 3, 4, and 5. Although located in five different villages, they appear on the map in almost a straight line. Each school has won a distinguished award in recent years. Since the schools are numbered rather than named, they have become known by their team names and their variety of mascots.

The Problem

Draw a map showing the relative locations of these five schools. Determine which school has won which award, and name the principal, team, and mascot of each school.

The Clues

Dr. Appleby is principal of the San Angelle School.

Mrs. Hurley's school has an ocelot.

Miss Montana's school mascot is a horse.

The mascots of the Bellemont school and PS#2 belong to the same family.

Mr. Gold's students sell T-shirts with tigers painted on them.

Bellemont is immediately to the east of Lakeport.

The school that won the creativity award has an English Bulldog as a mascot.

The team of the Jonesville Irish won the Science Fair.

A fierce dog lives at the middle school.

Ms. Barrow is principal at PS#1.

The best debate team is at the school next to the one with an Irish setter for a mascot.

Ms. Barrow is afraid of the tiger at the school next door.

The Mustangs won this year's football tournament.

Mrs. Hurley's school excels in music and is next in line after Miss Montana's school.

Ms. Barrow works in the town just before Alexandria.

The Irish and the Wildcats are at opposite ends of the district.

The Alexandria Bengals belong to Public School #2.

THE NEWLYWEDS

John Tolliver and his new bride Betsy went to Mason's Department Store to buy furnishings for their new home. Since Betsy's father had given them a generous check as a wedding gift, they were able to buy almost everything they needed, charging only $100 to their personal account. In just one trip, they bought a sofa, a chair, and three tables for the living room, as well as a bed with matching side tables. Moving to the Appliance Department, they then purchased a stove, a refrigerator, and a microwave oven. Since they still had money remaining, they returned to the Furniture Department and selected an additional chair and table for the living room, a double dresser to match their new bed, a dining room table with a set of matching chairs, and a breakfast set for the kitchen.

The total cost of the kitchen purchases was one and one-half as much as the total spent for living room furnishings. The appliances cost twice as much as the breakfast set, which was the same price as the sofa. The dresser was half the price of the dining room furniture, the cost of which was equally divided between the table and the set of chairs. The living room sofa cost $500, and the living room and bedroom tables cost $50 each. The total cost of the bedroom furniture was $400 more than the dresser, which equalled the cost of the dining room table. The dresser cost one-third more than the living room chairs. What was the amount of the couple's wedding check?

WATSON'S DILEMMA

The Clues:

The general manager of the condominium complex worked until 10:00 P.M. on weekends.

Joan and Tommy had been engaged for six months when the murder occurred.

Mr. Vice often flirted with Miss Whittington.

The knife found in Mr. Vice's yard had Suzanne's fingerprints on it.

The manager reported to police that he had seen Miss Whittington at 9:45 P.M. Saturday.

The neighborhood newsboy said that Mr. Morgan frequently left the building with Alex Burton's daughter.

In high school, Elva had threatened to get even with Joan if she didn't leave Elva's boyfriends alone.

When her body was found, Joan had a bullet in her shoulder and a knife wound in her chest.

When police tried to locate Mrs. Jordan after the murder, they learned that she had left on the 6:30 A.M. plane Sunday for Chicago.

When the manager saw Miss Whittington, she was holding her shoulder and appeared pale but otherwise seemed all right.

In looking through Joan's desk Sunday, the police found a substantial insurance policy naming Tommy Morgan as beneficiary, and a handwritten card inviting Joan to Suzanne's condo for a late dinner on Saturday.

The threads found in the victim's hair matched Tommy's red plaid jacket.

Miss Whittington's body was found at 6:00 A.M. Sunday.

The police learned that Joan had gone to Mrs. Jordan's condo at 9:30 P.M. Saturday.

According to the county coroner, the victim had been dead for eight hours when her body was found.

The night clerk, who took over the front desk at 9:30 P.M., said that he had seen no one leave the building between 9:45 and 10:15 P.M. Saturday.

The dirt on the bottom of Tommy's shoes came from the same area of the part as the dirt found under Suzanne's accelerator pedal.

The bullet taken from Miss Whittington's shoulder matched the gun owned by Mrs. Jordan.

The police lifted several sets of Tommy's fingerprints from Suzanne's condo.

Spots of Miss Whittington's blood type were found in Suzanne's car.

The manager saw Tommy Morgan go to Suzanne's condo at 10:15 Saturday night.

Blood stains of the same type as Joan's were found on the carpet in the hall outside Elva's condo.

Suzanne's bedroom window overlooked Mr. Vice's back yard.

The day manager said that Mr. Vice was in the lobby when he left.

On Sunday morning the police noticed that the service elevator near the kitchen entrance was switched to OFF on the first floor.

Elva shot at an intruder in her condo at 9:30 P.M. Saturday.

A knife with Miss Whittington's blood on it was found in Mr. Vice's yard.

It was obvious from the condition of the body that it had been dragged a long distance.

Mr. Morgan disappeared after the murder.

A neighbor told police he had seen Miss Whittington go to Suzanne's condo at 9:55 P.M. Saturday.

Only one bullet had been fired from Mrs. Jordan's gun.

Police were unable to locate Suzanne Burton after the murder.

The victim's body was found in the park.

THE LAND OF THE SPHERES

Long ago on the massive continent of Pangaea there existed a nation which its inhabitants called Cartel. Now, the people of Cartel were of two tribes: the Cubes and the Spheres. Although all of these people had existed on Cartel for many centuries, neither tribe had been native to the area. Somehow over the years the Spheres had gained control, although the Cubes were in the majority. In order to preserve their way of life, the Spheres maintained strict command of the land. Only Spheres could hold office in government, and the Spheres dictated the curricula of the schools. Spheres lived in good homes, inherited all the finest quality of life, and always had the run of the land. Spheres became Spheres by birth; it was not possible for a Cube to graduate into Spheredom.

The Cubes, on the other hand, were slaves to the Spheres. Their children could attend school until the age of ten, but they were taught by Cubes (who were not well-trained) in the ways required by the Spheres. Their villages were poor, with meager living quarters occupied by several families together. They ate only what they could produce, and they were allowed to leave their village walls only when employed by Spheres to do their menial jobs.

One day a bright new Cube was born. He spoke differently from his parents and peers. He talked of leadership, of better ways of life, of victory and command. They called him Lars, after the Etruscan Lord, because somehow they knew he would help them to overcome their adversity. As Lars grew, the Spheres watched apprehensively. They saw in him a difference. And so, in a feigned effort to appease the misery of the Cubes, the Spheres voted to give Lars a post in the government. It was here that they made their fatal error.

The land of Cartel now has a new government. Run by Lars, it gives to the Cubes the rights of ownership, the best schools, and the finest ways of life. One cannot become a Cube, for Cubeship is hereditary. Although Cubes were for many years suppressed, they now are educated. It is the Spheres who now are the slaves.

Answer the following questions, and discuss your answers.

1. Do you think Lars should have taken over the Spheres' cities and exiled them to the former villages of the Cubes?

2. Should Lars be merciful on the Spheres, recognizing that they were only trying to preserve their own way of life?

3. Should the younger Spheres be allowed to hold some important government positions?

4. Should the new generation of Spheres be punished for the years of pain that their ancestors inflicted on the older Cubes?

5. Would you answer differently if the Cubes were the Black tribes of South Africa? If you had been born a Sphere? If Cubes were Puerto Ricans in New York City?

Appendix B:
Solutions to Problems
in Text

PAGE 18

We know that Jessica is the same height as Richard. Since Marlene is taller than Jessica (thus taller than Richard), he is likely to prefer Tania, who is the only one of the three girls who is shorter than he is.

PAGE 326

The New London Problem

	PS1	PS2	PS3
Town	Jonesville	Alexandria	San Angelle
Principal	Ms. Barrow	Mr. Gold	Dr. Appleby
Award	Science Fair	Debate	Creativity
Team name	Irish	Bengals	Bulldogs
Mascot	Setter	Tiger	English Bulldog

	PS4	PS5
Town	Lakeport	Bellemont
Principal	Miss Montana	Mrs. Hurby
Award	Football	Music
Team name	Mustangs	Wildcats
Mascot	Horse	Ocelot

PAGE 327

The Newlyweds

1. Organize (classify) all purchases according to room.
2. Fill in prices as provided by clues or by computation from clues.
3. Calculate total of purchases.
4. Subtract $100 from total cost, since the couple charged $100 over and above the amount of the check.

Living Room	Sofa	$500	Bedroom:	Bed	$ 300
($1000)	2 Chairs	$300	($800)	2 Tables	$ 100
	4 Tables	$200		Dresser	$ 400

Dining Room	Table	$400	Kitchen:	Breakfast Set	$ 500
($800)	Chairs	$400	($1500)	Appliances:	$1000
				Stove	
				Refrigerator	
				Microwave Oven	

Cost Summary:	Living Room	$1000
	Dining Room	$ 800
	Bedroom	$ 800
	Kitchen	$1500
TOTAL COST:		$4100
Less $100		−$100
AMOUNT OF CHECK:		$4000

PAGE 111

Watson's Dilemma

Searching for her fiancé, Tommy Morgan, Joan Whittington went to Elva Jordan's condo at about 9:30 P.M. Mistaking her for a prowler, Elva shot at Joan, wounding her in the shoulder. Feeling guilty about her mistake, but still a little pleased at the opportunity to pay Joan back for all those years of misery, Elva revealed that Tommy had been seeing Suzanne Burton. Her pain dulled by anger, Joan then went to Suzanne's condo at 9:55 P.M. and, finding the door ajar, walked in. Alas, Suzanne was waiting behind the door and jumped on Joan, stabbing her to death. At 10:15, Tommy arrived as planned, pulled Joan's body into the service elevator, went to the first floor, and switched the elevator to OFF. He then dragged her out the back exit to Suzanne's car and drove to the park, where he abandoned her body in an area full of mud. It had been a plot that Suzanne and Tommy, who were in love but greedier than wise, had dreamed up, thinking Tommy would be wealthy on receipt of Joan's insurance. While Tommy got rid of Joan's body, Suzanne opened her bedroom window and threw the knife far into Mr. Vice's yard in the hope of implicating him in the murder. After Tommy returned, he and Suzanne left town

PAGE 245

Scoring Key for NASA Moon Survival Task

(15) Box of matches (little or no use on moon in absence of oxygen)

(4) Food concentrate (supply daily energy needs)

(6) 50 feet of nylon rope (useful in tying injured, help in climbing)

(8) Parachute silk (protection against sun's rays)

(13) Portable heating unit (useful only if party landed on dark side)

(11) Two .45 caliber pistols (self-propulsion devices)

(12) One case dehydrated milk (food, mixed with water for drinking)

(1) Two 100-lb. tanks of oxygen (fills respiration requirement)

(3) Map of moon's constellations (essential for navigation)

(9) Life raft (CO_2 bottles included with raft may be used for self-propulsion across chasms, etc.)

(14) Magnetic compass (no magnetized poles on moon; thus of no use)

(2) 5 gallons of water (replenishes loss from perspiration)

(10) Signal flares (distress call within line of sight)

(7) First-aid kit (oral pills or injection medicine valuable)

(5) Solar-powered FM receiver-transmitter (communication when in range of mother ship)

PAGE 20

1. Numerical Sequences

   48 is 8×6; 35 is 7×5; 24 is 6×4, 15 is 5×3, etc.
   (Each multiplicand is reduced by one for the next product.)

2. Letter Sequences:

   The correct answer is ADD, completing the second part of the sequence, AABBAACCAADD.

3. Mixed Sequences:

In this pattern, the numerals increase by one, while the letters increase by one between the numerals. Therefore, the correct answer is **X3XXX**.

PAGE 22

a. white:black::up:down
b. top:bottom::up:down
c. iris:eye::finger:hand
d. bay:sea::village:city
e. white:black::up:down
f. meat:drink::milk:eat
g. poverty:wealth::rich:poor
h. sock:foot::mitten:hand
i. mansion:room::skyscraper:office

Index